Deconstructing Behavior, C

Edward R. Morey

Deconstructing Behavior, Choice, and Well-being

Neoclassical Choice Theory and Welfare Economics

palgrave
macmillan

Edward R. Morey
Department of Economics
University of Colorado
Boulder, CO, USA

ISBN 978-3-031-36711-3 ISBN 978-3-031-36712-0 (eBook)
https://doi.org/10.1007/978-3-031-36712-0

This Palgrave Macmillan imprint is published by the registered company Springer Nature Switzerland AG
The registered company address is: Gewerbestrasse 11, 6330 Cham, Switzerland

Preface

As with all choices, you can now err in two ways: you want to read this book, so spend the money and time. Regrettably, you end up disappointed, so worse off. Or you choose not to but would have enjoyed it, so you miss a chance to be better off. You did but shouldn't have, or you should have but didn't.

I've spent 40 years modeling behavior: teaching, researching, and estimating environmental damages. My economic niche includes applied choice theory, welfare economics, and valuing things we like that are not directly bought or sold. The adventure included litigation: estimating $ damages from environmental injuries caused by corporations. This required an ability to defend, in litigation, my behavioral assumptions. Because I am anxious and hyper-vigilant, I allocated thousands of hours—a mistake?—to keep that wolf at bay: agonizing about defending my assumptions against assaults from opposing economists and lawyers. The ordeal led me—I was hesitant—on a second adventure: investigating research on behavior and choice in philosophy, psychology, neuroscience, evolutionary biology, and animal behavior. This book is what I have learned and concluded about behavior and how economists model it. While it is aimed at those with economic interests, it is philosophical—digging down by questioning—hopefully not to fantasy. Don't worry; there is no math(s), though I tell my students, "It will require critical thinking." Be playful (analytically) with the ideas: try them on, and don't discard one simply because you don't believe it—beliefs, correct or not, fuel behavior.

Those at the cutting edge of the research in a specific field will find my knowledge solid, though not always cutting edge. My perspective is armchair panoramic, panoptic.

The pandemic upset our routines by adding and eliminating constraints. For better or worse, families were forced to spend more time together and less time with everyone else. Still, we are at increased risk of sickness and death. Such changes have changed how we now live—a natural experiment for scientists who study behavioral changes. There have been opportunities to reflect on what we do and why. Think about how your expenditures, relationships, and time allocations have changed and why. More or less exercise? Divorced, newly married, or both? Less restaurant time, more Netflix? New pleasures, new worries? What now? Did you make all the right choices?

The pandemic coincided with my retirement from the University of Colorado. I stumbled into pursuits. Two include more biking and nordic skiing: a goal is to suffer more—a remnant of my Lutheran youth. Besides, anaerobic exhaustion is calming. I've allocated more time to this book. New pursuits include learning to do stuff with my left hand with my eyes shut, understanding first-order predicate logic, and improving my vertical jump. [My upcoming NBA tryout? I started jumping up rocks while walking the dog. I ended up unable to walk and was scheduled for back surgery. Edward's follies (behavioral errors)?] Have I maximized my well-being? These examples are reallocations of my time: I spent my career thinking more about your demand for activities than whether you purchase oranges or apples. What you buy has changed—yet it all comes down to how you spend your time. You are the limited time you have on earth; goods come and go; they only accompany your experiences—you are a sequence of experiences.

The foundation of applied economics is an individual's behavior can be predicted and explained by assuming the individual is always choosing their highest-ranked available path forward—a behavioral model called *neoclassical choice theory*, NCT. People, including most behavioral scientists, don't buy it. I critique the details—my conclusions surprised me. The distinction between wanting and liking is paramount.

I start by developing a souped-up NCT that includes everything one might care about, not just market goods and services. I have a lifelong interest in valuing things that are not directly bought and sold, e.g., environmental amenities. I allow for uncertainty and risks—*expected utility theory* is a restrictive example. I deconstruct NCT's axioms into their components and consider what it implicitly, not explicitly, assumes—a lot is implicit.

Entities whose behavior is consistent with NCT are the species *economici* (sing. *economicus*).[1] Economists assume economici and homo sapiens are the same species, so *homo-economici*. [NCT is a 19th Century relic of British protestant creationism: humans, and only humans, were created in his image.] I distinguish between the two species, asking where in the animal kingdom, if anywhere, one might find an economicus.

I'm disinclined to believe that human behavior is explained by assumptions fundamentally different from those that explain animal behavior, so consider the behavior and WB of animals. Doing so provides a broader perspective on NCT. All animals sense and perceive: they see, hear, feel, interpret, and respond. All behavior results from the same evolutionary forces. Humans and slugs are 70% identical in DNA; it's 99% with chimps. And, like us naked apes, other animals experience emotions, have relationships, learn, and pass the learning on. We are not that different from a hungry bear searching for breakfast, or Giacomo, my dog, chasing a ball.

Animals, including humans, have beliefs—some consistent with the best science—and beliefs affect behavior. For example, consider the role of beliefs in the recent US Presidential election. Does NCT assume your beliefs are correct?

Emotions—fear, anger, lust, embarrassment, boredom—affect behavior. Sad to say, sensations, perceptions, and emotions don't play an explicit role in NCT—the economicus brain is a Skinnerian black box. If an economicus has emotions, they run deep; on the surface, he is drab, like faded yellowish/brown wallpaper. What we do depends on what we want, and what we want depends on our emotional state. And humans don't understand that what they want will be different when they are in other emotional states. So, while economics books don't talk about sensations, emotions, and beliefs, I will.

[1] I have nouned the Latin adjective *economicus.* More proper would be *entitas economicus* (economic entity).

Scientists who model the behavior of animals, plants, planets, and photons deem their models "behavioural". Economists substitute "choice" for that adjective, imagining humans choose how to behave, given their options. However, not all behavior is chosen: few humans believe animals choose, and no physicist says the moon chooses its path. So, what is a choice? There is no agreement, and NCT is inconsistent with "choice" in the street sense.

NCT has "choice" in its title because economists believe there is something right, better, or good if what is experienced was chosen by the individual experiencing it. And because economists believe humans choose how to behave. Most everyone believes this. The belief that choice is good has its roots in the Enlightenment, secular humanism, and the liberalism of John Stuart Mill. Economists, like everyone else, bring their implicit ones to the party.

Welfare (well-faring) *economics* arose in parallel with NCT. Many economists believe it's the way to determine whether a behavior or policy is right or wrong: the ethical goal is to increase social well-being, a function of only the WB of each member of society. Others reject this—welfare economists don't understand why. I explain; this requires contrasting welfare economics with WB's role in other ethics, such as virtue and duty-based. While one can believe in NCT and reject welfare economics or vice-versa, the two are often conflated, further confusing our understanding of both.

After teaching environmental economics for years, I developed a critical-thinking course, "Economics, Ethics, and the Environment"—critiquing welfare economics and environmental ethics. Each student researched a topic of mutual interest. Because topics pushed beyond the environment, I generalized the course to "Ethics, Happiness, and Choice".[2] Over the last decade, my evolving notes and lectures morphed into a book.

[2] I punctuated "…Choice". rather than "…Choice."—the right " to the left of the period. This is called *logical punctuation* (Yagoda 2011 and Pinker's *The Sense of Style*). A period (or comma) will not appear between the left and right quotation marks unless it is part of the quotation. I am violating an American-style rule (not a British rule)) that the ending quotation mark comes after the period. The American rule is illogical: logic dictates that what is between quotation marks is what is quoted. This rule exists because a long-dead typesetter decided that type like "choice". disturbs the eye.

I write as if we're friends having an informal conversation, directing your attention to exciting and insightful theories and studies of behavior. The difference between us is that I have spent more time studying this literature. I will avoid words and expressions you don't need to know; I won't hedge or overly qualify. [E.g., I avoid diluting adjectives.] I won't *signpost* ("Now, I will tell you about... Then I will talk about..."). I will be specific. Since it is a conversation, there will be numerous "I", "me", and "you", and you and I will have roles in the examples.

Since it's a friendly conversation, you have obligations; one is giving me a break with qualifiers such as "most" and "mostly"—I mostly avoid them! When anyone discusses a theory or research study, it is possible to immediately and legitimately object: descriptions and interpretations often need to be further qualified to make them bombproof. [Lawyers try to make legal documents bombproof, resulting in a thickness of prose that overwhelms nonlawyers.]

If, with effort, you can't comprehend, I am at fault. You will have to think hard in places. So, please give me enough rope and stick to garrote myself. I am an academic, so writing clearly is an alien endeavor: success is not guaranteed.

But, if we are talking, why all the footnotes—it's a conversation? Because they are critical to the task at hand. References appear at the end of each chapter, whereas footnotes are details and asides about things on that page—conversations include asides. Footnotes are either hated or embraced. Authors often compromise and put the footnotes at the end, making them endnotes—readers who prefer footnotes are appalled. Try not to conclude the footnotes mean the book is a tome—hopefully, it isn't. You are free to ignore them. But, if you want to excavate, they and the references are the places to start. View them as links embedded in the transcript of our conversation: the book is a guide for exploring further, so it requires clear directions (footnotes and references).

Research advances. Unfortunately, articles and books are static. To uncover the latest findings, go to Google Scholar, locate a source I discuss, and then search articles that cite it.

Have fun, and if you have questions or comments, email me at Edward.Morey@colorado.edu. Also, check www.EdwardMorey@org for updates on the book and the research discussed. Thanks.

Thanks to many, including Alexa, Douglass, Giacomo, George, Neil, Mike, Sally, Sofie, and Tina. Many thanks to the three reviewers for their comments and helpful suggestions. If not for my philosophy, psychology, economics, and environmental-studies students, this book would not exist. Their questions, corrections, and arguments were instrumental. I learned a lot. The remaining errors, flaws, and omissions are, woefully, my fault.

Boulder, CO, USA
Rossland, BC, Canada
September 2023

Edward R. Morey

Contents

About the Author

Edward R. Morey is an Emeritus Professor of Economics at the University of Colorado, Boulder. He's taught in Canada, Italy, and Norway. Economic courses include micro theory, econometrics, natural resources, environmental, mathematical, welfare, philosophy, and environmental valuation.

His Ph.D. is from the University of British Columbia where he studied choice theory, natural resource economics, and environmental economics. While this first book, Edward has published articles in the *American Economic Review*, *Ecological Economics*, the *Journal of Environmental Economics and Management*, the *Review of Economic Statistics*, and the *Journal of Public Economics*, among others. They have been cited almost five-thousand times—a decent number. Edward's rep is that he is too theoretical for applied economists but not enough for the theorists. He has consulted for the US EPA, the Department of Justice, the governments of Canada and Italy, a number of States, and several North American tribes. Most of this work estimated damages from environmental injuries (e.g., PCBs and oil spills)—a litigious business. He spends much time on his six bikes and six pairs of skis. Too much? In the middle of the night, he studies Italian. Finishing his second marble sculpture, teaching a course on Buddhism and economics, becoming a better writer, and achieving tranquility are moving targets.

Abbreviations

CBT	Cognitive Behavioral Therapy
CRH	The Corticotropin-Releasing Hormone
CV	Compensating Variation
DPD	Dissociative Personality Disorder
ES	Ecological Systems
EV	Equivalent Variation
fMRI	functional Magnetic Resonance Imaging
GABA	Gamma-Aminobutyric Acid
GW	Global Warming
HPA	Hypothalamus/Pituitary/Adrenal System
HRAP	Highest-Ranked Available Path
lpm	Letters Per Minute
MDS	Mesolimbic Dopamine System
NB	Nota Bene
NBT	Neoclassical Behavior Theory
NCT	Neoclassical Choice Theory
PI	Pareto Improvement
RP	Readiness Potential
SSRI	Selective Serotonin Reuptake Inhibitor
VP	Ventral Pallidum
WB	Well-Being
WC	Welfare Consequentialism
WTA	Willingness-To-Accept
WTP	Willingness-To-Pay

List of Figures

List of Tables

CHAPTER 1

Introduction

The distinction between behaviors and choices (a choice being a chosen behavior) pervades my perspective. So does the distinction between what is desired and what will be liked.

It is critical to distinguish between modeling and judging behavior—deciding which behaviors are right and wrong. We all like to judge others and pronounce actions and policies right or wrong, particularly wrong. Sometimes our behaviors and thoughts are ethical: we are virtuous or do the right thing for ourselves and others. Sometimes we are unethical: we have wrong thoughts and do wrong to ourselves or others. Of course, what you find unethical, I may find ethical. There are numerous ethics (methods for parsing right from wrong), and, not surprisingly, they have different and often conflicting ways of parsing right from wrong. I review prominent ethics and contrast them with *welfare economics*, the ethic many economists use to judge behavior.

In my introductory economics course, I say that economists assume people choose what they perceive best for them, subject to their circumstances (constraints). And—what they perceive as best for them is, in fact, best for them. At every point, you choose your best path forward. Everyone else does the same—no one makes well-being-reducing choices. If I appear to act contrary to my well-being (*WB*),[1] it is because I have

[1] Going forward, I will abbreviate "well-being" with "WB."

E. R. Morey, *Deconstructing Behavior, Choice, and Well-being*,
https://doi.org/10.1007/978-3-031-36712-0_1

unusual tastes or constraints. This is the conventional economic choice theory: assumptions meant to predict and explain what you will do and why. It is called a "choice" theory because economists believe behaviors are chosen behaviors, in contrast to believing you have little or no conscious control.

Chapter 2 lays out the explicit and implicit details of a/the conventional economic theory of behavior. I will call it *Neoclassical behavior theory*, *NBT* for short. I occasionally refer to it as "my NBT" because it is my modern take on neoclassical choice theory. It emerged in the nineteenth century's last half as the economic theory of human behavior. It remains the one first taught and is the foundation for almost all empirical research in economics. However, many of its assumptions are implicit, and some seem incorrect.

To behave according to this theory has implications for how brains work. Since NBT is my conception of modern neoclassical theory, I will use "NBT" to refer to Assumptions 1–9 of Chapter 2 and neoclassical choice theory in general, unless the context is the theory's historical development. Then I will use "neoclassical choice theory," *NCT*.

If you behave according to NBT, a researcher needs to identify only your constraints (which paths are available) and your ordering to predict your behavior. She would then predict that you will move to Maine with Mary and become a stonemason if Maine, Mary, and masoning are part of your highest-ranked available path.

If a path is unavailable, one cannot experience it. My wife desires to dine with Springsteen, but paths that include Bruce accepting her invitation are unavailable. For me, Bruce is also out, along with drinking great wines and the apartment overlooking Central Park. In contrast, for Bruce, who suffers bouts of depression, depression-free paths, and paths of anonymity are unavailable. While economists are explicit about which paths you can't afford money-wise, you face additional constraints (e.g., your health, gender, age, fitness, culture, morals, and obligations). Economists typically do not model these as explicit constraints.[2] It is argued that they are not constraints. This is because they can be challenging to model, so it is easier to say that such things affect your ordering of paths. It is also because economists interpret actions as choices rather than constrained behavior. ["The new mom chose to feed her new baby",

[2] The pandemic-imposed constraints including where we could not go. And an increased risk of sickness and death.

rather than "The new mom had to feed her baby."] I attribute more behavior to constraints than many economists, though I am not alone.[3]

Determining someone else's ordering is difficult. A researcher could ask whether you rank higher Path *q* or Path *g*, but economists are hesitant to believe that if you answer "*q*", you rank *q* over *g*. So, we assume that if an individual chooses *q* over *g*, she must rank *q* over *g*—whatever one does must be best for them, given their constraints. So, if I drink motor oil and beat the kids, it must be a component of my best path, given my constraints.

While NBT assumes an ordering of paths and selecting the highest-ranked available path (*HRAP*),[4] both are questionable. Maybe you don't know your ordering or even have one. Moreover, while many believe they act in their best interests (choose their HRAP), they are convinced that others don't. It is difficult to look at a specific choice and determine whether it is inconsistent with the theory—NBT allows for wild and crazy behaviors.

Research by psychologists, behavioral economists, and neuroscientists demonstrates that humans have common quirks that can lead to what I will call *flawed choosing*, suggesting that we won't always experience our HRAP.[5]

[3] My research has focused on constraints such as skills (e.g., skiing, fishing, and biking), personality (e.g., extroversion and competitiveness) life constraints (kids, BMI, fitness, and health), and mental health. These are all constraints that are exogenous to the individual when a path must be selected. They are different from how behavior is affected by what is deemed unacceptable.

Adam Smith, in his *Theory of Moral Sentiments* (1759/2002), argues that many behaviors are avoided because they violate "moral sentiments" (one's moral sense): selecting Path *j* is simply wrong, so it is not selected. More recently, Amartya Sen (1997) formally distinguishes between which paths are available given the external constraints imposed on the individual, the set *S*, and the subset of those available paths that are personally admissible, the subset *K(S)*: the individual selects a path from *K(S)*.

[4] Acronyms are bad practice but better than a four-word subject. I do it when the expression appears numerous times, sometimes in the same paragraph. If it has been a while, I will repeat the full expression.

[5] Flawed choosing needs to be contrasted with psychological terms such as ***abnormal behaviors***, ***mental disorders***, ***mental illnesses***, and ***pathologies*** of mind, mood, or behavior. Abnormal and pathological behaviors do not necessarily violate the NBT Assumptions, and flawed choosing does not imply the individual has a mental disorder.

An important question is whether these common quirks violate any NBT Assumptions. Two common quirks are ***duration bias*** and ***empathy-gaps***. Duration bias is we fail to appreciate that we will adjust to the good and the bad. What makes us happy today (e.g., yesterday's pay raise) will not make us happy forever. And, even though we would be distraught immediately after a diagnosis of a permanent disability, we will adjust more than we can imagine, eventually returning to a state of happiness (or unhappiness) that can approach what it was before the diagnosis. Duration bias is we incorrectly imagine we won't adjust and make choices based on our false premise. For example, when I am anxious, I am inclined to believe it will persist unless I take a pill or drink; mistakenly, I believe the anxiety won't abate by itself, so I drink and pill too much.

Empathy-gaps are a lack of empathy for one's other selves. One can lack empathy for their future self or oneself in a different emotional state. The hypothesis is your ordering of paths varies with your emotional state. The gap is that individuals choose as if they will always have their current ordering. For example, when you are angry, you choose based on your angry ordering, so often choose a path that is not highest-ranked after the anger abates. Research on duration bias, the *emotional empathy-gap*, the *future-self empathy-gap*, and *incentive-salience effects* are presented in Chapter 8; Chapter 9, the *endowment effect*.

While economists assume the ordering is a preference ordering, economists are vague on why a path is "preferred." Economists presume if you rank Path *w* higher than Path *e*, you would be better off with *w*, or you desire *w* more than *e*, or both. The difference between *w* being better and *w* being more desired is critical, but economists do not make the distinction.

So, what does "better off" mean? Does it mean more pleasurable sensations (more orgasms and less pain)? Does it mean experiencing more positive thoughts and fewer negative thoughts—more "I'm successful." Less, "I'm a bad person."? Does it mean more *emotional WB* (experiencing more positive emotions and fewer negative ones, e.g., more happiness, less sadness)? Does it mean more life satisfaction (*life-satisfaction WB*)? It depends on who you ask, and "better off" often goes undefined. From now on, I define better off as more WB and WB as pleasurable sensations, positive thoughts, emotional WB, and life-satisfaction WB. [Not all species are capable of experiencing them all.] Confusingly, "happiness" is often used as a catchall. Researchers and authors are typically not specific.

What it means to be happy has drastically changed over the ages (Chapter 5). Currently, happiness is a chemical/electrical brain state—many of my students hate that happiness is a choreographed dance of brain synapses, choreographed by God-knows-who or what.

* * *

Turning from explaining to judging behavior, a researcher can build a theory to explain and predict what you will do without judging whether your behavior is ethical. Yet, some economists want to judge behaviors and policies right or wrong—they want to make ethical judgments. Welfare economics (defined in Chapter 4) assumes that a society's ethical objective should be maximizing its citizens' welfare (well-faring). It is a type of *welfare consequentialism*: how an act affects the WBs of society's members should be the sole determinant of whether it's right/ethical/moral. So, whose WB counts? Who is a member? Do Italians count in Canada? And, if so, as much as Canadians? How about beavers and moose? Economists presumptuously exclude the WB of beavers and moose, though nothing in NBT specifies their omission. Consider the implications of expanding who counts to other species, even if you believe their WB should not count. When it comes to humans, welfare economists punt on the issue of which humans should count.

Few moral philosophers are welfare consequentialists.[6] The few that are reject the WC of welfare economics.

People reject WC: believing that while how an act affects everyone's WB should be a criterion in judging whether it is right or wrong, it should not be the sole criterion.[7] Unfortunately, welfare economists don't deal

[6] *Moral philosophy* has two meanings: how one parses right from wrong behaviors and inclinations, or it can refer to a set of specific assumptions that parse right from wrong. To avoid confusion, I will refer to the latter as an *ethic*. *Moral philosophers* are individuals who study ethics. It is important to distinguish between moral philosophers and individuals who adhere to a specific ethic. E.g., one can believe right and wrong are determined by God's words without being a moral philosopher. One can be a moral philosopher that adheres to no specific ethic, or one can be a moral philosopher that defends a specific ethic such as virtue ethics or utilitarianism. At one extreme is the Oxford philosopher Bernard Williams (1929–2003), who suggested that philosophy might have nothing to contribute to ethics (Williams 2006).

[7] "Act" or "action"? Much of the time, they are synonyms, so interchangeable, but not always. I use both, going with the one that sounds more natural, given the context.

with the fact that others reject WC as the right ethic to parse right from wrong.

Using WC (including welfare economics) to judge right from wrong is difficult—other ethics share this difficulty. Consider first a society of one individual—George. Since WC does not have to consider how his behavior will affect others, the best ethical outcome, from the perspective of WC, is the outcome best for George. If George always chooses his best path, the moral imperative is to constrain him as little as possible—a world of no laws or restrictions and vast resources—the Tea-Party dream. If, alternatively, George, left alone, would sometimes not choose his best path, WC suggests sometimes forcing him, for his own good, to do things he would not choose to do. For example, George would be better off if a foreign agent stopped him from drinking motor oil.

Things get complicated if society has more than one member, and their behaviors directly affect each other. For example, consider a society of two people: George and Fred. George paints his house purple and fills his yard with plastic statues of Snow White and the Dwarfs: the visual effect brings joy to his heart. Unfortunately, it makes Fred, the neighbor, sick. On the other hand, Fred loves to get drunk and belt out—badly, and over and over—the swan song from the tragic opera "La Traviata". And WC requires that George's welfare be weighed against Fred's welfare, though welfare economics does not have rules for doing this.

Welfare economists can't imagine ethics where whether an act is right or wrong is independent of WB. Such ethics are common. I was brought up with an ethic that right vs. wrong was all about serving God, honoring God, and following his rules. The objective was not to experience pleasurable sensations: most were sins. Rejecting WC isn't limited to religious ethics: Kantian ethics, for example, emphasizes doing one's duty—happiness is OK though not the objective. Virtue ethics is about being virtuous, not about being happy.

* * *

Returning to explaining choice and my second sentence, "Most of us are mostly aware of our actions and perceive them as our own, actions we choose." We believe we make choices, but what is a choice, and do we make choices? What does it mean to choose Path *e* over *c*? Part II considers what it means to choose and whether we make choices. Let's agree that if Path *c* is the only available path, there isn't anything to choose—choice requires two or more available paths. For example, prison inmates don't choose to stay in on Saturday night—going out is not available, and people with no money and no credit can't choose to buy a new Mercedes or choose not to. In contrast, people with money who are not incarcerated can afford—money-wise—many different paths of goods and services, so they seem to have more choices.

It is tempting to conclude that the goods you buy and consume are the goods you chose to buy, and this is the conclusion everyone jumps to, including economists. But is it true? If you have $100 to spend on groceries, thousands of bags would cost $100 or less. If you walk out of Safeway with 3 pears, chocolate cookies, and a steak, a bag costing $58, your brain, body, and upbringing could have required it.

Economists typically think of constraints as external to the individual, but you are also constrained by who you are. Heavy people cannot win bike races with mountain stages, and I can't go downhill fast on my mountain bike because it would make me too anxious—anxiety is a chemical brain state I was born with. Besides—my wife won't let me ride a motorcycle, though she will let me go heli-skiing.[8] What is a choice cannot be assessed independently of a constraint? Consider how current choices (marriage and donuts) lead to future constraints. The ultimate constraint is reality, and the ultimate reality is your weeks are numbered—four thousand, give or take (Oliver Burkeman 2021).

As noted above, many people, including behavioral psychologists, reject the economic assumption that people always behave in their best interests, arguing and demonstrating that people make bad choices. A bad choice, however, is still a choice. As will be discussed (Chapters 9 and 10), numerous prominent physicists and neuroscientists don't believe we make choices in the world's street sense. For example, if your unconscious determines you will propose to Wilma, and before you buy the ring, your conscious brain provides you with the experience of choosing to propose, did you choose to propose to Wilma?[9] A substantial body of neurological evidence suggests that the final determinant of whether you do *x* or *y* is

[8] Heil-skiing makes me anxious but includes moments of euphoric pleasure.

[9] A few readers of earlier drafts have insisted that unconscious means "passed out", and that I should use "subconscious". Quoting Michael Craig Miller, M.D. (2010), former Senior Editor, Mental Health Publishing, Harvard Health Publications, "As a general rule, then, in most of the professional literature where mental functioning is concerned (including not just psychoanalysis, but also psychiatry, psychology, and neuroscience,

unconscious. Before the behavior is initiated, the conscious part of our brain provides us with the perception of choosing—an *illusion of choice*. I review this research; you can "choose" how much you choose to believe.

There is also the physics of *causal determinism*: what you do this moment, and the next, is entirely determined by the world's configuration of atoms and the laws of physics, including your brain's atomic configuration. Both causal determinism and behavior determined by the unconscious brain raise the issue of whether you should be held responsible for your behavior, be it right or wrong.

Economists implicitly adopt "weak" *free will*. Free will is a common expression in philosophy; economists might define it as the ability to choose freely. Philosophers differ regarding what it is and whether it is consistent with choice. If we want to explain behavior, economists need to ask how much behavior is chosen, starting by understanding the neurology of choice and the philosophical disagreements about choice.

* * *

All will be investigated by referencing recent research. The goal is to introduce you to the philosophy and scientific research that has helped me evaluate economics as a social science and welfare economics as an ethic. Of course, many students of economics are already versed in parts of this literature. My mental reveries scratch surfaces in philosophy, ethics, psychology, neuroscience, evolutionary biology, and animal behavior. Wandering is fun and has led me to think about behavior and choice in new and weird ways. I hope to convey a bit of that weirdness. Philosophical zombies are dissected, asking whether a zombie can be an economicus.[10]

A few warnings are appropriate: what is new here is how the different literatures are brought together, packaged, and interpreted, along with my deconstruction of NCT: I am presenting research by others by analyzing and questioning. I bring new insights and contributions to the discussions. Since there is ignorance and disparate views on how brains

among others), writers—like Freud—tend to use the word 'unconscious' rather than 'subconscious'. Although the word 'subconscious' continues to appear in the lay literature, it is rarely defined carefully and may or may not be synonymous with 'unconscious'."

[10] There are movie zombies, voodoo zombies, and philosophical zombies. Philosophical zombies appear in academic discussions of consciousness. Philosophical zombies and humans are indistinguishable, but with zombies, no one is home.

work, research findings and speculations are sometimes in conflict—so question the research and pursue the conflicts, starting with the references and links. The goal is to introduce and critique the literature, not revere it.

There will be environmental examples because I have spent my life studying environmental economics. Thinking about the environment, including its living non-human inhabitants, highlights the economic approach to ethics and how it differs from other ethics. For example, if individual animals have moral standing and people make them suffer, there are drastic implications for what is and is not economically efficient. These implications are worth considering, even if you reject them. A related belief, rejected by welfare economics, is an ecosystem, a species, or a place (e.g., the Grand Canyon) can have value separate from the value you and others ascribe to it. I survey non-economic values.

My examples will push the boundaries of propriety and taste—this is intended. There will be religious examples: religious doctrine is how many distinguish right from wrong (sin). Sexual desire, drugs, and perverse behaviors make excellent examples; they push buttons. Sex is conspicuous in ethics—for instance, is sex for fun moral or a sin? Does its morality depend on which body parts are involved or who it is with, and if so, why? The implications of our ethical assumptions are appreciated after they have taken us to abhorrence.

Final warning: would learning what you now believe is incorrect make you happier? Consider what Dr. Victor Frankenstein had to say, lamenting the creature he created,[11]

> You seek for knowledge and wisdom, as I once did; and I ardently hope that the gratification of your wishes may not be serpent to sting you, as mine has been... Learn from me ...how dangerous is the acquirement of knowledge and how much happier that man is who believes his native town to be the world, than he who aspires to become greater than his nature will allow. —Mary Shelley (1823)

[11] When possible, there is a link to a person when their name first appears—not available in print copies. Use them to find an author's related most recent articles. A list of these embedded links is at www.EdwardMorey.org

Do you know what will make you happy, and if so, will you take that path? Dr. Frankenstein did not. Could he have chosen a different path? Do any of us choose our path?

While I carefully chose the order to present the topics, and while they collectively form a whole, nothing terrible will happen if you read the chapters in the wrong order or skip some: most stand alone or at least teeter alone. Jumping around within a chapter isn't advised though skimming a section is OK. The book has five parts. Part I (Chapters 2 and 3) is a neoclassical theory of behavior. Chapter 4 is welfare economics. Neoclassical choice theory and welfare economics are birds of a feather.

Part II distinguishes between wanting and liking. Well-being is defined along with the history of happiness. The last chapter in II expands on whether all the different kinds of WB are commensurable and whether all the different bearers of WB are comparable. Common quirks, incorrect beliefs, and flawed choosing are investigated in Part III. The endowment effect is the most famous quirk. At issue is whether quirks violate the assumption of neoclassical choice theory. Incorrect beliefs are rampant.

Part IV, "Choice or the illusion of choice," asks, "What is a choice?" And do humans and other animals make them? It draws from the neuroscience on the conscious experience of choosing, the physics of choice, and the philosophical literature on free will and choice. Finally, Part V adds to our conversation about welfare economics and contrasts it and WC with other ethics such as virtue, Kantian, and Buddhist. And it introduces the ethics of prominent ethicists who are economists but neither welfare economists nor even welfare consequentialists.

* * *

You can determine a lot about a book by how often a word, phrase, or name appears. *Utility* and *preferences* don't much: both are suitcase words—packed with various meanings.[12] In contrast, *WB* (for well-being) often appears with the adjective *emotional* or *life-satisfaction*. *Behavior* will be ubiquitous: it is critical to distinguish between it and

[12] Ken Binmore (2021) argues that this is the word's charm: in his assessment, maximizing utility only means one behaves consistently, and it does not matter what the individual is being consistent with respect to. So, there is no need to equate utility with happiness or well-being. He does note that people often behave inconsistently.

He notes the word traces "its origins to the Latin *utilitas*." and its use by "Daniel Bernoulli [1700–82] in discussing the St. Petersburg Paradox."

a choice (a chosen behavior), and the same goes for *wants/desires* vs. *likes*. You will encounter *neurons*, *synapses*, *readiness potential*, and the *mesolimbic dopamine system*. Also, *anxiety*, *happiness*, and *emotional-dependent orderings*; philosophical terms include *will*, *free will*, *duty*, and *virtue ethics*. Other vital words and phrases include *beliefs* and *incorrect beliefs*, *bias*, *flawed choosing*, and *violations of choice theory*. Non-economist names you will encounter include Mark Bear, Jeremy Bentham, Kent Berridge, Daniel Dennett, Rene Descartes, Epicurus, Leon Festinger, Michael Gazziniga, Dan Gilbert, Jonathan Haidt, David Hume, Henry and William James, Daniel Kahneman, Benjamin Libet, J.S. Mill, Shaun Nichols, Richard Nisbett, Martha Nussbaum, Derik Parfit, Frank Ramsey, Jean-Jacques Rousseau, Bertrand Russell, Peter Singer, Cass Sunstein, Timothy Wilson, and Daniel Wenger. Many references are non-economic. There are numerous references authored by behavioral economists, but my perspective is broader.—I am not a behavioral economist. There is more on animal behavior, and Buddhist thought than you will find in most econ. books. There are many environmental examples. Neoclassical references are limited to textbooks and historical works.

References and Sources

Binmore, Ken. 2021. *Early utilitarians*. Springer.

Burkeman, Oliver. 2021. *Four thousand weeks: Time management for mortals*. Farrar, Straus and Giroux.

Morey, Edward, Terry Buchanan, and Donald Waldman. 2002. "Estimating the benefits and costs to mountain bikers of changes in trail characteristics, access fees, and site closures: Choice experiments and benefits transfer."*Journal of Environmental Management* 64 (4): 411–422. https://doi.org/10.1006/jema.2001.0513. https://www.webofscience.com/wos/woscc/full-record/WOS:000176543000008.

Morey, Edward, Jennifer Thacher, and William Breffle. 2006. "Using angler characteristics and attitudinal data to identify environmental preference classes: A latent-class model." *Environmental & Resource Economics* 34 (1): 91–115. https://doi.org/10.1007/s10640-005-3794-7. https://www.webofscience.com/wos/woscc/full-record/WOS:000236615400006.

Morey, Edward, and Mara Thiene. 2012. "A parsimonious, stacked latent-class methodology for predicting behavioral heterogeneity in terms of life-constraint heterogeneity." *Ecological Economics* 74: 130–144. https://doi.org/10.1016/j.ecolecon.2011.12.005 . https://www.webofscience.com/wos/woscc/full-record/WOS:000301277000015.

———. 2017. "Can personality traits explain where and with whom you recreate? A latent-class site-choice model informed by estimates from mixed-mode lc cluster models with latent -personality traits." *Ecological Economics* 138: 223–237. https://doi.org/10.1016/j.ecolecon.2017.03.038. https://www.webofscience.com/wos/woscc/full-record/WOS:000402215800022.

Pinker, Steven. 2015. *The sense of style: The thinking person's guide to writing in the 21st Century*. Penguin Books.

Sen, Amartya. 1997. "Maximization and the act of choice." *Econometrica: Journal of the Econometric Society*: 745–779.

Shelley, Mary Wollstonecraft. 1823. *Frankenstein: Or the modern Prometheus*. G. and W.B. Wittaker. https://books.google.com/books/about/Frankenstein.html?id=5twBAAAAQAAJ.

Smith, Adam. 1759/2022. *The theory of moral sentiments*. Vol. 1. Ireland: J. Beatty and C. Jackson and The Gutenberg Project. https://www.webofscience.com/wos/woscc/full-record/WOS:000283912100003.

Thacher, Jennifer, Edward Morey, and Edward Craighead. 2005. "Using patient characteristics and attitudinal data to identify depression treatment preference groups: A latent-class model." *Depression and Anxiety* 21 (2): 47–54. https://doi.org/10.1002/da.20057. https://www.webofscience.com/wos/woscc/full-record/WOS:000229157100001.

Thaler, Richard. 2015. *Misbehaving: The making of behavioral economics*. New York, NY: W. W. Norton & Company.

Williams, Bernard. 1985/2011. *Ethics and the limits of philosophy*. Fontana Press 1985 Routledge 2006/2011.

Yagoda, Ben. 2011. "The rise of "logical punctuation"." *Slate*. https://slate.com/human-interest/2011/05/logical-punctuation-should-we-start-placing-commas-outside-quotation-marks.html.

PART I

Neoclassical Choice Theory and Welfare Economics

CHAPTER 2

Economicus: Assumptions of a Neoclassical Theory of Behavior and Their Implications—My Take

The Goal of a Theory of Behavior Is to Explain the Behavior of Individual Entities: The Sequence of *Paths* Each Will Experience

There is more than one theory of behavior and choice in economics. It's the same in psychology and neuroscience.[1] Here I present a theory of behavior fundamentally neoclassical, extending what is taught in principles of economics courses. Its first nine assumptions are my take on neoclassical choice theory. While I teach it to undergraduates, I don't necessarily take it as truth or the best theory of behavior—in my defense, I am not the sole economist in this boat.

The *neoclassical behavior theory* presented here, hereafter, *NBT*, allows for risks and ignorance. It extends consumption, and consumption paths, to include the environment, public goods and bads, and aspects essential to economists in labor and other applied fields such as urban/regional and demography. It extends paths to include all that may make any economicus better or worse.

[1] While economists emphasize the word "choice", other fields use *decision theory*, *judgment*, and *behavior*. As an alternative to the neoclassical perspective, there is the newish field of *behavioral economics*.

E. R. Morey, *Deconstructing Behavior, Choice, and Well-being*,
https://doi.org/10.1007/978-3-031-36712-0_2

It is "an NBT" rather than "the NBT". I will avoid the word *choice*: economists tend to use it rather than *behavior* because they assume human behaviors are chosen. Think of choice theories as a subset of theories of behavior, keeping in mind that many don't assume behaviors are consciously chosen. Think of NBT as a framework for discussing behavior and asking questions about behavior and choice. It is presented as a theory of how entities behave, not how they should behave. And, at this early point, the issue is understanding the theory, not whether it does or does not explain behavior. Later, research will be presented on whether you and others behave consistent with the NBT Assumptions. I am offering my take on modernized neoclassical choice theory, not embracing it.

A dividing line between theories of behavior is whether their intent is to predict without judgment. Or whether it also predicts what you do is best for you, given your constraints. If the behavior predicted is deemed ethically right, ethics has crept aboard: there is something right about the behavior. Contrast a choice theory with, for example, a theory to explain the moon's position relative to the earth (Newtonian physics). It would never cross a physicist's mind to suggest their theory implied there was something right or wrong about the moon's path. In contrast, welfare economists believe that choosing your highest-ranked available path, HRAP, is, in many situations, the right thing to do.

Simply put, NBT assumes an economicus does what is best for it, given what is available.[2] This chapter provides details. An economicus is an entity whose behavior is consistent with my first 9 Assumptions. A plant, animal, machine (Rob the Robot or a toaster), or even a human might qualify—whether you believe economici exist is up to you. While NCT was postulated to explain the behavior of humans, many humans are convinced it does not apply to other humans. The following entities could be economici; it depends on whether they follow the rules of NBT (Fig. 2.1).

At this point, I will not restrict NBT to humans: doing so could mean there are no real economici—maybe economici are mythical, like angels and dragons. The behaviors of clams, chimps, and humans all have the same evolutionary root, and all are motivated to propagate their genes. If a theory of behavior explains the behaviors of complex organisms, like

[2] How one conceives of and defines "best" will be a big deal.

Fig. 2.1 Economici? A dog, an economist, a clam, a robot, a cactus, and a chimpanzee

humans, wouldn't we expect it to also explain the behaviors of simpler organisms, like clams and cacti, so why exclude them? I worry that if a theory can't explain the behavior of a bivalve, how could it possibly explain the behavior of more complex organisms? Considering clams makes us think more deeply about behavior and choice. Psychologists, neuroscientists, and behavioral economists believe that economici don't exist. To find a real one, we should examine the behaviors and motivations of dogs, clams, and toasters. I would argue that my NBT, Assumptions 1–9, applies to clams and toasters—yes, toasters. I'm not so sure about dogs and cats.

We need a theory of animal behavior if we want to consider the welfare of non-human animals, so why not a theory that covers all animal behavior? [Don't worry! I'm not going to sweat whether toasters are happy.]

As with all scientific theories, a behavior theory starts with a set of definitions and assumptions that contain no contradictions. Logical deduction determines what they together imply/guarantee. What goes in [the assumptions and definitions] determines what comes out [the predictions]. Another name for a prediction is a hypothesis: *if such and such conditions hold, a certain outcome will result*. A theory may predict that if the price of gasoline rises, you will buy less, and it may predict that if you wear a red dress, a Saturday-night date is more likely. Remember the distinction between what the assumptions imply and whether you and others act consistently with them. Later chapters present evidence on whether humans and other animals do.

While you and I would like to believe we are logical, humans, as a species, didn't evolve to be logical or to limit our thinking to the assumptions on the page: we unconsciously add our beliefs, making it difficult for us to avoid faulty logic.[3] So, when we consider what the NBT Assumptions imply and don't imply, we need to ensure we don't add our beliefs as implicit, additional ones. Since many of us are familiar with NCT and its predictions, we will be tempted to suppose the standard predictions

[3] For example, my students often accept the non sequitur: "Living things need water; fish need water, so fish are living things." They only see that their reasoning is illogical when I replace "fish" with "washing machines". Why the faulty logic? Humans know that fish are alive, so "fish are living things" is, by itself, a correct statement, and so miss the "so". They mistake water being *necessary* for living things with water being a *sufficient* condition for life.

before I have specified all the necessary assumptions. To keep us in line, there will be sentences, "Assumptions 1-X neither preclude nor imply...."

A Neoclassical Behavior Theory (NBT)

NBT is simply a set of definitions and assumptions. Since what a theory predicts depends precisely on what is and is not assumed, the definitions and assumptions must be precise. NBT consists of two definitions and nine assumptions: the standard neoclassical ones are deconstructed into their components.

NBT is limited to predicting the behavior of *economici*.

Definition 1: An *economicus* is an entity whose behavior and objective are consistent with Assumptions 1–9.

The definition does not imply that the entity is a human: that would be a *home-economicus*, a particular type of economicus. Likewise, it does not imply that the entity is alive: it could be a computer program, a robot, or even a fridge, as long as its actions are consistent with Assumptions 1–9. They don't imply human economici, but it is not precluded.

If you look at the textbook descriptions of NCT, an "individual" or an "agent" is the subject rather than a "person," "human," or "pig". Human is, I believe, implicit. It's the word "individual", which my wife believes is restricted to people. You can, if you insist, restrict, by assumption, the theory to homo-economici, but keep in mind the possibility that there are none.

The curt description: the assumption (economicus), the method (logic), and the conclusion (behaves like an economicus) (Fig. 2.2).

A *path*:

Definition 2: *A path is an imaginable life as it would unfold through time, starting now. It includes the goods, services, and inputs the entity would consume/use through time on that path (its consumption path). It includes its job, what it would know at different points in time (its knowledge path), what other entities would consume (other's consumption paths), what other entities would know, plus the entity's relationships (social, sexual, work),*

Fig. 2.2 Dante, the Inferno, Gustave Dore llus

> *the relationships of other entities, and the environment (who is now and will be the future Prime Minister of England, air qualities, crime rates, etc.), Uncertainty and ignorance are part of every path, and so are beliefs.*[4]

For economici, there are typically many paths forward, but all end. A life (an existence) is a sequence of paths taken. An economicus' paths are not quite like those in Yosemite: they can't be loops, and one can't turn back, and the entity must continue forward at the speed of time: deviations would be time travel to the past or future.

A goal of NBT is to predict the sequence of paths an economicus takes. [Keep in mind that an economicus's behavior is not influenced by all path components.]

If you were taking an introductory microeconomics course, a path would be defined by the amounts of each market good you would consume on that path, and it would be called a *consumption bundle*. Except, the behavior of humans is influenced by more than market goods.

There is a path, call it *Path k*, in which I would be married to Shirley for eight years, have a poodle named Fred, smoke Camels, no one would be starving, and Trump is re-elected in 2024. On another path, *Path f*, I would be married to George, not know about global warming, have a cat, drink zinfandel rose, many people would be starving, and Michael Bloomberg would be the US President. Each sequence of paths taken is a different life. Since economici don't have perfect information, paths include uncertainties.

[4] Another term for path would be *state-of-the-world*. I picked *path* because I will discuss different types of states (emotional states, brain states, states of nature, etc.). I have broadened the concept of a *consumption bundle* to include everything that might affect an economicus. In an earlier draft, I used *bundle*, but found that a bundle is interpreted as something experienced now, rather than a path through time (a sequence of present bundles). This expansion beyond the consumption bundle isn't new; John Harsanyi (1920–2000), the 1994 Nobel laureate in Economics, included (1977) "health, social status, job situation family situation, etc." I also considered the word *prospect*, where a prospect is a set of uncertain outcomes, each associated with a probability of occurrence. The words *prospect* and *gamble* are often used when considering choice when there are uncertainties.

Note the word *imagine* in the definition and remember that humans can imagine the impossible, and *imaginable* does not mean *available*.[5] So by my definition, a path can't have non-imaginable components. What is imaginable can change over time and varies across individuals: it depends on what they have seen and experienced. For example, inhabitants of the N. American plains had sets of paths vastly different from their contemporary, Adam Smith. Consider animals; humans have larger imaginations than chimps, and chimps' brains are larger than canines, so my set of imaginable paths is larger than my dog's: Giacomo has never imagined a trip to Bangkok or the taste of 1961 Chateau Rothchild. At this point, you are asking, "What's with the imaginable restriction? I have never heard an economist use the word imagination". I will explain but note that it limits the number of paths.

The path definition ended with, "*Uncertainty and ignorance are part of every path, and so are beliefs.*" "Uncertainty," as I am using the term, neither implies nor precludes *probabilities of occurrence* associated with uncertain events. While every path includes uncertainties, the definition does not require that these uncertainties be expressible as probabilities, where the probability of an outcome is a number between zero and one, inclusive, and the probability of something happening is one.[6]

Your beliefs consist of things that you think are correct: they represent that which is the case. For example, Bob's belief that "the world is flat" means that somewhere in his neurons is stored a representation of

[5] If an entity has experienced something or is programmed to do something, it is imaginable. Imaginable paths are not limited to experienced paths.

[6] For example, if the only two possible outcomes are rain tomorrow or not, then the probability of it raining, *Prob(r)*, or not, *Prob(nr)*, is one. Probability is often formally defined as follows: for all possible outcomes ($k=1,2,\ldots,K$): $Prob(k) \geq 0$ for all k, $Prob(some\ k)=1$, and $Prob(j\ or\ k)$ for all j and k equals $Prob(j)+Prob(k)$ if outcomes j and k are mutually exclusive. These three conditions are called *Kolmogorov's Probability Calculus*.

For economists, *uncertain* outcomes fall into two categories: those where it is possible, because of one's beliefs/knowledge, to associate probabilities (e.g., the probability it will rain tomorrow) and uncertain events where, because of a lack of priors, you are unable to associate probabilities with the different possible outcomes. The former are *risky* events. The latter are uncertain situations where you can identify the possible outcomes, but you are unable to associate probabilities with them. E.g., whether it will rain tomorrow is associated with an estimated probability based on weather models, weather data, and painful joints, but if there were neither weather models nor data, and nothing ever hurt, there would be no basis for a probability estimate, and we would be clueless as to whether it will rain tomorrow.

this subject and predicate. And it bubbles up whenever the earth's shape becomes relevant to behavior. [I don't walk around constantly thinking about how 2 plus 2 is 4, but I become conscious that it is when I need to do sums in my head.] Beliefs are often described as "affective attitudes", "affective" meaning they affect behavior. Yours are yours, and mine are mine. They include how you think the world works, including what you think will happen if Event A happens; will it cause Event B or C? Most are mundane, e.g., my belief that squirrels have tails and I have feet. They vary in strength: how confident you are that it is correct: your confidence in it being the way you think it is.[7] People express the strength of a belief with terms like "probable," "unlikely," and "for sure," but they can also be expressed as probability numbers; *Subjective probabilities* to distinguish them from other uses of "probability," such as "frequency of occurrence".[8] For example, until recently, I believed, with about 60% confidence, that I had had the Covid virus. I still believe I had it, but now

[7] A probability of .5 (50%) would indicate that both it and not it has an equal chance of occurring. Subjective probabilities are often described as how much you would wager on a proposition. For example, consider the proposition that Biden will win reelection. If you would wager, at most, 66 cents for a bet that will pay nothing if Biden is not reelected and one dollar if he is, your subjective probability is .66 (you believe the odds are 2 to one that he will be reelected).

Not everyone agrees that beliefs can have degrees. An alternative view is that you either believe something or you don't. This alternative view would argue that you either believe in God, or you don't: "if you doubt his existence, you are not a believer." Philosophers don't all agree on what a belief is (Eric Schwitzgebel 2019).

[8] What you believe is *subjective* in that it is internal to you (you are the *subject* of that belief). Consider the following: I believe it will rain tomorrow and Trump won the election; I believe in our Lord and Savior, Jesus Christ, I believe the stock market will fall, and I believe a real Burger-King Whopper must taste better than their new non-meat Whopper. These beliefs of mine. For each my confidence in its truth is subjective. [In contrast, *objective* is "it is what it is." Size, for example, is objective (as in Box B is bigger than Box C). See Sumner (1996).]

The word "probability" has a number of different but overlapping interpretations, including *classical*, *logical*, *evidential*, *frequency*, *subjective*, and *propensity* (Alan Hajek 2019). What I call subjective probabilities are more formally known as *subjective Bayesian probabilities*; their origin traces back to Frank Ramsey (1903–30) and Bruno De Finetti (1906–85). Their contributions to probability theory laid the foundation for expected utility theory (discussed soon) and game theory. While Ramsey made significant contributions to economics (I studied him in graduate school), economics was a sideline encouraged by John Maynard Keynes. Ramsey was an early twentieth-century philosopher, logician, and pure mathematician—not bad for someone who died at age 26. There is a recent biography (2020) by Cheryl Misak, *Frank Ramsey: a sheer excess of power*.

my confidence hovers closer to 99%. Your confidence in your beliefs—your subjective probabilities—may not align with probability estimates based on the best available data and best scientific practices. Looking ahead, I will define beliefs inconsistent with the best available data and scientific practices as *incorrect beliefs*.

Semantic/declarative knowledge (e.g., $2 + 2 = 4$ and Justin Trudeau is the Prime Minister of Canada) is a *correct belief*. In contrast, *procedural* knowledge (e.g., how to snowboard) is not a type of belief. Procedural knowledge is "knowledge-how"; declarative knowledge is "knowledge-that".

Economists don't often use the word "beliefs" or discuss how they are formed or updated, which is unfortunate.

Assumption 1: *At every point in time, an economicus is on one path*

Economicus can't be on two paths at the same time. N.B. (*nota bene*) does not imply that it is always on the same path. The definition makes this impossible: paths include uncertainties, and as time passes, many become certainties, ending the paths with those uncertainties.

Assumption 2: *At every point in time, an economicus has one ordering of all paths—1st, 2nd,—An economicus has an ordering if, for all paths j and k, either Path j is ranked higher than Path k, Path k is ranked higher than Path j, or paths j and k have the same rank.*[9]

Assumption 2 says that if an economicus is presented with any two paths, it knows, at least operationally, which path is ranked higher. It does

[9] This complete ordering is, by definition, transitive. *Transitivity* is defined as if *Path j* is ranked at least as high as *Path c* and *Path c* is ranked at least as high as *Path a*, then *Path j* is ranked at least as high as *Path a*. Sometimes, transitivity is casually, but incorrectly, defined as if *Path j* is ranked strictly higher than *Path c* and *Path c* is ranked strictly higher than *Path a*, then *Path j* is ranked strictly higher than *Path a*. This is not transitivity but *quasi-transitivity*. Transitivity implies quasi-transitivity, but quasi-transitivity does not imply transitivity: quasi-transitivity is a weaker relationship. Relaxations of transitivity will be relevant when incomplete orderings are discussed.

Distinguish between the word *ordered* and the word *rank*: paths are *ordered*; the *rank* of a path is its "position number" in the ordering. For example, the path with two paths ordered above it has the rank "3rd".

not require conscious awareness of the ordering nor imply anything about the criterion to use to order paths, so it does not imply or exclude an ordering based on WB or wants/desires. It does not preclude orderings with lexicographic properties.[10] And it neither implies nor precludes the existence of paths with the same rank.

Something caused an economicus to have its current ordering, but Assumption 2 is silent on the cause. It excludes entities with multiple simultaneous orderings battling for dominance. It excludes orderings that depend on how the paths are *framed*.[11]

Assumption 2 limits the orderings to paths that are imaginable.

Since humans have big imaginations, a home-economicus's set of paths is humongous, making a list of how they are ordered longer than all Google searches put end to end. This makes me wonder why an economicus would have a complete ordering of all paths given that 99.9999% aren't available to it—and never will be. A neurophysiologist would wonder where and how this humongous amount of useless information is stored. Why would evolution allocate space? While my dog imagines fewer paths than I imagine, he still imagines many (sleep on a rug, sleep on his bed, get a drink, run straight, run left, bark once, bark twice). And since his brain is smaller than mine, I wonder where a *canis economicus* stores his ordering.

There is also the question of whether it can rank minutely different paths. E.g., *paths i* and *j* differ only in the pattern of your mother-in-law's paisley drapes and the shades of her cat's tail hairs. Assumption 2 precludes economicus from saying, "I don't know how to order them."—complete means complete. Assumption two is consistent with you giving them the same rank.

Assumption 2 implies nothing about how quickly an ordering can change; it specifies that, at every point in time, economicus has one. If you are a

[10] Commodity x lexicographically dominates y, if, all else is the same, the path with more x is always ranked higher independent of the amount of y. For example, chocolate is lexicographically preferred to scotch, if for sets of paths that are identical except for their amounts of chocolate and scotch, paths with more chocolate are ranked higher.

[11] Framing is how the path is presented; it does not affect the components of a path. For example, patients and their loved ones more often adopt a directive that says "allow natural death" than one that says "do not resuscitate" even though they mean the same thing (Sandy Venneman et al. 2008). Orderings influenced by framing violate Assumption 2. Dino Borie and Dorian Jullien (2020) propose a framework for explaining them. Framing has also been described as a salience effect (see Chapter 4).

homo-economicus, it is consistent with your ordering depending on your emotional state (mad, sad, sexually aroused), and it is consistent with your emotions fluctuating wildly. It is consistent with your ordering changing from minute to minute.

Assumption 3: *An economicus's ordering of any two paths, j and k, is independent of what other paths are, or are not, imaginable.*

I can imagine driving, walking, or biking to Montreal, but I can't imagine getting there by transmutation. If I'm an economicus, Assumption 3 says that my ordering of paths that vary in terms of bike vs. walk can't change if I come to imagine a transmutation option. Consider marriage: currently, I can imagine a path where I am married to Alex and another where I am married to Spencer, but, at the moment, I can't imagine a path where I am married to Scout. I rank the Spencer path higher than the Alex path. If I start to imagine a path where I am married to Scout, my imagining can't influence how I rank the Spencer path vs. the Alex path.

Assumption 3 may appear innocuous; it isn't. For example, imagine I have abandonment issues that cause me to rank Spencer higher than Alex because Alex is a flight risk, and I am certain Spencer will not leave me. Spencer does not dance, but Alex does, and I love to dance. Then something makes marriage to Scout imaginable, and married, we would dance, dance, dance—Scout is a great dancer. Imagining a married life dancing with Scout causes me to hate the idea of a life of no more dancing, driving me to now rank Alex higher than Spencer. Assumption 3 precludes this.

Assumption 4: *An economicus's ordering does not change in the time-span behavior is modeled.*

An economicus's ordering is stable, at least for a while. Typically, a minimum length is implicit in empirical work. For example, an economist estimates the demand functions for different fruits because she wants to use those estimates to predict future weekly demand for bananas and strawberries. This estimation exercise requires everyone's ordering of paths to be constant during the data collection period and remains so over the period she wants to predict. If the orderings change, the estimated model predictions would be based on the wrong orderings.

Assumption 4 is rarely made explicit.[12]

Assumption 5: *Most paths are unavailable, and an economicus* must experience an available path.

In explanation, many paths are blocked from the get-go, and all paths run into roadblocks. I don't have the physical talents to play in the NHL or dance with the NYC Ballet, and neither does my dog. I'm not smart enough to understand quantum mechanics. And while imaginable, paths that include me dating Carla Bruni are unavailable. And paths that are certain about tomorrow's weather are available to none of us, but paths with weather forecasts are.

Which paths are available varies a lot, e.g., Warren Buffet can afford paths where splendid wines are drunk every night, but I cannot. This does not mean Warren will take such a path; it means he could. On the other hand, paths that include being married to Taylor Swift or playing in the NHL aren't available to Warren, even though he has mucho dinero. Which paths are available to you depends on your resources and what is happening. Your resources include intelligence, abilities, age, appearance, propensity to work, education, friends, and inheritance. What is happening includes prices, wage rates, who is the President of France, pollution, public goods, and whether Taylor exists and, if so, what kind of guys or women she likes.

The passage of time reveals what has happened to now; this restricts which paths are available going forward. If I have recently gained thirty

[12] An exception is *De Gustibus Non Est Disputandum* (In matters of taste, there can be no disputes) by George Stigler and Gary Becker (1977).

The establishment of the proportion that one may usefully treat tastes as stable over time and similar among people is the central task of this essay.

If I understand, they are not arguing that everyone has the same, and stable, ordering, but rather a lot of changes in an individual's behavior over time can be explained by changes in which paths are available, and across individuals by differences in which paths are available. In a bit of a dig,

the problem of [changing tastes] is abandoned at this point to whoever studies and explains tastes (psychologists? anthropologists? phrenologists? sociobiologists?).

As I note earlier, I believe differing constraints can explain a lot of why you and I behave differently, but they can't explain all the differences. 1977 was long ago.

pounds and learned about global warming, every available future path must start with a heavier me who knows about global warming. Even though I would like to begin the future lighter and less knowledgeable. The passage of time turns probabilities into certainties: Today, there is a 70% chance it will not rain tomorrow, so paths without rain tomorrow are still possible. The arrival of a rainy tomorrow will make my choice today to suntan tomorrow no longer available. See Fig. 2.3: everything is going smoothly for Scout, then it rains; it wasn't supposed to.

The black boxes are points in time where what is available changes. The blue arrows are the paths available at each point. The thick one is the path taken. A stop sign indicates that the current path is no longer available. Scout had planned a sunny day at the beach, but unexpected rain blocked that path, so Scout was forced to take a different path. But then, given her chosen path, her rich aunt dies, and suddenly, she can afford more goods and services.[13]

Unplugging my toaster would drastically limit its available paths to one path—not making toast.

The objective of a theory of behavior is to explain and predict how behaviors will change when what is available changes (a price or income increases, partner leaves). The objective is to explain and predict an economicus's sequence of paths as the set of available paths changes.

I have defined feasibility more restrictively than in many descriptions of NCT. In those, just one constraint is explicit, the budget constraint (an economicus can't purchase what it can't afford). Assumption 5 excludes paths that are not affordable in terms of income and wealth; it also excludes paths that are unavailable because of ability, intelligence, cultural restraints, laws, and moral commitments.[14] Other agents' orderings reduce, for you, which paths are available. E.g., paths with Bob as a friend are not available if he dislikes you. More rights for you, political and otherwise, increase your set of available paths, but they reduce those

[13] I drew the figure so after it rains there are three paths going forward, and her aunt dies of a broken neck in two of them. If she had chosen the lowest path, the aunt would still be alive: because on that path Scout would have called an ambulance. Or maybe the other two included Scott breaking her aunt's neck. As drawn, the spouse leaves no matter which path Scott chooses.

[14] Neoclassical choice theory does not explicitly mention duties (self-imposed constraints), commitments, or responsibilities. The economics philosopher Daniel Hausman (2011), an exception, views moral commitments as important determinants of behavior, but treats them as a determinant of the ordering rather than as a constraint.

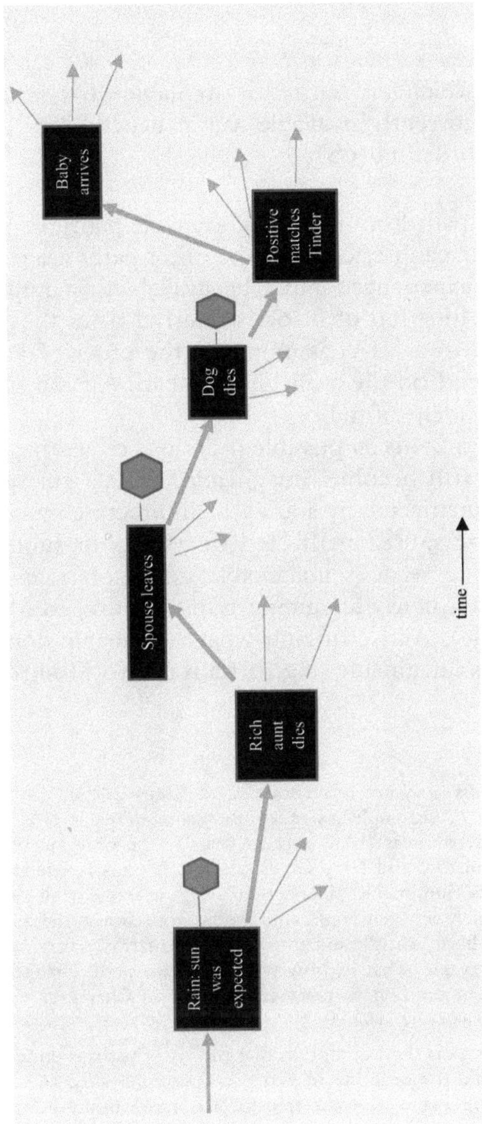

Fig. 2.3 Scout's paths over time

available to me: your right to do something constrains me from stopping you.

Assumption 6: *An economicus's ordering of paths* can't depend on which are currently available (6a), and which are currently available can't depend on their current ordering (6b).

So, eliminating a path from the set of available paths, or making additional paths available, can't affect how the other paths are ordered. Since the path currently experienced must be available, 6a implies that the ordering can't be a function of it. 6a is referred to as the *independence of irrelevant alternatives* (IIA) assumption: the order of Path *j* relative to Path *k* can't depend on the availability of Path *h*.[15] 6b says that what is available is independent of the ordering.[16]
The largest set in Fig. 2.4 is all possible orderings of all imaginable paths: if an unimaginable path becomes imaginable, this set enlarges. Assumption 3 is the subset unaffected by adding or subtracting imaginable paths. Assumption 6a is the subset unaffected by adding or subtracting available paths. [Changing what is imaginable does not necessarily change what is available (e.g., newly imagining transmutation to Montreal does not make it available). And changing what is available does not necessarily change what is imaginable (e.g., a train trip to Montreal becoming

[15] Another name for 6a is *choice coherence* (David Kreps 2013). The *weak axiom of revealed preference*, *WARP*, accomplishes much the same thing as IIA but is a restriction directly on behavior, whereas IIA is a restriction on the ordering of paths (Andreu Mas-Colell, Michael Whinston, and Jerry Green (1995). If 6a is violated, the individual's choices can be, in Kreps' judgment, "incoherent". His example: you order coffee and pie, you are given a choice between apple and cherry, you choose the apple. The waiter then says, "Oh, we also have peach", and this added alternative makes your change your order to coffee and cherry pie. That is, how you order two paths changes when another path becomes available. Assumption 6a takes center stage in Chapter 9 where I discuss a common quirk, the *endowment effect*.

[16] Assumptions 2, 3, 6, plus the assumption that the set of paths is finite (an assumption I haven't made) imply that the ordering of paths can be represented by a *utility function* that is unique up to increasing monotonic transformations. A utility function is a mathematical function that associates a number with each path as a function of its components such that a higher-ranked path is associated with a larger number. I will rarely mention utility functions or the number the function associates with each path (called *utility*).

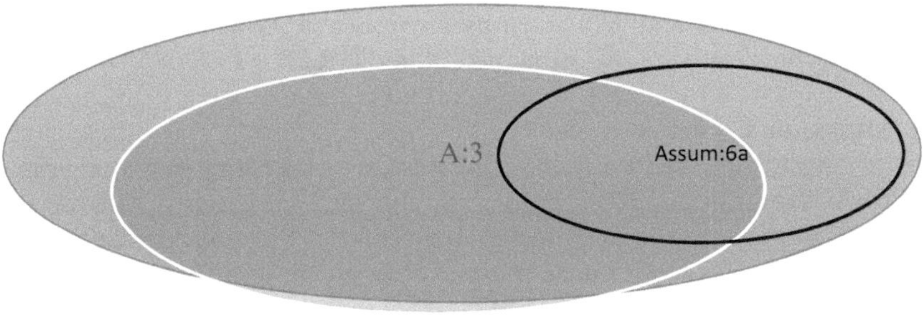

Fig. 2.4 Orderings, at a pt. in time consistent with Assum. 3 and 6a

affordable does not mean it wasn't previously imaginable).] The intersection of Assumptions 6a and 3 represents the set of orderings that are not influenced by changes in imaginable or available paths.[17] NBT restricts orderings to the intersection of the Assumption 3 and 6a sets.

> Assumption 7: *At every point, economicus takes one of its highest-ranked available paths (HRAPs).*[18]

Assumption 7 is an *optimizing axiom*. Optimization mistakes are not allowed.

Even if the ordering of paths is constant, which paths are available changes because time continuously updates our knowledge about the world and its future. This, by itself, will cause the HRAP to change.

* * *

My path definition, along with these seven assumptions, is a theory of behavior. If Assumptions 1–7 hold for Lady Gaga, and you know her

[17] That part of Assumption 6a that isn't part of Assumption 3 is the set of orderings that are unaffected by what is available but affected by what is imaginable. That part of Assumption 3 that isn't part of 6a is the set of orderings that are unaffected by what is imaginable but affected by what is available.

[18] Implicit is the restriction that there exists a HRAP (or paths). Assumption 7 is typically stated as a single highest-ranked available path, but there could be a number of available paths that are all tied for the highest rank.

ordering of paths and which paths are available, you can immediately identify which path she will now take if her HRAP is unique.

The path taken will vary across economici because what is imaginable, orderings, and what is available differ. Assumptions 1–7 is a behavioral theory. Still, there isn't anything in these seven assumptions that imply that an economicus makes conscious choices, consciously debates the alternatives, or that the debating influences what they experience.

Assumption 5 (economicus must experience an available path), along with 1–4 and 6–7, leads to the NBT's primary prediction: demand curves usually slope down (price increases cause demand to decrease).

A weakness, or strength, of Assumptions 1–7 as a theory of behavior is it assumes nothing about the ordering criterion, making Assumptions 1–7 consistent will every possible ordering criterion. They are, for example, consistent with a randomly generated ordering or an ordering based on how many times the letter *q* appears in the description of each path.[19] With Assumptions 1–7, the brain of an economicus is B.F. Skinner's black box, so there is no need to consider psychology or cognitive neurology.[20] The downside, and the upside, is that the ordering "is what it is", Assumptions 1–7 don't preclude nor imply that your chosen path is, in any sense, *best* (better for you than any other available paths). So, economists add a few additional assumptions.

While I have not seen the word *senses* or *sensations* in describing NCT, I'm pretty sure economists presume economici have senses, so let's make that explicit.

[19] While Assumptions 1–7 are consistent with one's ordering being randomly generated, it precludes higgledy-piggledy behavior: Assumption 4 restricts behavior to what is feasible. You might find Assumptions 1–7 with each entity's ordering randomly generated at each choice occasion, preferable to NCT. In explanation, everyone agrees that behaviors are limited to feasible behaviors, and what is feasible at a choice occasion is largely determined by prior behavior.

[20] In the twentieth century's first half, economists worked hard to purge choice theory of psychology. At the same time, psychology was dominated by behavioralism (led by Skinner); it considered the brain a box not worth opening—only behavior matters. While psychology has left behavioralism behind, economists still have principled blindness when it comes to the brain. Neoclassical choice theory predates modern neuroscience and behavioral economics.

Assumption 8a: *Economici have senses: they are sentient. And the sensations experienced and their intensities depend on which path* is taken.

Humans have six senses: sight, hearing, touch, taste, smell, and proprioception.[21] Bats have echolocation; humans don't. A sensation is the awareness of a stimulus through one or more senses; they enable an economicus to observe its environment (outside stimuli), so the ability to change its behavior in response to changes in its environment (respond to environmental stimuli). For example, head for the shade when the sun gets too hot and run out the back door when you hear a wolf howling at the front door. My refrigerator senses its internal temperature and set temperature but is sightless; in contrast, fridges in development have cameras that can sense whether it contains milk. My toaster senses which button (*bread*, *bagel*, or *defrost*) I pushed and whether its lever was pushed down. It sends electricity to its heating coils when it senses my push.

Eating an ice-cream cone produces a different melody of sensations than getting a massage. Animals experience pain, a sensation, and try to avoid the behavior that caused it.[22] Economicus is motivated to repeat the behavior that caused a positive sensation. If the theory is Assumptions 1–8a, animals are not excluded.

But what about plants? Natalie Angier (2009) describes how plants sense their surroundings and react in extraordinary ways. Charles Darwin and his son wrote a book (Darwin and Darwin 1896, 2004) about how plants respond to stimuli. Everyone agrees that plants are sentient—they gather information about their environment and change their behavior

[21] Animals have nerve receptors that fire only when a specific stimulus is encountered. For example, you have taste receptors on your tongue that only fire in the presence of sweets, and others that only fire in the presence of sours, and you have receptors on your retina that only fire if they experience the color red. Such firings are transmitted to your brain. These are sensations. Physiology and experiments indicate that there is more similarity in a sensation within a species than across species; for example, seeing is more similar across humans than between humans and frogs.

[22] An animal does not even need a backbone to experience pain. After using pain-inducing chemicals on spiders, Thomas Eisner (2015), the recently deceased "father of chemical ecology", concluded, "I have no doubt they did [experience pain]...we came to the conclusion that invertebrates perceive pain, and that their sensory basis for doing so may not be much different from our own."

based on what they sense. For example, they move toward sources that enhance their WB (light, nutrients, water) and exude chemical defenses when their WB is attacked by pests. They even share resources with other plants depending on their relative needs. The neuro-botanist Stefano Mancuso (Eric Bremmer et al. 2006; Mancuso and Alessandra Viola 2015) further claim that while plants do not have a central brain, they process information and their different parts communicate (signal). They share information in ways that are analogous to how animal brains work: they have cells that behave like neurons. He does not claim that plants experience pleasure or pain, but it makes one wonder. Many botanists reject his claim that plants are intelligent; it comes down to how you define intelligence.[23] He defines it as the ability to solve problems.

What about robots? My Roomba vacuum cleaner senses walls and drop-offs and changes its behavior (directions) when it encounters walls and drop-offs. It can also identify objects using its camera and artificial intelligence. The ability to sense things—including pain and pleasure—requires neither self-awareness nor a mental map of what is happening. Assumption 8a neither implies nor precludes economicus from having thoughts and emotions.

Assumption 8a implies an entity without sensors isn't an economicus. Since plants and animals have sensors, Assumption 8 does not exclude them. It also does not exclude toasters, refrigerators, or computer programs. It excludes inanimate objects such as rocks and steel bars.

I believe that advocates of NCT believe/suppose economici are sentient, but Assumption 8a is not listed as an assumption.

Assumptions 1–8a imply that a sequence of sensations is associated with each path.

Assumption 8b: *An economicus's ordering of paths is determined, at least in part, by the sequence of sensations* that would be produced by each path.

That is, whether Path *j* is ranked higher than Path *k* is determined, at least in part, by the sensations that would be produced by each.

[23] Mancuso was recently attacked by vegetarian extremists (Roberta Scorranese 2021): their reasoning was that saying plants have feelings makes it more OK to eat meat. He rejects their reasoning, but there is a logic to their conclusion.

Assumption 9a: *An economicus's ordering of paths is based on its WB (well-being), WB, accounting for the uncertainties. The more WB economicus associates with a path, the higher is its rank. And WB is determined, in part, by sensations.*

The phrase "accounting for uncertainty" is to be interpreted broadly, allowing different economici to account for uncertainty differently.[24] Assumptions 1–9a don't imply an economicus will always take the available path that would have produced the most WB. From now on, for brevity, I will omit the qualifier "accounting for the uncertainties". Note that 9a neither precludes nor implies that the economicus orders paths by their expected level of WB—*expected* meaning *statistical expected value*—details later.

Or

Assumption 9b: *An economicus's ordering of paths is based on its wants and desires. Paths that are more wanted/ desired/are ranked higher. And wants and desires are determined, in part, by sensations.*

Or

Both 9a and b: the two orderings are identical.

NBT (neoclassical behavior theory) is Assumptions 1–9, and any entity whose behaviors and motivations are consistent with Assumptions 1–9 is an economicus. The choice theory taught in introductory microeconomics courses is a restrictive case of NBT.[25] What is known as *Expected utility theory* is as well—details soon. After discussing Assumptions 9a and

[24] I initially wrote, "in a statistical sense". But for econometricians "statistics" implies the use of probability measures. Assumption 9a neither requires nor precludes probability measures.

[25] Typically, in introductory microeconomics courses, a path consists of only the goods and services you would personally consume on that path—your *consumption bundle*: other important path components are ignored. Which consumption bundles are available is only restricted by prices and income—the *budget constraint*. There is no future (it's a one-period world); there are no risks, and you have full knowledge—there is no ignorance.

b and then the implications of Assumptions 1–9, I will consider additional assumptions you may want to add.

The distinction between 9a and 9b is critical: it is the distinction between an economicus getting what it wants and getting what will increase its WB. Imagine three possible paths, *j*, *k*, and *l*, such that your WB-ranking is *k*, *l*, and *j*, and your wanting-ranking is *k*, *j*, and *l*. The two orderings differ, but Path *k* is ranked higher than *l* in both. Picture the degree of overlap between two paths as a continuum of correlations. If 9a and b both hold, the correlation is 1.0; the other end is -1.0, the midpoint 0 meaning uncorrelated. My guess is that many believe that the WB-ranking and the want/desire-ranking are either identical or highly positively correlated. In contrast, Buddhism believes the default correlation is negative and defines enlightenment as a state of being where 9a and b merge. Wow! economicus is enlightened.[26] The amount of actual overlap is an empirical question. A later chapter assesses the research.

At this point, WB[27] and *wants* and *desires* are not explicitly defined but determined by sensations, at least in part.[28] Being more explicit will require specifying economicus's experiential capabilities. Dogs, humans, and refrigerators have different experiential capabilities. While they all have temperature receptors, dogs and humans, but not refrigerators, have smell receptors, and dogs' receptors are more sensitive. Humans can think abstractly and can self-reflect; dogs and refrigerators can't. So, the specifics of WB are different for dogs, humans, and refrigerators.

Assumption 9 allows for two broad but distinct ordering categories: a WB criterion and a want/desire fulfillment criterion. So, without further assumptions, the ordering criterion is still unclear.

A question. Does making the ordering criterion either WB or wants and desires (Assumption 9) further restrict what entities can be economici? Or expressed another way, can entities that are neither animals

[26] Buddhists talk about "craving" rather than wanting and desiring, a synonym with a negative edge, "craving" chosen to draw their critical distinction between want fulfillment and WB (see, for example, Stephen Batchelor 2015).

[27] What *WB* means is often ignored. One view is that it does not matter what it means: it is "in the eyes of the beholder," like *porn*. I reject this. Another view is that WB means more *utility*, but this just defines WB as an ill-defined word, *utility*, a lousy synonym for WB. My students think utility means more than it does, and while some surveyors ask people about their WB, no one asks them about their utility.

[28] Looking ahead, *wants* and *desires* are synonyms. For some economici, *drives* and *instincts* might be more appropriate words.

nor plants have WB or have wants and desires? Sure! For example, when broken, an entity exhibits less WB (being well). WB for a machine or computer program is increasing in how well and long it performs its dictated tasks and at what cost. So, performance reflects the user's WB. [I wish my word processor, WORD, exhibited more WB, particularly the part that "corrects" my grammar.] I defined WB as emotional WB, life-satisfaction WB, and pleasurable sensations, but not all entities are capable of experiencing all three. Machines, for example, are incapable of emotional WB and pleasurable sensations. And most species can't experience life satisfaction. Experiential capabilities vary with DNA by species and across individuals within a species. Keep in mind that animals, like machines, do not get to pick their capabilities.

Assumption 9a implies one concept of *value*, *economic value*, in that higher-ordered paths have more value. Since orderings depend on economicus's WB, objects don't have objective/inherent value, only extrinsic value. Without 9, there would be no such thing as economic value.[29]

Assumption 9a also implies that expanding the set of available paths can't decrease WB (having additional options never hurts—even a million colors of house paint).

With either 9a or 9b, the ordering need not depend on every path component. For example, while who is the Prince of Denmark is a component of every path, it does not have to affect an economicus's ordering: if three paths are identical except for whether it's Hans, Bob, or Hamlet, and the economicus is indifferent to who is the Prince, the three paths would all have the same rank. Your ordering might depend on each path's malnutrition rate, while mine depends only on what I would get to eat: I'm indifferent to what the wife, kid, and dog consume.

Reasons for why an animal's ordering depends on what other animals are doing include: (1) Their behaviors negatively affect it (they are smoking, driving drunk, or trying to kill and eat it). (2) Their behaviors positively affect it (they nurture, protect, and leave around half-eaten carcasses. (4) Animals care about their position (status, influence) relative

[29] So, for you, apples, the smell of roses, and the existence of a pristine ecosystem only have value if including them in a path would increase that path's rank. Values depend on the orderings of paths, so commodities only have value if they affect the ordering; value, or lack of, isn't an objective characteristic of a commodity.

to other animals, particularly their peers, and (5) animals sexually desire one another.

For humans, their ordering depends on each path's present and future components. And many humans put less weight on path outcomes the farther they occur in the future—they discount the future. There is nothing in Assumptions 1–9 that implies economici have the cognitive ability to consider the future—and there is also nothing that precludes it.

Knowledge, or its absence (ignorance), could be a factor in how an economicus orders paths. All else constant, I am likely to rank higher paths where I don't know the black spot on my toe is toe cancer, even if I can find out for free. Knowledge and ignorance are commodities, like peanut butter.[30] My ordering could also depend on freedom or rights (Free speech? Free Love?) I would have in each path. And it could depend on whether you have those same rights.

At this point, you might wonder why an entity could have an ordering not based on either WB or want fulfillment (Assumption 9a or b). A straightforward answer is that entities neither select their ordering nor their ordering criterion. Instead, your ordering is imposed by genetics, God, parents' parenting skills, and other past experiences, which you can now do nothing about. In evolutionary genetics, the objective of plants and animals is to increase the probability they will pass along their DNA, which is different from making them better off. What ordering a God would impose depends on which god, but the one in my church was not into WB or reducing suffering while people are alive. And he was into maximizing the ill-being of most dead people—those in hell.

NBT assumes economicus's ordering is given and assumes nothing about its creation. Economists don't seem to care where it came from—but they should. Quoting the economic philosophers Franz Dietrich and Christian List (2013) and then Samuel Bowles (1998):

[30] Recently, Ananda Ganguly and Joshua Tasoff found that 16% of the university students sampled were willing to forego payment of $10 to avoid learning whether they had genital herpes. David Eil and Justin Rao (2011) have found that people will pay to not learn about their IQ or how attractive others find them. Check out Kate Sweeny et al. (2010).

> Preferences are exogenously given in that the standard theory can't explain how they are formed. An *agent's* preferences are simply taken to be an essential but inexplicable feature of the agent's personal identity.
>
> The axiom of exogenous preferences is as old as liberal political philosophy itself… Reflecting this canon, most economists have not asked how we come to want and value the things we do.

If there is no theory of how a WB ordering is created, any is possible, and my WB could mean sticking pins in my eyes and drinking antifreeze. If I am an economicus, eyeball pin-sticker, it is either because I have a bizarre ordering or terrible options. If economists could explain the ordering's creation and evolution, they would be better able to predict behavior. Your ordering is determined by genetics and learning, but both words are absent from economic theories of choice.[31]

[31] There is a small literature on the formation of your ordering, not much by economists. In one strain (going back to Kelvin Lancaster 1966), an ordering of goods and services is derivative of a more basic ordering in terms of the characteristics of those goods and services, but it does not ask where the ordering in terms of characteristics came from or how and why it might change over time. In the ordering-formation literature, a distinction is made between worlds of complete and incomplete information. In a world of incomplete information, experiencing different commodities and activities provides information (experiencing what Vegemite tastes like) that might cause you to modify your ordering of paths. Also, belief formation and their evolution affect your orderings. Dietrich and C. List (2016) model your ordering in terms of the motivational salient properties of each path (the properties you pay attention to), causing your ordering to change as properties gain or lose salience. "For example, after having suffered from gallstones, an agent may form his or her preferences over various kinds of food on the basis of whether they are healthy and may no longer be interested in whether their taste is rich (something he or she cared about before the illness)." The salience of choice is discussed in Chapter 4.

In the 1998 *J. of Economic Literature*, Bowles reviews how economic institutions (markets, families) influence your ordering. I have modeled (Morey and Mara Thiene 2017) one's ordering as a function of one's personality. See the references to the determinants of the ordering in Dietrich and List (2013) and the book, *Preference Change: Approaches from Philosophy, Economics, and Psychology* (Till Grune-Yanoff and Sven Hansson 2009). For another take, see D. Hausman (2011) who views the determination of one's ordering as a challenging process of weighing WB, desires, moral obligations, and beliefs, so subject to change. Philosophers discuss the logic (or illogic) of changing one's ordering.

WB-Comparable and WB-Commensurable

Assumptions 2 and 9a require that all paths and their components are *WB-comparable*, which requires that all the kinds of WB are *WB-commensurable*. If there isn't complete WB-comparability and commensurability, the ordering is incomplete, contradicting Assumption 2.[32]

Explaining: distinguish between kinds of WB and *bearers of WB*. Feeling safe is a kind of WB, whereas door locks are a bearer (producer) of this kind of WB, and so are security services.[33] A bearer is a producer of one or more kinds of WB. A path is a bearer, and so are each of its components. Since, for me, the taste sensation sweet-'n-salty is one kind of WB, bacon covered in maple syrup, and caramels with sea salt are bearers of this kind of WB; all else constant, I order paths with more sweet-'n-salty higher.

An ice-cream cone is a bearer of multiple kinds of WB, including pleasurable taste, gustatory and visual sensations, positive thoughts, and positive emotions (*happiness*). At the same time, its consumption can decrease other kinds of WB: my later thought: *I'm depressed because my diet is ruined.*

Distinguish between comparing kinds of WB (a sense of calm vs. sexual pleasure) and comparing bearers (a meditation class vs. a willing sexual partner).

WB-comparability is a property that two paths either have or don't. If two bearers aren't WB-comparable, they are *WB-incomparable* (Chang 1997). Paths *h* and *k* are WB-incomparable if none of the following statements are correct: *h* is ranked higher than *k*, *k* is ranked higher than *h*, or *h* and *k* have the same rank. They are WB-comparable if one, and only one, of these statements is correct. For example, if Path *k* is identical to Path

[32] It is sufficient, but not necessary, to make the ordering incomplete. Sen (1997) lists "*process significance* (preferences may be sensitive to the choice process... and (2) *decisional inescapability* (choices have to be made whether or not the judgemental process has been completed)." Sen (2018) lists *epistemic inadequacy*: "we quite often do not know all of the consequences that will follow from taking one action rather than another."—another term for lack of full information.

[33] For some, guns are a bearer of feeling safe; for others, they are bearers of fear. Political philosophers have used *freedom*, *equality*, and *pleasure* as examples of kinds of WB and the Bill of Rights as a bearer of freedom and equality. Philosophers concerned with the motivators of choice typically use the word *value* rather than WB. Ruth Chang (1997) is responsible for the adjective *bearers* to keep clear the distinction between kinds of WB and the bearers that produce the different kinds of WB.

h, except Path *k* has *x* more pandas in the wild, but *y* has fewer teachers in your daughter's school, and if you can determine which path you rank higher, these two paths are WB-comparable. [WB-(in)comparability is a pair-wise property[34]:]

WB-comparability is a property that two path components have or don't have. Components *x* and *y* are pair-wise WB-incompatible if increasing the amount of one component while decreasing the other makes the new path WB-incomparable with the initial path. For example, skiing, *s*, and eating chocolate, *c*, are not WB-comparable if increasing *s* or *c* while decreasing the other makes this new path WB-incomparable with the initial one. In contrast, here are a few examples of comparability: I would give up my friendship with George for two apples, my friendship with Phil for five apples, and for no finite number of apples would I give up my friendship with Wanda. I would give up my right to free speech for the freedom to do whatever else I please, but I would not give up free speech for 12 ice-cream cones. A complete ordering of paths based on WB means you know whether and at what rate you would trade any path component for any other path component, be it friends, The Bill of Rights, or cheeseburgers. The rate can be zero or infinite—extreme examples of WB-comparable.

Figure 2.5 shows what paths are ranked or not ranked when there at WB-incomparabilities.

Since it's a figure, paths are limited to three components: the rate of global warming, *gw*, the individual's consumption of market goods, *m*, and her positive personal relationships, *r* (familial, sexual, and platonic (friendships)). In Fig. 2.5, *m* increases as one moves left, *r* increases as one moves forward, and the rate of *gw* declines are one moves up, *lgw* for less *gw*. The intersection can represent any path. The axes are deviations from it. Paths with at least more of one and not less of the others are in the upper-left front quadrant, Quadrant A. Paths with less of at least one, but not more of the others, are in the lower-back right quadrant, Quadrant G. Label the quadrants alphabetically, A-H, going counter-clockwise, starting with A top left. Complete WB-comparability means the individual can rank every conceivable pair of paths.

But what if some path components are WB-incomparable? Paths in Quadrant A are still ranked higher than the origin path, and paths in G

[34] If Paths *j* and *k* are incomparable, and Paths *k* and *l* are incomparable, that does not imply *j* and *l* are incomparable.

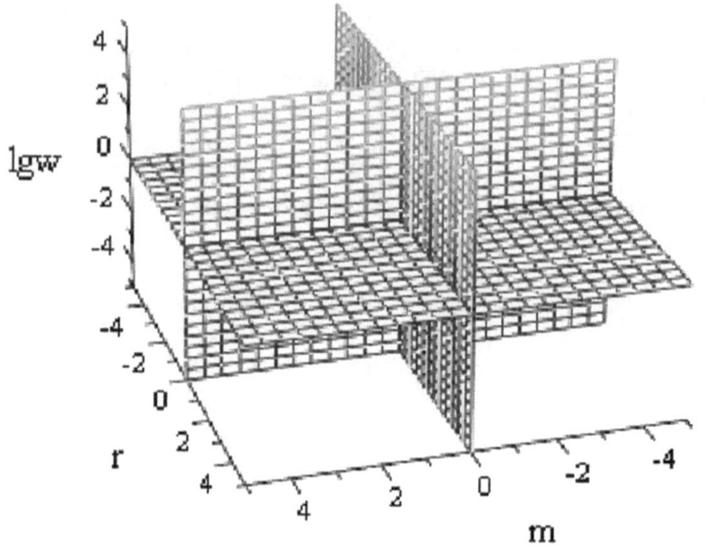

Fig. 2.5 m-*r*-*lgw* paths

are still lower. Which other rankings remain depends on what is and isn't comparable.

If nothing is comparable, only Quadrants A and G paths are ranked relative to the origin path.

What if *m* and *r* are WB-comparable, but *gw* is WB-incomparable with both? Then, paths on the horizontal plan through the origin (*gw* constant) are also ranked related to the origin path. Paths in Quadrants B, C, and D interiors are unranked relative to the origin path. These paths have less *gw* and less of either *m* or *r* than the origin path. Paths in Quadrants E, F, and H interiors are also unranked relative to the origin path. These paths have more *gw* and more *m* or *r* than the origin path.

Alternatively, what if *gw* and *m* are WB-comparable, but *r* is incomparable with both? Then, all paths on the vertical plane through the origin (*r* constant) are ranked related to the origin path. Paths in Quadrants B, E, and F interiors are unranked relative to the origin path. These paths have more r and either less m or more gw than the origin path. Paths in Quadrants C, D, and H interiors are also unranked relative to the origin path. These paths have less *r* and more *m* or less *gw* than the origin path.

To summarize, if a path component is not WB-comparable with other components, paths with different levels of that component often can't be ranked.

* * *

WB-incommensurability: WB of kinds *A* and *B* are WB-incommensurable if you cannot compare them in terms of WB (David Wiggins and Nien-he Hsieh. For example, it requires you to be able to compare music's sensual pleasure with the relief from finding out pandas won't be going extinct. Complete commensurability means you have a complete ordering over all conceivable *packets* of different kinds of WB. Incomplete commensurability means you can't order all the WB-packets.[35] In philosophy, the practice is to use the words "comparable" and "incomparable" when comparing goods, activities, and paths and to use the words "commensurable" and "incommensurable" when comparing kinds of WB (Chang 1997).[36]

Feeling safe and being in love are WB-incommensurable if you cannot order all packets that vary only in feeling safe and experiencing romantic love. Likewise, if you can't compare the grief from the loss of a loved one with global warming existential-angst, they are WB-incommensurable.[37] [The pandemic is caused both death and a reduction in CO_2 emissions.]

Complete WB-commensurability implies an economicus can order all packets in terms of utility, with packets differing by kinds and magnitudes

[35] You will still have a partial ordering of packets. For example, if all the kinds of WB generated by eating different types and quantities of chocolate are commensurable, there will an WB ordering over packets that vary only in the types and quantities of chocolate eaten. There can also be a partial ordering in that Packet *c* generates more WB than Packet *m*, while there are packets that generate more WB than *c* but less than *m* but can't be ranked relative to each other.

[36] I add the prefix "WB-" to both "comparable" and "commensurable" because one can compare based on criteria besides WB, so comparability does not always mean *WB-comparability*. And because a few economists have used "commensurable" to mean the ordering of paths is complete and has no lexicographic properties, which is different from how I define *WB-commensurable*. See Clive Spash and Nick Hanley (1995), David Pearce (1998), Mika Rekola (2003), and Jonathan Aldred (2006).

[37] Even if Packets *h* and *k* are WB-incomparable, they still can be comparable in terms of specific kinds of WB (e.g., Packet *k* generates more happiness than *h*, but less life satisfaction). And Packets *h* and *k* being comparable does not imply that either is comparable with any other packets.

of WB. E.g., picture a three-dimensional graph with *satisfaction*, *calm*, and *pleasurable sensations* on the three axes. Each point in Fig. 2.6 represents a different packet. The black WB package (dot) has positive amounts of satisfaction and calm but no pleasure, whereas the green has pleasure but no satisfaction or calm. If an individual can't order every packet, she suffers from WB-incommensurability. Alternatively, if I could always order paths that vary only in the amounts of contentment and excitement they produce, contentment and excitement are, for me, WB-commensurable.

WB-commensurability gives a second and equivalent way of defining pair-wise WB-incompatibility for two components. Commodities *s* and *c* are WB-incomparable if the kinds of WB produced by *s* are incommensurable with the kinds produced by *c*.[38]

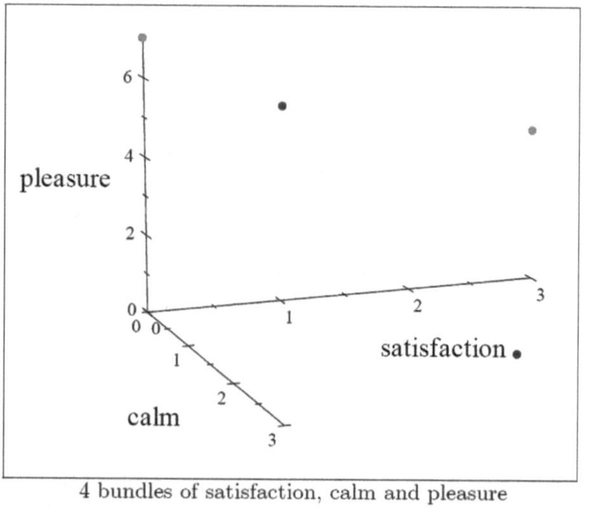

Fig. 2.6 Four combinations of satisfaction, calm, and pleasure

[38] Incomparability of a bearer can be discontinuous: at some levels, you can WB-compare and at other levels you can't. For example, while I'm not sure I could compare all possible income reductions with all possible reductions in the rate of global warming, I know I could compare a few of them: for example, ten dollars less income with a 10% less *gw* is ranked higher than my current path. All that is needed for WB-incomparability is that there are income reductions where I wouldn't be able to order the current path vs. a 10% reduction in *gw* combined with any of those income reductions.

Complete WB-commensurability is necessary for complete WB-comparability.

You can guarantee that WB-incommensurabilities will never occur if you are willing to assume there is just one type of WB. If so, whether two kinds of WB are commensurable is a non-issue. Nevertheless, many people, including economists and philosophers, are *WB pluralists* (a philosopher would say *value pluralists*): we believe there is more than one kind of WB, more than one way to be better off. Daniel Kahneman and Angus Deaton (2010), two recent Nobel laureates in Economics, are WB pluralists. The Harvard legal scholar Cass Sunstein (1993) makes a compelling case for WB pluralism. The utilitarian Jeremy Bentham (1748–1832) was not a WB pluralist: he was a WB monist; WB is pleasure (a unidimensional pleasure/pain continuum), a sensation that varies by magnitude and duration.[39] The philosopher and legal scholar Donald Regan is, I believe, a rare example of a modern WB monist.[40]

Aristotle, a WB pluralist, argued that many kinds of WB are WB-incommensurable; many modern philosophers agree (Martha Nussbaum 2012)—many regular people agree.[41] If not all kinds of WB are commensurable, Assumptions 2 and 9a are violated: economicus does not have a complete ordering of paths based on WB. Chapter 7 provides more

[39] Locke (1700/1975 and Sheridan 2016) believed the same. Whether the utilitarian J.S. Mill was a WB pluralist is a matter of debate. She identifies him as one because he counts "music, virtue, and health as major pleasures" (M. Nussbaum 2012). In contrast, Mark Schroeder (2012) in his survey of Value Theory, notes that "whether Mill properly counts as a pluralist about value depends on whether his view was that there is only one value — happiness — but two different kinds of pleasure which contribute to it, one more effectively than the other, or whether his view was that each kind of pleasure is a distinctive value."

[40] Quoting him (1997): "In this volume, I am the 'designated eccentric', appointed to take a position no one else would touch with a barge pole,...Specifically, I believe the following two propositions: (1) There is one and only one sort of value that matters to practical reason in the final analysis. This unique final value is G.E. Moore's 'good' ['good' as in approved of]. (2) Given any two items (objects, experiences, states of affairs, whatever) sufficiently well specified so that it is apposite to inquire into their (intrinsic) value in the Moorean sense, then either one is better than the other, or the two are precisely equal in value."

[41] Philosophers accept the idea that some kinds of WB are commensurable (e.g., the pleasure of a cold drink and the pleasure of an ice-cream cone), but they reject that all kinds of WB can be compared. For example, the WB loss generated by environmental injuries and animal extinctions might not be comparable with the WB gain generated by a cold soda.

detail and summarizes the arguments for and against bearer-of-WB-comparability and WB-commensurability.

In contrast, if one adopts Assumptions 9b instead of 9a, there will not be a complete ordering unless there is complete comparability of bearers of want/desire fulfillment. And this requires complete commensurability of all the different wants and desires.

Cardinal WB?

Assumptions 2 and 9a don't imply that WB has cardinal properties; they also don't preclude it. If an individual's WB is *weakly cardinal*, she can order paths in terms of WB; and she can, in addition, order differences between paths in terms of WB. She can comprehend whether a shift from Path *j* to Path *k* would increase her WB more or less than a shift from Path *c* to Path *f*. If her WB is *strongly cardinal*, she can also comprehend whether the ratio of the WBs associated with Paths *j* and *k* is greater than the ratio associated with Paths *c* and *f*. For example, an individual whose WB ordering is strongly cardinal could comprehend that a shift from j to k would increase her WB three times more than a shift from *c* to *f*.[42]

Complete WB-comparability and commensurability don't imply that WB has cardinal properties.

Implications of NBT (Assumptions 1–9)

Bivalves and plants order paths consistent with Assumptions 1–9. I am not sure about dogs. Consider a computer program that orders words alphabetically and selects the highest-ranked available word. And words that start with the letters *a*, *c*, *f*, or *ba* are unavailable. It would select

[42] Consider numbers. Numbers are ordered in that 10 is larger than 5 and 5 is larger than 3. In addition, numbers are weakly cardinal in that the differences between numbers can be ordered. E.g., the difference between 10 and 5 is greater than the difference between 6 and 3. An ordering where the differences can be ordered is, at least, *weakly cardinal*. Numbers also have the property that the ratios of numbers can be ordered. For example, 10/5 is larger than 5/3. If an ordering has this ratio property it is *strong cardinality*. Strong cardinality implies weak cardinality. In contrast, consider the ordering properties of letters (a, b, c, ...). Letters are ordered in that alphabetically "c" comes before "m" but a difference between any two letters is meaningless, so differences between letters can't be ordered, and neither can their ratios. So, letters have an ordering, but that ordering has no cardinal properties: no one claims the letter *q* divided by the letter *m* is greater than the letter *d* divided by the letter *w*.

bb, the "size of a shot fired by an air rifle". The program selects its most wanted path, the *bb* path. Consider my refrigerator: the relevant components of every path are internal temperature, set temperature (set by me), and whether the refrigeration is on or off. The paths are ordered by how much it is too hot or cold: the smaller the absolute difference between the internal and set temperatures, the higher the path is ranked. If there are two paths where the temperature is 5 degrees too warm, the one with refrigeration on is ranked higher than the one with it off. If the internal temperature is either at the set level or too cold, it experiences/chooses to turn off the refrigeration; if it is too hot, it experiences/chooses on. It is doing the best it can; it is being well. Life and consciousness aren't required. If Assumptions 1–9 apply to humans, they also apply to philosophical zombies, creatures that, by definition, have no conscious experiences.

Assumptions 1–9 do not imply that economici have thoughts or emotions. These assumptions do not require a memory except for knowing the ordering. And they don't imply that economici are self-aware. They don't even imply that economici are conscious. Assumptions 1–9 do not require that an economicus is a living plant, animal, or human. Assumptions 1–9 imply rationality in the weakest sense. And Assumptions 1–9 don't imply that WB has cardinal properties.

Assumptions 1–9 don't imply that the path experienced was chosen (consciously or unconsciously), which makes me wonder why NCT includes the adjective *choice*. Here I am defining choice in the street sense: you have a choice if you could have behaved differently. Assumptions 1–9 apply to worms, but many humans believe that worms are *incapable of choice*: worms have limited options, and evolution has programmed their instincts to crawl, dig, and eat to maximize gene transmission.[43] Does incapable of choice apply to you as well? This is discussed in Part II.

Assumptions 1–9 imply that there is no randomness in behavior. By this, I mean that if two economici at a point in time have the same ordering of paths and the same available paths, both will take the same path.

[43] "Worms exhibit dietary choice, they hunt for high-quality food and leave hard-to-eat bacteria...Using laser ablations and mutant analysis, we show that AIY neurons serve to extent roaming periods and are essential for food seeking" (Boris Shtonda and Leon Avery 2006).

Assumptions 1–9 are consistent with taking a path with future doom and gloom written all over it. For example, paths that include a daily bottle of Beefeaters—it tastes great and, at the time, feels good—even though the economicus knows it will soon lead to a massive drop in future WB. Such drinking could be part of economicus's best available path if the weight it puts today on future WB is less than it puts on immediate WB. As noted earlier, Assumption 9a is consistent with any type of, and degree of, what economists call *temporal discounting* (discounting the future).

If you subscribe to an ethic that assumes more WB is the goal, then whether Assumption 9a holds (the ordering is based on WB) is critical. Welfare economics is such an ethic: anything that increases the WB of a member of society is ethically right as long as it does not decrease the WB of other members. If more WB is the ethical goal, Assumptions 1–9a support the argument that Robin Crusoe[44] should have unlimited freedom: he can do no wrong, so restricting Robin's freedom is wrong/ unethical. Suppose more WB is the ethical goal, and Assumption 9b is correct, but not 9a. In that case, Robin will not even do what is ethically right for himself, eliminating the ethical justification for unlimited freedom. Assumption 9a, combined with the ethic that more WB is ethically preferred, implies something right about an economicus's behavior, at least from its perspective—this is the ethical creep I mentioned earlier.

Alternatively, if you subscribe to an ethic that assumes the goal is to fulfill more wants and desires, then if for Robin, Assumption 9b holds, but not 9a, Robin can do no wrong.

An Important question is whether humans violate the NBT Assumptions (Assumptions 1–9). Much of Part II is devoted to this question.

Expected Utility Theory, EUT, Is a Restrictive Case of NBT (Assumptions 1–9)

Expected utility theory (EUT)—developed in the twentieth century—restrictively specifies how one chooses in an uncertain world. To start, it assumes WB is cardinally meaningful.[45] Specifically, economici can order

[44] The classic example of a society where no one else is affected by anyone's behavior.

[45] EUT is a prominent form of *Decision theory* which is an umbrella term for theories designed to model choices in an uncertain world. It is an interdisciplinary endeavor with contributions from statisticians, philosophers, theorists, and economists. It also includes, or not, game theory and social-choice theory. For introductions to Decision Theory and

WB differences (at least weakly cardinal).[46] It also requires that a probability of occurrence is associated with every uncertain event. It is a restrictive case of NBT and predicts economicus will choose the available path with the highest expected WB.

An example of expected WB: imagine that you and your partner prefer having a girl over no child and no child over having a boy. You can, with certainty, have a baby, and the probability it is female is 0.5. Your cardinal WB from not having a baby is 0. If you have a child, your expected WB is the WB associated with a girl multiplied by 0.5, plus your WB with a boy multiplied by 0.5. If WB with a girl is 1 and WB with a boy is -0.5, the expected WB with a child is 0.25, which is greater than zero. So having a child would maximize expected WB. The ordering of alternatives would be the same if the WB from a girl was 0.5 and from a boy −1, but in this different cardinal situation, EUT says you would choose to not have a baby because the expected WB from having a baby is less than expected WB without one.

John von Neumann (1903–1957) and Oscar Morgenstern (1902–1977) famously demonstrated that an economicus will choose the available path that maximizes their expected WB if one adds to Assumptions 1–8 and 9a four additional assumptions.

1. Differences in WB can be ordered, and
2. A probability can be associated with each set of uncertain alternatives in each path.
3. A continuity assumption, and
4. An independence assumption.[47]

EUT, see Martin Peterson (2017), Katie Steele and Orri Stefánsson (2016), and Ray Briggs (2017).

46 Imagine that Path *j* generates more WB than Path *k*, Path *k* more than Path *s*, and Path s at least more than Path *t*. EUT assumes the individual knows whether going from *k* to *j* increases WB more, less, or the by the same amount, as going from *s* to *t*. If WB has this property, the ordering of paths is, at least, *weakly cardinal*. See the earlier discussion of weak and strong cardinality.

47 Consider first the continuity assumption expressed as an example. The upcoming US Presidential election is part of every path. Imagine you rank Donald higher than DeSantis, and DeSantis higher than Harris, all else the same. The continuity assumption says that there must have been a specific probability, p_d, such that you would have been indifferent between a path where DeSantis wins for sure, and a path where Donald wins

Subjects violate the independence assumption in many choice situations, so EUT is not ideal for explaining choices in an uncertain world.[48]

EUT has two forms: explaining how one should choose in a world where outcomes are probabilistic (the normative form) and describing how people choose (the descriptive form). EUT is a descriptive theory, a restrictive case of Assumptions 1–9a.[49] Unlike many choice modelers, I never understood why a human would or should always choose to maximize expected WB. I implicitly questioned the continuity and independence assumptions, but without knowing it.

What Else Has Been Presupposed (Implicitly Assumed)? What, if Any, Additional Assumptions Would You Want to Add?

Presuppositions are things you take for granted (pre-suppose), imagining others do as well. Since tacit, economists rarely think about them, so there is no way of knowing what is presupposed unless one asks. Which, if any,

with probability p_d and Harris wins with probability $(1\text{-}p_d)$. This assumption is restrictive but not drastically so.

More restrictively, independence implies, all else constant, that if you ranked Donald higher than DeSantos, you ranked—for every p—a race between Donald with probability p and Harris with probability (1-p), higher than a race between DeSantis with probability p and Harris with probability (1-p). Independence says adding Harris to a race that was initially between Donald and DeSantis cannot influence your cardinal ordering between Donald and DeSantis.

48 See Jonathan Levin (2006) and Kahneman and Amos Tversky (1979). A famous example, the *Allais Paradox*, is from 1953 by the French economist and Noble Lauate, Maurice Allais. Subjects are presented with two different gambles and asked to indicate which alternative they prefer in each gamble. Many respondents' two choices together imply that they are violating the independence axiom. Johan Lehrer (2010) has a nice vacation-choice example. Kahneman and Tversky suggest that the violation occurs because people value sure things (an outcome with certainty) more than is consistent with the independence assumption.

49 Note again the phrase "WB, accounting for the uncertainties" in Assumption 9a: EUT restrictively assumes that the ordering criterion is expected WB. Uncertainty can be accounted for in ways besides a probability-weighted expected value. For example, if one is extremely risk-averse one might order paths by the least amount of WB that could be realized in each path, a maxi–min strategy—a strategy consistent with NBT but inconsistent with maximizing expected WB.

of the following additional assumptions (10–12) have you already implicitly included and now want to make explicit? What have you not already implicitly assumed but now want to? Adding could serve two purposes. (a) Adding 10–12 in sequence further restricts the set of entities whose behavior the theory explains. And (b) Adding each gives the entity more ways to experience a path, and this will allow us to be more specific about what it means for different sorts of economici to increase their WB. For example, adding Assumption 10 means the theory no longer applies to robots and toasters.

I will adopt the following terminology: continue to label any entity whose behavior is consistent with Assumptions 1–9 as an *economicus*. Entities whose behavior is consistent with Assumptions 1–11 are *super-economici*. Those whose behavior is consistent with Assumptions 1–9 plus Assumption 13 are *homo-economici*. If Assumptions 1–9 hold, but not 10, 11, or 13, the entity is a *primitive-economicus*. What increasing WB means is different for super and primitive economici. Deem Assumptions 1–11 *NBT Plus*. If Assumptions 1–9 plus 12 hold, the entity is a *choice economicus*, and if Assumptions 1–12 hold, the entity is a *super choice economicus*.

Assumption 10a: *Economici experience thoughts and emotions. Both are provoked by past and present sensations, perceptions, memories, knowledge, cognitive abilities, plus past thoughts, and emotions.*

A perception is a type of thought, how one interprets a sensation. A perception can depend on what caused the sensation: pain caused by a fall, knee surgery, or a mobster hitting you with a bat. If touched, you sense the touch, but how you perceive it depends on who is doing it. An elk sees and smells a wolf (sensations), and these sensations cause a perception. A sensation is necessary but just part of what produces the perception.

A perception is a thought, but not all thoughts are perceptions. While *thoughts* are challenging to characterize, I hope we all agree that thoughts are the product of thinking, and thinking is a cognitive process involving neurons firing. And we agree that a thought is a discrete mental state (they come and go) and differ from sensations. Thoughts can be conscious or unconscious: unconscious thoughts are ones you are unaware of. Many thoughts are questions: Why is the dog hungry, and where is the nearest restaurant? Saying "around the corner" is a spoken thought.

A belief is a type of thought (a stored thought) that the individual regards as true. "It's a 1964 Malibu." "Assumption X implies Assumption Y." "Trump made America great again, and if not for a Democratic conspiracy, he would still be President." Subjective probabilities are beliefs. "It is likely to rain tomorrow." "That bus is going to hit that car."

Humans typically believe that few other animals can think and that only humans have thoughts about anything other than the immediate past and future. Independent of what people believe, not much is known about animal thinking. Whether a machine can have thoughts is debated.

There is no agreed-upon definition or theory of *emotions*. There isn't even agreement on how many there are.[50] Emotions are viewed from three perspectives: "as experiences, as evaluations, and as motivations" (Andrea Scarantino and Ronald de Sousa 2018). For example, anger and arousal are experienced; they are evaluations of what's going on and motivate action. Emotions differ on numerous dimensions making it challenging to come up with a one-size-fits-all definition:

> *…some emotions are occurrences (e.g., panic), and others are dispositions (e.g., hostility); some are short-lived (e.g., anger) and others are long-lived (e.g., grief); some involve primitive cognitive processing (e.g., fear of a suddenly looming object), and others involve sophisticated cognitive processing (e.g., fear of losing a chess match); some are conscious (e.g., disgust about an insect in the mouth) and others are unconscious (e.g., unconscious fear of failing in life); some have prototypical facial expressions (e.g., surprise) and*

[50] Until recently the number was finite: The Confucian text *Liji* (*Book of Rites*) lists seven; Descartes lists six. In the 1970s, the psychologist Paul Ekman listed six. Now there are 27 with fuzzy boundaries (Alan Cowen and Dacher Keltner 2017). New ones include aesthetic appreciation, awe, awkwardness, empathetic pain, and nostalgia (Melissa Dahl 2020).

There is constructed-emotion theory (Lisa Barrett 2017a, b): while there are basic ones, some are constructed based on one's language and culture. Not everyone buys it. It suggests that if you can give the feeling a name, it is an emotion. Consider *Force Majeure* ["a vague sense of humiliation that accompanies an instinctual flight response to a perceived danger. named for the Swedish film in which a man runs away from his family to save himself from an avalanche and thereby is diminished by his fear"] And, *Itchy Teeth* ["the restless urge to explode your own life by doing something that can't easily be undone." I am tempted], and Liegasm ["The sick pleasure of knowing you're lying and getting away with it"] (Editors, NY Magazine 2020).

others lack them (e.g., regret). Some involve strong motivations to act (e.g., rage) and others do not (e.g., sadness). Some are present across species (e.g., fear) and others are exclusively human (e.g., schadenfreude [pleasure from another's misfortune] (Scarantino and de Sousa 2018).

Emotions have physiological components (e.g., hormonal, cardiovascular, and facial expressions) that can be observed. Still, emotions are more. They're simultaneously physiological and mental states: the same physiological state can be associated with either a positive or negative emotion depending on what is being experienced (e.g., pursued by a lion or watching a horror flick) and who is experiencing it.

It seems that one could have thoughts even if one cannot experience sensations, but I'm not prepared to argue the point.

Assumption 10a implies that each path is associated with a sequence of thoughts and emotions. Assumption 10a, like Assumption 8a, limits what can be an economicus: no more toasters or robots, at least for now.

Assumption 10b: *An economicus's ordering of paths (either in terms of WB or in terms of wants and desires) is determined, at least in part, by the sequence of thoughts and emotions* that would be produced by each path.

Whether Path *j* is associated with more WB than Path *k* is determined, in part, by the thoughts and emotions it would produce. And whether Path *j* is more wanted/desired than Path *k* is determined, in part, by the thoughts and emotions that each would produce. Assumption 10a is necessary but not sufficient for Assumption 10b. For humans, WB-enhancing emotions include pleased and relaxed, and disgust reduces WB.

Assumptions 10a and b don't imply the individual is self-aware.

Assumption 11: *Economici are self-aware*

Self-awareness is the "ability to take oneself as the object of one's own attention and thoughts," recognize yourself as a physical object, separate from all else, and recognize that what you feel belongs to you. In nature, there are degrees of self-awareness: it consists of five distinct cognitive abilities, and only humans seem to have the ability to think abstractly and symbolically.[51] Many other species have one or two, and a few have four.

Assumption 11 further limits whose behaviors the theory explains. My dog fails the standard test for self-awareness: he has been known to bark at himself in the mirror, even after I drew a blue dot on his forehead while he was napping. [Researchers draw a blue dot on the animal's forehead while it is sleeping. They place a mirror in the room and wait behind the one-way glass to see what it will do when it wakes up. If, when seeing itself in the mirror, the animal touches its forehead, it self-recognizes, and they conclude it is self-aware. Professor Gordon Gallup came up with this test when he cut himself shaving, seeing, in the mirror, blood. Chimps tend to touch the blue dot.] A few species (the higher primates, elephants, dolphins, magpies, and possibly pigs) have passed this mirror test, but not everyone is convinced it is a self-awareness test. E.g., self-awareness does not require visual self-recognition.[52] Assumption 11 excludes robots, cacti, most animals, a couple of humans I know, and new babies.

Assumption 11 introduces the possibility of "I" and "me" thoughts, such as *Wanda loves me*: one can't think reflectively about oneself without self-awareness. *I'm happy* (or *content*, *excited*, *awed*, *calm*, *relaxed*, *proud*, *superior*, *free*, *liked*, or *depressed*). So are, *I'm satisfied*; *I'm accomplished*, or *I'm a Fuck-up*. So, *I want to go skiing*. For the religious, *I am experiencing God's grace*, and *I'm a sinner.*

Thoughts About NBT Plus

Like NBT, NBT Plus does not require much in the way of logic or rationality. Super-economici are no more rational than primitive economici; Assumptions 10 and 11 add a bit of cogitating.

[51] This is one definition of self-awareness; feel free to replace it with another. In philosophy, self-awareness is one type of consciousness. The five types are awareness of yourself in relationship to your immediate physical environment (knowing where your body ends and the world starts), awareness of interactions with other members of your species, the ability to reflect on yourself over time, the ability to reflect on your feelings, and the ability to think about yourself symbolically and abstractly (Mark Leary and Nicole Buttermore 2003). Giacomo has, at least, the first two.

[52] For a video on self-recognition by an elephant go to http://www.pnas.org/content/suppl/2006/10/26/0608062103.DC1.

Assumptions 9–11 raise questions about how sensations, thoughts, and emotions map into WB and into wants and desires. Consider all the different things that affect your WB: sensual pleasures (tastes, sounds, sights), happiness, contentment, excitement, a sense of calm, relaxation, a meaningful/rich life, satisfaction (including life satisfaction), other positive thoughts (including those about the future), learning, pride, loving, being loved, a sense of accomplishment, interactions with others, interactions with animals and nature, being free, being equal or being superior, justice being served, different sorts of personal pain, anxiety, worry, depression, hunger, thirst, embarrassment, fear, sadness, anger, feeling sick, experiencing disability, your reactions to these by others, negative thoughts, loneliness, discriminated against, feeling inferior, and feeling controlled. Assumptions 9–11 force me and you to think about their mapping to WB. For example, it requires that all these diverse sensations, thoughts, and emotions are commensurable, and each can be separated from the act or situation that produced it. Wow!

But—I don't recollect seeing the words, *sensations*, *perceptions*, *thoughts*, or *emotions* in the standard economic literature on choice. Economists don't talk about them. This is unfortunate: they are what make us feel alive.

Assumptions 8, 10, and 11 (self-awareness) imply a self—a me—who experiences the world with sensations, thoughts, and emotions, all from a personal me perspective. There is a me embodied in every super-economicus, a me who experiences sensations, thoughts, and emotions as his.[53] In contrast, when my dog experiences pain and perceives danger, he reacts, but he does not consciously think about it as his pain and a danger to him because there is no conscious him for my dog. Self-awareness complicates mapping sensations, thoughts, and emotions to WB; the same for mapping to wants and desires.

Together with Assumptions 8, 10, and 11, Assumption 9b is David Hume's (1711–76) view of human nature: emotions, not reason, drive

[53] The late Harvard psychologist Daniel Wegner (1948–2013) Wegner has an insightful definition of the self: "The sense we have that we are agents who do things and experience things, and who in some regard are the same from one time to another. This sense of identity is inherent in the aspect that James (1890) called the 'knower,' the self that is the seat of experience, the self that is doing all our thinking and living. Another way of conceptualizing identity is the self as the object one can think about, the aspect that James called 'known'."

Another take on the self, a Buddhist take, is that it does not exist, it's empty—*no-self*.

behavior—"Reason is, and ought only to be the slave of the passions and can never pretend to any other office than to serve and obey them" (Hume 1740/2002).

With Assumptions 8, 10, and 11, the researcher and policymaker must consider what WB means for super-economici: economici with sensations, perceptions, thoughts, and emotions. I think WB can depend on them all, but how much weight each gets varies across super-economici and can vary over time for an individual super-economicus. And for some individuals, some kinds of WB might not be comparable (WB-incommensurable).

For Kahneman and Deaton (2010), kinds of WB fall into two categories: *emotional WB* and *life-satisfaction WB*. I prefer three categories. Their first is "the emotional quality of an individual's everyday experiences—the frequency and intensity of experiences of joy, stress, sadness, anger, and affection that makes one's life pleasant or unpleasant."[54] This component of WB is only relevant to economici that experience emotions, so only super-economici.

Life-satisfaction WB, in contrast, is economicus's thoughts about how well their life is going. This component of WB is relevant to economici that have thoughts and are self-aware, so, again, super-economici. Life-satisfaction WB is the thought component of WB.

Standard survey questions about emotional WB include: "Did you experience a lot of stress (enjoyment, happiness, anger, sadness, stress, worry) yesterday?" Another is "How happy are you these days?" where happiness (unhappiness) is adopted as a catchall for all the components of emotional WB. In contrast, a life-satisfaction question, "Rate your life on a ladder scale of 0 to 10 where '0 is the worst possible life for you', and '10 is the best possible life for you'" Another is "How satisfied are you with your life these days?" Unfortunately, few researchers ask emotional WB and life-satisfaction questions.

Until recently, those studying WB had either not thought about the distinction between emotional WB and life-satisfaction WB or viewed the distinction as unimportant because they incorrectly believed the two were influenced by the same factors in the same ways. This isn't the case, and the distinction is critical. For example, after a crucial dollar amount, more

[54] Emotional WB is sometimes defined as the ability to manage one's emotions. It is not how I am defining it here.

income will increase your life-satisfaction WB but not necessarily your emotional WB.

My third category is *sensations WB*: all else constant, WB increases (decreases) with the duration and intensity of pleasurable (displeasurable) sensations. Orgasm is a classic example of a pleasurable sensation. For me, and as noted, the taste of sweet-n-salty is near the top. The sensations associated with burning skin and inability to breathe are displeasurable, as is hunger. All else constant, economici repeat behaviors that produce pleasurable sensations and don't repeat behaviors that produce displeasurable sensations. But "All else constant" is essential. Gasping for breath could increase overall WB if it, for example, ends with you winning the Boston Marathon.

I don't recollect seeing a survey that asks people about the number and intensities of their pleasurable sensations. Doctors and nurses often ask, "On a scale of 1–10, how much does it hurt?"

* * *

Do you want to require WB to have cardinal properties or require that it has no cardinal properties?

As noted earlier, Assumptions 2 and 9a imply that economicus has, at a minimum, a complete ordering of paths based on WB. However, assumptions 2 and 9a neither imply nor preclude WB from having cardinal properties. Because of this, you might want to replace Assumption 2 with the assumption that the ordering must have cardinal properties. Or you might want to replace 2 with an ordering that does not have cardinal properties.

Assumption 2:	*At every point in time, an economicus has one ordering of all paths—1st, 2nd, …. An economicus has an ordering if, for all paths j and k, either Path j is ranked higher than Path k, Path k is ranked higher than Path j, or paths j and k have the same rank.*
Assumption 2(Cardinal):	*At every point in time, an economicus has one ordering of all paths—1st, 2nd, …. An economicus has an ordering if, for all paths j and k, either Path j is ranked higher than Path k, Path k is ranked higher than Path j,*

	or paths j and k have the same rank. And, economicus can rank the shift from i to k relative to a shift from l to m.
Assumption 2(Ordinal):	*At every point in time, an economicus has one ordering of all paths—1st, 2nd, ... An economicus has an ordering if, for all paths j and k, either Path j is ranked higher than Path k, Path k is ranked higher than Path j, or paths j and k have the same rank. And economicus can't rank a shift from i to k relative to the shift from l to m.*

Deem economici who conform to Assumption 2(Cardinal), *cardinal economici.* Deem economici who conform to Assumption 2(Ordinal), *ordinal economici.* So, why would you want to replace Assumption 2 with one of these more restrictive assumptions?

Some history: nineteenth-century neoclassical economists adopted Assumption 2(Cardinal) because they thought cardinal WB was necessary to predict behavior. They were wrong. In the late nineteenth century, economists figured out that cardinal WB in a world of certainty adds nothing to the model's predictive power[55]; the theory with Assumption 2(Cardinal) and the theory with Assumption 2 predicts the same thing: economicus will experience their highest-ranked available path. He will experience it whether he comprehends it's associated with a lot more, or a bit more, WB than the second-ranked available path. And, if he can't comprehend such differences, he still goes with the HRAP. If the two available paths are to marry Shirley and have five kids or marry Fred and adopt two, and the Fred path is associated with more WB, you marry Fred—end of story.

Since Assumptions 2 and 9a generate identical predictions to Assumptions 2(Cardinal) and 9a, and since 2(Cardinal) further restricts who the

[55] Dropping the assumption that WB is cardinal was first proposed by the German economist and mathematician Andreas Voigt in 1893, but he has been largely forgotten, with the credit going to Vilfredo Pareto (Torsten Schmidt and Christian Weber 2008). The switch from cardinal to ordinal was solidified by R.G.D. Allen and Hicks in 1934—they stated there was no need for cardinal WB in choice theory.

theory applies to, it was dropped from NCT.[56] But do you replace it with Assumption 2, an assumption that does not exclude cardinality, or do you replace it with Assumption 2(Ordinal), which, together with 8a, bans cardinal WB? NBT adopts Assumption 2, but for most of my career, I thought 2(Ordinal) was assumed. The distinction is between allowing for cardinal WB in a theory where its existence is superfluous to explaining behavior and banning cardinal WB because the WB of economici and humans don't have cardinal properties.

How to decide? Cardinal WB is not required to explain behavior in a world of uncertainty. It is, however, required if one assumes economici maximizes expected WB (expected utility theory, EUT). Proponents of EUT require Assumption 2(Cardinal).

Another reason to suppose cardinal WB is that you believe that many economici have it. We want to believe that we can comprehend and compare whether a shift from Path k to m would increase WB more or less than a shift from c to l. Humans describe their sensations, perceptions, and emotions in cardinal ways. For example, the perceptions and emotions I experience seem to have intensity ("The taste sensation I get from chocolate ice cream is a bit more pleasurable than from vanilla, but the pleasure sensation from tutti-frutti is way more pleasurable than from chocolate."). Wouldn't you expect WB to be cardinal if sensations, perceptions, and emotions have cardinal properties? For example, I would like to think that a starving me obtaining enough to eat would increase my WB more than my current WB would increase if someone gave me their new SUV in exchange for my old SUV.

But I could be deluded in imagining that my WB has cardinal properties. Perhaps my WB is ordinal. It is an unanswered neurological research question.

Would you expect evolution to lead to cardinal WB? Since we live with uncertainty, it depends on the evolutionary advantages of cardinal WB over ordinal in a world of uncertainty.[57] I don't know.

[56] If a theory's predictions don't change if a restrictive assumption is removed, the assumption should be removed. At least William of Ockham (1287–1347) thought so: if a restrictive assumption is removed, the theory applies in more situations. Use *Ockham's razor* to shave away unnecessary restrictions. Replacing an ordering with cardinal properties (which is an ordering of paths with intensity added) with only an ordering is such a generalization/relaxation.

[57] Recollect, that cardinal WB does not affect behavior when there is certainty.

If WB depends on sensations, thoughts, and emotions, and if behavior is motivated by WB, understanding your behavior requires understanding how your sensations, thoughts, and emotions map into your WB. While explaining this mapping is beyond my pay grade, the map depends on which experiences have or don't have cardinal properties.

Whether WB has cardinal meaning and to what degree is an empirical question. So are whether sensations, thoughts, and emotions have cardinal properties.

Another implicit assumption

Assumption 12: *Before a path is taken, an economicus has the experience of consciously choosing some components of that path. And that perception of choosing caused them to take a path* with those components.

Assumption 12 is a choosing axiom; it makes economicus consciously in charge of which path will be experienced—if you are an economicus and 12 holds, you choose, and this determines the path you take—so you are responsible for your behavior. It adds to economicus's sense of self (who they are) and the belief that others are responsible for their behaviors. [Jurists often wonder if a person should be held morally accountable if their behavior wasn't chosen. For example, shouldn't Pinocchio be excused for not listening to his father: Geppetto forgot to carve him ears. We find children, the insane, and animals not morally responsible, but there are exceptions: in 1386, the French hanged a pig for murdering a child—it had flopped down, suffocating the kid.]

A reason to adopt Assumption 12 is many humans believe it's true—at least for humans. [Of course, you can't choose every component of your path. For example, that Mexico is south of the U.S., and Trudeau is currently Canada's P.M. are path components I'm experiencing (same for you), but I chose neither Canada's P.M. nor the U.S.'s location. And, while what you consume and do is a component of my path, typically, I don't get to choose what you consume or do.] Assumption 12 is critical to the economic sense of choice and the ethics of economics, and it's crucial in ethics that assume more freedom is better than less.

Assumption 12 embeds two assumptions:

Assumption 12a: *Before a path is taken, an economicus has the experience of consciously choosing* at least some components of that path.

And Assumption 12b: *This perception of choosing* caused them to take the path they did.

A necessary condition for 12a is consciousness: the ability to experience conscious mental states.[58] Therefore, assumptions 10a and 11 are required. While 12b requires 12a, 12a does not imply 12b. If you experience choosing (12a), but that experience does not, in fact, influence what you experience (12b), you suffer from the *illusion of choice*. People, including economists, accept Assumption 12b as the gospel. However, many eminent neurologists reject it. Their reasons are presented in Part II.

Assumption 12 implies an economicus can consciously retrieve his ordering, and could, if so inclined, tell a researcher which alternative he would choose in any set of alternatives.[59] Without this conscious knowledge, you wouldn't be able to do this, and researchers wouldn't be able to learn about your ordering simply by asking you (something I have done many times in surveys).

More significantly, it implies that economici experience the available path with the most WB because they went through a conscious process—choosing. If Assumption 12 is violated, the predictions of NBT and NBT Plus won't change, but the path taken wouldn't be consciously chosen, making me, and probably you, hesitant to say, "Economicus made a

[58] This is one definition of consciousness (Robert Van Gulick 2018). "On one common reading, a conscious mental state is simply a mental state one is aware of being in ...Conscious states in this sense involve a form of *meta-mentality* or *meta-intentionality* in so far as they require mental states that are themselves about mental states. To have a conscious desire for a cup of coffee is to have such a desire and also to be simultaneously and directly aware that one has such a desire. Unconscious thoughts and desires in this sense are those we have without being aware of having them" (Van Gulick 2018). Thoughts are conscious if you are aware of them.

[59] You can be self-aware without being aware of your ordering of paths. If you are consciously aware of your ordering and your constraints, you know whether you are doing the best you can. Alternatively, if you do not consciously know your orderings, you have no conscious awareness that you are doing the best you can. In which case, your incentive to keep doing the same thing, if you have such an incentive, must be unconscious.

conscious choice."[60] A question concerning Assumption 12 is whether it is consistent with Assumptions 1–9 and, if so, what *conscious choosing* means. Without Assumption 12, the path taken could be determined entirely by an unconscious process—a simple process (the HRAP). There isn't anything to think about, either consciously or unconsciously.

If you insist, you can add Assumption 13.

Assumption 13: *Economici* are Homosapiens.

With it, the theory limits itself to explaining the behaviors of humans who behave in a manner consistent with Assumptions 1–9. Earlier, I laid out reasons for not limiting my NBT to humans; researchers are more likely to find economici among the entities who reside in zoos, forests, and gardens than at football games. And, if we exclude non-human animals but want to adopt an ethic that gives more standing to them or asserts humans have a duty to them, we will need a different model for animal behavior and WB.

One reason to include Assumption 13 is that many people want to believe, and need to believe, that humans are superior and separate from the animal kingdom. A way to separate us from the beasts is to assume human behaviors are chosen and animal behaviors are not. If one is in this category, one needs their theory of human behavior to be a choice theory that does not apply to other animals.

Assumption 13 implies Assumptions 8a, 9a, 10a, and 11, making them redundant if all living humans have sensations, thoughts, and emotions and are self-aware.

So, What to Say About an Economicus, a Person or Thing that Follows the Rules?

NBT, like more theories of behavior, assumes one theory of behavior explains the behavior of all humans: the way people think and perceive the world, along with their sense of self, is universal. Henrich, Steven Heine, and Norenzayan (2010) explain it [not what they believe].

[60] If you do not have conscious awareness of your ordering, the path you experience isn't determined by an conscious thought process, even if you are experiencing choosing. If so, if you believe you can correctly describe why you do what you do, you are wrong.

> We all have the same hardwiring, so we must all make choices in the same way...The fund analyst in NYC operates with the same axioms as the subsistence farmer in Peru.

My NBT even expands the applicability to other living things. The assumption that all human behavior can be explained by one set of assumptions is based on two things: (a) We all share the same genome, the *human genome* ("23 chromosome pairs with a total of about 3 billion DNA base pairs...24 distinct human chromosomes: 22 autosomal chromosomes, plus the sex-determining X and Y chromosomes."). And (b), Significant differences in how humans perceive and think and what motivates them have not been observed. The latter, (b), is because, until recently, no one looked. Even today, most behavior research is done on *WEIRD* people (Western, Educated, Industrialized, Rich, and Democratic), often undergraduate psychology or economic majors. Remember that NCT was created by old, white, male protestants, many of whom lived in nineteenth-century Great Britain—they were not thinking about explaining the behaviors of "savages" and other foreigners.

Maybe one theory of behavior can't explain the behaviors of all humans. Recent research indicates that when it comes to how we think and perceive the world, WEIRDS are the statistical outliers. Paraphrasing Henrich et al. (2005, 2010): the universality assumption has been under assault, starting in the 1960s when fundamental differences in visual perception across cultures were observed. It turns out that people's sense of fairness, how they decide, their sense of self, their moral reasoning, and even their brain scans vary significantly by culture, and WEIRD people are typically the statistical outliers. The point is how individual humans behave varies by population and culture.

Home-Economicus Is a Western Sort of Guy

Economicus can't have an inconsistent ordering of paths. In addition, his behavior is directed, without flaws, to the HRAP. Every kind of WB is commensurable for him: he's a Western ideal. Formal logic was first studied in Ancient Greece, infusing how we in the West view thinking, decision-making, and choice. Asian thinking tends to be more intuitive, holistic, and accepting of what Westerners view as contradictions.[61] In Ancient China, there was nothing comparable to the Ancient Greek system of formal logic; instead, a dialectic (method of reasoning and deciding) was developed that allows for contradictions, and this approach infused Asian thinking. Of course, we all do both types, and thinking patterns vary widely within a culture, but how people think and value different ways of thinking varies across cultures.[62]

Research by the psychologists Emma Buchtel and Ara Norenzayan (2008) demonstrates that Asians think more intuitively, judging intuitive reasoning as more reasonable than analytic reasoning. Their article starts with a quote on analytical versus intuitive thinking from a Chinese scholar in 1939. Expressing the Chinese view:

> ... We see an opposition of 'logic' versus common sense, which takes the place of inductive and deductive reasoning in China. Common sense is often saner because the analytic reasoning looks at truth by cutting it up into various aspects, thus throwing them out of their natural bearings, while common sense seizes the situation as a living whole... Logic without such common sense is dangerous... (Dr. Yutang Lin)

Different ways of thinking aren't just an East/West thing. For example, southern Italians think more holistically than Northern Italians, and working-class Southern Italians think more holistically than middle-class Southern Italians. Richard Nisbett, a social psychologist, has been a pioneer in finding cross-cultural differences in cognition and evidence supporting the hypothesis (the *Social Orientation Hypothesis*) that these differences are due to culture rather than genetic or linguistic differences.

[61] To clarify the distinction, quoting Joseph Henrich et al. (2010): *Holistic thought involves an orientation to the context or field as a whole, including attention to relationships between a focal object and the field, and a preference for explaining and predicting events on the basis of such relationships. Analytic thought involves a detachment of objects from contexts, a tendency to focus on objects' attributes, and a preference for using categorical rules to explain and predict behavior. This distinction between habits of thought rests on a theoretical partition between two reasoning systems. One system is associative, and its computations reflect similarity and contiguity (i.e., whether two stimuli share perceptual resemblances and co-occur in time); the other system relies on abstract, symbolic representational systems, and its computations reflect a rule-based structure.*

[62] Learning about logic, marginal analysis, and benefit–cost analysis might cause one to reason more analytically, causing economists to believe man behaves logically.

Do Any Economici Exist, or Are They Mythical Creatures? And Does It Matter?

Parts II and III are devoted to reporting on and discussing the recent psychological, neurological, philosophical, and behavioral economic research on the behavior of humans and other animals. In brief, Assumptions 1 and 4 are on solid footing: you can live only one life at each point in time, and you can't do the impossible. Concerning Assumption 2 (an economicus has a complete ordering of all paths), it's hard to imagine why it would be true. Based on the evidence that will be presented, I doubt whether Assumptions 7 (you experience your HRAP) and 9a (paths with more WB are consistently ranked higher) apply to all, or even some, humans, and doubt whether they apply to chimps, dolphins, and elephants. The realism of others is also in doubt.

But! No theory's assumptions realistically describe all the situations where it is applied—the apple that fell on Newton's head was not falling in a vacuum. Theories are not necessarily rejected because they assume unrealistic stuff. Milton Friedman's stance was that realism is immaterial, and all that matters is whether the predictions do a good/adequate job predicting behavior. A more nuanced view is a model that adequately predicts behavior because its assumptions, while not realistic, approximate reality. Of course, adequately predicting is a matter of degree: different applications of NCT, including NBT and NBT plus, explain how people react, in aggregate, to changes in their constraints (estimated aggregate-demand curves slope down and shift out when aggregate income increases), but they are not adept at explaining the behavior of specific individuals.[63] NCT has been applied to estimate the demands for thousands of goods and services, public goods, environmental quality, and fishing sites—you name it. And the results are used to inform policy by estimating how demand will change if, for example, a price changes or what an average person will pay for a quality change.

[63] A cynic might argue that NCT predicts, for individuals, just one thing: if you can't afford to buy q units of x, you won't. Picturing an individual's demand function for a particular good (price on the horizontal axis, units purchased on the vertical). At current prices, most people do not purchase most goods and won't start purchasing them if their prices fall. I have never purchased a Bugatti, inline roller blades, or liver, and won't even if their prices fall 50%. And for much of what we do purchase, we also don't necessarily buy more when the price drops—I can't drink more Coke Zero. Individual demand functions for goods are flat over large ranges in price.

Economists have used it to estimate how much the demand for cigarettes by teenagers will drop if the tax on cigarettes increases and estimate willing to pay for improvement in environmental quality. I have spent my life estimating site-specific recreational demand as a function of environmental conditions, and my estimates have informed damages estimates in numerous NRDAs (Natural Resource Damage Assessments). To summarize, different versions of NCT are widely used in research and to inform policy.

Neoclassical choice theory, including my NBT, is an idealized caricature of how an individual behaves, and its creation motivated by the mathematizaton of economics, starting in the nineteenth century. Caricatures intentionally distort. NCT has morphed into a story about choice based on optimizing, a self-appealing story. It is also a simple story. Be that as it may, the current economicus is quite different from economic man as conceived by Alfred Marshall (1842–1924), and his conception is different from Adam Smith's (1723–1790). Economicus continues to evolve; hopefully, he will grow into a more complicated and flawed creature who behaves but does not always choose his behavior—behavioral man—a subject of Behavioral Economics. What is unfortunate is that the current economicus is the character that most economics students encounter, but this is starting to change.

Before further discussing behavior and choice, Chapter 4 jumps to welfare economics: how many economic ethicists parse right from wrong actions. Chapter 5 returns to behavior and choice, absent ethical considerations. I return to ethics in Chapters 11 and 12, briefly surveying other ethics.

References and Sources

Aarts, Henk, and Ap Dijksterhuis. 2003. "The silence of the library: Environment, situational norm, and social behavior." *Journal of Personality and Social Psychology* 84 (1): 18–28. https://doi.org/10.1037/0022-3514.84.1.18. https://www.webofscience.com/wos/woscc/full-record/WOS:000180072500002.

Aldred, Jonathan. 2006. "Incommensurability and monetary valuation." *Land Economics* 82 (2): 141–161. https://doi.org/10.3368/le.82.2.141. https://www.webofscience.com/wos/woscc/full-record/WOS:000237867900002.

———. 2013. "Justifying precautionary policies: Incommensurability and uncertainty." *Ecological Economics* 96: 132–140. https://doi.org/10.1016/j.ecolecon.2013.10.006. https://www.webofscience.com/wos/woscc/full-record/WOS:000328712600013.

Angier, Natalie. 2009. "Sorry, vegans: Brussels sprouts like to live, too." *The New York Times*, December 21. https://www.nytimes.com/2009/12/22/science/22angi.html .

Barrett, Lisa. 2017a. *How emotions are made: The secret life of the brain*. Vol. 2017a. New York: Houghton-Mifflin-Harcourt.

———. 2017b. "The theory of constructed emotion: An active inference account of interoception and categorization." *Social Cognitive and Affective Neuroscience* 12 (1): 1–23.

Batchelor, Stephen. 2015. *After Buddhism: Rethinking the dharma for a secular age*. Yale University Press. https://yalebooks.yale.edu/book/9780300224344/after-buddhism/.

Borie, Dino, and Dorian Jullien. 2020. "Description-dependent preferences." *Journal of Economic Psychology* 81. https://www.sciencedirect.com/science/article/pii/S0167487020300726.

Bowles, Samuel. 1998. "Endogenous preferences: The cultural consequences of markets and other economic institutions." *Journal of Economic Literature* 36 (1): 75–111. https://www.jstor.org/stable/2564952.

Brenner, Eric D., et al. 2006. "Plant neurobiology: An integrated view of plant signaling." *Trends in Plant Science* 11 (8): 413–419.

Briggs, Ray. 2017. "Normative theories of rational choice." Stanford Encyclopedia of Philosophy. Stanford University. https://plato.stanford.edu/title/Briggs/.

Buchtell, Emma, and Ara Norenzayan. 2008. "Which should you use, intuition or logic? Cultural differences in injunctive norms about reasoning." *Asian Journal of Social Psychology* 11 (4): 264–273. https://doi.org/10.1111/j.1467-839X.2008.00266.x. https://www.webofscience.com/wos/woscc/full-record/WOS:000260535300002.

Chang, Ruth. 1997. "Introduction." In *Incommensurability, incomparability, and practical reason*, edited by Ruth Chang. Cambridge, MA: Harvard University Press.

Cowen, Alan, and Dacher Keltner. 2017. "Self-report captures 27 distinct categories of emotion bridged by continuous gradients." *Proceedings of the National Academy of Sciences of the United States of America* 114 (38): E7900-E7909. https://doi.org/10.1073/pnas.1702247114. https://www.webofscience.com/wos/woscc/full-record/WOS:000411157100009.

Cox, James, et al. 2006. "An scn9a channelopathy causes congenital inability to experience pain." *Nature* 444 (7121): 894–898. https://doi.org/10.1038/nature05413. https://www.webofscience.com/wos/woscc/full-record/WOS:000242805400048.

Dahl, Melissa. 2020. "If you can say it, you can feel it: Some scientists believe you have infinite emotions so long as we can name them." *New York Magazine*, February 2.

Darwin, Charles, and Francis Darwin. 1896/2004. *The power of movement in plants*: Gutenberg. https://gutenberg.org/ebooks/5605.

Dietrich, Franz, and Christian List. 2013. "Where do preferences come from?" *International Journal of Game Theory* 42 (3): 613–637. https://doi.org/10.1007/s00182-012-0333-y. https://www.webofscience.com/wos/woscc/full-record/WOS:000321919100004.

Dietrich, Franz, and Christian List. 2016. "Reason-based choice and context dependence: An explanatory framework." *Economics and Philosophy* 32 (2): 175–229. https://doi.org/10.1017/s0266267115000474.

Editors. 2020. "Liegasm, jealoushy, and feminamity: Introducing 78 new emotions." *New York Magazine*, February 3.

Eil, David, and Justin Rao. 2011. "The good news-bad news effect: Asymmetric processing of objective information about yourself." *American Economic Journal: Microeconomics* 3 (2): 114–138.

Eisner, Thomas. 2015. *For love of insects*. Harvard University Press.

Elwood, Robert. 2012. "Evidence for pain in decapod crustaceans." *Animal Welfare* 21: 23–27. https://doi.org/10.7120/096272812x13353700593365. https://www.webofscience.com/wos/woscc/full-record/WOS:000304787600005.

Ganguly, Ananda, and Joshua Tasoff. 2017. "Fantasy and dread: The demand for information and the consumption utility of the future." *Management Science* 63 (12): 4037–4060. https://papers.ssrn.com/sol3/papers.cfm?abstract_id=2370983.

Grune-Yanoff, Till, and Sven Hansson. 2009. "From belief revision to preference change." In *Preference change: Approaches from philosophy, economics, and psychology*, edited by Till Grune-Yanoff and Sven Hansson, https://www.webofscience.com/wos/woscc/full-record/WOS:000267874700008.

Hajek, Alan. 2019. "Interpretation of probability." Stanford Encyclopedia of Philosophy. Stanford University. https://plato.stanford.edu/.

Harsanyi, John C. 1977. "Morality and the theory of rational behavior." *Social Research*: 623–656.

Hausman, Daniel. 2011. *Preference, value, choice, and welfare*. Cambridge University Press.

Heckert, Justin. 2012. "The hazards of growing up painlessly." *The New York Times*.

Henrich, Joseph, et al. 2005. ""Economic man" in cross-cultural perspective: Behavioral experiments in 15 small-scale societies." *Behavioral and Brain Sciences* 28 (6): 795-+. https://doi.org/10.1017/s0140525x05000142.

https://www.webofscience.com/wos/woscc/full-record/WOS:000234696400022.

Henrich, Joseph, Steven Heine, and Ara Norenzayan. 2010. "The weirdest people in the world?" *Behavioral and Brain Sciences* 33 (2–3): 61-+. https://doi.org/10.1017/s0140525x0999152x. https://www.webofscience.com/wos/woscc/full-record/WOS:000279973200001.

Hicks, John, and Roy Allen. 1934a. "A reconsideration of the theory of value. Part i." *Economica* 1 (1): 52–76.

———. 1934b. "A reconsideration of the theory of value. Part ii. A mathematical theory of individual demand functions." *Economica* 1 (2): 196–219.

Hsieh, Nien-Hê. 2007. "Is incomparability a problem for anyone?" *Economics & Philosophy* 23 (1): 65–80.

Hume, David. 1740/2002. *A treatise of human nature*: Project Gutenberg. https://www.gutenberg.org/files/4705/4705-h/4705-h.htm .

Kahneman, Dan, and Amos Tversky. 1979. "Prospect theory: An analysis of decision under risk." *Econometrica* 47: 237–251.

Kahneman, Dan, and Angus Deaton. 2010. "High income improves evaluation of life but not emotional well-being." *Proceedings of the National Academy of Sciences of the United States of America* 107 (38): 16489–16493. https://doi.org/10.1073/pnas.1011492107. https://www.webofscience.com/wos/woscc/full-record/WOS:000282003700022.

Kahneman, Dan, and Robert Sugden. 2005. "Experienced utility as a standard of policy evaluation." *Environmental & Resource Economics* 32 (1): 161–181. https://doi.org/10.1007/s10640-005-6032-4. https://www.webofscience.com/wos/woscc/full-record/WOS:000231511500008.

Knight, N., and Richard Nisbett. 2007. "Culture, class and cognition: Evidence from Italy." *Journal of Cognition and Culture* 7 (3–4): 283–291. https://doi.org/10.1163/156853707x208512. https://www.webofscience.com/wos/woscc/full-record/WOS:000218409800006.

Kreps, David M. 2013. *Microeconomic foundations i: Choice and competitive markets*. Vol. 1. Princeton university press.

Lancaster, Kelvin J. 1966. "A new approach to consumer theory." *Journal of Political Economy* 74 (2): 132–157.

Leary, M. R., and N. R. Buttermore. 2003. "The evolution of the human self-tracing the natural history of self-awareness." *Journal for the Theory of Social Behaviour* 33 (4): 365-+. https://doi.org/10.1046/j.1468-5914.2003.00223.x. https://www.webofscience.com/wos/woscc/full-record/WOS:000187289700002.

Lehrer, Jonah. 2010. "Allias paradox." *Wired*, October 21.

Levin, Jonathan. 2006. "Lecture notes on choice under uncertainty for economics 202: Graduate microeconomics (first quarter), Stanford university." http://web.stanford.edu/~jdlevin/teaching.html.

Locke, John. 1700/1975. "On modes of pleasure and pain." *4th edition, An essay concerning human understanding Book II: Ideas*. Oxford: Oxford University Press. https://www.earlymoderntexts.com/assets/pdfs/locke1690book2.pdf.

Lyons, David. 1991. *In the interest of the governed: A study in Bentham's philosophy of utility and law*. Cambridge: Cambridge University Press. https://global.oup.com/academic/product/in-the-interest-of-the-governed-9780198239642?cc=us&lang=en.

Mancuso, Stefano, and Alessandra Viola. 2015. *Brilliant green: The surprising history and science of plant intelligence*. Island Press.

Mas-Colell, Andreu, Michael Whinston, and Jerry Green. 1995. *Microeconomic theory*. New York: Oxford University Press. https://www.webofscience.com/wos/woscc/full-record/WOS:A1979GR75700001.

Mercier, Hugo, and Dan Sperber. 2017. *The enigma of reason*. Cambridge MA: Harvard University Press.

Morey, Edward, and Mara Thiene. 2017. "Can personality traits explain where and with whom you recreate? A latent-class site-choice model informed by estimates from mixed-mode lc cluster models with latent -personality traits." *Ecological Economics* 138: 223–237. https://doi.org/10.1016/j.ecolecon.2017.03.038. https://www.webofscience.com/wos/woscc/full-record/WOS:000402215800022.

Nisbett, Richard, K. P. Peng, I. Choi, and Ara Norenzayan. 2008. "Culture and systems of thought: Holistic versus analytic cognition." *Reasoning: Studies of Human Inference and Its Foundations*: 956–985. https://www.webofscience.com/wos/woscc/full-record/WOS:000305482200050.

———. 2011. "Culture and systems of thought: Comparison of holistic and analytic cognition." *Psikhologicheskii Zhurnal* 32 (1): 55–86.

Nussbaum, Martha. 2012. "Who is the happy warrior? Philosophy, happiness research, and public policy." *International Review of Economics* 59 (4): 335–361.

Pareto, Vilfredo. 1909(Italian)/2014. *Manual of political economy: A critical and variorum edition*. Oxford: Oxford University Press. https://books.google.com/books?hl=en&lr=&id=43NYAwAAQBAJ&oi=fnd&pg=PP1&dq=pareto+manual+of+political+economy+&ots=9SbJExabbI&sig=nQsi46xq4Ts2z4fBHLeE9FzpWOI.

Pearce, David. 1998. "Cost-benefit analysis and environmental policy." *Oxford Review of Economic Policy* 14 (4): 84–100. https://doi.org/10.1093/oxrep/14.4.84. https://www.webofscience.com/wos/woscc/full-record/WOS:000078358100006.

Peterson, Martin. 2017. *An introduction to decision theory*. Cambridge: Cambridge University Press.

Plotnik, Joshua, Frans De Waal, and Diana Reiss. 2006. "Self-recognition in an Asian elephant." *Proceedings of the National Academy of Sciences of the United*

States of America 103 (45): 17053–17057. https://doi.org/10.1073/pnas.0608062103. https://www.webofscience.com/wos/woscc/full-record/WOS:000241969500076.

Reeves, Richard. 2008. *John Stuart mill: Victorian firebrand*. London: Atlantic Books Ltd. https://atlantic-books.co.uk/book/john-stuart-mill.

Rekola, M. 2003. "Lexicographic preferences in contingent valuation: A theoretical framework with illustrations." *Land Economics* 79 (2): 277–291. https://doi.org/10.2307/3146871. https://www.webofscience.com/wos/woscc/full-record/WOS:000182568500009.

Russell, Bertrand. 2009. *Unpopular essays*. Routledge.

Scarantino, Andrea, and Ronald De Soursa. 2018. "Emotion." Stanford Encyclopedia of Philosophy. Stanford University. https://plato.stanford.edu/.

Schmidt, Torsten, and Christian Weber. 2008. "On the origins of ordinal utility: Andreas Heinrich Voigt and the mathematicians." *History of Political Economy* 40 (3): 481–510.

Schroeder, Mark. 2012. "Value theory." Stanford Encyclopedia of Philosophy. Stanford University. https://plato.stanford.edu/.

Schwitzgebel, Eric. Fall 2019. "Belief." Stanford Encyclopedia of Philosophy. Stanford University. https://plato.stanford.edu/.

Scorranese, Roberta. 2021. "Mancuso, il botanico attaccato dagli estremisti vegani: Mi accusano di diffendere chi produce carne." *Corriere Della Sera*, September 21.

Sen, Amartya. 1997. "Maximization and the act of choice." *Econometrica: Journal of the Econometric Society*: 745–779.

Sen, Amartya. 2018. "The importance of incompleteness." *International Journal of Economic Theory*. https://doi.org/10.1111/ijet.12145.

Shtonda, B. B., and L. Avery. 2006. "Dietary choice behavior in Caenorhabditis Elegans." *Journal of Experimental Biology* 209 (1): 89–102. https://doi.org/10.1242/jeb.01955. https://journals.biologists.com/jeb/article/209/1/89/33408/Dietary-choice-behavior-in-Caenorhabditis-elegans.

Smith, Adam. 1759/2022. *The theory of moral sentiments*. Vol. 1. Ireland: J. Beatty and C. Jackson and The Gutenberg Project. https://www.webofscience.com/wos/woscc/full-record/WOS:000283912100003.

Spash, Clive, and Nick Hanley. 1995. "Preferences, information and biodiversity preservation." *Ecological economics* 12 (3): 191–208.

Steele, Katie, and Orri Stefansson. 2016. Decision theory. In *Stanford encyclopedia of philosophy*, edited by Edward N. Zalta: Stanford University. https://plato.stanford.edu/.

Stigler, George, and Gary Becker. 1977. "De gustibus non est disputandum." *American Economic Review* 67 (2): 76–90. https://www.webofscience.com/wos/woscc/full-record/WOS:A1977DA61600007.

Summer, Patricia. 2016. Locke's moral philosophy. In *Stanford Encyclopedia of Philosophy*, edited by Edward N. Zalta: Stanford University. https://plato.stanford.edu/

Sumner, L.W. 1996. *Welfare happiness, and ethics*. Oxford University Press.

Sunstein, Cass. 1993. "Incommensurability and valuation in law." *Michigan Law Review* 92: 779.

Sweeny, Kate, Darya Melnyk, and James Shepperd. 2010. "Information avoidance, who, what, when, and why." *Review of General Psychology* 14 (4). https://doi.org/10.1037/a0021288.

Van Gulick, Robert. 2018. "Consciousness." Stanford Encyclopedia of Philosophy. Stanford University. https://plato.stanford.edu/.

Varnum, M. E. W., I. Grossmann, S. Kitayama, and Richard Nisbett. 2010. "The origin of cultural differences in cognition: The social orientation hypothesis." *Current Directions in Psychological Science* 19 (1): 9–13. https://doi.org/10.1177/0963721409359301. https://www.webofscience.com/wos/woscc/full-record/WOS:000275063900002.

Venneman, S. S., P. Narnor-Harris, M. Perish, and M. Hamilton. 2008. ""Allow natural death" versus "do not resuscitate": Three words that can change a life." *Journal of Medical Ethics* 34 (1): 2–6. https://doi.org/10.1136/jme.2006.018317. https://webofscience.com/wos/woscc/full-record/WOS:000251836000002.

Von Neumann, John, and Oskar Morgenstern. 2007. "Theory of games and economic behavior." In *Theory of games and economic behavior*. Princeton University Press.

Watters, Ethan. 2013. "We aren't the world." *Pacific Standard* 6 (2): 46–53.

Wegner, Daniel. 2002. *The illusion of conscious will*. Cambridge, MA: MIT Press.

Weintraub, Karen. 2018. "The Swiss consider the lobster. It feels pain, they decide." *New York Times*. https://www.nytimes.com/2018/01/12/science/lobster-pain-swiss.html.

Wiggins, D. 1997. "Incommensurability: Four proposals." In *Incommensurability, incomparability, and practical reason*, edited by Ruth Chang. Cambridge, MA: Harvard University Press.

CHAPTER 3

What's More Likely? Economicus Was Created by Evolution or by God

Evolution Is Driven by the Survival of Genes, Not Their Containers

Evolution has two components: (1) genes generate traits in their containers (us and other living things). These traits increase or decrease the container's probability of passing its genes to the next generation. This causes the population stock of some genes to increase and others to decrease. And (2) when genes are transmitted, transcription errors occur; these are usually disastrous for survival but occasionally fortuitous.

Evolution takes place at the gene level rather than at the level of the organism—living things are simply copying machines. As the eminent evolutionary biologist Richard Dawkins explains in "The Selfish Gene,"[1]

> They are in you and me; they created us, body and mind; and their preservation is the ultimate rationale for our existence. They have come a long way, those replicators. Now they go by the name of genes, and we are their survival machines.

[1] In 2006, the book's thirtieth anniversary was celebrated with a conference at the London School of Economics (the biologist Alan Grafen and the zoologist Mark Ridley 2006).

E. R. Morey, *Deconstructing Behavior, Choice, and Well-being*,
https://doi.org/10.1007/978-3-031-36712-0_3

Evolution does not require happy gene-containers nor implies that the containers will become happier over time. Consider lust, the great contributor to sexual angst in teenage boys; this evolutionary trait increases reproduction, but rather than being happy, the container is, in Elvis' words, "All shook up." Likewise, evolution's aim isn't to maximize our WB: being happy and satisfied isn't an appropriate mindset for surviving in a world of hungry, brutish beasts—not for the beast nor the prey.

Of course, animals (and plants) suffering or dying because they lack the resources to survive and are less able to reproduce and nurture their children. But a lot of WB isn't required. If things are too good pre-kids, you won't have any, which wouldn't serve your genes.

A caution: genes typically influence multiple traits, but that does not mean each trait, by itself, makes it more likely the container will successfully reproduce; genes produce side-effect traits. Some side effects won't influence reproduction, and others, taken alone, will reduce the probability of successful reproduction. The textbook example: genes evolved to produce a trait, sickle-shaped blood cells. This happened in sub-Saharan Africa, where malaria was common and deadly. The sickle shape provides protection: the parasite needs round blood cells to prosper. Unfortunately, with the trait comes sickle-cell anemia, a negative side effect.

A secondary trait more germane to our topic is striving to acquire more resources, even after having enough to reproduce successfully. Genes that convey the desire to survive and reproduce will increase the probability of those genes surviving. But this desire becomes a side effect if it does not turn off when one has enough resources to survive and reproduce. For gene transmission, there is no advantage to turning the desire off.

Evolution, Typically Incremental, Gravitates Toward a Local Best Rather Than the Bestest Best (the Global Best)

Evolution wouldn't produce the perfection of economici; it proceeds from its current state in small steps. Recipients of drastically mutated genes (a big step) typically don't survive. Consider, for example, a species' current system for night vision. If better night vision will increase survival and reproduction, and if better night vision is a tweak away, evolution

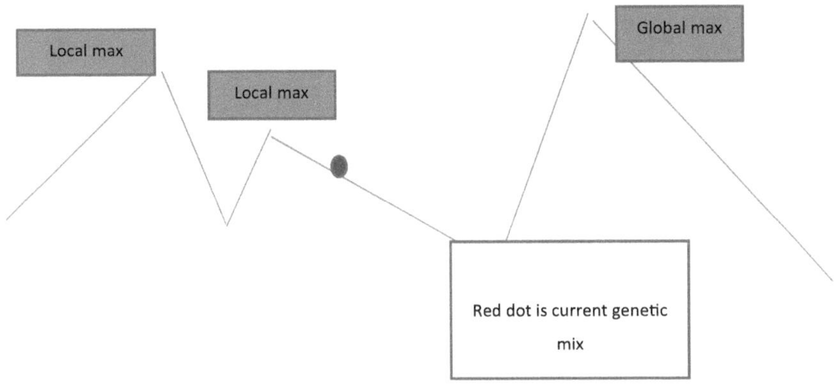

Fig. 3.1 Night-vision acuity on the vertical axis, genetic mix on horizontal

will improve night vision. Figure 3.1 shows that with small steps, evolution could move from the current position to the local max to its left, but it won't take us to the best possible night vision (the global maximum).[2]

If a better system is utterly different from the current one, it is improbable that evolution will get us there. This holds for our brain system as well as our vision. NYU psychologist Gary Marcus describes our brain, a product of evolution, as a "kluge": n. Slang, "A clumsy or inelegant solution to a problem," in his amusing and informative book *Kluge: The Haphazard evolution of the human mind* (2008). While it serves us well, our brain isn't a best mechanism; evolution isn't about perfection, but what the Nobel laureate Herbert Simon calls *satisficing*, doing well enough.

Humans suffer evolution's limitations: we mix beliefs with logic and inference. Marcus conjectures that formal logic, to the extent we practice it, isn't a product of evolution but something we learn in school and sometimes find useful. In the 1930s, the Russian psychologist Alexander Luria (1902–1977) went to villages in the mountains of Central Asia and interviewed indigenous, uneducated villagers. He told them that all the bears in a particular Siberian town are white. He then told them their neighbor had visited that town and saw a bear. Then he asked, "What

[2] Any marginal shift to the right would reduce survival rates.

color was the bear?" The typical answer was, "Ask my neighbor." Logic implies white. Tversky and Kahneman (1983) describe Linda:

> Linda is 31-years old, single, outspoken, and very bright. She majored in philosophy. As a student, she was deeply concerned with issues of discrimination and social justice, and also participated in anti-nuclear demonstrations. Which is more probable? 1. Linda is a bank teller. 2. Linda is a bank teller and is active in the feminist movement.

Modern literate respondents often illogically choose 2: the probability of two events co-occurring can't be greater than the probability of one occurring. We get it wrong because Linda sounds like a feminist. In a 2017 book, *The enigma of reason*, Hugo Mercier and Dan Sperber argue that humans did not evolve to be logical. Instead, we evolved to reason (create and give reasons/justifications), so other humans would accept our ideas and plans—we evolved to convince, not to be logical. And we evolved to be convinced by the reasons of others when it is in our interest. In this view, reasoning evolved to increase cooperation, not logical thinking.

NCT Emerged and Developed in Nineteenth and Early Twentieth-Century Britain, a Christian Creationist World Where Man Was Unique and in God's Image

In nineteenth-century England, only Christian males could be college professors. Developers of NCT include William Stanley Jevons (1835–1882), Francis Edgeworth (1845–1926), Marshall, and Hicks (1904–1989). If NCT is a religion, their writings form its Canon.

Jevon's diary and correspondence demonstrate that the originator of marginal utility believed in God and found no conflict between his Christian faith and science. Edgeworth (the creator of indifference curves) was a friend.[3] Marshall is the father of consumer's surplus; his father was "a devout Evangelical". Robert Frantz, in his 2005 book *Two Minds: Intuition and Analysis in the History of Economic Thought*, notes that Marshall,

[3] An indifference curve for Path j identifies all paths that are ranked the same as Path j.

> ...integrated his economics into his ideas about religion, character, duty, and intuition... Marshall also considered the joy brought about from religion as the 'highest joys of which men are capable.

Hicks advocated for an NCT where the ordering of paths has no cardinal properties (Assumption 2b). He was raised a Baptist. These gentlemen were aware of Darwin's theory but also seeped in creationist Christianity, so it shouldn't be a surprise that they adopted a theory of behavior where man is perfect—in God's image.[4] I don't know the depths of their faith, but their NCT is consistent with Christianity's view of man, assumptions evolution does not imply.

Creationism and NCT Are Symbiotic Bedfellows

The late nineteenth century drive toward mathematical formalism and logic in choice theory, led by Jevons, Marshall, and the Austrian Carl Menger, melded effortlessly with the idea that man is an optimizer—a goal was to make economics more science-like. Human behavior is difficult to mathematically model if human behavior results from the awkward process called evolution. Human behavior is easier to model if God created man, and man maximizes subject to his constraints.

Chapter 4 tackles welfare economics.

References and Sources

Dawkins, Richard. 1976. *The selfish gene*. New York: Oxford University Press.

Frantz, Roger. 2005. *Two minds: Intuition and analysis in the history of economic thought*. Springer Science & Business Media.

Grafen, Alan, and Mark Ridley. 2006. *Richard Dawkins: How a scientist changed the way we think*. Oxford: Oxford University Press.

Marcus, Gary. 2008. *Kluge: The haphazard evolution of the human mind*. Houghton Mifflin Harcourt.

Mercier, Hugo, and Dan Sperber. 2017. *The enigma of reason*. Cambridge, MA: Harvard University Press.

Simon, Herbert. 1982. *Models of bounded rationality*. Vols. I and II. New York: Wiley.

[4] If humans are logical and created in God's image, God must be logical, so not a holistic Yin-Yang kind of guy.

Tversky, Amos, and Daniel Kahneman. 1983. "Extension versus intuitive reasoning: The conjunction fallacy in probability judgment." *Psychological Review* 90 (4): 22. https://doi.org/10.1037/0033-295X.90.4.293. https://psycnet.apa.org/record/1984-03110-001?doi=1.

Additional Readings

Kaushik, Basu, and Luis Lopez-Calva. 2011. "Functionings and capabilities." *Handbook of Social Choice and Welfare* 2: 153–187. https://doi.org/10.1016/S0169-7218(10)00016-X.

Klein, Daniel, and Ryan Daza. 2013. "John R. Hicks. Ideological profiles of the economics laureates." *Econ Journal Watch* 10 (3): 366–377. https://econjwatch.org/ancillary/IPEL.html.

Mosselmans, Bert. 2015. "Jevons." Stanford Encyclopedia of Philosophy. Stanford University. https://plato.stanford.edu/title/Mosselmans/.

Schabas, Margaret. 1989. "Alfred Marshall, w. Stanley Jevons, and the mathematization of economics." *Isis* 80 (1): 60–73.

Wikipedia. "Alfred Marshall." Wikipedia. Wikipedia Foundation. http://en.wikipedia.org/wiki/Alfred_Marshall.

CHAPTER 4

Welfare (Well-Faring) Economics, Criteria for What Is Right and Wrong: My Take

Introducing welfare economics detours us from wondering about the determinants of behavior and choice. The topic is here, rather than later, because its foundation is the NBT prediction (with Assumption 9a, not 9b) that everyone maximizes their WB. For welfare economics, the moral objective is to maximize societal WB—where societal WB aggregates the WBs of society's members. Both NBT and welfare economics are about WB and maximization. In Chapter 12, other ethics will be reviewed and contrasted with welfare economics.

Four questions: (1) What is welfare economics? (2) Is it an ethic? Yes. (3) How do welfare economists differ from one another? And (4) how do they differ from other economic ethicists? Then utilitarianism is discussed. I was taught and have taught that welfare economics is a type of utilitarianism. I was wrong; it isn't. Welfare economics is an atypical form of *welfare consequentialism*: consequentialist in that whether an act or policy is right or wrong depends on its consequences—the adjective "welfare" because the only consequences that matter are the welfare (well-faring) consequences. Most welfare consequentialists are not welfare economists, and few moral philosophers are welfare consequentialists. People are not welfare consequentialists. Welfare economists who accept, without critical

Some parts of this chapter are revisions of sections of Morey (2018).

E. R. Morey, *Deconstructing Behavior, Choice, and Well-being*,
https://doi.org/10.1007/978-3-031-36712-0_4

thought, that welfare economics is the ethic for parsing right from wrong are not moral philosophers. The few economists who study ethics and argue that welfare economics is the preferred ethic are moral philosophers.

Welfare Economics Is a Method to Test Right from Wrong

Whether it is depends on how one defines welfare economics and right and wrong. This first section starts by defining an ethic. In the words of John Stuart Mill (1806–1893), an ethic is "a method to test right from wrong." Quoting from the *Journal of Economic Literature* article *Taking Ethics Seriously*, Hausman and Michael McPherson (1993).

> Welfare economists have sometimes thought that their techniques are virtually morally neutral because they rest on innocuous and uncontroversial moral premises such as the Pareto principle. But the standard definition of a social optimum compares social alternatives exclusively in terms of the goodness of their outcomes (rather than the rightness of their procedures) and identifies the goodness of outcomes with satisfaction of individual preferences. These commitments to value only outcomes and to measure outcomes only in terms of individual utilities are neither neutral nor uncontroversial. (see Sen 1979; and Sen and Williams 1982)

A *Pareto Improvement*, *PI*, is a change that increases the WB of some members of society without decreasing the WB of any other members. That a PI is always right, while obvious to welfare economists, is rejected by, and inconsistent with, other ethical criteria. Ethics that reject it include virtue ethics,[1] rights theory, Kantian and other duty-based ethics, those based on religion (sins are wrong, no matter how they affect WB), and ethics that judge actions right or wrong based entirely, or in part, on process and intent. Rawls (1971/1999) rejected the PI criterion, arguing that increasing the WB of the better off while holding constant the WB of

[1] Adam Smith was a virtue ethicist (McCloskey 2008); Smith suggested two guides for behavior: rules against abhorrent acts (killing, raping) and virtue for everything else (Smith 1759/2002; Fleischacker 2013). He thought the morality of an act depended on both the intent and the consequences, but if the intent was virtuous, the behavior is good, unless, of course, the outcome is disastrous. Virtue ("proper gratitude, kindness, courage, patience, and endurance") results from empathy for others, our sympathy for others—our "moral sentiments." Smith was not a welfare economist.

the worst off is wrong. To summarize, the Pareto objective is inconsistent with many other ethics, which leaves no doubt that it is an ethic.

"A moral principle can be viewed as a requirement to exclude the use of certain types of information in moral judgments" (Sen and Williams 1982). Welfare economics excludes the cause and the actor's intent unless they affect the WB produced. It also excludes from moral consideration how a policy or act affects the WB of individuals who are not members of society.

And welfare economics assumes that my behavior and choices are right for me and society if they don't affect others.

Quoting D. Hausman (2015), referring to economists, "they are [always] ready with advice on how to make life better."

So, welfare economics is an ethic: the moral objective is to maximize some aggregation of WBs, the aggregation over society's members.[2] But, at this point, skepticism is in order because I have not articulated welfare economics. And—some economists advocate ethics inconsistent with welfare economics, but welfare economics is the predominant ethic among economic ethicists.

Ethics judge actions. Actions include individual behaviors (eating peanuts, smoking in a crowded room, and driving drunk). They include government policies such as going to war, taxation to redistribute income, and taxing carbon emissions. Since economists think on the margin, the welfare-economic question is typically not whether the action is right or wrong, but what is the right amount—the right amounts of chocolate and global warming?

My first inclination was to use the words "good" and "bad" acts, but I will instead use "right" or "moral" and "wrong" or "immoral" as in "morally right" and "morally wrong". The words "good" and "bad" have innumerable meanings, so words that are easy to misinterpret.[3] Sound good? Morally right sounds pretentious but is more precise. Morally wrong means it should not happen for moral reasons. To appear less

[2] Some argue, in my view incorrectly, that it isn't an ethic but rather a valuable tool for moral philosophers because it shines a harsh light on consequences. A reviewer of one of my papers wrote, "So maybe a necessary stage of moral decision-making should be the rigid consequentialist phase: just stop and consider this apart from everything else." But, if one takes this view, one can't parse right from wrong policies based on welfare economics.

[3] Consider: "Phil is a good guy to take along if you want to pick up girls: he's friendly and nice but not attractive." Or "Boy is that pie good."

pretentious, I will typically drop the adjective "morally" and stick with "right" and "wrong".

Based on its criterion for right vs. wrong, welfare economics can, in theory, judge whether an act is right or wrong but often can't in practice. This is true of most ethics. Policymakers are lucky when an ethic indicates whether a particular act is right or wrong. Looking ahead, you may disagree with my characterization of welfare economics, citing examples of individuals who self-identify as welfare economists but who would disagree with my definition. This is OK: the objective isn't for you and me to agree on what welfare economists agree. Instead, the aim is to evaluate ethical assumptions.

It is crucial to know that almost everyone rejects welfare economics as a criterion to parse right from wrong. More on this, but after we list its commonalities. After fully articulating welfare consequentialism and economics, I address whether welfare economists are best described as utilitarians. This chapter also reviews the research on how people judge right from wrong.

Welfare Economists Are Consequentialists, Welfare Consequentialists

Welfare consequentialism (hereafter "WC") was defined above; now, it's detailed. First, I shift back and forth between WC (the general category) and welfare economics (an atypical type).[4] Then I list major concerns about WC as a criterion for parsing right from wrong. Even modern welfare consequentialists reject welfare economics (e.g., the Canadian philosopher L.W. Sumner and the Oxford philosopher John Broome).

After laying out these distinctions, I return to the relationship between welfare economics and utilitarianism. Benthamite utilitarianism was the original WC. And it is inconsistent with welfare economics; it is neither the face of modern WC nor modern utilitarianism.

Like economic theories of choice, there is no one set of assumptions that all welfare economists agree to. Nonetheless, they are all *consequentialists*: whether an action is right or wrong depends only on its consequences. The actor's intent is immaterial, and so is what was

[4] Since welfare economics is a subset of WC, if one rejects a tenant of WC, one rejects welfare economics, but one could reject welfare economics and still be a WC.

expected.[5] Consider the behavior of Harvey Weinstein. Consider the rape of Lucretia by Tarquin (Sixth Century BC He was the son of Rome's last king). Lucretia killed herself; Shakespeare wrote a poem about it; the rape and suicide were memorialized by Renaissance artists (Fig. 4.1).

The citizens of Rome found Tarquin's behavior so offensive they over-threw the king and established "'liberty' and the 'free republic of Rome'" (Beard 2015); so, the overall effect was, for Romans, WB increasing[6]—but the result of a rape. Suppose the past actions of Harvey Weinstein

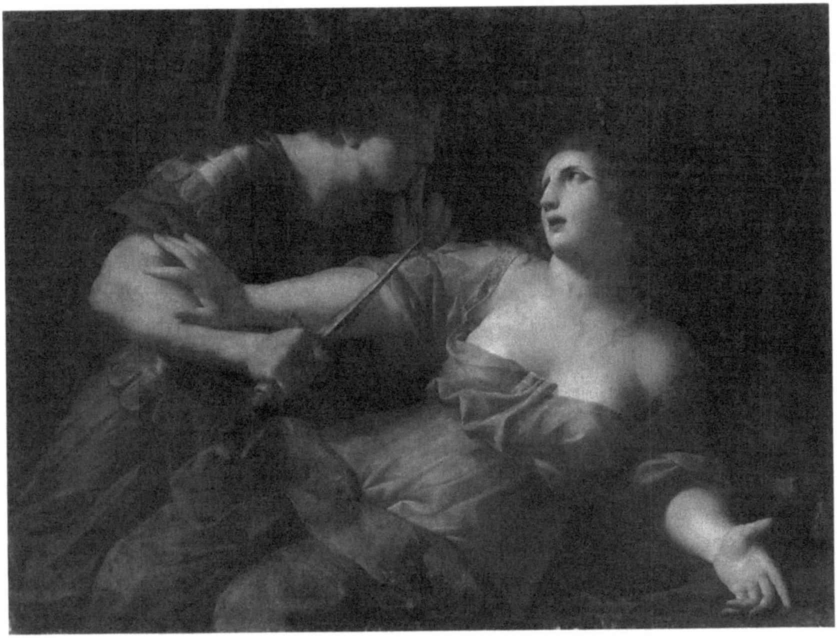

Fig. 4.1 The rape of Lucretia, Tarquinius and Lucretia, 1638, Giovanni Francesco Romanelli, Kunsthisforisches Museum

[5] At the other extreme are *processists* who judge on only the process that caused the act (e.g., a majority vote), not the consequences. For a summary of consequentialism, see Walter Sinnott-Armstrong (2015).

[6] One could argue. "This rape is almost certainly as mythic as the rape of the Sabines: assaults on women symbolically marking the beginning and the end of the regal period...

lead to less sexual harassment and fewer rapes (we will see). In that case, a welfare consequentialist could/would argue that while his behavior was objectional, and his victims suffered, his behavior increased WB. For welfare consequentialists, the same act can be right in some circumstances and wrong in others: it is determined by the act's consequences. When one thinks of modern welfare consequentialists, additional names include the U. of Mass. philosopher Fred Feldman and the Yale philosopher Shelley Kagan.[7]

These rape examples indicate that it can be difficult for a welfare consequentialist to determine right from wrong since the long-run consequences are unknown when the act occurs. Even if one waits and sees how the world plays out, there is still the issue of what can be attributed to the act.

People are not consequentialists; while they care about consequences, they also care about what caused them (the process), so they care about intentions, virtues, duties, commitments, and rights. Famous economic ethicists who have articulated different theories of right and wrong and who are neither welfare economists nor consequentialists include Dasgupta, Rawls, and Sen.[8,9]

Since welfare economists care only about WB, the only consequences that concern them are how the act affects the WB of individuals who matter—the consequences that matter are the welfare consequences—so they are welfare consequentialists. Recollect Assumption 9a: *An economicus's ordering of paths is based on its WB (well-being), WB, accounting for the uncertainties. The more WB economicus associates with a path, the higher its rank. And WB is determined, in part, by sensations.*

And recall the discussion of WB after Assumptions 10 and 11 were added.

But mythic or not, for the rest of Roman time the rape of Lucretia marked a turning point in politics, and its morality was debated" (Beard).

[7] Peter Singer, while a consequentialist, isn't a welfare consequentialist. Sinnott-Armstrong (2015) identifies Broome, Feldman, and Kagan as welfare consequentialists; they might disagree.

[8] For introductions to Rawls, see Jonathan Wolff (2010) and Leif Wenar (2017).

[9] It is common to lump together all economists who judge policies and call them welfare economists, but this is incorrect.

Before proceeding, again distinguish between an ordering based on WB and an ordering based on wants/desires. Consider the alternative assumption: Assumption 9b: *Paths that are more desired/wanted are ranked higher*. They generate the same ordering only when (1) paths that are more desired are associated with more WB, and (2) paths associated with more WB are more desired. Whether either, or both, approximate reality is an empirical question, but welfare economists assume, often implicitly, that they hold simultaneously (wants/desires ↔ WB). I point out the distinction here because while welfare economics' objective is WB, other ethicists specify fulfilling wants and desires as the ethical objective rather than increasing WB. Peter Singer (1997, 2011) is in this camp. I label this camp *want/desire consequentialists*. They are neither welfare economists nor welfare consequentialists (Table 4.1).

Welfare consequentialists are in I or VII. Want/desire consequentialists in VII or IX. In VII, (want/desires) ↔ WB. Welfare economists are a subset of I or VII, mostly VII. III includes Kantian ethics and the will of God. Category III ethics are alien to welfare economists. Ethicists who care about process and WB are in either II or V; many non-philosophers are in II or V.

Table 4.1 Different ethics in terms of whether want/desire fulfillment or WB are determinants of right from wrong

	Welfare consequentialist: only WB effects matter	*WB matters, but WB effects are not the sole determinant*	*WB effects play no role in determining*
Wants and desires play no role in determining	I: Only WB effects matter	II:	III: includes Kantian and religious conservatives
Wants and desires matter, but they are not the sole determinant	IV: **Empty** (if only WB effects matter, wants and desires can't unless they are always in sync with WB)	V:	VI
Want/desire consequentialist: nothing but wants and desires matter	VII: want/desires ↔ WB (the two orderings are identical)	VIII: **Empty** (if wants and desires matter, WB can't unless it is always in sync with wants and desires)	IX:

Two properties shared by all welfare economists, but few other welfare consequentialists, are (a) in the choice period, the individual's ordering of paths is exogenous, and (b) the individual must experience their highest-ranked available path. These standard-NCT assumptions (Assumptions 1–9) take a component of ethics off the table: how to lead an ethical life. Economicus can't choose to behave more ethically.[10] If my highest-ranked available path, HRAP, includes immoral behavior, I am immoral because I'm constrained to be immoral. In this sense, welfare economics is an unusual ethic: making me live a more ethical life requires coercion by the State or other exogenous agent. They cause me to act less immorally by constraining or rewarding me to produce fewer negative *external effects*. [I produce an *external effect* when my behavior directly affects another individual. External effects can be positive or negative. Second-hand smoke from my cigarette is an example of a negative external effect; my beautiful garden produces positive external effects.]

Most welfare economists assume that only humans count but don't have a criterion for which humans matter/count. They don't justify or explain why just humans (Fig. 4.2).

This contrasts with other welfare-based ethics, which assert and defend criteria such as *all individuals who can feel pain should count*, or *all sentient individuals should count*. When applying welfare economics, welfare economists typically accept their employer's definition of who matters.[11] Not surprisingly, what is right or wrong in WC comes down to who is included. A huge issue is whether future humans count and, if so, how much relative to us. The issue of future humans is further

[10] If one defines an ethic as personal rules for living more ethically (being virtuous, having empathy, respecting authority, etc.), welfare economics isn't one. Looking ahead, I suspect most welfare consequentialists embrace the possibility that you can choose to act differently than you do, even though NBT precludes this.

[11] For years I consulted for NOAA and the US Justice Department estimating the dollar damages associated with environmental injuries resulting from oil spills, mine tailing, and toxic wastes. This makes me, and the economists I worked with, prime examples of welfare economists. Damages to non-citizens and damages to future citizens are not included, nor are damages to other species. If I were valuing the damages from emissions in Paris, I would have accepted a dictate to estimate damages only for French citizens residing in Paris.

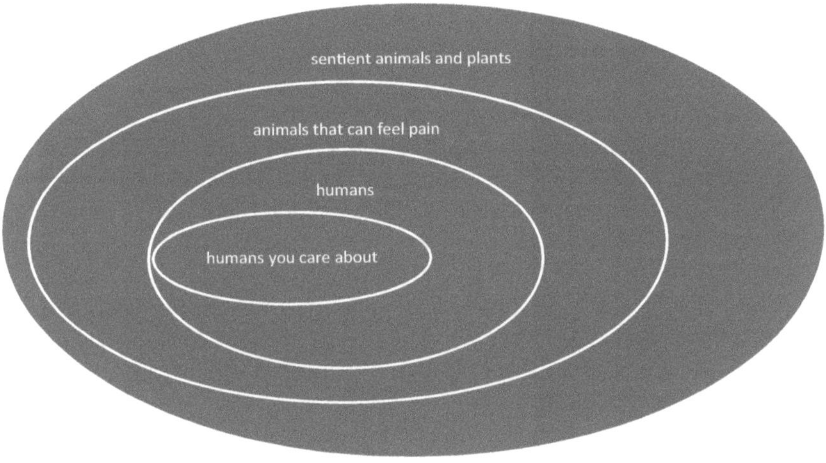

Fig. 4.2 Individuals—Who counts?

complicated because current humans affect the number of future humans. Within WC, welfare economics is restrictive regarding who counts.[12]

Welfare economists agree that the relevant consequence is how society's WB is affected. And this depends only on the WB of each member of society. Let's call the WB of society's *societal WB*.[13] Actions that increase societal WB are right, those that decrease it are wrong, and those that increase societal WB more are righter (morally preferred). Welfare economists impose the PI criterion on the social welfare function.[14,15]

Think what WC implies about a trade: if the seller's and the buyer's WBs are increased by the trade, and if the production and consumption of

[12] One could be a welfare economist (an unusual one) and include everything that can feel pain or everyone sentient. I lean toward everyone who can feel pain.

[13] I chose the adjective "societal" rather than "social" to make clear that I am not referring to the specific type of WB one might get from socializing with others.

[14] Interestingly, any policy can be made a PI by banning the losers from the roles of society—one can't argue that who counts, and who does not, isn't an ethical judgment.

[15] Pareto (1848–1923), in his later years, frustrated with how mathematical economics theories failed in the real world, turned to sociology. He came to believe that men act non-logically "but they make believe they are acting logically."—he could have been a twenty-first-century psychologist.

what is traded decrease no other individuals' WB, the trade is, by assumption, necessarily right. Moreover, this trade could even be right if it makes third parties worse if they are not made too worse.

Above I mentioned rights (as in the "right to free speech" or the right to vote). People believe in inalienable rights. And if you have the right to do something, it is wrong (according to *Rights Theory*) for me to interfere with your ability to exercise that right (your right is a constraint on everyone else). Welfare economists do not recognize inalienable rights; they would, for example, talk about the right amount of free speech in the same way they would about the right amount of pollution. Welfare economists advocate for property rights because they believe that having and enforcing property rights will increase societal WB, not because they believe in an inalienable right to own stuff.

Honest welfare economists agree that increasing efficiency is neither necessary nor sufficient to increase societal WB. An act is efficiency increasing if the gain to the gainers, in money terms, is large enough so that the gainers could compensate any losers for their loss and still be gainers. [The compensation does not have to occur for the act to be efficiency-increasing.] An increase in net real wealth (in $) does not imply societal WB has increased[16]; money income isn't an accurate measure of WB. This is unfortunate since money is easy to count. An example demonstrates that an efficiency increase can decrease societal WB. Donald, a rich guy, would be willing to pay you $1000 for a ring you inherited from your mother. You treasure the ring but are poor, so you would sell it for $200. So, selling it to him for more than $200 but less than $1000 would make both of you better off. And, if no one else would have been affected by the transfer, societal WB and efficiency would have increased. However, Donald steals it, saving himself $200. The stealing is efficiency increasing but does not necessarily lead to an increase in societal WB. For Donald, it is an additional trinket; for you, a treasure lost (your WB went down more than his increased, causing societal WB to decline—if that comparison has meaning). While welfare economists agree on all this, for better or worse—and trying to be relevant—it is common for

[16] Measuring wealth is, itself, difficult. To measure a society's aggregate wealth, one must include things besides the present value of its GDP stream. For example, an increase in pollution or a decrease in a county's natural resource stock both affect its wealth, but neither is included in GDP.

talking heads (sometimes those same welfare economists) to misleadingly suggest that more efficient means more societal WB.[17,18]

A few ethicists argue that increased wealth (increased efficiency), not increased WB, should be the criterion to parse right from wrong—Posner is in this camp. These ethicists are not welfare consequentialists; they are *wealth consequentialists*.[19] Few academic normative economists are wealth consequentialists.

So Much for What Welfare Economists Agree On

Some welfare economists assume many don't that societal WB should be the simple sum of each member's WB. I will refer to this simple sum as *aggregate WB*, so when I refer to aggregate WB, I mean the simple sum, and when I refer to societal WB, I mean the more comprehensive concept.[20] Aggregate WB is invariant to how WB is distributed across society's members; it is impartial to which member experienced it.[21] If

[17] Harold Hotelling (1938) argued for using efficiency increasing alone as a criterion for increasing societal WB: if society invoked a sequence of efficiency-increasing policies (ignoring who won and who lost at each step), eventually everyone would end up with more WB. The merit of this argument depends on the questionable assumption that the sequence of efficiency-increasing policies has the property that each policy is random concerning who wins and losses. It also requires that the policies tend to be of equal WB-increasing magnitudes. He was clear that one specific efficiency-increasing policy would not necessarily increase societal WB. See Hotelling (1938), the Nobel Laureate John Hicks (1939), I. M. F. Little (1950), and Scitovsky (1951).

[18] Numerous economists blurt "more efficient is better than less efficient." Quoting Broome (1998): "*They* [welfare economists] *have slipped from identifying efficient states, which can be done without interpersonal comparisons, to claiming that efficient states are better than others, which generally one cannot. Robbins was right about this.*"

[19] The Federal judge and legal scholar Richard Posner (1983) argues that, while wealth and welfare are not the same thing, they are related, and that the goal of increased wealth, as compared to increased welfare, provides an ethical justification for honesty, commitment, etc., because these characteristics decrease the cost of market transactions. (A welfare consequentialist would advocate dishonesty if it would increase societal WB). Posner's view mimics the Keynesian view that prosperity is better than depression—just because.

[20] An aside: some welfare consequentialists argue that the least cost way to increase societal WB is to decrease suffering, a different and appealing perspective.

[21] Consider whether you would choose the maximization of aggregate WB as the ethical criterion under two different scenarios: (1) you are an *impartial spectator* choosing whether a group should adopt this objective, or (2) you know you will be a member,

maximizing aggregate WB is the moral objective, individuals, as individuals, are unimportant—they are simply containers that generate WB. And whether society consists of many or only one big one is immaterial.[22] Many welfare economists are unwilling to go this far, wanting, for example, to allow the possibility that the WB of some members should count more, for example, citizens more than foreigners or those at the bottom of the WB ladder. Other welfare economists believe that economists have no expertise in determining a fair distribution of WB[23] and, as discussed next, believe that WB can't be compared across individuals.

Welfare economists don't all agree on what WB means or how it should be measured.[24] Some assume WB is simply emotional WB/happiness, some that it's life-satisfaction WB, and some a combination. Some, like me, add pleasurable sensations.

Welfare economists differ on whether WB is cardinally meaningful (e.g., WB = 4 is twice as much as WB = 2) or only ordinally meaningful (4 is more than 2, but degrees of more are not comprehended).

They also disagree about whether the overall levels of WB are comparable across individuals (measurable on the same scale).[25] Incomparable across individuals is a common assumption. Consider four camps of welfare consequentialists: ordinal/comparable, ordinal/incomparable, cardinal/comparable, and cardinal/incomparable (Table 4.2).

so are not an impartial spectator, but do not know your specific position in the group. The second is choosing behind a *veil of ignorance*. Hume and Adam Smith considered the impartial spectator; Harsanyi and the economist and moral philosopher John Rawls (1971/1999) considered the veil. Harsanyi (1977) argues that an individual whose objective is to maximize his expected WB would, behind the veil, choose maximizing average WB (maximizing aggregate WB). Rawls (1971/1999), making different assumptions, reaches a different conclusion. That an impartial spectator might choose to maximize aggregate WB.

[22] Increasing aggregate WB does not necessarily increase societal WB unless everyone's WB has equal weight, and societal WB is aggregate WB.

[23] Non-expertise is commonly stated in introductory microeconomics. For example, "Exactly how far policymakers should go in promoting equity over efficiency is a difficult question that goes to the heart of the political process. As such, it is not a question economists can answer" (Krugman and Wells 2014).

[24] Chapter 5 extends the discussion and review of the different ways WB can be defined.

[25] Whether WB is comparable across individuals is different from whether bearers-of-WB are comparable.

Table 4.2 Cardinal, ordinal, comparable, incomparable

	WB is comparable across individuals	*WB isn't comparable across individuals*
For an individual, different levels of WB are cardinally meaningful	Cardinal/comparable	Cardinal/incomparable
Are only ordinal	Ordinal/comparable	Ordinal/incomparable

Getting your head around ordinal/comparable is challenging; it's easiest for cardinal/comparable. If everyone's WB is a number on the same cardinal scale (cardinal/comparable), aggregate WB has cardinal meaning.

As noted in Chapter 2, whether WB has cardinal meaning is an unanswered empirical question. People think they comprehend and rank changes in WB, but that does not make it so.

Whether it is possible to compare WB across individuals is also an empirical question. People assert such comparisons. "I am not as happy as George but am happier than Glen, who is always depressed." Or "Donald stealing my mother's ring increased his happiness less than it decreased mine." While, at the same time, admitting that we can't be sure about such comparisons. There are two issues: whether it is meaningful to compare your WB to mine and, if so, how to do it.

If WB is ordinal/non-comparable, adding WB numbers across individuals makes no sense. However, a welfare consequentialist can still ask whether a rule could exist that would take everyone's ordering of paths and spit out a societal WB ordering of sets of paths. Ideally, a rule that worked for all possible individual orderings. They would want to impose ethical restrictions on the rule. For example, if every member of society ranks a *Set X* higher than *Set Υ*, the rule must rank *Set X* higher in terms of societal WB.[26] Kenneth Arrow (1961/1963, 2012) proved that if this and a few other reasonable ones are imposed, no rule can exist that would work for all possible individual orderings (this is Arrow's famous impossibility theorem). So, if each of us only has an ordering of paths, and if

[26] *Set X* is the set of paths taken by each member of society in scenario *X*.

these orderings are WB-incomparable across individuals, for many individual orderings, it will be impossible to order sets of paths in terms of societal WB.[27]

I was surprised when I learned that rules exist for ordinal/comparable—I am having trouble getting my head around comparable but not cardinal.

Consider the following Rawlsian rule: *Set X* is associated with more societal WB than *Set Υ* if, and only if, the individual with the least amount of WB in *Set X* has more WB than the individual with the least amount of WB in *Set Υ*. [They don't have to be the same individual.] That is, *Set X* is morally preferred to *Set Υ* only if the worst off is better off with Set *X*.

This rule is inconsistent with dictatorship (no individual's ordering can be the sole determinant of the societal ordering. It also has the desirable property that how it ranks *X* vs. *Υ* does not depend on what other sets are available. And it is consistent with the ***independence of irrelevant alternatives restriction***. Despite these desirable properties, The Donald would not like this rule.

To implement this Rawlsian rule, two things are required: one has to be able to identify the individual in each set who experiences the least WB and then determine which one is worse off. Usually, with ordinal rankings, who has the least WB is meaningless.

But what if everyone has the same ordering? Anyone who knows the ordering can observe who in Set *X* is experiencing a path ranked lower than everyone else's. Same for Set *Υ*. If this lowest-ranked path in Set *X* is higher than the one in *Υ*, *X* is preferred to *Υ*.[28]

[27] Ordinal/incomparable, a mantra of much of twentieth-century choice theory, leaves welfare economists nothing to conclude other than Pareto Improvements (Deteriorations) are right (wrong). Robbins (1938) famously pointed this out. "He maintained that if economics was to have the objectivity of a science, economists may not make interpersonal comparisons and may not, in their capacity as economists, argue for or against any policy or change of policy that would make some people better and others worse off" (Scitovsky 1951). Bucking this ordinal/incompatible trend, numerous Cambridge (e.g., Pigou 1932/2017; Kahn 1935) and some American economists (e.g., Irving Fisher and Frank Knight) continued to advocate, sometimes implicitly, for comparability, arguing that we all have a similar capacity for WB, such that similar amounts of money generate similar amounts of comparable WB. See Scitovsky for additional details on the varying views on welfare economics in the twentieth century's first half.

[28] But, only if you assume the individual who experiences the lowest-ranked path is the one with the least WB—a reasonable conjecture, but ….

What if the identifier does not know the ordering? Can the lowest-ranked experienced path in a set be identified? Eliminate every path an individual chose from the set of experienced paths when there were at least two experienced paths in their feasible set. [If Bob chose the Disney path, and I chose the St Moritz path, and Bob could afford St. Moritz, the Disney path is not the lowest-ranked experienced path.] If only one path is left, it is the lowest-ranked experienced path. If more than one path is left, look for paths many could have chosen, but only one or a few did: these are paths chosen by individuals with limited options. The individuals choosing one of the remaining paths are likely those with the least WB. One could choose the guy with the least money income. This would make sense if everything that matters is a market commodity, but that is not the case.

Comparing the worst offs in Sets X and Υ: Set X is preferred if someone in either set had a choice between these two worst paths and chose the X one.[29] I am stopping here; we are beyond my pay grade.[30]

[29] It would be easier to find the highest-ranked available path in each set: people are choosing their HRAP, not their lowest-ranked available path. Consider the rule that Set X is morally preferred to Υ if and only if the greatest amount of WB experienced in X exceeds the greatest amount in Υ. E.g., if Putin is best off in Set X and Elon is best off in Υ, and Putin's WB in X exceeds Elon's in Υ, X is morally preferred.

[30] I recollect reading that paths are ordinal/comparable if everyone's *WB* function (utility function) is unique only up to one common increasing monotonic transformation. [Define $\text{WB}_i(k)$ as the function that identifies the amount of WB individual i would get from Path k. WB_i^* is an increasing monotonic transformation of the function WB_i if $\text{WB}_i^* = \varphi_i(\text{WB}_i)$ such that the derivative of $\varphi_i(\text{WB}_i)$ is positive. One "common transformation" means $\varphi_i = \varphi$ (that it's the same function for everyone).] The increasing monotonic part implies that each individual has only an ordinal ranking of paths, but it does not imply that everyone has the same ranking. So, what does $\varphi_i = \varphi$ add? Since it is a restriction on the transformation φ_i but not a restriction on the WB function, it does not imply that everyone has the same ranking (what I assumed in my example).

If one knows everyone's $\text{WB}_i(k)$ function and which path each is experiencing, one can identify a WB number for each individual, WB_i, rank them from highest to lowest, and decide that the individual with the lowest WB number is the individual with the lowest WB. However, if one then monotonically transforms the $\text{WB}_i(k)$ functions using different monotonic transformations for different individuals, who has the lowest WB number will change, even though no one's ranking of paths has changed. But it will always be the same individual if everyone is subject to the same transformation φ. [E.g., if you multiply everyone's WB by 3 or square everyone's WB, the ordering of individuals in terms of WB will not change.] This is all well and good, but it is not clear to me why the individual identified is objectively worst off.

Welfare Consequentialism (WC), Including Welfare Economics, Scares Moral Philosophers Because Anything Goes If It Increases WB

In WC, no act nor behavior is inherently right or wrong. Lying isn't inherently wrong; it is morally right if it increases societal WB; the same goes for breaking promises and derelictions of duties. There is no inherent right to free speech nor equal treatment under the law. There's no proscription on racial, cultural, or sexual discrimination. There is no right to liberty, so there is no limit on the amount the government can interfere in your life. Since speaking freely increases the WB of those speaking, but it often decreases the WB of those who must hear it, WC requires restrictions on speech.

For welfare economists, the sources of an individual's WB are irrelevant for determining right from wrong. Consider the implications. The emotional WB the neighbor kid gets from his mother's love is worth no more, nor less, than the emotional WB he gets from torturing cats. My decrease in WB from knowing that people are starving counts for no more than the decrease in WB I experience from having neighbors who are ethnically different. Abhorrent is that the WB I get from causing others to suffer, or their misfortune, counts as much as the WB I get from helping a friend or loved one.

If the sources of an individual's WB are irrelevant for determining right from wrong—the WB counts no matter how despicable or disgusting its source is. Looking ahead to research on disgust, the pleasure George gets from having sex with a dead chicken he bought at the supermarket, then roasted and enjoyed for dinner, counts. [Of course, WC must consider that the WB of others could decrease if they were to know what George was up to.[31]]

Imagine the sources of an individual's WB are irrelevant, and the moral objective is to maximize aggregate WB. Then, any act that increases aggregate WB is right (morally preferred) no matter how the WB was generated. Start with a simple example from Sen (1970), an economic

[31] Mill did not discuss chicken sex but rejected counting external effects of this sort, providing further evidence that he was neither a utilitarian nor a welfare consequentialist. Reacting to the argument that society can limit drinking simply because it decreases security and weakens and demoralizes society. Mill angrily responded that if this is harm, then we would all, wrongly, have an interest in everyone's "moral, intellectual and physical perfection" (Reeves 2008).

ethicist and Nobel laureate but not a welfare consequentialist. Consider a society of two individuals, Lewd and Prude, where Prude gets WB by denying Lewd pleasure, and Lewd gets WB by making Prude do something he does not want to do.

> Society has to rank three states: (A) no one reads Lady Chatterley's Lover, (B) only Prude reads it, or (C) only Lewd reads it. Prude, being a prude, does not want to read it but prefers he read it rather than Lewd: Prude hates the idea of Lewd enjoying the book. Best for Prude is no one reads the book. Lewd, on the other hand, would enjoy the book, but loves the idea of Prude being forced to read it. No one reading the book is Lewd's worst outcome.

To the discern of many, Prude being forced to read the book could increase aggregate WB: both Prude and Lewd are better off if Prude, rather than Lewd, reads it, and while Prude would have more WB if no one reads it, this may be more than offset by the great pleasure Lewd gets from Prude being forced to read it. Objectors, including Sen, would argue that forcing Prude to read a book he hates can't be the moral high ground. Also, objectors would object to having to include both the pleasure Lewd would get from Prude being disgusted and the pleasure Prude would get from Lewd not having the pleasure of reading the book. Shifting examples, Bob's pleasure from living in a neighborhood of straight, white people could mean that keeping others out is WC morally preferred to an integrated neighborhood.

If the sources of an individual's WB are irrelevant and the moral objective is to maximize aggregate WB, WB generated by ignorance counts as much as WB generated by learning. There is nothing inherently wrong with fake news: it increases the WB of some. There is also nothing inherently right about real news: it decreases the WB of some. The pleasure I get from believing global warming isn't real counts as much as the WB I would get from a great ski day or pulling a drowning kid from a ditch.

If one takes WC to the extreme, one can create examples that would make almost everyone scream "NO": No to awful acts that could be justified by WC. These include torture, racial discrimination, sadistic acts, dictatorial rule, and killing humans for fun and sport.[32] Anything can be morally justified by WC simply by arguing that doing it would increase

[32] Welfare consequentialists tend to argue that while despicable acts could in theory increase WB, this is unlikely in practice when one takes account of those who suffer from

societal WB. One could reject the assumption that the sources of WB are irrelevant, but one would not be a welfare economist. Welfare economists include the negative WB impacts of my actions on others, but they would never deem specific sources of my WB as immoral per se.

In contrast, Harsanyi did: arguing that society should, on ethical grounds, exclude from WB pleasures and pains caused by lack of information, misinformation, and morally objectionable orderings (those based on racism, sexism, sadism, maliciousness)—orderings that lead people to trample on the dignity and equality of others (Harsanyi 1977).[33] He was not a welfare economist. As a Hungarian Jew in 1944, he worked in a forced-labor unit, escaping from the train at the Budapest station as his unit was sent to an Austrian concentration camp (Harsanyi 1994).

Consider the implications of adding to WC the welfare-economic assumption that everyone maximizes their WB subject to their constraints (there is no flawed choosing). This makes, for many, welfare economics even more objectionable. It is more objectionable because the assumption implies it is always wrong to interfere in actions that affect no one other than the actor. You and the government have a moral imperative not to intervene when I beat my head against the wall, drink 12 shots of tequila, or try to commit suicide—unless someone else would be negatively affected—affected a lot. In contrast, a welfare consequentialist who recognizes a choice would reduce WB would be morally compelled to intervene, even if it would not decrease anyone else's WB. We believe other people make mistakes, and we are happy to intervene.

And finally, there is the complaint that welfare economists don't require that everyone counts and everyone's WB counts equally.

Are Welfare Economists Utilitarians?

The Dictionary of Bad Definitions

Utilitarian, *n.*

Etymology < post-classical Latin *utilitarius* >

despicable acts. Of course, their suffering is not taken into account if the sufferers are not members of society.

[33] An important question is who determines what orderings are immoral. And if society decides an ordering based on hate is immoral, there is the further issue of whether an ordering is, or isn't, hate-based. And, if hate is deemed immoral, how does one determine what a hate-filled person's ordering would be if he were hatred free?

A person who studies, worships, or is otherwise obsessed with the word *utility*.

> Economists must be utilitarians because they are always talking about utility. (Shakespeare's brother Bob, 1604, in *My letters to Will*)

Whether welfare economists are utilitarians needs clarification. Why? (1) Economists are led to believe (I was) that welfare economics is grounded in the ethic called utilitarianism—this is incorrect. Welfare economists need to be clear on what they assume and believe—they need to be precise. We should not be misleading ourselves or our students. (2) Utilitarianism is objectionable to many—a dirty word—so why unnecessarily call yourself a utilitarian? [Even without the title, many would still find the ethics of welfare economics objectionable.] (3) And it is of interest to understand how the label "utilitarian" came to be associated with welfare economics: it is because Benthamite utilitarianism was the first welfare consequentialist ethic out of the gate, so, for a long time, it was reasonable, and initially not misleading, to refer to all welfare consequentialists as utilitarians. There are different sorts of welfare consequentialists, so it is misleading to label them all utilitarians when most are not.

So, what is utilitarianism, and how does it relate to welfare economics? The first difficulty with answering is that few modern moral philosophers are welfare consequentialists, and those few do not self-identify as utilitarians—it has a bad name in large spheres of moral philosophy.

So, I start with whether welfare economists adhere to the classic utilitarianism of Jeremy Bentham (1748–1832), the founder of utilitarianism?[34,35] Most do not. Benthamite utilitarianism is WC if WB

[34] Utilitarianism was developed and popularized by Bentham's *Introduction to the Principles of Morals and Legislation* (1789). Humans and other animals experience only pleasure and pain which can be netted and then added across individuals (his *felicity calculus*). An action is moral if it increases aggregate net happiness. The first sentence of the book says it all,

> Nature has placed mankind under the governance of two sovereign masters: pain and pleasure. It is for them alone to determine what we ought to do, as well as to determine what we shall do.

[35] Initially, Bentham did not call it utilitarianism. John Stuart Mill adopted the term after seeing it used in a novel, unaware that Bentham had earlier used the word in a

is pleasure minus pain. Welfare consequentialists, including welfare economists, take a broader view of WB. Pain may cover all the things that would cause a spider's WB to suffer, but many things that decrease the WB of my dog and I are not physical pain (the firings of specific types of muscular nerve cells), and pain does not always cause a decrease in our WB. Chewing on sticks to dislodge one's baby teeth hurts, but the puppy persists. On the way to the dentist, my tongue plays with the loose tooth trying to find the amount of pushing that hurts best. After a competitive bike ride, the leg pain tells me I worked hard, a goal. And I know the pain will be gone in the morning. The opposite is pain you do not control and won't go away, which might be an illness symptom. It causes a decrease in WB. The word pleasure is also too narrow for humans. Like pain, pleasure is a sensation. Some pleasures (the taste of good chocolate, orgasm) are specific to certain body parts. A pleasure can cause enjoyment, but it can also cause suffering—I am upset with myself for eating those tasty onion rings. Or, it can go the other way: consider poor Fyodor Dostoevsky going on about "the enjoyment, of course, of despair; … in despair there are the most intense enjoyments" (Dostoevsky 1884/1996). Whether a pleasurable or painful sensation increases WB depends on the circumstances in which it occurs. He was a pain and pleasure guy; welfare economists are not.

Also, in Benthamite utilitarianism, net pleasure has cardinal meaning, and everyone's pleasure is measured on the same cardinal scale (cardinal, comparable). Also, the moral objective of Benthamite utilitarianism is to increase aggregate net pleasure, defined as the sum of aggregate pleasures minus aggregate pains. He advocated maximizing aggregate WB, limiting WB to one pain/pleasure continuum.

letter (Reeves). Mill suggests that Plato was the first utilitarian (Mill 1879). "To each his due" suggests actions should be assessed on the basis of how they affect welfare. The expression "the greatest happiness of the greatest number," while popularized by Bentham, can be traced back to the philosopher Francis Hutcheson, a founding father of the Scottish Enlightenment (Reeves). One root of utilitarianism is Epicurus. Bentham claimed inspiration from Hume. When he came across Hume's discussion of morality, he felt as though "scales had fallen from his eyes" (quoted by Gottlieb 2016) "It appears there was never any quality recommend as a virtue, or moral excellence, but on account of it being *useful* or *agreeable* to a man *himself*, or to *others*" (Hume 1758/2011). Hume differed from Bentham in that Hume was noting how people judge, not how they should judge, and he did not think WB was quantifiable (Gottlieb 2016).

And this includes the pleasure and pains of all animals that can experience either, independent of species. For Bentham, the pleasures and pains of ducks count as much as yours and mine, and all count equally, including spider pain.

> The day may come when the rest of the animal creation may acquire those rights which never could have been witholden from them but by the hand of tyranny. The French have already discovered that the blackness of the skin is no reason a human being should be abandoned without redress to the caprice of a tormentor. It may one day come to be recognized that the number of the legs, the villosity of the skin, or the termination of the os sacrum [whether one has a tail] are reasons equally insufficient for abandoning a sensitive being to the same fate. What else is it that should trace the insuperable line? Is it the faculty of reason or perhaps the faculty of discourse? But a full-grown horse or dog is beyond comparison a more rational, as well as a more conversable animal, than an infant of a day or a week or even a month, old. But suppose the case were otherwise, what would it avail? The question isn't, can they reason? nor can they talk? But, can they suffer? (Bentham 1789/2017)

Holding all else constant, imagine two worlds: in the first, I get 10 units of net pleasure, and Wilbur, a pig, gets -5, and in the other, the numbers are switched. The Benthamite utilitarian is indifferent/impartial: who gains and loses is immaterial if the net gain is unchanged. This *impartiality* is critical to his utilitarianism (Driver 2014) but not welfare economics. Welfare economists typically do not require that members' WB get equal weight. The objective of Benthamite utilitarianism is to maximize aggregate WB, but many welfare economists don't assume societal WB is aggregate emotional WB, a critical difference.

Benthamite utilitarianism would judge a behavior as moral or immoral by whether it increases or decreases aggregate WB in his pleasure/pain sense. And a larger increase in aggregate WB is preferred to a lesser increase. He would judge the singer Lana del Rey smoking another cigarette wrong if her pleasure is less than the displeasure produced by her second hand smoke. Welfare economists, in contrast, would ask whether the act increases societal WB, defining WB more broadly, not necessarily counting Lana's and everyone else's WB, equally. Neither welfare economics nor Benthamite utilitarianism implies your act is moral simply because it increases your WB. As noted earlier, since economicus is constrained to maximize his WB, economicus is constrained to act

Bentham—immorally if an act increases his personal WB but decreases aggregate WB. Economici are derogatorily referred to as *psychological egoists* or *egoists*—which is true if an egoist is defined as someone who cannot act contrary to their self-interest. Whether Bentham believed humans are egotistical is a matter of debate: he left open the possibility that humans can choose to act contrary to their WB. If so, Benthamite-Lana may decide to not light up if her smoking would reduce aggregate WB.[36] To make Economicus Lana's behavior moral, someone would have to interfere.

In Table 4.1, Bentham utilitarianism is a subset of Sets I or VII, and so is welfare economics, but they have minimal or no overlap.[37]

The first place to look past Benthamite utilitarianism is the supposed utilitarianism of John Stuart Mill, but I will skip over him for now: he is

[36] Bentham is contradictory: sometimes saying we are egoists, but sometimes giving us the ability to act contrary to our self-interest. In *The Book of Fallacies*, Bentham (2015) says,

> In every human breast, rare and short-lived ebullitions, the result of some extraordinary strong stimulus or incitement excepted, self-regarding interest is predominant over social interest: each person's own individual interest, over the interests of all other person taken together.

This sounds like an endorsement of egoism except for the part

> rare and short-lived ebullitions, the result of some extraordinary strong stimulus or incitement excepted,"

which is often omitted replaced with "…"), this sounds like an endorsement of egoism.

In contrast, in *An Introduction to Principles of Morals and Legislation* (1789/2017) he says,

> There is no case in which a private man ought not to aim to produce his own happiness and of that of his fellow-creatures; … Every act that promises to be beneficial on the whole to the community (himself included) each individual ought to perform of himself; … Every act that promises to be pernicious on the whole to the community (himself included) each individual ought to abstain from;…

There are differing interpretations as to what Bentham meant (see, e.g., Driver 2014; Din widdy and Twining 2004; Lyons 1991).

[37] Looking ahead, to get overlap, welfare economists must assume that only emotional WB matters, that the emotional WB of all animals matters equally, and that WB is cardinally meaningful.

complicated.[38] I will also jump over the influential utilitarian Henry Sidgwick (1838–1900) to the twentieth century.[39] Simply put, there is no one modern utilitarian ethic but several overlapping ethics. For example, *act utilitarianism*, *rule utilitarianism*, and *preference utilitarianism*. Act utilitarianism, like Benthamite utilitarianism, makes the objective maximizing aggregate WB—act by act. Whereas the objective of rule utilitarianism is to identify rules—rules that apply to everyone—that will, overall, lead to maximizing aggregate WB.[40] The different varieties agree that WB isn't simply pleasures minus pain. And none are Benthamite utilitarianism.

Interesting is preference utilitarianism. Peter Singer states, "my ethical position is a form of preference-utilitarianism:" "I approach each issue by seeking the solution that has the best consequences for all affected. By 'consequences', I understand that which satisfies the most preferences, weighted in accordance with the strength of the preferences" (Singer 1997). A noted difference between him and Benthamite utilitarianism is that for Singer, the objective is to fulfill an individual's *interests*, achieved by giving the individual what they prefer, even if it causes them more

[38] In partial explanation, Mill complicated the simplicity of Benthamite utilitarianism by arguing that higher pleasures should count more than lower ones (sex, drugs, and rock'n'roll). See, *Utilitarianism* (Mill 1879/2004), and Reeves). The deceased Bentham rolled over at Mill's notion of utilitarianism. In 1879, Mill's book was perceived as the voice of utilitarianism, but Jevons (1879) argued that if one drops the assumption that all feelings fall on the same pleasure/pain univariate measure, it is no longer utilitarianism. Quoting Jevons (1879) critique of *Utilitarianism*,

> Nothing can be more plain, too, than that Mill himself believed he was dutifully expounding the doctrines of his father, [and] of his father's friend, the great Bentham...His Essays purport throughout to be a defense and exposition of the Utilitarian doctrine.... but there is a wide gulf between what he intends and what he achieves... I [Jevons] make it my business therefore in this article to show that Mill was intellectually unfitted to decide what was utilitarian, and what was not.

[39] Sidgwick wrote the influential *The Method of Ethics* (1874/1907/2014) which was both a defense and explanation of utilitarianism (Driver (2014)). He critically pointed out the problem of total emotional WB versus average emotional WB: suggesting that the goal should be to maximize the product of average emotional WB and population size.

[40] One argument for rule over act utilitarianism is that act utilitarianism provides no justification for moral rights or obligations—anything goes if it increases aggregate WB (Harsanyi 1977). Whereas the general rules produced by rule utilitarianism provides guidelines (rights and obligations) for behavior. So, for example, rule utilitarianism warrants the banning of slavery, while in act utilitarianism whether enslaving someone is moral or immoral is determined case by case. The other difference is that an individual undertakes an act taking as given the behavior of others, whereas a chosen rule applies to everyone, so affects the behavior of others.

pain and less pleasure or even less emotional WB. He defines preferences as "wants, needs, and desires" (Singer 2011). He does not advocate for maximizing aggregate WB, so while he is a consequentialist, he is a *want/desire consequentialist*. Singer does not believe fulfilling wants and desires always increases WB. His advocacy for fulfilling wants and desires, rather than increasing WB, is that they are easier to observe and measure. He counts the wants and desires of all species equally, giving all animals equal standing.[41] Singer defines "basic equality" as when everyone's interests get equal consideration (impartiality) and argues that equal consideration is morally preferred over unequal consideration. Singer (2011) describes his preference utilitarianism as extending the utilitarian views of his Oxford professor R. M. Hare (1919–2002).[42]

In 1977, Harsanyi (1977) proposed preference utilitarianism. He pointed out (as psychological studies confirm) that individuals don't always maximize, subject to their constraints, their WB: he argued individuals violate the assumptions of NCT based on misbeliefs, emotions, etc. He distinguishes between what he calls *true preferences* (an ordering based on personal WB) and *manifest preferences* (an ordering consistent with behavior). Harsanyi's moral objective is to maximize WB based on true preferences—but after deleting WB caused by morally objectionable acts.[43]

The preference utilitarianisms of Singer (2011), Hare (1981), and Harsanyi (1977) all have a rules component. They argue that society should determine what is morally right based on rules that, if followed, would, over time, lead to satisfying more wants and desires. The rules will not suffice in complicated cases, and critical thinking will be required. They agree that preferences based on illogical or bad information should not count. While Harsanyi excludes the fulfillment of immoral wants and desires (hate, sadism, etc.), I have not found anything by Singer or Hare that indicates they agree. Singer emphasizes the equal consideration of everyone's interests; his textbook, *Practical Ethics* (2011), says nothing about inappropriate interests.

[41] Singer is a founder of the animal-rights movement—*Animal Liberation* (1975/2009).

[42] For an introduction to R. M. Hare, see Anthony Price (2016). Of interest is also *Early Utilitarians* (Binmore 2021).

[43] It isn't clear whether such subtractions are possible. How would one determine what a malicious racist's ordering would be if they were neither a racist nor malicious?

Contrasting with preference utilitarianism, welfare economists are concerned with welfare/WB, not want and desire fulfillment per se. And preference utilitarians like Singer include the preferences of non-humans. And many welfare economists reject the notion that preferences and WB have intensities that can be compared across individuals. Another difference is that preference utilitarianism gives everyone equal weight, as does Benthamite utilitarianism, while welfare economics does not require this.

Welfare economics does not distinguish between true and manifest WB: self-assessed WB and WB are the same?[44] Preference utilitarianism explicitly admits the possibility that you don't know what is best for you. One can be a preference utilitarian without assuming everyone experiences their HRAP, whereas NCT and welfare economics assumes the individual always experiences their HRAP. Preference utilitarians admit flawed choosing in terms of WB. If they believe someone makes a flawed choice, they advocate for paternalism (limiting and directing the individual's behavior against their wishes). For example, imagine that your teenage daughter is inclined to cut herself (not uncommon). Welfare economics says to let her cut unless the cutting negatively affects others. A preference utilitarian would advocate sending her to therapy and throwing away the knives—even if her cutting affects only her. Or imagine that I, when given the opportunity, poke pins in my eyes and fail to save for retirement. A preference utilitarian may stop the poking and force saving. If no one else is affected, the welfare economist has no grounds for interfering. [In determining whether to restrict my behavior, a preference utilitarian should consider that forcing me to save for retirement conflicts with my desire for freedom.]

Some economic ethicists agree with Singer that the moral objective is satisfying more wants and desires rather than increasing WB. As I characterized Singer, they are want/desire consequentialists. In Table 4.1, want/desire consequentialists are restricted to VII and IX. If they admit choices that violate preferences, as most do, they are in Set IX. D. Hausman (2010) critiques the divide between WC and want/desire consequentialism.

I end this comparison of utilitarianism and welfare economics with their implications for redistributing wealth. An imperative of Singer's preference utilitarianism is that once the basic needs of you and your loved

[44] Self-assessed WB is sometimes called *subjective WB*: from the subject's perspective.

ones have been met, you should allocate all remaining time and income to reduce the suffering of those individuals who are suffering the most, irrespective of their relationship to you, or their species—to do otherwise is wrong. This conclusion follows from his assuming (1) preferences have intensity, (2) preferences can be compared across individuals (even between spiders and humans), (3) a dollar spent will fulfill the most wants and desires if it's spent helping those who are currently suffering the most,[45] (4) one can choose to not pursue their own interests, and (5) the moral objective is to increase aggregate want and desire fulfillment. In his textbook Practical Ethics, Singer admits he is asking a lot. His examples deal with our moral imperative to help desperately poor people. His assumption that everyone should count equally, independent of species, implies a moral imperative to reduce animal suffering. And reducing the suffering of food animals could be cheaper than serving the interests of desperate humans.

Welfare economists would not advocate Singer‘s imperative because they would not, as we have discussed, accept all his assumptions. For one, they would reject (4): economicus can't do this; he must maximize his personal WB (or desire fulfillment) subject to his constraints. So, for the welfare economist, behaving more morally must be imposed on the individual.

If a welfare consequentialist, or welfare economist, adopts (3) and the moral objective is to maximize aggregate WB, they would conclude that it is right (moral) that the State redistributes from the well-off to the worst off.[46] But many reject (3).[47] Given all these differences, welfare economists are not preference utilitarians.

[45] This assumption is akin to what economics defines as *diminishing marginal utility*: something we teach as a law to students in principles of microeconomics.

[46] Everyone would consider that progressive tax rates could influence the incentive to work.

[47] Bentham also advocated for the redistribution of wealth from the best off to the worst off. While Bentham did not articulate modern "diminishing marginal utility," he did feel that an additional dollar spent by someone well-off would increase net pleasure less than if were spent by a worst off, and Bentham's goal was to maximize aggregate pleasure minus pain. Quoting Bentham, "the more remote from equality are the shares [of wealth] possessed by the individuals in question, in the mass of the instruments of felicity, –the less is the sum of the felicity produced by the sum of those same shares" (Bentham 1789/2017).

Welfare economists are also not rule-utilitarians: welfare economists typically think about whether a specific act or policy would increase aggregate or societal WB rather than suggesting ethical rules that would, on average, increase aggregate or societal WB.[48]

Besides Not Being Utilitarians (Benthamite, Rule, or Preference), Welfare Economists Differ from Other Modern Welfare Consequentialists

Some modern welfare consequentialists reject the assumption that an individual can WB-order all possible paths, arguing that there are different kinds of WB and that not all are commensurable. One could believe only welfare consequences matter, but it is impossible to compare all the different types. As noted in Chapter 2, the commensurability of WB is the foundation of NCT and welfare economics—pervasive non-commensurability would be a blow to both.[49]

In contrast, some welfare consequentialists who believe all paths can be WB-ordered reject the additional assumption that individuals always maximize their personal WB. They reject it either because they believe in mistakes or believe a few individuals choose their path to maximize aggregate WB. [If individuals can do the latter, how to live an ethical life is a component of WC.]

Some modern welfare consequentialists (e.g., a former World Bank chief economist, Kaushik Basu) argue that WB isn't just emotional and life-satisfaction WB. Instead, they assert that WB also increases with knowledge, the extent to which one is fulfilling their capabilities, and even simply having more capabilities—even if they fail to increase emotional or life-satisfaction WB.[50]

[48] The aim of *social-choice theory* (List 2013) is to identify rules (functions) to identify what is morally preferred based on its welfare consequences. For example, there is the well-researched question of how different voting schemes (rules for decision-making) succeed and fail to distinguish between right and wrong policies.

[49] NCT survives limited non-commensurability but with wounds. For example, if all the kinds of WB associated with the consumption of market goods are commensurable, but these kinds of WB are not commensurable with those associated with non-market experiences such as religion and time with friends. Chapter 6 has more details.

[50] The view, that WB is increasing in capabilities, even if they are unrealized, is widely associated with Sen and M. Nussbaum (Sen 1980a; Nussbaum 2006, 2011; Kaushik and Lopez-Calva 2011; Robeyns 2016).

According to this view of WB, you can have more even if you don't feel it or realize it. And you could be better off even though you feel worse if, for example, the newly acquired knowledge makes you anxious and depressed.

One can, of course, be an economic ethicist who adheres to an ethic where the WB of society's members is important, but WB isn't the only thing of importance (II or V in Table 4.1). If so, one is neither a welfare economist nor a welfare consequentialist.[51] This is OK: no rule says economists who care about parsing right from wrong actions must only care about WB. What one is called if one cares about WB, but not only WB depends on how much one thinks WB should matter relative to other things, such as being virtuous or fulfilling your duties. I will call them *NotOnlyWB ethicists*.

We now turn to research on how regular people judge right from wrong. If you view yourself as a welfare consequentialist or a welfare economist, it is enlightening to know that few accept your view that only welfare consequences matter. Also disturbing to an applied welfare economist like myself is people, while concerned with their WB, do not believe that maximizing societal WB is the moral objective or that PIs are always right. Summarizing by paraphrasing Aristotle, if Joe Schmo and the intellectuals who study ethics reject welfare economics, I, as a lifelong welfare economist, should stop and pause.

The Moral Judgments of Regular People: They Don't Ascribe to the Ethics of Welfare Economics

People don't determine whether an act is right or wrong solely on its effect on WB. For them, the WB of almost everyone else plays no role in deciding right from wrong. Research in moral psychology indicates that typical Western research subjects judge morality (of an act or a person) using two criteria: (1) justice/fairness (treating others in proportion to their actions and intent—they should get their just desserts)[52] and (2) caring for others and protecting them from harm. Harming others is

[51] One could even be an economic ethicist who believes that how an act influences WB is irrelevant to determining whether the action was right or wrong. The moral imperative could be fulfilling the will of God. My friend Mike is in this category.

[52] If justice and fairness depend on intent, and not just consequence, it is inconsistent with WC.

wrong; caring for others is right; those who harm should be punished, and those who care for others, and reduce harm, should be rewarded.

Non-Western adults and religious conservatives add two additional criteria: (3) loyalty to your community/group, respecting its authority, and fulfilling your obligations to the group. And (4) an ethic of holiness (humans are God's creations and are morally obligated to not degrade that holiness). Describing this perspective:

> People are bearers of something holy or god-like and have moral obligations to not act in ways that are degrading to or incommensurate with that holiness. The ethic of divinity requires that people treat their bodies as temples, not as playgrounds, and so personal choices that seem to harm nobody else (e.g., about food, sex, and hygiene) are sometimes moralized (for a further elaboration of moral foundations, see Haidt & Graham 2007). In sum, the high-socioeconomic status (SES), secular Western populations that have been the primary target of study thus far appear unusual in a global context, based on their peculiarly narrow reliance, relative to the rest of humanity, on a single foundation for moral reasoning (based on justice, individual rights, and the avoidance of harm to others; cf. Haidt & Graham 2007). (Henrich et al. 2010)

One way to observe and measure moral diversity is to present research subjects with descriptions of different behaviors and ask how they judge them (right or wrong?). Judgment varies with the respondent's socioeconomic status, political orientation (liberal vs. conservative), and religiousness. Researchers also ask what criteria the respondent considered when judging an act right or wrong. The research objective is to determine whether the criteria vary across individuals.

Jonathan Haidt (2012), his coauthors, and others have tested respondents' reactions to *harmless acts* (acts that cause no physical or psychological damage, except possible offense—acts that occur in private). Three examples (Haidt, Silvia Koller, and Maria Dias 1993):

> A woman is cleaning out her closet, and she finds her old [American or Brazilian] flag. She does not want the flag anymore, so she cuts it up into pieces and uses the rags to clean her bathroom.
>
> A man goes to the supermarket once a week and buys a dead chicken. But before cooking the chicken, he has sexual intercourse with it. Then he cooks it and eats it.

> A brother and sister like to kiss each other on the mouth. When nobody is around, they find a secret hiding place and kiss each other on the mouth passionately.

Surveying in three cities (two in Brazil, plus Philadelphia), the authors asked about such activities. They found that high-socioeconomic Americans view such acts as causing no harm and are not immoral—just activities that go against social convention. In contrast, the poor and the religious (more so in Brazil) find such acts immoral simply because they invoke disgust or disrespect. Moreover, Western democracies typically legislate to reduce harm, not to eliminate harmless acts. [There are exceptions, such as laws against homosexual acts between consenting adults.] In contrast, religious states such as Iran and the Vatican ban numerous harmless acts.

Jesse Graham Haidt, and Brian Nosek (2009 at https://doi.org/10.1037/a0015141) identify five moral dimensions: harm/care, fairness/reciprocity, ingroup/loyalty, authority/respect, and purity/sanctity. Conservatives give weight to each dimension, whereas liberals care mainly about the first two.

In their 4th Study, respondents were asked what they would have to be paid to voluntarily do different sorts of distasteful things. The following are their examples for each criterion:

> (Harm) Kick a dog in the head, hard
>
> (Fairness) Say no to a friend's request to help him move into a new apartment after he helped you move the month before.
>
> (Ingroup) Burn your country's flag (nobody else sees you do it)
>
> (Authority) Make a disrespectful hand gesture to your boss, teacher, or professor.
>
> (Purity) Get a blood transfusion of 1 pint of disease-free blood...from a convicted child molester.

Their Figure 4 graphs their findings with "self-reported political identity" on the horizontal axis (very liberal to very conservative) and "Average amount required to violate taboos" on the vertical axis. To be unfair, everyone needed the most money, and the amount did not vary by political orientation (their top solid line). As one becomes more conservative, one needs more money to violate an ingroup, authority, or a purity taboo. It is the opposite of harm: the more conservative, the less money is needed to harm. Except for fairness, liberals and conservatives put different weight on these five dimensions of morality.

It isn't easy to reconcile these ethical criteria with WC, especially if each gets a similar weight. Criterion 2: *caring for others and protecting them from harm* is the one with an obvious link to societal WB. Following Criterion 1: *justice/fairness (treating others in proportion to their intentions and actions—they should get their just deserts* can decrease societal WB. I should care for others if their behavior indicates they deserve care. None explicitly say that increasing the WB of yourself and others is morally preferred.

Trying to reconcile the four criteria to WC and welfare economics, one could awkwardly argue that observing what the observer regards as disloyalty, disrespect, or injustice matters to the observer solely because it reduces the observer's WB. And caring for others, who need and deserve care, is right only to the extent it increases the recipient's and caregiver's WB. Justice, disloyalty, etc., are of moral relevance because they affect WB. Many disagree. Consider the football players who knelt in protest when the US National Anthem was played. Did they do it because it increased their WB, and did others object because the kneeling decreased their WB?—both groups would say no.

A welfare consequentialist who isn't a welfare economist (e.g., Harsanyi) may, alternatively, try to reconcile the four criteria fully or partially with WC by arguing that WB obtained by being disloyal, disrespectful, or unjust should not count in determining societal WB. A welfare economist would shudder at this suggestion.

The introduction-to-microeconomics text I used, Krugman and Wells (2014), concludes that a PI is a right act. And, given a societal goal, achieving it at a lower cost is morally preferred. These two pillars of welfare economics are not in sync with how many of us judge specific policies and behaviors. The four criteria imply an individual will conclude a PI is wrong if they view the gainers as undeserving (e.g., lazy) and conclude a Pareto Deterioration right if the losers deserve punishment. The same justice issues pertain to whether society should strive to minimize the costs of achieving a goal; are the recipients of the savings deserving? There are two interpretations: (1) If WB is reduced by an act because it violates someone's sense of justice and fairness, it isn't a PI—so there are few or no PIs. Or, if a policy is a PI (no one's WB declined), it is still wrong, meaning a PI can be wrong.

Additional Evidence That People Are Not Welfare Consequentialists: Trolley Problems

Philosophers like thought experiments; one favorite is the *Trolley Problem*. Their findings indicate that we often behave inconsistent with WC. The hypothetical-trolley scenario has numerous variations, but at issue is whether it is right or wrong for you (or someone else) to kill (or let die) one person to save five. The brake-less trolley is barreling down the tracks, soon to derail on a curve killing all five onboard. You're standing on a footbridge with a fat guy. If you trip or push him, he falls on the track, and his large body stops the train. [Your body is too small to stop the train.] Or, an empty trolley is barreling down the tracks and will run over five people crossing the tracks unless you throw a switch that will divert the trolley onto another track, where it will run over one person. If everyone at risk is a productive member of society, a welfare consequentialist would always throw the guy or the switch. If presented with the switch story, subjects often say they would throw the switch, but if presented with the fat-guy version, few are willing to trip or push the fat guy, even though switching and pushing lead to the same number saved. Since welfare consequentialists care only about consequences, they would always switch or push (Fig. 4.3).

Or a third version: you are standing by the track next to a switch. The fat guy is on the footbridge. If you throw the switch rather than diverting the trolley onto the other track, it trips the trap door the fat guy is standing on, and he drops to his death on the track. When you

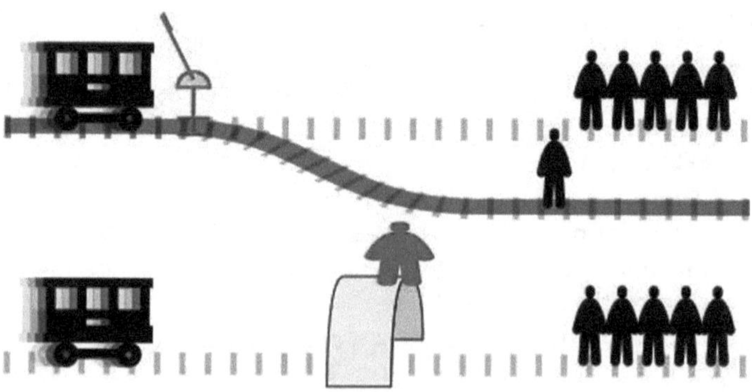

Fig. 4.3 Trolley problems

were both on the bridge, you might not have pushed because you were afraid you would get into a life-or-death struggle with someone bigger. That worry is eliminated with the trap door. Still, few are willing to trip the trap door. Every welfare consequentialist always would. If you would not, you are not a welfare consequentialist.

The British philosopher and podcast host David Edmonds' explanation goes to intent. The intent is to kill the fat guy if you hope to stop the trolley with his body—he needs to die for the trolley to stop—his death could not be construed as *collateral damage*. In contrast, if one switches the trolley to the other track, there is no intent to kill anyone, and once the trolley is on the other track, the five are saved even if no one is on the other track. The poor guy crossing the other track is simply collateral damage—no one is responsible for killing him. In summary, we judge actions both on consequence and process. Tweaks to the scenario are critical.[53] For example, whether it is you or someone else deciding.

Conclusions and Qualifications

Questions addressed: What are the ethics of welfare economics? What is utilitarianism? And what are their ethical distinctions and similarities? The ethics of welfare economics is a unique type of WC and quite different from utilitarianism. The latter comparison is complicated by there being various forms of utilitarianism and by hesitancy among moral philosophers to self-identify as utilitarians. Who is what and why depends on how

[53] If a subject's serotonin levels are enhanced by the SSRI citalopram, they are less inclined to push the fat guy, particularly if they are an empathetic person (Crockett et al. 2010; Crockett 2012, 2013; Siegel and Crockett 2013). [SSRI for *Selective Serotonin Reuptake Inhibitor*.] The decision to kill one to save five can be made using the executive-functioning part of your brain, thinking through the consequences, and then choosing the best outcome, which is to kill one to save five. Or it can be driven by your moral empathic inclination not to harm an innocent person "I can't kill someone." How much your choice is based on moral inclination versus consequence depends on the type of person you are, the amount of time you have to decide, your emotional state, and the situation's emotional salience. Greene et al. (2001, 2004) found, using fMRI imaging, that when the moral decision is more up-close-and-personal, there is more activation of the emotional-processing centers of your brain (e.g., the amygdala and posterior cingulate gyrus), so more conflict between emotion and reasoning. The more emotionally salient the situation (pushing the fat guy is more personal and emotional than flicking a switch), the more your decision is based on the moral imperative not to harm. Thus, decreasing the probability that you will kill the one to save the five. Serotonin is thought to strengthen your natural aversion to doing harm.

welfare economists and utilitarians are defined and identified and how WC is defined. There is no book of official definitions, and you might object to some of mine. This is OK—but I hope you come away averse to suggesting that welfare economists are utilitarians but believing welfare economics is a type of WC, quirky like utilitarianism, but different. And a sort that other welfare consequentialists shun.

What to conclude about welfare economics? First, welfare economists should question why few besides economists subscribe to it. And they should not be surprised that everyone does not accept the policy recommendations it implies. A vital distinction between welfare economics and other forms of WC (including utilitarianism) is welfare economists assume individuals always choose their HRAP. Much research in psychology and behavioral economics indicates this assumption is wrong. That welfare economics dictates that actions that do not affect others should, ethically, not be messed with depends on a violated assumption.

An economist concerned with ethics and WB may want a WC ethic that does not adhere to the specific trapping of welfare economics. Alternatively, an economist concerned with ethics and WB, but not only WB might adopt an ethic based on welfare consequences and intent (or duty, rights, or whatever). An economist concerned with ethics might adopt an ethic where WB plays no role in determining right from wrong; for example, one could adopt a Kantian ethic. As Hicks admitted, "one also has the right to an economics free of utilitarian assumptions." And an economist can remain a scientist who is just trying to model—without judgment—behavior.

But then again, utilitarian could mean someone who talks much about utility.

Chapters 12 and 13 will continue our conversation on ethics. Now I return to behavior and choice.

References and Sources

Arrow, Kenneth. 1961/1963. *Social choice and individual values*. New York: Wiley.

———. 2012. *Social choice and individual values*. Vol. 12. New Haven, CT: Yale University Press.

Beard, Mary. 2015. *SPQR: A history of ancient Rome*. New York: W.W. Norton.

Bentham, Jeremy. 1789/2017. *Introduction to the principles of morals and legislation*. Early Modern Texts. www.earlymoderntexts.com/assets/pdfs/bentham1780.pdf.

———. 2015. *The book of fallacies*. Edited by Philip Schofield. Oxford: Oxford University Press. https://books.google.com/books?hl=en&lr=&id=hLW6BwAAQBAJ&oi=fnd&pg=PP1&dq=Jeremy+bentham+book+of+fallacies&ots=C2DPjzxwNg&sig=0ORA-e3g-zZxKm-aEmtp2JfnOOM#v=onepage&q=Jeremy%20bentham%20book%20of%20fallacies&f=false.

Binmore, Ken. 2021. *Early utilitarians*. Cham: Springer.

Broome, John. 1998. "What's wrong with poverty?" *London Review of Books*, 2.

Crockett, Molly. 2012. "Molly Crockett on brain chemistry and moral-decision making." *Philosophy Bites*. https://philosophybites.com/2012/07/molly-crockett-on-brain-chemistry-and-moral-decision-making-originally-on-bioethics-bites.html.

———. 2013. "Models of morality." *Trends in Cognitive Sciences* 17 (8): 363–366. https://doi.org/10.1016/j.tics.2013.06.005. https://www.webofscience.com/wos/woscc/full-record/WOS:000323458700001.

Crockett, Molly, Luke Clark, Marc Hauser, and Trevor Robbins. 2010. "Serotonin selectively influences moral judgment and behavior through effects on harm aversion." *Proceedings of the National Academy of Sciences of the United States of America* 107 (40): 17433–17438. https://doi.org/10.1073/pnas.1009396107. https://www.webofscience.com/wos/woscc/full-record/WOS:000282512000069.

Dinwiddy, John, and William Twining. 2004. *Bentham: Selected writings of John Dinwiddy*. Stanford, CA: Stanford University Press.

Dostoevsky, Fyodor. 1884(Russian)/1996. *Notes from the underground*. Project Gutenberg. https://www.gutenberg.org/ebooks/600.

Driver, Julia. 2014. "Stanford encyclopedia of philosophy, the history of utilitarianism." September. https://plato.stanford.edu/.

Fleischacker, Samuel. 2013. "Adam smith's moral and political philosophy." Stanford Encyclopedia of Philosophy. Stanford University. https://plato.stanford.edu/title/.

Gottlieb, Anthony. 2016. *The dream of enlightenment: The rise of modern philosophy*. New York: W. W. Norton.

Graham, Jesse, Jonathan Haidt, and Brian Nosek. 2009. "Liberals and conservatives rely on different sets of moral foundations." *Journal of Personality and Social Psychology* 96 (5): 1029–1046. https://doi.org/10.1037/a0015141. https://Www.Webofscience.Com/Wos/Woscc/Full-Record/WOS:000265305100007.

Greene, Joshua, Leigh Nystrom, John Daley, and Jonathan Cohen. 2001. "An fMRI investigation of emotional engagement in moral judgment". *Science* 293 (5537). https://doi.org/10.1126/science.1062872.

Greene, Joshua, Leigh Nystrom, Andrew Engell, John Daley, and Jonathan Cohen. 2004. "The neural bases of cognitive conflict and control in moral judgment". *Neuron* 44. https://doi.org/10.1016/j.neuron.2004.09.027.

Haidt, Jonathan. 2012. *The righteous mind: Why good people are divided by politics and religion*. New York: Pantheon Books.

Haidt, Jonathan, and Jesse Graham. 2007. "When morality opposes justice: Conservatives have moral intuitions liberals may not recognize." *Social Justice Research* 20: 18.

Haidt, Jonathan, Silvia Helena Koller, and Maria Dias. 1993. "Affect, culture, and morality, or is it wrong to eat your dog?" *Journal of Personality and Social Psychology* 65 (4): 613.

Hare, Richard Mervyn. 1981. *Moral thinking: Its levels, method, and point*. Oxford: Clarendon Press; New York: Oxford University Press.

Harsanyi, John C. 1977. "Morality and the theory of rational behavior." *Social Research*: 623–656.

Harsanyi, John. 1994. "Nobel address: Biographical." https://www.nobelprize.org/prizes/economic-sciences/1994/harsanyi/biographical/.

Hausman, Daniel. 2010. "Hedonism and welfare economics." *Economics and Philosophy* 26 (3): 321–344. https://doi.org/10.1017/s0266267110000398. https://www.webofscience.com/wos/woscc/full-record/WOS:000283912100003.

Hausman, Daniel. 2015. "Economics, philosophy of." In *International encyclopedia of the social & behavioral sciences: Second edition*, 99–104. Elsevier. https://www.rep.routledge.com/articles/thematic/economics-philosophy-of/v-1.

Hausman, Daniel, and Michael McPherson. 1993. "Taking ethics seriously: Economics and contemporary moral philosophy." *Journal of Economic Literature* 31 (2): 671–731. https://www.jstor.org/stable/2728513?origin=JSTOR-pdf.

Henrich, Joseph, Steven Heine, and Ara Norenzayan. 2010. "The weirdest people in the world?" *Behavioral and Brain Sciences* 33 (2–3): 61-+. https://doi.org/10.1017/s0140525x0999152x. https://www.webofscience.com/wos/woscc/full-record/WOS:000279973200001.

Hicks, John. 1939. "The foundations of welfare economics." *The Economic Journal* 49 (196): 696–712.

Hotelling, Harold. 1938. "The general welfare in relation to problems of taxation and of railway and utility rates." *Econometrica* 6 (3): 242–269.

Hume, David. 1758/2011. *Essays and treatises on several subjects*. London: John Long LTD London (1758) and Project Gutenberg (2011). https://www.gutenberg.org/ebooks/36120.

Jevons, Stanley. 1879. "John Stuart Mill's philosophy tested." *The Contemporary Review, 1866–1900* 36: 521–538. https://www.webofscience.com/wos/woscc/full-record/WOS:A1970H895500002.

Kahn, Richard 1935. "Some notes on ideal output." *The Economic Journal* 45 (177): 1–35. https://www.jstor.org/stable/2224577.

Kaushik, Basu, and Luis Lopez-Calva. 2011. "Functionings and capabilities." *Handbook of Social Choice and Welfare* 2: 153–187. https://doi.org/10.1016/S0169-7218(10)00016-X.

Krugman, Paul, and Robin Wells. 2014. *Microeconomics*. 4th ed. New York: Worth.

List, Christian. 2013, Winter. "Social choice theory." Stanford Encyclopedia of Philosophy. Stanford University. https://plato.stanford.edu/title/.

Little, I. M. D. 1950. *A critique of welfare economics*. Oxford: Oxford University Press.

Lyons, David. 1991. *In the interest of the governed: A study in Bentham's philosophy of utility and law*. Cambridge: Cambridge University Press. https://global.oup.com/academic/product/in-the-interest-of-the-governed-9780198239642?cc=us&lang=en&.

McCloskey, Deirdre. 2008. "Adam Smith, the last of the former virtue ethicists." *History of Political Economy* 40 (1): 43–71. https://doi.org/10.1215/00182702-2007-046. https://www.webofscience.com/wos/woscc/full-record/WOS:000253416700002.

Mill, John Stuart. 1879/2004. *Utilitarianism*. 7th ed. London: Longmans, Green, and Company, Project Gutenberg. https://www.gutenberg.org/cache/epub/11224/pg11224-images.html.

Morey, Edward. 2018. "What are the ethics of welfare economics? And, are welfare economists utilitarians?" *International Economic Review* 62 (2): 29. https://doi.org/10.1007/s12232-018-0294-y. https://link.springer.com/article/10.1007/s12232-018-0294-y.

Nussbaum, Martha. 2006. *Frontiers of justice: Disability, nationality, species membership*. Cambridge, MA: Belknap Press.

———. 2011. *Creating capabilities: The human development approach*. Harvard University Press.

Pigou, Arthur. 1932/2017. *The economics of welfare*. 1st ed. New York: Routledge: Taylor and Francis Group. https://www.taylorfrancis.com/books/mono/10.4324/9781351304368/economics-welfare-arthur-pigou.

Posner, Richard. 1983. *The economics of justice*. Cambridge, MA: Harvard University Press.

Price, Anthony. 2016, Winter. "Richard Mervyn Hare." Stanford Encyclopedia of Philosophy. Stanford University. https://plato.stanford.edu/.

Rawls, John. 1971/1999. *A theory of justice*. Cambridge, MA: Harvard University Press. https://www.webofscience.com/wos/woscc/full-record/WOS:000281657300017.

Reeves, Richard. 2008. *John Stuart Mill: Victorian firebrand*. London: Atlantic Books Ltd. https://atlantic-books.co.uk/book/john-stuart-mill/.

Robbins, Lionel. 1938. "Interpersonal comparisons of utility: A comment." *Economic Journal* 48 (192): 635–641. https://doi.org/10.2307/2225051. https://www.webofscience.com/wos/woscc/full-record/WOS:000203610800002.

Robeyns, Ingrid. 2016. "The capability approach." Stanford Encyclopedia of Philosophy. Stanford University. https://plato.stanford.edu/.

Scitovsky, Tibor. 1951. "The state of welfare economics." *The American Economic Review* 41 (3): 303–315. https://www.jstor.org/stable/1802104.

Sedgwick, Henry. 1874(first)/1907/2014. *The method of ethics*. 7th ed. New York: The Macmillan Company. The Project Gutenberg. https://www.gutenberg.org/files/46743/46743-h/46743-h.htm.

Sen, Amartya. 1970. "The impossibility of a Paretian liberal." *Journal of Political Economy* 78 (1): 152–157.

———. 1979. "The welfare basis of real income comparisons: A survey." *Journal of Economic Literature* 17 (1): 1–45.

———. 1980a. "Equality of what?" In *The tanner lectures on human values*, edited by S. McMurrin. Cambridge: Cambridge University Press.

Sen, Amartya, and Bernard Arthur Owen Williams. 1982. *Utilitarianism and beyond*. Cambridge: Cambridge University Press.

Siegel, Jennifer, and Molly Crockett. 2013. "How serotonin shapes moral judgment and behavior." *Sociability, Responsibility, and Criminality: from Lab to Law* 1299: 42–51. https://doi.org/10.1111/nyas.12229. https://www.webofscience.com/wos/woscc/full-record/WOS:000325924700006.

Singer, Peter. 1975/2009. *Animal liberation. Animal rights*: Springer. https://www.webofscience.com/wos/woscc/full-record/WOS:000329385300023.

———. 1997. A philosophical self-portrait. In *The Penguin Dictionary of Philosophy*, edited by Thomas Mautner. London: Penguin Books.

———. 2011. *Practical ethics*. Cambridge: Cambridge University Press.

Sinnott-Armstrong, Walter. 2015, Winter. "Consequentialism." Stanford Encyclopedia of Philosophy. Stanford University. https://plato.stanford.edu/.

Smith, Adam. 1759/2022. *The theory of moral sentiments*. Vol. 1. Ireland: J. Beatty and C. Jackson and The Gutenberg Project. https://www.webofscience.com/wos/woscc/full-record/WOS:000283912100003.

Wenar, Leif. 2017, Spring. "John Rawls." Stanford Encyclopedia of Philosophy. Stanford University. https://plato.stanford.edu/title/Wenar/.

Wolff, Jonathon. 2010. "Philosophy bites." *On John Rawls: A Theory of Justice*. http://philosophybites.com/2010/02/jonathan-wolff-on-john-rawls-a-theory-of-justice.html.

Additional Readings

Bentham, Jeremy. 1996. "Chapter 17." In *The collected works of Jeremy Bentham*, edited by J. H. Burns and H. L. A. Hart. Oxford: Oxford University Press.

Bentham, Jeremy, and John Bowring. 1839. *The collected works of Jeremy Bentham*. Vol. 2, Part I. https://www.google.com/books/edition/Works_of_Jeremy_Bentham_Volume_2_Part_1/98FdDQEACAAJ?hl=en.

Dietrich, Franz, and Christian List. 2016. "Reason-based choice and context dependence: An explanatory framework." *Economics and Philosophy* 32 (2): 175–229. https://doi.org/10.1017/s0266267115000474. https://www.webofscience.com/wos/woscc/full-record/WOS:000378589900002.

Edmonds, David. 2013a. "David Edmonds on trolley problems." *Philosophy Bites*. https://philosophybites.com/2013/09/david-edmonds-on-trolley-problem.html.

———. 2013b. "Would you kill the fat man?" In *Would you kill the fat man?* Princeton: Princeton University Press.

Gottlieb, Anthony. 2000. *The dream of reason: A history of western philosophy from the Greeks to the renaissance*. New York: W. W. Norton.

Haidt, Jonathan. 2008. "The emotional dog and its rational tail: A social intuitionist approach to moral judgment." In *Reasoning: Studies of human inference and its foundations*, 1024–1052. https://www.webofscience.com/wos/woscc/full-record/WOS:000305482200055.

Knight, Frank. 1944. "Realism and relevance in the theory of demand." *Journal of Political Economy* 52 (4): 289–318.

Mill, John Stuart. 1859/2011. *On liberty*. London: Walter Scott Publishing Company and Project Gutenberg. https://www.gutenberg.org/ebooks/34901.

———. 1987. "Bentham." In *John Stuart Mill and Jeremy Bentham, utilitarianism and other essays*, edited by Alan Ryan. London and New York: Penguin.

Pareto, Vilfredo. 1909(Italian)/2014. *Manual of political economy: A critical and variorum edition*. Oxford: Oxford University Press. https://books.google.com/books?hl=en&lr=&id=43NYAwAAQBAJ&oi=fnd&pg=PP1&dq=pareto+manual+of+political+economy+&ots=9SbJExabbI&sig=nQsi46xq4Ts2z4fBHLeE9FzpWOI.

———. 1971. *Manual of political economy*. New York: A. M. Kelley.

Raz, Joseph. 1986. *The morality of freedom*. Oxford: Clarendon Press.

Sen, Amartya. 1971. "The impossibility of a Paretian liberal: Reply." *The Journal of Political Economy* 79 (6): 1406.

———. 1975. "Is a Paretian liberal really impossible: A reply." *Public Choice* 21: 111–113.

———. 1980b. "The welfare basis of real income comparisons: A reply." *Journal of Economic Literature* 18 (4): 1547–1552. https://www.jstor.org/stable/2724063.

Smith, Adam. 1791/2022. *An inquiry into the nature and causes of the wealth of nations: By Adam Smith*. Vol. 4. JJ Tourneisen and JL Legrand. https://www.gutenberg.org/ebooks/3300.

PART II

Wanting, Liking, Well-Being, and Incommensurability

CHAPTER 5

From Aristotelian to Modern Happiness: Eudaimonia to Hedonic Hotspots

A Brief History of Happiness and WB

Thomas Jefferson inscribed an American's Right to the pursuit of happiness.[1] In 1843, the cranky, contrarian essayist, Thomas Carlyle, pointed out.[2]

> Every pitifulest whipster [whippersnapper, wannabe hipster] that walks within a skin has his head filled with the notion that he is, shall be, or by all human and divine laws ought to be, 'happy.' His wishes, the pitifulest whipster's, are to be fulfilled for him; his days, the pitifulest whipster's, are to flow on in an ever-gentle current of enjoyment, impossible even for the gods.

The Pre-Enlightenment Western View of Happiness

An Ancient View of Happiness

Aristotle (384–322 BC) distinguished between pleasure and *eudaimonia*, often translated as happiness; though scholars translate it as "human flourishing" or "living well": others think it best to not translate it. For

[1] The right to pursue it, not the right to it.

[2] Carlyle coined economics the "dismal science".

E. R. Morey, *Deconstructing Behavior, Choice, and Well-being*, https://doi.org/10.1007/978-3-031-36712-0_5

Aristotle, the goal was eudaimonia, a way of life (pursuing certain activities), rather than pleasurable sensations and positive emotions—one was a happy camper if they died having lived a meaningful life. This required a life of *arête* (excellence) in all activities, including "morally virtuous activities". In addition, you had to experience a life of *reasoning*. Why? Because humans have the unique ability to reason, part of our nature. Things are best utilized if they do what they were uniquely designed to do: hammers should pound nails, and humans should reason.

Different activities produce different physical and mental sensations, and it's difficult to separate them from the activities. Pleasurable sensations feel good. The activities that promote eudaimonia may not produce pleasure. Aristotle had nothing against pleasure: it just wasn't top shelf.

Aristotle outlined two incompatible paths to eudaimonia: the practical social/political life and the intellectual life. The first requires the practical virtues—appropriate amounts (not too much, not too little) of courage, temperance, generosity, honor, friendliness, and wit, to name a few. In contrast, the intellectual virtues include a commitment to studying philosophy or science and educating the young to pursue truth and reason.

> At the same time, Aristotle makes it clear that in order to be happy one must possess other goods as well—such goods as friends, wealth, and power. And one's happiness is endangered if one is severely lacking in certain... advantages—if, for example, one is extremely ugly, or has lost children or good friends through death. But why so?... Aristotle's reply is that one's virtuous activity will be, to some extent, diminished or defective if one lacks an adequate supply of other goods. Someone who is friendless, childless, powerless, weak, and ugly will simply not be able to find many opportunities for virtuous activity. (Shields 2014)

Eudaimonia requires luck, position, and resources, so only accessible to elites. Animals can't have it (they can't reason), and one must be old—kids have not lived long enough. Sex, drugs, and rock'n'roll won't do it, no matter how pleasant the sensations; sensations do not cause a life to be happy or unhappy. For Aristotle, living a virtuous life is right for you and society: he was an early advocate for *Virtue ethics* (one is ethical if one is virtuous, see Chapter 12).

In contrast, Epicurus (341–270 BC) viewed happiness as pleasurable sensations, positive emotions, and less pain and suffering—a happy life is a tranquil life. Epicurus was all for a virtuous life, but unlike Aristotle, he thought people should be virtuous because it would make encounters with others more pleasant (cheating and lying could lead to injury or worse). There are similarities with Buddhism: trying to fulfill desires and cravings causes more cravings, plus stress; tranquility is as good as it gets. Benthamite utilitarianism has roots in Epicurean happiness.

The Medieval (Middle Ages) View of Happiness: Happiness = Heaven
Paraphrasing Lotario dei Segni (Lotario of the Signs), before he became Pope Innocent III in 1198 (Fig. 5.1),

> Men and women are simply vile. Conceived in the stench of lust and formed of the filthiest sperm, we spend our earthly days in misery, toil, and degradation. (Quoted by McMahon 2006)

Worldly happiness was not expected; a good life was devout. Happiness was being blessed by God in the afterlife.

> Suffer for virtue's sake, medieval Christians were told, and you will be rewarded with an eternity of heavenly bliss. (Holt 2006)

Medieval-Christian happiness is a sensation, so not Aristotelian—and available only in heaven: a sensation achieved, eventually, by first serving King, Church, and tradition, and by Stayin'Alive—life was "nasty, brutish, and short", with an occasional drunken feast. Thomas Aquinas (1225–1274), a Dominican monk and Aristotelian scholar, allowed for a bit of worldly happiness, distinguishing between perfect happiness (*beatitudo*) and imperfect happiness on earth (*felicitas* or *beatitudo imperfecta*). If an individual has sufficient resources and abilities and plays her cards right, she gets *duplex felicitas* (both kinds of happiness).

Why Does Society Care Whether You Are Happy? The Enlightenment and the Reactions to It

The *Enlightenment* (late seventeenth to late eighteenth century) was a revolution in thinking, an intellectual movement that proposed reason, logic, and evidence as the tools for decision-making—"The Age of Reason"—a reaction to things being done based on tradition, the Church, and the monarchy. It followed in the footsteps of the scientific revolution

Fig. 5.1 Lotario dei Segni: Pope Innocent III

in the sixteenth and seventeenth centuries. [It should be interpreted as wanting to shine the light of reason on questions, not when we were necessarily first enlightened by the truth.]

It advocated for the individual, for thinking for oneself, for self-determination, and in summary, for *autonomy*.

> [The Enlightenment] The period during which modern identity was forged...People become the source of power and authority...The individual has the right to decide, personally, for all of their actions. (Todorov 2010, a modern French/Bulgarian essayist)

While these ideas go back to ancient Athens, they combined the old ideas in new ways and applied them to the common man. The American and French Revolutions were motivated by it and are expressions of it. In the fourth century, St. Augustine divided actions into two types: a means to an end and those we directly enjoy. And the one we should enjoy is worshiping God. The Enlightenment opened the door to enjoying worldly things.

Enlightenment thinkers include Francis Bacon (1561–1626), Baruch Spinoza (1632–1677), John Locke 1632–1704), Denis Diderot (1713–1784), Voltaire (1694–1778), Hume, Immanuel Kant (1724–1804), and Isaac Newton (1642–1726). We in the West are children of the Enlightenment and can thank it, for better or worse, that we, as individuals, have standing and that our personal welfare counts for something. Without this revolution in thinking and importance, there would be no WC or welfare economics.

While Enlightenment thinkers advocated for scientific thinking, that individual autonomy is of value is an ethical position, not a scientific discovery. Its endorsement was not based on research in psychology, sociology, or neuroscience; there was none. Instead, it was a negative reaction to the medieval ethic that the suffering of ordinary people was unimportant.

The early nineteenth century saw a partial pullback. The reaction, the Romantic Age, added back sensations, emotions, and mystery—think of English poets such as Lord Byron, Percy Shelley, and Samuel Coleridge, and painting by Eugene Delacroix, Casper David Friedrich, and J. M. W. Turner.

The works of Jean-Jacques Rousseau (1712–1778) bridge from the Enlightenment to Romanticism. Thank him for equating welfare with happiness (Fig. 5.2):

> ...the love of happiness is the sole principle of all human actions.

NB the distinction between (1) giving importance to the individual and his WB and (2) defining WB as happiness. The Enlightenment caused the first; Romanticism solidified happiness as the goal—the Romantic Age was the age of feelings and emotions.

Individualism and the right to happiness: have a dark side: boredom and frustration. As the Norwegian philosopher Lars Svendsen notes, before the Enlightenment, life was largely determined by the constraints of tradition, religion, and staying alive. Now we must choose a *lifestyle*

Fig. 5.2 Rousseau

(Buddhist, or bass fisherman, or Buddhist bass-fisherman?),[3] and we expect our choice will make us happy. So, we experience frustration and disappointment when it does not—so try another. There are potential costs to having the right and resources to worry about happiness, including boredom, indecision, frustration, and anxiety. Except for monks and nobility, boredom is a modern emotion: "A 'privilege' of modern man."

An Eastern View

There is an Eastern-Western happiness distinction. Buddhism, for example, teaches that the pursuit of happiness is destined to fail and that pleasures are fleeting, a belief consistent with recent research. Right process, rather than consuming, is the path to Buddhist WB, making the Buddhist practice of a good life closer to the ancient Western practice

[3] A *lifestyle* is "essentially a set of practices maintained for a period of time."

than to modern Western practice. It as an ethic will be discussed in Part III, Chapter 12. Buddhist practice and WB are discussed in Chapter 6.

The Late Nineteenth-Century View(s) of Happiness

Bentham and Mill defined happiness as Epicurus did, as Rousseau did. Happiness is positive minus negative feelings, where these sensations have both duration and intensity.[4] Epicurus and Bentham, and maybe Mill, are what philosophers call *pleasure hedonists*—guys who equate good with pleasure. Bentham and Mill are typically viewed as founders of utilitarianism; whether Mill was depends on what of his you read and how you read between the lines (Figs. 5.3 and 5.4).

Epicurus and Bentham equated happiness with emotional WB. Mill's view of happiness and WB is complicated: Mill considered freedom to choose a component of WB, independent of whether it increases happiness or affects behavior. At issue is whether the pleasure one gets from an activity depends on the process or circumstances that made it possible. For example, would forcing you to eat a piece of cake that you would have chosen diminish the pleasure of eating it? [More on freedom in the section on Mill in Chapter 12.]

Perceptions influence the assessment of life satisfaction; for example, was the enjoyment experienced the result of a misperception—"I foolishly believed Wanda loved me but now realize my time with her was a sham." Other concerns include recollection errors, false projections, expectations, self-delusion, and discounting past and future sensations. WB is complicated: one economicus may order on emotional WB, while another on life-satisfaction WB. Some researchers ask happiness questions, thinking it is the best measure of WB, while others ask life-satisfaction questions. Imagine policies that increase one but not the other. Research

[4] Mill, but not Bentham, argued that while two activities might be equally pleasurable, pleasure produced by high-brow activities generates more social good than pleasure produced by low-brow activities. Mill argued that the social worth of a pleasure depends on how it was produced.—In his view, Rousseau's pleasure from reading Shakespeare was better than his pleasure from picking his nose, and Rousseau's pleasure from scratching his butt was better than his pig's pleasure from Rousseau scratching the pig's butt—because his pig was a pig. There is more on this ethical distinction in Chapter 12. You might disagree with my assessment and argue Mill thought high-brow activities produce more pleasure. If you interpret him in that way, there is no need to judge social good based on anything other than pleasure.

Fig. 5.3 Jeremy Bentham embalmed

suggests that a permanent increase in income causes a long-run increase in life-satisfaction WB but only a short-term happiness bump.

In both research and popular culture, it is often unclear what a writer or speaker means when they use the words "happiness" or "WB"—often, they have not settled on what they mean.

Independent of how one defines individual WB, a critical ethical question is whether WB is the criterion that should be used to determine whether an act or policy is right or wrong. Welfare economists say "yes"—Part III discusses moral philosophies that answer "no".

Turn now to a materialist view of modern happiness.

Fig. 5.4 John Stuart Mill

Modern Happiness: A Chemical State of Mind

Happiness is a Brain State[5]

> Some things make our brains feel good; some things make us feel bad. For example, being cold or having a cold is unpleasant, and eating toast feels good. (Robert Frank, Cornell economist and *NY Times* columnist)

The modern scientific view—a view my students hate—is happiness is simply a brain state, a mixture of chemical and electrical activity in the brain that causes you to feel good. [I like to exercise till exhaustion. Why? Because afterward, endorphins dance through my brain, the "endorphin rush", as effective as cocaine.]

[5] Your "brain" includes your entire nervous system.

Dualists and Materialists

Materialists believe the mind and brain are the same—everything has a physical explanation, including our thoughts, emotions, and consciousness—the mind isn't ethereal. In contrast, *Dualists* distinguish between the brain, a physical thing, and the mind, an immaterial spirit, believing that while much is explained by physics and chemistry, the human mind transcends the physical.[6] For dualists, the mind creates feelings and thoughts that are incapable of ever being explained with physics or chemistry—so magical.[7]

Rene Descartes went to great lengths to defend dualism. Why? Because he wanted to defend Catholic doctrine? Because he did not want to be labeled a heretic?[8] While few neuroscientists are dualists, the man on the street won't abandon it. While he accepts physical explanations for most things, he is hesitant to believe who we are and what we feel is solely the result of a chemical/electrical stew. I think of one student, an army officer from the South, who shuddered in protest whenever I suggested he was a "material boy", baffled that I would even imagine such a thing (Fig. 5.5).

[6] For a modern questioning of materialism, see Thomas Nagel's (1974) essay, What is it like to be a bat?—fun. Nagel, an NYU philosophy professor emeritus, argues that while one can't reject the argument that the experience of mind is the result of a chemical stew, it's hard to argue it's just that, at least not without a theory of how the stew generates our sense of self and the feeling we are experiencing. But! no such theory [now] exists. He questions whether it's even possible to have a theory that equates every mental state with a specific and physical brain state, at least within the confines of modern physics.

[7] Dualists are not required to believe that the magic extends beyond the minds of men; they are not required to believe in God, and one could, arguably, believe in God and not be a dualist. Conversely, you can believe some magic exists without believing it affects your mind.

You might prefer the word "supernatural" to "magical"; as in, outcomes not consistent with the current laws of nature.

[8] During the Enlightenment, philosophers went to great lengths (Hume being the poster boy) to not be labeled a heretic, atheist, or unbeliever. One criticized religion in code. Hume was not surprised when [because Rousseau's book *Emile* contradicted the notion of original sin] the city of Paris issued an arrest warrant. Writing to Rousseau's English host, Hume noted that Rousseau "had not the precaution to throw any veil over his sentiments; ...he could not wonder that all the zealots were in arms against him." Concern was warranted; it was only in 1697 that Britain hung its last person for blasphemy, Thomas Aikenhead.

Fig. 5.5 Rene Descartes

People, including Descartes, are willing to accept physicality for everything non-human.[9] But not me. Unwilling to accept mind over matter, I am a material boy living in a material world made of physical matter with lots of chemical and electrical connections, and so are you. We are moistly sophisticated robots (machines/automata); in the 1874 words of the famous British biologist and materialist T. H. Huxley, I am a "conscious automata". So are you, unless you are a zombie (sentient, but no one is home). I have no way of telling; I hope my wife isn't one. [Zombies raise are a problem for materialism: the existence of zombies is inconsistent with materialism, and proof of a zombie would confirm dualism.[10] Zombies can't be happy; they can't feel.]

9 "Descartes held that non-human animals are automata" (Kirk 2023). they have no conscious experiences, and their behavior is wholly determined by physical mechanisms. Descartes considered, but rejected, the idea of a machine that looked and behaved like a human being (a zombie).

10 The argument: if zombies and humans are physically identical but humans have conscious experiences and zombies don't, then conscious experience can't be the result

Science hasn't proven all our thoughts and actions are embodied in our brain, but the alternative requires an acceptance of processes and agents (spirits) that don't adhere to the laws of physics and chemistry. Most people believe in things inconsistent with the laws of physics. Many physicists do not. For example, most of us are at least a bit superstitious. Human dualism is difficult for humans to abandon—many religions and cultures teach dualism—imagining the mind transcends the brain is comforting—it makes people feel superior to other animals. And besides, we don't know how the brain does what it does—it is even hard to imagine knowing how it works—making it easy to believe there is magic (or magick).

Happiness: A Brain State
Happiness is associated with a whole class of brain states, many overlapping, each state producing a different kind of WB experience. So, in theory, science could identify a set of brain states and define happy as one or more of those states.

So, What Is a Brain on Happiness? Your Brain in a Nutshell

Happiness, like all feelings, is neural activity in the brain; increased happiness is just more of some neural activity and less of other sorts. You eat an ice-cream cone, pet a dog, or, God forbid, play Wordle because you hope these activities will change the synapses in your brain in ways you will experience as nice—happier is simply a matter of modifying your brain state. This section is about how that works. While my interest in the brain started with the psychology of choice and then progressed directly to neuroscience, there is a new field in economics called *neuroeconomics*. Few departments offer courses. While I did not encounter the neuroscience of WB and choice through the lens of neuroeconomics, this chapter draws, in part, from the textbook, *Neuroeconomics 2nd edition,* edited by the neuroeconomists Paul Glimcher at NYU and Ernst Fehr at the University of Zurich. Each chapter is written by imminent researchers. The other textbooks I draw on are *Neuroscience: exploring the brain*

of body parts—humans and zombies have the same parts. Therefore, if zombies exist, human consciousness arises from the mind, not the physical brain.

3rd edition by Mark Bear, Director of the BEAR Lab at MIT, Barry Connors, Professor of Medical Science at Brown, and Michael Paradiso, the Director of the Center for Vision Research at Brown. And *Cognitive neuroscience: The biology of the mind* (4th ed.) by Michael Gazziniga, Richard Ivry, and George Mangun.[11] Gazziniga is at the U. of California Santa Barbara, Ivry at U. of C. Berkeley, and Mangun at the U. of C. San Diego (Fig. 5.6).

The human brain contains approximately 86 billion neurons.[12] Collectively, neurons generate sensations and feelings[13] and embody your knowledge (your dog's name and your skateboarding skills), memories,

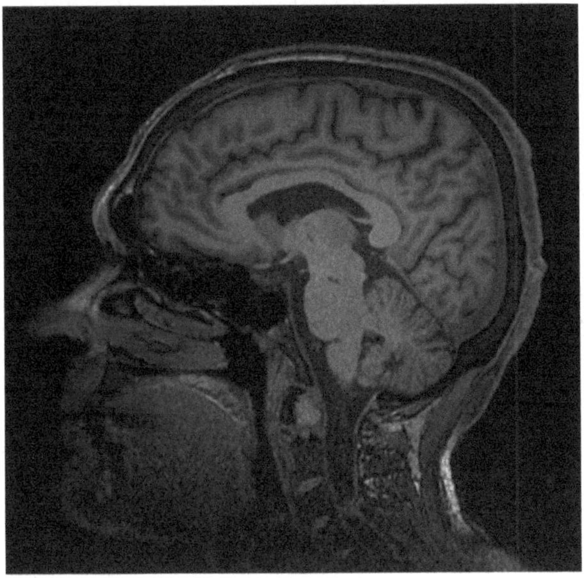

Fig. 5.6 An economist's brain

[11] For a short introduction to the brain see "Perception Lecture note: the brain" (Heeger 2022). The notes include fantastic pictures.

[12] Everyone used to say 100 billion, but Suzana Herculano-Houzel counted 86 billion by turning five brains into soup and counting the number of nuclei (2016).

[13] The burning of a muscle is an unpleasant *sensation* (a physical sensation); your interpretation of that sensation is a perception that you may find pleasing.

tastes, and goals. Neurons generate your behavior. The *cell body* of each houses its *nucleus* and power source. Neurons communicate; each neuron has a transmission tower called an *axon*, and one or more antennas (receiving towers), called *dendrites*.

Axons vary drastically in length; the sciatic nerve runs the length of your leg; many axons traverse from one brain part to another—these are long-distance transmission lines; most are orders-of-magnitude shorter (Fig. 5.7).

The end of the axon, the *axon terminal*, is stocked with chemicals called neurotransmitters (e.g., serotonin and dopamine). Each axon terminal almost touches one or more antennas (the receptors on other neurons' dendrites). The gaps, called *synapses*, are 20 billionths of a meter wide. Neurons communicate across these gaps: an axon terminal releases packets of its neurotransmitter; these cross the gaps and bond with the receptors on other neurons' dendrites. Those have gated channels that open to receive the neurotransmitter.

Axons can branch (divide), so synapse with many receptors; sometimes, these receptors are all on the same recipient neuron; sometimes, they are on different neurons. You have sixty trillion synapses—give or take. Many neurons synapse with the dentrites of many neurons.

When an electrical impulse is transmitted down a neuron's axon, its terminal releases neurotransmitters (Fig. 5.8). The technical term for this electrical impulse is an *action potential*. A neuron's axon only fires (experiences an action potential) after its dendrites are the recipients of sufficient amounts of the neurotransmitter (Fig. 5.9).

There are many types of neurons and neurotransmitters.[14] We all know about serotonin and dopamine. GABA (gamma-aminobutyric acid), norepinephrine, encephalin, and anandamide are others that explain pleasure and reward-seeking.

Your neurons determine who you are, what you do, and how you feel. How does that work? All the details are not known, but many are. Genetics, experiences, and what you ingest affect your neurons; they affect the number and efficacy of the synapses. "Neurons that fire together wire

[14] Most neurons connect only with other neurons, but some also connect with muscles, glands, and other tissues. The firings of neuromuscular cells cause your heart to beat and your feet to move as you walk down the street. Nerve cells in the skin transmit touch to the brain, and neurons in the eyes start the process of seeing.

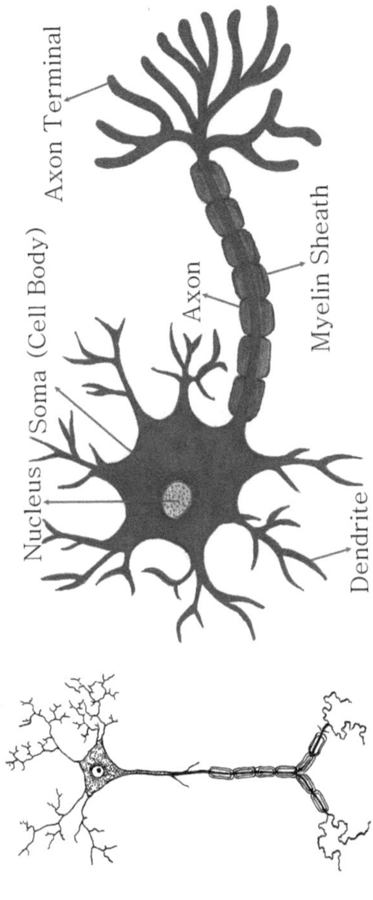

Fig. 5.7 Two friendly neurons

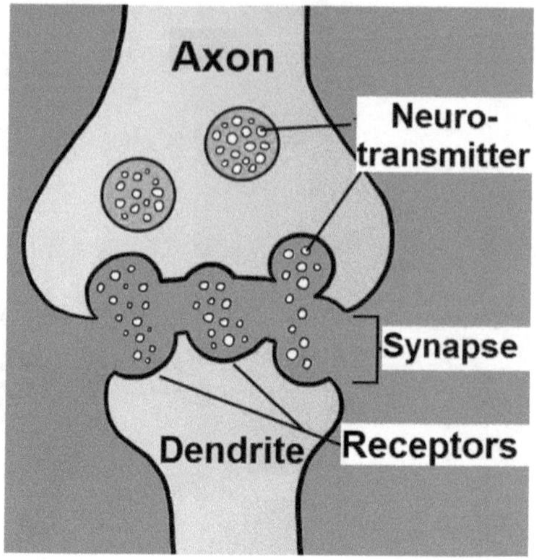

Fig. 5.8 Neurotransmitters bounding across a synapse

together." And "Neurons that fire out of sync lose their link." *Wiring together* means the number of synapses they share increases, and each's effectiveness (efficacy increases). A neuron firing alone will not strengthen the link between itself and a post-synaptic neuron; the link will weaken. However, if many neurons simultaneously shoot neurotransmitters at the same neuron, all the links will get stronger.

Consider all the things that can change the efficacy of a synapse: the amount of the neurotransmitter stored in the axon terminal, the amount it releases and for how long, and the receptiveness of the dendrites on the recipient neuron. These are influenced by what you have experienced: the road trip to Yellowstone when you were twelve, the toast at breakfast, and you're reading this book. There are temporary modifications (short-term memories); others last a lifetime. Learning modifies neural connections, and learning and pleasures share many neural pathways. Like rats pushing bars for pellets, we learn behaviors that get reinforced, and pleasure is one type of reward. Your ordering of paths—if you have one—is embedded in your neurons.

Mice are afraid of cats unless a neurologist snips specific neural connections, and then they are not—it has been done.

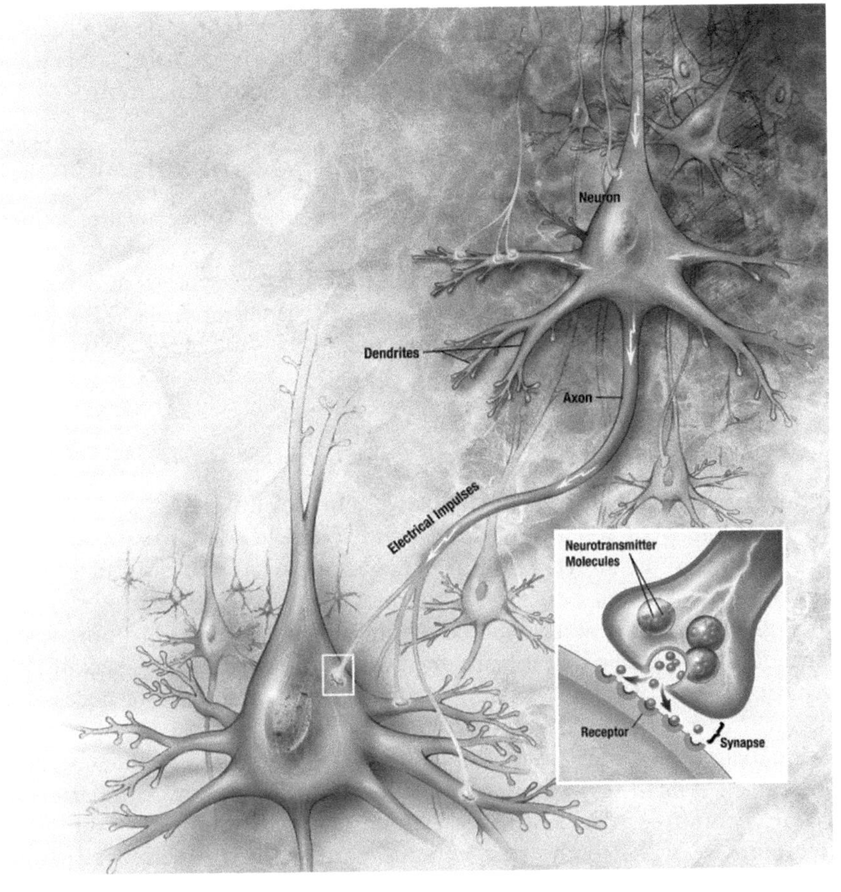

Fig. 5.9 An action potential

You recognize an object as a cat because your brain contains a neural synaptic imprint of a cat (an *engram*, a *memory trace)*. It is a cat when enough neurons in your cat imprint fire.[15] My previous dog was white, so

[15] Your hippocampus plays an important role in how you store episodic memories (what you got for your birthday). Recent research using electrodes implanted in epilepsy patients indicates that each episodic memory is encoded in about 2% of the neurons in your hippocampus (millions of neurons), so "each neuron contributes to the representation of at most a few memories" (Wixted et al. 2014). See Douglas Quenqua (2006). The good

when the corner of my eye glimpses a white pillow on the floor, I register Sofie. That we like sweets and adolescent males pursue girls rather than learning Latin is determined by neural connections and hormones.

Neurologists, Like Economists, Model Behavior

They hope to determine how your brain chooses between alternatives: is it determined by what you desire (Assumption 9b) or what you will like (Assumption 9a), and whether they are they in sync (a and b). For rats, "pleasure" is their WB. [No one is asking lab animals WB or life-satisfaction questions, and it is easier to manipulate the pleasure of a sweet than WB.]

Choosing/Seeking, Pleasure, and the Mesolimbic Dopamine System

Economists use the word "choose," and neuroscientists use "seek". While we often like what we sought/chose and seek/choose what we will like, you can choose what you will not like and like what you did not pursue. Choosing/seeking is behavior; liking, by itself, isn't a behavior; it's a feeling. [When I throw the ball, Giacomo seeks it (chooses to pursue it); at academic cocktail parties, many seek wine rather than soda—seeking is a behavior.] The path you experience is the result of seeking, not necessarily liking.

We believe we seek/pursue a commodity or an experience because realizing it will increase our WB (we will like it). It is a foundation of welfare economics: NBT with 9a assumes the path pursued is the available path we will like the best and the path we will experience. [Some economists say it does not matter whether we end up liking what we wanted: what matters for behavior is desires (Assumption 9b), not likes. This is discussed below.] But is 9a true? While we often like what we sought and seek what we will like, you can seek what you will not like and like what you did not pursue.

The *mesolimbic dopamine system*, MDS, plays a critical role. "Meso" is Greek for middle, the brain's approximate center. The "limbic" includes the under chamber (the hypothalamus), the seahorse (the hippocampus), and the almond (amygdala). Included are clumps of neuron cell bodies

news is that if you lose a few thousand neurons, you will still remember your wedding, or at least parts.

in the VTA (*ventral tegmental area*) Fig. 5.10). ["Ventral tegmental," from Greek, means "belly-covering"; it sits on the floor of the midbrain, covering its belly.] These neurons have long axons that project into the prefrontal cortex and nucleus accumbens. Since they all emit dopamine, the clumps and their axons are called the MDS.

In Fig. 5.10, note the axons, the black line starting in the VTA that branches out when it enters the frontal cortex. When these axons fire, dopamine is released in the frontal cortex. If a rat presses a bar and gets a reward, axons in the MDS fire, and dopamine is released in the frontal cortex, causing the rat to quickly learn to keep pressing. If the bar is rewardless, pressing does not lead to more pressing. Unless, when the rat presses, the researcher stimulates the rat's mesolimbic dopamine axons. [She implanted electrodes in these axons.] Then the rat quickly learns to keep pressing. It persists until it collapses in exhaustion. It continues even if each press causes a painful electrical shock. Alternatively, suppose a rat is administered a drug that blocks the dopamine receptors in its

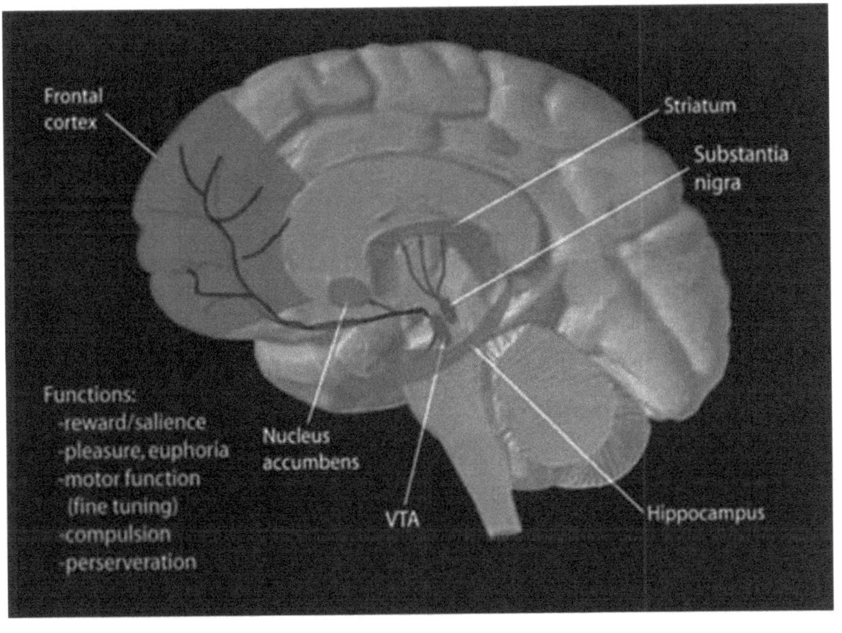

Fig. 5.10 The mesolimbic dopamine system

frontal cortex.[16] In that case, the rat never learns to push the bar even if every press causes a dopamine release, caused by either a real treat or the researcher electrically stimulating the axons.

In a 2006 study in *Nature* (Pessiglione et al. 2006), human subjects had to choose quickly and repeatedly between two symbols on a computer screen. After each choice, the individual was shown whether they had won £1. The probability of winning was always higher for one symbol (60% vs. 40%). The objective was to see how quickly the subject figured this out. Subjects who had taken a dopamine-enhancing drug were the quickest to learn, subjects who took an inhibitor were the slowest, and those on a placebo were in between.

We, and rats, are motivated to seek/choose alternatives that cause dopamine to synapse with receptor neurons in our frontal cortex. This is a positive from an evolutionary perspective if the actions that produce a dopamine rush increase reproduction. The pursuit of sex releases dopamine. Cocaine, nicotine, and methamphetamines are fast ways to get the dopamine to flow, causing many to pursue these drugs—including lab rats.[17] But snorting coke does not typically confer an evolutionary advantage. [Keith Richards, who has five children, could be an exception.] Sugar cravings can be as intense as the craving for cocaine. In the past, seeking sweet, high-calorie foods conveyed an evolutionary advantage. [Note that foods with high sugar concentrations ferment into alcohol.]

When and how much dopamine is released when one gets the reward? How much when an expected reward does not occur? How much when the individual observes a cue that makes a reward more or less likely?

Initial answers came from a 1990 experiment with monkeys: if, when a light starts flashing, the monkey pushes the left bar, he gets juice. While learning the task, the dopamine flows when the monkey gets the juice. However, after he has learned to associate the light (a cue)[18] with the

[16] A drug that blocks the receptors on a neuron's dendrites from accepting (bonding with) the released neurotransmitter.

[17] Here, "flow" is the firing rate of dopamine neurons. Dopamine's effectiveness is enhanced by how long it remains in the synapses (before reuptake) and the recipient neurons' receptiveness.

[18] A cue for a specific outcome is a stimulus you associate with that outcome. Palov trained dogs to associate an initially neutral stimulus (e.g., a light coming on or a sound)

juice, the dopamine flows not when he gets the juice but when the light flashes—when the monkey knows he will get the juice if he pushes the bar. fMRI (*functional magnetic resonance imaging*) indicates it's the same for us: after learning, dopamine isn't released by the reward itself (biting into and tasting a great burger), but before when you know it will happen, when you realize a desire/want will be fulfilled, not when it's fulfilled.

What happens if, after the monkey learns to associate the light with the juice, the expected juice does not appear when he pushes the bar? There is still a burst of dopamine when the light flashes, but then the dopamine level drops below baseline right after the juice should have arrived—reducing his motivation to push the bar again. Alternatively, if more than the expected amount of juice is delivered, its arrival causes a second burst of dopamine—increasing his motivation to push the bar again. Dopamine release motivates behavior: one explanation is that if the reward is better than expected, more dopamine flows; if the reward is less than expected, less flows.

Summarizing: when the cue for a positive outcome occurs, there is a burst of dopamine. Then, when it's reward time, a second occurs if the reward is better than expected. Dopamine drops if the reward is worse than expected. And there is neither a burst nor a drop if the reward is as expected. The error-prediction hypothesis assumes that the magnitude and burst's direction depend on whether the outcome was better than expected, worse, or as expected.

An additional wrinkle: a monkey experiment with different cues, each associated with a different probability of getting the juice (e.g., 0%, 25%, 50%, 75%, and 100%). When cued, the amount of dopamine that flows depends on which cue is presented: the higher probability associated with it, the more information it conveys to the monkey. See Fig. 9 from an experiment by Christopher Fiorillo, Phillipe Tobler, and Wolfram Schultz (2003 at https://doi.org/10.1111/1468-0297.00261).

There are five graphs, one for each cue probability; the second, for example, shows the Monkey's dopamine spikes when the cue signals a 25% probability of juice; the fifth represents the cue that guarantees

with either a positive or adverse outcome, changing the stimulus into what is now called a *Pavlovian cue*, a learned/conditioned cue. A cue is a potentially influential observation that occurs right before you make a choice. Some cues are consciously observed (you hear the phone ring), but others you record subliminally. For a thirsty you, a cue could be you seeing someone enjoying a Pepsi rather than a Coke.

the reward. When the monkey sees the cue that signals the reward will arrive with certainty, there is a big spike when that cue appears, but there is no spike when the certain reward arrives. Overall, the dopamine spike when the cue appears is increasing in the probability that the cue means a reward. Conversely, the dopamine spike when a reward appears is decreasing in these probabilities. To summarize, the lower the probability that a cue means a reward, the smaller the initial spike, but the larger the spike if the reward appears.

In a 2008 economics paper, Andrew Caplin and Mark Dean suggest dopamine "update[s] the 'value' humans and other animals attach to different stimuli and actions. And this changes the probabilities associated with the alternatives." The sequence of dopamine releases measures the outcome's value relative to its expected value, according to them. A caution: don't interpret their "value" to necessarily mean providing pleasure. A better word would be "reinforcing", as choices that result in the release of dopamine are repeated; the choice may not produce pleasure. I now turn to that issue.

Wanting Versus Liking

It has been known for over sixty years that releasing dopamine causes wanting/seeking, leading to the initial, reasonable conjecture that dopamine release causes both wanting and pleasure (a type of liking). If correct, it would mean dopamine neurons are both wanting and liking neurons. This conjecture was accepted as true.

However, findings over the last few decades by the neuroscientist Kent Berridge and others contradict this conjecture. They find that the neural pathways for liking are separate from those for wanting and that choice is driven by wanting rather than liking. Choice is based on Assumption 9b (based on desire/wanting, not WB (9a)).

The Berridge lab separated liking a food from wanting it: measuring liking using facial and mouth expressions (lip-smacking and Yuk face). [Using facial expressions to measure emotions goes back to Darwin's 1873 book, *The Expression of the Emotions in Man and Animals.*]

If the neurologist blocks or destroys the relevant dopamine axons, a rat will not seek food: it will starve rather than walk across the cage for food. Nevertheless, it will eat with relish a sweet food placed on its tongue, expressing all the gestures a hungry carnivore exhibits when enjoying a cheeseburger—the food is liked but not wanted. Conversely, in rats whose dopamine axons have not been severed, stimulating these axons causes more dopamine to be released, which causes the craving for food to increase but not the liking (no additional lip-smacking).

> Research on humans and animals suggests that liking and wanting [seeking] are mediated by separate circuits in the brain. Berridge and his colleagues have, for example, shown that how much you like a sweet is independent of how much dopamine is flowing. Drugs like antipsychotics that inhibit dopamine activity reduce people's desire for pleasure, but don't make that pleasure less intense (Bear et al. 2020)

Consider the distinction between sexual desire and sexual pleasure. As people age, their sex drive (their seeking) diminishes, but when sex occurs, it's often enjoyed more than when they were eighteen. Alternatively, imagine yourself as an adolescent taking an antidepressant that blocks the ability to orgasm. Yet, you're aroused and want sex—an awful, unliked state.

Research neuroscientists occasionally cut or stimulate human neural pathways to locate sites that cause extreme seizures. Wilder Penfield (1891–1976) pioneered the technique in 1950: the "Montréal Procedure". Picture the top of your brain exposed with electrodes attached at numerous locations. See a photo at https://www.pnas.org/doi/abs/10.1073/pnas.44.2.51.

In some studies, patients could choose how often to self-stimulate each implant; surprisingly, they stimulate the sites that produce an experience they describe as a potential for pleasure that never comes, sites that deliver a pleasurable sensation less often. Go figure!

My friend Bob paid a thousand dollars for a power meter for his bicycle (don't even ask). He had to have it but, as he would readily admit, having it would not, and did not, increase his WB. A famous philosophical example demonstrates how desiring and liking can differ. Imagine an addictive drug that causes neither pain nor pleasure, but once addicted, you wake up desiring it, a feeling neither pleasurable nor painful. Once addicted, if you don't take the drug within an hour of waking, you experience pain. If the drug were free and if your ordering of paths was determined by desiring rather than liking, you would choose to become addicted: why?—because you would fulfill a lot of desires for free. The example is from the Oxford philosopher Derek Parfit (1942–2017). You want your seeking and liking systems in sync. You don't want to be like

Marcel Proust's fictional self, Charles Swann, in his (1913) book Swann's Way: Charles spent his life desiring a woman he knew he would not like.

Remember why the distinction between wanting and liking is essential: if they do not line up and choice is based on wanting rather than liking, what you choose will not always make you better off; it could even make you worse. Neuroscientists agree that wanting is driven by the mesolimbic dopamine system but somewhat disagree on how dopamine affects wanting. And the disagreement is critical to NBT, ethics, and the pursuit of happiness.

How much you want alternative A versus B may depend on your recollection of how each previously affected your emotional WB or how you expect each would affect it. Or it may depend on the desires/wants you are experiencing, which might be unrelated to the rewards you expect each alternative to produce.[19] Advocates of choice theories that order paths based on experienced WB should hope that wants/desires are in sync with WB expectations and that individuals experience the WB they expected to experience.

The Wanting/Liking Disagreement: The Incentive-Salience Hypothesis *vs. The* Reward-Prediction Error Hypothesis

One hypothesis (*incentive-salience*) is dopamine influences choice by directly influencing wanting. The other hypothesis (*reward-prediction error*) is dopamine indirectly affects choice by influencing expected emotional WB—and wanting is determined by expected emotional WB. There is data both in support and in conflict with each hypothesis. Some evidence is consistent with both.

A critical distinction is whether dopamine directly drives learning: the reward prediction hypothesis says yes, and incentive-salience says no. "Chapter 18: From Experienced Utility to Decision Utility" in the textbook *Neuroeconomics* critiques, compares, and debates the two

[19] Neuroeconomists, and, surprisingly, non-economic neuroscientists, use the word *utility*: separating *decision utility* (the measure (of value) you use to decide which alternative to choose from *experienced utility* which is how emotional WB is affected by the alternative chosen. Experienced utility is what I have defined as emotional WB. So, terminology-wise, they separate what you will like from what you choose. They then separate decision utility into its possible components: *remembered utility* (how it felt last time), *predicted/expected utility*, and *wanting* (*incentive salience*).

hypotheses. The chapter is jointly written by Berridge and John O'Doherty. O'Doherty, the director of the Caltech Brain Imaging Center, advocates for the reward-prediction error hypothesis and Berridge for incentive-salience.

The Incentive-Salience Hypothesis

This hypothesis is associated with Berridge and his lab. *Incentive salience* is fancy for serious wanting (a strong urge—conscious or not) compared to run-of-the-mill wanting. The *incentive* is to choose the most *salient* (striking, attention-grabbing).[20] An initial motivator for the hypothesis was a Berridge finding. By removing or blocking dopamine, rats can be manipulated to not want what they would like (e.g., food). And they can be manipulated, with dopamine, to want what they will not like

[20] Salience, attention, and working memory: Paraphrasing the neurologist Amishi Jha (2021), envision working memory as the whiteboard in your brain. On it is written what you are actively remembering. However, its capacity is limited, and the writings on it quickly fade if they are not continuously traced over. What is written is what you are attending to (the objects of your attention). They can be external stimuli (e.g., the stop light or a person's expression), internal (your thoughts, emotions, and long-term memories), or both.

There are millions of things that you could pay attention to, but your working memory can only hold on to a few, so your brain must ignore much of the information out there. So, what do you attend to? A complicated question! Attention is the mechanism that allows you to attend to some things and in-attend to others.

Your attention can be highly focused like the beam of a flashlight or broadly focused like a spotlight, but it can't do both simultaneously. Either can be external or internal. And your focus can be self-directed or usurped. The scope of your focus and what it is attending to is constantly changing, which is usually a good thing from a survival perspective. For example, if you're lying in the grass viewing the stars and hear a rattle and hiss, your focus will immediately and involuntarily shift to focus narrowly on the sounds, and the stars disappear from your working memory.

Salient objects are objects (or characteristics of objects) that draw our focus—often stuff you didn't consciously choose to focus on. The snake is a dramatic example: immediate threats to our well-being are highly salient—a good thing but only if the threat is real. Salient for you might not be for me, and its strength will vary with your physiological and emotional state. For example, seeing someone smoking a cigarette is salient to someone who has recently quit, and a Pepsi ad will push you toward drinking a Pepsi rather than a Coke even if you prefer the taste of Coke, but more so if you are thirsty. Salient objects pull your attention away from what you were attending to so often are viewed as distractions.

Why do we care about salience? We veer toward the alternative that draws our attention.

(e.g., a shock). This implies that wants are not always based on expected emotional WB.

To summarize, wanting is separable from liking, and wanting is driven by dopamine. This separation motivated his lab to seek the brain part that produces pleasure. Five pleasure hotspots have been identified.

The Pleasure Sensation

So, if dopamine isn't the pleasure neurotransmitter and the mesolimbic dopamine system, MDS, isn't the pleasure pathway, what causes pleasure? By 2012, Berridge and others identified two hotspots.

So why are they hedonic hotspots? Micro-dosing their neurons with the neurotransmitter *enkephalin* makes a sweet taste sweeter, and so does the neurotransmitter *anandamide*. Anandamide is "the brain's version of the active ingredient in marijuana." [Ananda is Sanskrit for bliss.] Releasing these opioids causes anandamides to flow, which feedback to the axon terminal, causing more enkephalin to flow (a positive feedback loop).

> One of these lies in a subregion of the nucleus accumbens called the medial shell"; the nucleus accumbens is a small part of the MDS. (Kringelbach and Berridge 2012)
>
> The other is found within the ventral pallidum, the VP, a deep-seated structure near the base of the forebrain that receives most of its signals from the nucleus accumbens. (Kringelbach and Berridge 2012)

Your VP is between your nucleus accumbens and your amygdala. Destroying a rat's ventral pallidum makes a sweet taste yucky. [Thousands of rats get brain parts destroyed in the interests of neuroscience.[21]] Stimulating the ventral pallidum can make something yucky produce pleasure.

Three more have been identified in the last decade, along with some *cold-spots*. [Dosing a cold-spot reduces the pleasure of a sweet.] Hotspots

[21] The pleasure parts of human and rat brains are similar. Unlike a rat, a human has a large cortex, giving it the ability to ruminate about what they feel. But a rat does not need these higher brain regions to experience pleasure, nor do humans. In the 1940s and '50s, thousands of people got frontal lobotomies (a procedure that intentionally destroys cortex), and while after they suffered from bad decision-making, they didn't experience a decrease in their ability to experience pleasures—they still liked food and sex.

are tiny (a few cubic millimeters in a rat), and micro-dosing near one does not increase pleasure (Nguyen, Erin Naffziger, and Berridge 2021). Recent research has zeroed in on their locations. The hotspot in the medial shell is at its front; there is a cold-spot at its rear (Morales and Berridge 2020). The VP hotspot is at the back end of the VP; there is a hedonic cold-spot at the front.

Axons project from the VP and the medial shell to the *orbitofrontal cortex* and the *insula cortex,* where the experience of conscious pleasure is produced (the *pleasure gloss*), each containing a hotspot (Morales and Berridge 2020; Nguyen et al. 2021). The orbitofrontal cortex "adjusts this feeling based on inputs from other brain regions" (Kringelbach and Berridge 2012). Human neural activity in the orbitofrontal cortex (observed by neuroimaging) is significantly correlated with pleasure.

The other hotspot is in the brain stem, in the *pontine parabrachial nucleus* (Pecina and Berridge 2005; Soderpalm; Berridge 2000; Morales and Berridge 2020). The five hotspots are a coordinated network: pleasure can be enhanced by dosing any of them, stimulating all. The hotspot in the VP plays a critical role in that blocking its neuroreceptors is sufficient to negate the effects of dosing one of the others (Ho and Berridge 2014) (Fig. 5.11).

It is Fig. 5.10 with the liking pathways replacing the wanting/desiring pathway. The right-most dot is the hotspot in the brain stem. The upper left is in the insular cortex; the lower left is in the orbitofrontal cortex. The third from the left is in the medial shell, and the fourth from the left is the VP hotspot. See also the authors' figures, the "Paths to Pleasure, at https://www.scientificamerican.com/article/new-pleasure-circuit-found-brain/, the first figures at https://www.sciencedirect.com/science/article/pii/S2352154621000358, and https://www.sciencedirect.com/science/article/pii/S0031938420304662.

Where do I get dosed?

While micro-dosing to find hedonic hotspots has come from animal studies, human neuroimaging studies indicate that they are activated even by cognitive pleasures such as the arts. See, for example, Eloise Stark, Peter Vuust, and Kringelbach (2018). They hypothesize that the default-mode network plays a central role in WB; it is "a key resting state that is most active when we are not directly engaging in tasks" (Gusnard et al. 2001). Many of our pleasure centers are in it. Further evidence is that breakdowns in our pleasure centers can lead to mood disorders.

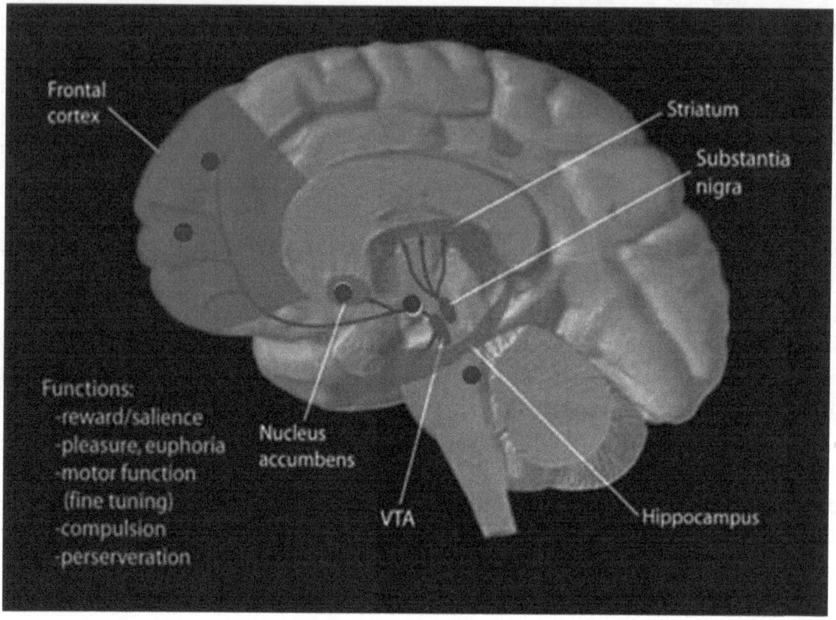

Fig. 5.11 Pleasure hotspots and pathways

Kringelbach and Berridge (2017) review the literature on the relationship between emotions and pleasure centers.

* * *

Some people experience more pleasure because they consume more of what makes the enkephalin and anandamide flow. Lucky others inherit more and better enkephalin/anandamide synapses. Past experiences can also strengthen them. Twenty percent of Americans have a FAAH gene mutation that increases the flow of anandamide.[22] The gene encodes to produce the enzyme *fatty acid amide hydrolase* (FAAH). This enzyme breaks down anandamide. The mutation causes less FAAH, so less anandamide is broken down, and more flows. People and mice with this

[22] The probability of inheriting this gene mutation varies by ethnic group; while it's 21% for Americans of European descent, it's 14% for Han Chinese living in China and 45% for Yoruban Nigerians (Friedman, (2015) referring to data from the HapMap project).

mutation tend to be less anxious and recover from bad experiences more quickly.[23] So to experience pleasure, you want parents who are inherently good at experiencing pleasure, and you want experiences that strengthen the pleasure synapses you were born with.

Most neuroscientists agree that wanting is typically determined by remembered and expected WB. Quoting from the text *Neuroeconomics*:

> That is, we ordinarily desire an outcome to exactly the same degree that we predict the outcome will be liked, and most predictions about future experienced utility [WB] are based on how liked the outcome was in the past.

[There is a 2012 economic study (Benjamin et al. 2012) that tends to support this conclusion. The study asks hypothetical choice questions; for example, "Would you choose a job that pays $80K/yr. and you have time to sleep 7.5 hrs/night or a job that pays $140K with 6 hours to sleep?" After you answer, the researcher asks which scenario would make you happier. The study estimates that in 83% of the questions asked, the subject chose the alternative they expected would generate the most happiness. If we make a leap and believe the subjects always chose their most desired alternative, the study implies that 83% of the time, the alternative most desired was the one they expected to like the most.]

According to the incentive-salience hypothesis, sometimes (17%?), the intensity of the desiring/wanting for one of the alternatives is excessive. This happens when a cue for that alternative occurs when the individual is in a physiological state (hungry, aroused, tired, etc.) that increases their receptiveness to the cue. For example, you are thirty and see someone enjoying a Pepsi rather than a Coke. When a cue occurs, and you are receptive, the dopamine spike is compounded, causing you to want the alternative associated with that cue above and beyond what would be warranted by its expected effect on your emotional WB. You choose

[23] Researchers (Dincheva et al. 2015) recently inserted the mutated gene into mice to see how their behavior would be affected. Compared to normal mice they were more adventurous and had better connections between their amygdala (a fear-processing center) and their prefrontal cortex. Then the mice (mutated and normal) were conditioned to fear a neutral tone. [This was achieved by pairing the tone with an electric shock.] Later all were repeatedly exposed to the same tone but without the shock. The mutated mice more quickly learned to not fear the tone. The researchers got the same results when they compared humans with and without the gene mutation.

Pepsi over Coke even though you would have enjoyed the Coke more. [Remember that dopamine is released when a cue for the outcome occurs before the outcome is experienced.] For example, the clock striking six is a cue for a hungry Giacomo that dinner will soon arrive and for me to drink wine. A second cue for us both is the smell of his burger cooking. These cues trigger the release of dopamine, directly and excessively increasing our desire for the alternative associated with these cues, making me overly inclined to drink and Giacomo to stand next to his bowl.

Experiments by Cindy Wyvell in the Berridge lab have measured the combined effect of a cue and physiological receptiveness. "Rats were first trained to press one of two levers to obtain sucrose pellets. They were conditioned to associate a Pavlovian cue (30 sec. light) with free sucrose pellets" (Wyvell and Berridge 2000). Then on test day, the rats had different amounts of amphetamines injected into their nucleus accumbens, "putting the rat's brain in an elevated state of dopamine activation." They were then set free to press, or not press, one or both levers. No sucrose pellets were rewarded or given, but the cue was presented at intervals. Light off, all the rats pressed both levers, but more the lever they had associated with the pellet. Light on (the cue), they all pressed the "sucrose" lever more than when the light was off, but they did not increase how often they pressed the other lever. All expected.

With the light on, the number of times the sucrose bar was pressed increased with the dosage, but the dose did not affect how often the other bar was pushed. That is, the activation of the dopamine system only influenced cue-specific behavior.

With a separate test, she showed that the amphetamines did not increase liking, so the rate of lever pushing was not increased by liking, only by wanting. To summarize, the cue increased sucrose-lever pushing, and more so, the more the rat's physiological state was amped up. The more the rat was amped up, the more salient the cue.

One might view incentive salience as expected WB multiplied by a constant k, so when k equals 1, the individual wants what they expect to like, but if k is more or less than 1, wanting deviates from liking. And the extent a cue affects k depends on the individual's physiological state. The implication for NBT is that what the individual chooses will not always make them better off. And this is more likely to occur when they experience cues and are in a receptive physiological state. You often make flawed choices when you are tired, aroused, intoxicated, etc., and a cue for the bad alternative appears.

Consider the 83% estimate noted above, keeping in mind that the choices were hypothetical. In the work sleep study, there was no cueing (no pictures of comfortable beds flashed on the screen). And we can presume the subjects were at their physiological baseline (e.g., not tired). This makes me conjecture that in the real world (where cues are numerous and people are often not at their physiological baseline), wanting and expected liking line up less than 83% of the time. Whether getting it wrong at least 17% of the time is a big deal is a matter of interpretation. Some choices (like Coke or Pepsi) don't affect long-term WB, but others can (e.g., having unprotected sex without birth control).

Pedro Bordalo et al. (2022) review the new and growing economic literature on salience's role in choice, much by them, including (2012a, 2013, 2020).[24] They (2022) define a stimulus as salient "when it attracts the decision maker's (DM's) attention bottom up," that is, automatically and involuntarily.[25] And note that "markets abound with salient stimuli." And, in my words, not theirs, they distort choice away from the HRAP based on WB. They drive a wedge between an ordering based on WB (Assumption 9a) and an ordering based on wants and desires (9b). In their words,

> In sum, many choice instabilities typically explained using a smorgasbord of ingredients such as probability weighting, reference points, menu effects, and exotic preferences can be viewed as the product of a well-documented and fundamental psychological force: bottom-up attention to contrasting, surprising, and prominent stimuli. (2022)

The Reward-Prediction Hypothesis

This hypothesis, proposed by Schultz at Cambridge, is dopamine flows when the expectation of future rewards needs correcting. It flows whenever new information indicates the current expectation is wrong. New information comes in two forms: the magnitude of your last reward and sometimes a cue before the next reward is expected. A temporary increase

[24] See also Dietrich and List (2016). Bordalo et al. (2012b) suggest salience can explain the endowment effect: what's salient shifts after the good is obtained.

[25] Framing effects are a type of bottom-up stimuli.

in firing rate (a positive spike) signals to expect more (your current expectation is too low). A negative spike signals expect less. No spike signals no need to correct.

When a cue associated with an alternative appears, it tells your brain that you should associate a larger reward with that alternative. And the taller the spike, the more you need to revise upward the expected reward. If there is no cue, there is no pre-reward spike because, since the last reward, there is no new information.

A positive dopamine spike when the reward arrives signals that it was better than expected, so you should expect even more in the future. A negative spike when the reward arrives signals the opposite.

In summary, the spikes start a process that brings expected WB more in line with the WB that will be experienced. [Recollect that the axons of these dopamine neurons project widely.] Discussions of this hypothesis typically use the word *learning*: you learn, through reinforcement, better what to expect. When the prediction error is large, there is more to learn.

The primary evidence for the hypothesis that dopamine flow is a gauge of the prediction error is that the dopamine spike when a cue is presented is larger the more the cue guarantees the reward. And the observation that the magnitude of the dopamine spike when the reward occurs (up, down, or not at all) depends on how much the reward deviates from the expected reward. These two observations are evidence for the hypothesis in that they are what it predicts. However, they are not proof because they are consistent with other hypotheses.

A problem with testing the reward-prediction error hypothesis is that while neuron firing rates can be directly observed (what Fiorillo did), prediction errors can't. So, researchers proxy them based on assumptions, ones that not everyone accepts. Studies show that firing rates are correlated with the estimated prediction errors, but no current studies prove that firing rates are correlated with the actual prediction errors.

In addition, Berridge points out that the above experiment would produce results consistent with the prediction-error hypothesis, even if it is wrong. This will happen if the incentive-salience hypothesis (his hypothesis) is correct. And, if during the experiment, the physiological states of the subjects are all the same and constant (e.g., all the rats are equally thirsty or not). And, wanting will be mislabeled as prediction error. So, according to Berridge, a distinction between wanting and prediction error will only appear if there is variation across subjects in their physiological states. Studies have not included such variation.

A finding that conflicts with the reward prediction error hypothesis is that rats can learn without dopamine. For example, even after most of their dopamine neurons have been destroyed, they can learn to dislike a taste they liked (Berridge and O'Doherty 2013).[26]

That said, many neuroscientists support the reward prediction error hypothesis.

The reward prediction error hypothesis implies that dopamine does not directly drive wanting but indirectly influences it by updating expected emotional WB. Concerning Assumption 9a (paths are WB-ordered) and 9b (paths are want/desire ordered), the reward prediction error hypothesis and its supporting data are consistent with paths being ordered based on desiring/wanting (9b)—not in WB (9a). Still, desire is correlated with expected WB. A neurological mechanism continuously uses new information to update expected WB. If the reward prediction error hypothesis is correct, your ordering is based on expected WB, not actual WB, so things can still turn out badly. You expected the beautiful house with the beautiful wife would make you happy, so you got both, but you might have been better off living elsewhere with someone else—a point made by the Talking Heads.

Summarizing

Both hypotheses hypothesize that choice is driven by wanting/desiring, often by the expected WB associated with each alternative. The link between wanting and expected WB is weaker if the incentive-salience hypothesis is correct. If correct, the link weakens when cues proceed the choice, and the chooser is in a physiological state that makes her hyper-receptive to the cues. In such cases, the incentive-salience hypothesis predicts you will often choose something other than what you would have liked the most. In the reward prediction hypothesis, dopamine drives learning (changing expected values when new information arrives). In the incentive-salience hypothesis, dopamine drives wanting, not learning.

The neurological data supports the conjecture that choices are based, at the decision point, on wants rather than likes (Assumption 9b, not 9a). I am no expert in judging between the two hypotheses. Still, I find the incentive-salience hypothesis appealing and intriguing because it is more in line with models and data from psychology that indicate we often act

[26] But it seems that some types of learning do require dopamine (Berridge and O'Doherty 2013).

against our self-interest (see Chapters 7 and 8). It is also in line with literature on addiction that suggests how much you want something does not necessarily reflect how much you will like it. In one exciting study (Marco Leyton et al. 2005),

> cocaine users were given a drug that lowered their dopamine levels. In the lowered dopamine state, cues indicating the availability of the drug were rated as less desirable. When given the drug, however, the users' feelings of euphoria and the rate of self-administration were unaffected. That is, with reduced dopamine, study participants still liked the drug in the same way (reinforcement was unchanged), even though they didn't particularly want it. (Gazzaniga et al. 2014)

Or the reverse, the recovering addict encounters a positive cue while in an elevated physiological state, which makes them temporally want the drug more than they will like it. So, they take it even though they know that their past use was a mistake and know that taking it now is a mistake (Ber nheim and Rangel 2004).

As a choice modeling welfare economist, I find the incentive-salience hypothesis both more intriguing and more troublesome because, if correct, you and I don't always maximize our WB. [The reward prediction-error hypothesis is more in line with maximizing our WB, so I should hope the incentive-salience hypothesis is eventually rejected. Nevertheless, seeing apple carts upset spikes my emotional WB—when I don't have a cart or apples in the game.]

What about economists and ethicists who don't care about WB? If you are an economist who only cares about predicting behavior, Assumption (9b) is consistent with both hypotheses and the neurological data.

If you are an ethicist (economic or otherwise) for which want/desire fulfillment is the ethical objective (rather than maximizing WB), go with 9b: it is consistent with both hypotheses (both imply 9b). And it means that individuals pursue want fulfillment, the ethical objective, from their perspective.

Findings in neuroscience are coming fast and furious, and new research could negate or confirm the results reported above. One possibility is that dopamine plays two roles: in one part of your brain, a gauge of prediction error, and in another, a gauge of salience. Gazzaniga et al. (2014) describe a study by Masayuki Matsumoto and Okihide Hikosaka (2009) that recorded firing rates for dopamine neurons in the brain stem:

> One subset of dopamine neurons responded in terms of valence [*reward or punishment*]. These cells increase their firing rate to stimuli that are predictive of reward and decrease their firing rate to aversive stimuli (Figure 12.19a). A greater number of dopamine neurons, however, were excited by the increased likelihood of any reinforcement, independent of whether it was a reward or a punishment, and especially when it was unpredictable (Figure 12.19b). The first response class is similar to what would be expected of neurons coding prediction errors, the second to what would be expected of neurons coding salience or signaling things that require attention.

I leave it to you to decide when and if it would be better for NCT to be explicit about the basis for ordering. My preference is to be explicit, and the neurological evidence indicates it is based on wants, not likes.

A More Macro View: Pleasures, Emotions, Temperaments, and Happiness

Consider four sorts of happiness: (1) a pleasurable sensation (the taste of Valrhona chocolate, coming in from the cold), (2) a positive *emotion*, (3) being in a good *mood*, and (4) having a good *temperament*. Happiness is one of the *effects* experienced. Affect is the general term for emotions, feelings, and moods.

Emotional WB Is a Suite of Emotions, But What Is an Emotion? And How Are They Formed?

An emotion is a conscious experience. As was discussed in Chapter 2, while there is no universally agreed-upon definition, psychologists generally agree that it has at least three parts: a "physiological reaction to a stimulus, a behavioral response, and a feeling." Feelings are subjective in that I can't know how what I am feeling differs from what you are feeling or what a bat, or another animal, is feeling. For example, Giacomo is happy (or appears so) when playing in the snow, catching things, and pouncing on stuffed animals—the sight of an airborne stuffed animal is a stimulus. On the other hand, most of us imagine slugs are incapable of emotions—we don't know for sure.

Emotions and moods are of limited duration, and the emotion's duration is shorter than a mood but more intense. And, unlike emotions, moods don't have an "obvious trigger." For example, the fear experienced when you hear a snake in the grass is an emotion, whereas being anxious for long periods for no reason is a mood, a mood disorder. A semi-permanent mood is a temperament, a component of your personality.

Emotions such as disgust, fear, anger, happiness, sadness, and surprise are considered basic emotions: they are, arguably, hardwired, shared by everyone, and characterized by the same facial expression in every culture. The Big-Bad Wolf knew Goldie Locks was afraid when he saw the whites of her eyes.[27] Check out faces for emotions at https://www.humintell.com/2021/01/the-universality-of-facial-expressions-of-emotion/.

More complex emotions include bored and embarrassed; they are learned and vary culturally. Romantic love is a complex emotion, one not associated with any facial expression. Current thinking is that there isn't a one-stop emotion center in your brain—not surprising given all the different emotions and that brain regions serve multiple roles—but the amygdala and hypothalamus play a significant role. Emotions have two dimensions: positive or negative (pleasant or unpleasant) and intensity. For example, a little sadness can be pleasant.

Emotion Formation

If the goal is to make someone happier, we hope to enhance their ability to form the emotion happy. Emotions have three components: a physiological response, a behavioral response, and a feeling. There are several contrasting theories of emotion formation; they differ in the order the components occur—which comes first. Two primary and historical theories of emotion are the *James-Lang Theory* and the contrasting *Cannon-Bard Theory*. The James-Lang theory hypothesizes that the first response to the stimulus is physiological (e.g., sweating, increased heart rate), and the conscious feeling we experience—the emotion experienced—is a reaction to these physiological changes. So, the unpleasant sensations I experienced when I arrived at the home of my high-school prom date (terror and anxiety) were caused by my body's sweating and shaking and my inability to swallow. [Willam James (1842–1910) was a

[27] If B. B. Wolf had had his two amygdale surgically removed, he would not have recognized Goldie's fear: individuals with severe amygdala damage do not process fear as do you and I do, in part because they do not automatically focus on eyes (see Adolphs et al. 2005).

noted philosopher and the father of psychology in the US. He suffered from depression and insomnia and used chloroform as a sleep aid. His brother was the novelist Henry James. Carl George Lang (1834–1900) was a Danish physician. They separately, but within a year of each other, proposed the theory.] In contrast, the Cannon-Bard Theory (Walter Cannon and Phillip Bard) hypothesizes that your brain processes the physiological change and the conscious feeling simultaneously. And the feeling processes faster, so first you feel nervous and then sweat.

There are other theories. One class is *Appraisal Theories*: the sexy grizzly bear sitting alone at the bar winks at you; first, you do a quick harm/benefit risk appraisal (often unconsciously).[28] Your appraisal has two components: what does the wink mean for me, and can I cope? Based on your appraisal, you feel fear, sexual arousal, disgust, or whatever. This feeling may be associated with physiological changes, but that isn't required. Then, based on which feeling is experienced, you run, offer to buy the bear a drink, or remain alone in the corner with your Michelob Light. Appraisal theories explain why you and I may experience different emotions when we are winked at. Appraisal theories sharply contrast with the James-Lange theory, which starts with a physiological response to a stimulus.

The (Stanley) Schachter and (Jerome) Singer Theory (1962) blends Appraisal theories with the James-Lange theory. It hypothesizes that (1) emotions are influenced by both the physiological and cognitive reactions to the stimulus, (2) the physiological response sometimes proceeds the thinking part, and (3) people identify the emotion and gauge their degree of arousal based on how physiologically they are revved up. Their theory was proposed to explain the results of their famous experiment where they injected subjects with adrenaline (a potent stimulant), telling half of them that they were being injected with adrenaline. The other half were told they were being injected with vitamins. Each subject then interacted with an individual who behaved either angrily or euphorically. [The subject thought the other person was another subject, but it was a research assistant.] After interreacting with the other individual, subjects falsely told they were injected with vitamins attributed their emotional state to the individual's behavior. Those told they were injected with adrenaline attributed their emotional state to the adrenaline.

[28] James liked scary-bear examples.

Another theory, the *Construct Theory* of emotions (Barrett), hypothesizes that some emotions are cultural constructs. In this view, embarrassment, for example, isn't a hardwired emotion but instead constructed.

> in the same way that they see color or the way they perceive behaviors in others…Color is a continuum of wavelengths, yet … experienced categorically….
>
> Physical movements are continuous in the same way that the visible light spectrum is continuous. People are constantly moving and doing things—that is, they are constantly engaging in "behavioral actions". Yet, behaviors are perceived as discrete acts …
>
> People are compelled by their own experiences to believe that emotions exist as natural-kind entities, yet a century of research has not produced a strong evidentiary basis for this belief. To date, there is no clear, unambiguous criterion for indicating the presence of anger or sadness or fear. (Barrett 2006)

According to Construct Theory, the bear's wink causes a physiological change. Then you assess your past experiences with bears (winking and not) and other bar winkers. Then you categorize the experience, in your language, as fear, attraction, embarrassment, or whatever. Then you act.

Summarizing the theories of how emotions form, the jury is still out, but all start with a stimulus that causes a physiological change, a behavioral change, and a feeling.

While happy is considered a primary emotion, it can have different forms: joyful, gleeful, delighted, euphoric, etc. Happy is either one type of emotional WB or a synonym for it, and how it arises depends on which theory of emotional WB you subscribe to. Happiness that persists without an obvious trigger is better described as a mood than an emotion, but for simplicity of exposition, include a happy mood in emotional WB.

Your Brain in a Mood

A necessary condition for happiness is the absence of negative emotions and moods such as anxious or depressed. Anxiety and depression don't always have identifiable triggers. Most of the mood research is on mood disorders, most often anxiety or depression.

Anxious

Unsolicited anxiety is a barrier to emotional WB. In addition to precluding happiness, it affects our behavior: we avoid situations that provoke it; we do things to reduce it and don't do things we would have done if we weren't anxious. For example, when I called Patricia to ask her to the prom, I was anxious, so I had a flow chart of what to say in response to everything I thought she would say. When she accepted, my flow chart was good for nothing; I hung up in a panic. Our prom was a disaster.

When you perceive danger, you experience fear and the flight-or-fight response (our stress response), making you more able to survive the threat. Your amygdala receives an external stimulus (you hear a gunshot) that shouts danger. The warning is passed through your hypothalamic and pituitary glands to your adrenal glands, which react by pumping *cortisol* (a stress hormone) into your bloodstream.[29]

Your hypothalami release CRH, the *corticotropin-releasing hormone*; it binds with receptors in your pituitary glands. This causes each pituitary gland (you have two) to release ACTH (the *adrenocorticotropic hormone*); it binds with receptors in your adrenal glands, which produce cortisol. The cortisol channels energy away from needs that aren't immediate, such as growth, digestion, and immunity. This hypothalamus/pituitary/adrenal system is called the *HPA axis*. This neurological and hormonal pathway that kicks in when your body registers the gunshot is your *excitatory system*—the pathway that generates excitement (Fig. 5.12).

You also have an *inhibitory system*, a neurological and hormonal pathway that calms you; the two systems work to keep your excitement commensurate with the danger. As part of the inhibitory system, the hippocampus monitors the amount of cortisol emitted. If it's deemed too much, a message is sent to the pituitary gland through the hypothalamus. "Cut down" on the cortisol release: GABA neurons release the neurotransmitter GABA. In the post-synaptic neuron, the GABA attaches to neurons in the hippocampus with GABA receptors, causing these neurons to fire. Their firings start the chain of events leading to less cortisol, a negative feedback loop.

[29] Cortisol shouldn't be confused with *adrenaline*, another hormone released by your adrenal gland when a threat is detected; adrenaline increases heart rate, sweating, and muscle tension.

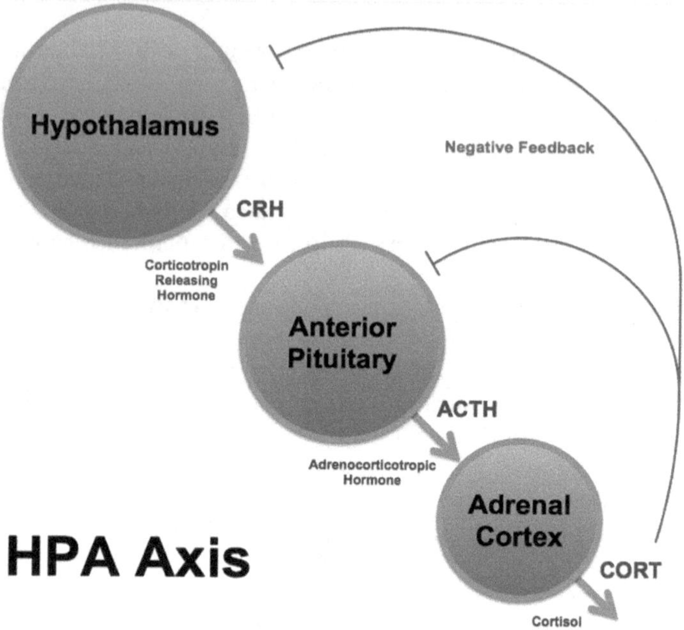

Fig. 5.12 The HPA axis

Both the excitatory and inhibitory messages pass through the hypothalamus. Ideally, both systems are balanced, and you only freak out when freaking out is appropriate. However, genetics, prior experiences, and learning can cause a stress response when there is no danger. These experiences can be low-level and chronic (a *generalized anxiety disorder*) or short and extreme (a *panic disorder*). Either way, the amygdala works too much or the hippocampus too little.

Three drugs reduce anxiety: benzodiazepine (e.g., Valium), alcohol, and SSRIs. They do this by modifying neural synapses. Valium and alcohol temporarily reduce stress by enhancing the inhibitory system: the GABA receptors in the hippocampus become more receptive to GABA after the Valium or alcohol has attached to them. Like others who suffer from a generalized anxiety disorder, I make my GABA receptors more receptive by self-administering wine. A nickname for Valium is "Mother's little helper," which is the name of a 1996 Rolling Stones song about how Valium got your mom through the day.

No one is sure why SSRIs reduce anxiety, but they often do. They keep the released serotonin in the synaptic gap longer by inhibiting its reabsorption by the axon terminal that emitted it. Most of the serotonin-emitting neurons in your brain have cell bodies in one of the nine Raphe (ridge) nuclei at the base of your brain.

Their axons project into diverse parts of the brain (one axon can synapse with hundreds of thousands of neurons spread all over the place, and the effects of serotonin releases can last for hours). These neurons influence brain activities, including emotions and moods such as happiness, fear, and aggression (Fig. 5.13).

While an SSRI immediately causes serotonin to remain longer in the synapses, it, unlike alcohol and Valium, does not immediately reduce anxiety; that can take weeks. [This is why your doctor may prescribe Valium for a few weeks even though you have started on Prozac.] So, it's not the increased serotonin per se that reduces the anxiety. One relevant finding is that the increased serotonin causes, in the hippocampus,

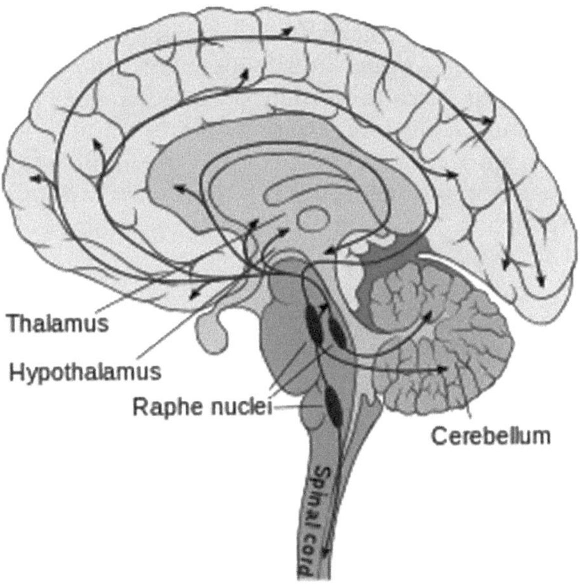

Fig. 5.13 Your Raphe nuclei and their serotonin pathways

an increase in the number of receptors for the neurotransmitter glucocorticoid. Researchers speculate that this strengthens the inhibitory system, so it reduces the release of cortisol.

Eating chocolate causes serotonin to flow. You can reduce anxiety by learning not to be inappropriately stressed. When there is a threat, other things are also happening around us; these can become misleading cues: things that aren't dangerous (*benign stimuli*—it was raining when you heard the gunshot). You learn, incorrectly, to go into stress mode when one or more of these other things occur, even when there is no threat—you have learned to associate rain with danger. Like a rat that experiences a sight or sound cue paired with something unpleasant, we learn that when that sight or sound occurs, we imagine something terrible will happen, and our mind and body prepare. *Cognitive Behavioral Therapy* (CBT) and its extensions can break the link: you learn to no longer associate the stimulus with the threat. Like drugs, re-learning changes the number and effectiveness of your synapses.

Besides unwarranted anxiety, there is warranted stress: fear and anxiety caused by being at risk. Many people are in circumstances with a high probability of injury, death, sickness, and hunger. Warranted anxiety can be reduced by reducing these probabilities. For example, knowing the kids won't starve will lessen the anxiety of most parents. [Independent of how you feel about Obamacare, assuring access to healthcare will reduce anxiety. On the other hand, Obamacare has put those who hate it in a bad mood. An important question is how long these bad moods will last. The anxiety reduction will continue if the access continues.]

Depressed

If you are depressed, you are unhappy, and we all occasionally experience depression. Unfortunately, many suffer from chronic depression, making it a leading cause of disability and unhappiness. "Perhaps 20% of the population will suffer a major, incapacitating episode of depression during their lifetime" (Bear et al. 2020). Like anxiety, depression causes behavioral changes: a shutting down, a decreased responsiveness to stimuli—an ice-cream cone is no longer worth the trouble.

Anxiety and depression often go together, and SSRIs are effective for anxiety and depression. Why are they effective for depression? One answer is the *monoamine hypothesis of mood disorders*. There are two monoamine neurotransmitters: serotonin and *norepinephrine*. Explaining: your brain contains three mood-critical *diffuse modulatory systems*. Figures 5.10 and

5.11 illustrate the diffuse modulatory systems for dopamine and serotonin. Each consists of a clump of cell bodies, all with axons spewing their neurotransmitter far and wide. The serotonin system modulates the diffusion of serotonin; the dopamine system diffuses dopamine. There is also a diffuse modulatory system for norepinephrine; its clumps are in your brainstem.

The monoamine hypothesis is that depression results from a deficit in either the serotonin or norepinephrine diffuse modulatory system. The evidence that SSRIs work as an antidepressant through these two diffuse systems is (1) SSRIs keep the effects of serotonin release working longer (inhibit reuptake), (2) another effective antidepressant drug (*imipramine* (Tofranil)) inhibits the reuptake of both serotonin and norepinephrine, (3) a few drugs for other ailments cause depression by messing up the release of serotonin, and (4) drugs that inhibit the enzyme MAO—MAO destroys serotonin—are antidepressants. These drugs are called MAO inhibitors; they effectively treat depression but are now rarely prescribed. They can cause severe high blood pressure when consumed with red wine and aged cheese.

A different but overlapping theory of depression is the *diathesis-stress hypothesis*. Depression, like chronic anxiety and other mood disorders, is caused by hyperactivity in the hypothalamus/pituitary/adrenal system, the HPA axis (see Fig. 5.12). This system is implicated in all theories of anxiety and depression. The adjective "stress" because stress distorts the HPA; the adjective "diathesis" because mood disorders have a genetic component; some people are predisposed. "Animal studies are highly suggestive" (Bear et al. 2020) that hyperactivity in the HPA results in depression. There is also strong evidence that infants who experience nurturing and stimulation are better able to respond to stressors in adulthood, making them less likely to develop mood disorders. Conversely, lousy pre-natal care and neglecting the baby can lead to an adult with a hyperactive HPA.

Genes, monoamines, and early childhood experiences are implicated in mood disorders. So, what does all this have to do with happiness and emotional WB? A way to increase emotional WB in adults is to make sure babies are nurtured and stimulated. In adults, depression and chronic anxiety can be treated with CBT and drugs. Electroconvulsive therapy (inducing a seizure by zapping your brain with electricity) can effectively treat major depression, but it also zaps your short-term memory—think of it as setting the reset button. And psychedelics are starting to show promising results.

Pervasive Happiness (a Happy Person) and WB

The happiness from an experience/stimulus is typically fleeting, and these experiences are intermittent, not pervasive. So, neurologically, what causes persistent emotional WB? Not being chronically anxious or depressed is necessary but not sufficient. Having strong enkephalin/anandamide synapses also helps.

By many definitions, WB requires the experience of happiness (emotional WB) and a sense of meaning in your life (life-satisfaction WB). One relevant finding is that high reported happiness is correlated with the feeling you have a meaningful life, suggesting a neurological connection between the two.

The neurobiology of persistent happiness is sketchy, and the neurobiology of meaningfulness is an informed scribble. Experiencing meaning in your life must, however, have a neurobiological foundation. For example, there is a suggestion that the brain mechanisms that give you pleasure from chocolate also cause persistent meaningfulness.

Based more on observation than on neurobiology, we each have our own quasi-set level of emotional WB/happiness, which we can easily deviate from in the short run but not in the long run—a hypothesis Adam Smith subscribed to. This is discussed in Chapter 6. Studies on identical twins separated at birth indicate that happiness has a genetic component. One large study finds that approximately 33% of the variation in happiness across individuals is explained by genetic variation. The paper "Genes, Economics, and Happiness" finds that a feature on a serotonin transporter gene positively correlates with reported happiness.[30] People that inherit this feature grow stronger happiness-related synapses.

[30] It's the 5-HHT gene and "much is known about the way different versions of this gene influence transcription, metabolism, and signal transfers between genes…efficient variants of this gene have been shown to moderate the influence of stress on depression, …and [are] linked to optimism" (De Neve et al. 2012). It's unlikely a single gene can explain all the variation in a complex feeling, like happiness, and that huge samples are required if the researcher hopes to find links between specific genes and behavior. Quoting further, "We do not claim that 5-HTT determines happiness, nor do we exclude the possibility that several other genes may play a role in accounting for the influence of genes on happiness."

Defining Happiness in Non-biological Ways Is Difficult—But, Like Porn, You Know It When You See

Dictionary synonyms for modern happiness include pleasure, joy, bliss, felicity, and contentment, but these are not all the same. The physical feelings associated with contentment differ from what it feels like to laugh. Happiness varies on multiple dimensions; for each, there is intensity and duration: short and intense or less intense but longer-lasting. Possible antonyms include unhappiness, sadness, grief, pain, and depression. Which words should be synonyms or antonyms is a tricky business. For example, pain often leads to unhappiness, but pain is neither necessary nor sufficient for unhappiness.

> Happiness is the sublime moment when you get out of your corset at night. (Joyce Grenfell [1919-1978]—actress, comedienne, and singer-songwriter)
>
> What we call happiness in the strictest sense of the word comes from the (preferably sudden) satisfaction of needs which have been dammed up to a high degree. (Sigmund Freud)

Most Economists Talk About Preferences, not Happiness or WB

Recollect Assumption 9a vs. 9b (an ordering based on WB vs. desire/wanting). Given that pleasure (liking) and desiring (wanting) have different neurological pathways that are not necessarily in sync, whether your ordering is based on WB (9a) or desire (9b) is important. Either way, whether path *a* is ranked higher than path *b* depends on their respective electrical/chemical brain mixtures.

When economists think about you being better off, they typically think this is achieved by experiencing a higher-ordered path of goods and experiences. But! There are more direct ways to feel better—drugs, for example? I ask my students whether they would take a drug that would make them happier. Most say "No". [I'm always surprised, given that quite a few college students are prescribed SSRIs, and most drink alcohol.] When I ask for an explanation, the first response is typically, "There would be bad side effects." When I asked what they would do if they knew there were no undesirable side effects, many students still wouldn't take the drug. And their reasons change to, "It would be wrong/unnatural/dishonest to achieve happiness in this way." This implies they care not only about happiness but also about the process that achieved it—an outcome, meaning they care about both consequences and process (see Chapter 4 and Part III).

Another way to make you better off is to change your ordering so the path you are experiencing moves up in the orderings. Economists typically avoid this possibility, but marketers embrace it—also Buddhists.

Is an Economist Concerned with Policy a WB Doctor?

Most people, including most economists, don't think of economists as WB doctors. Whereas mental-health therapy typically tries to increase WB one patient at a time, macroeconomic policy tries, I imagine, to simultaneously increase the WB of thousands, if not millions. As an undergraduate, I switched from psychology to economics. The welfare objective of clinical psychology and welfare economics is the same, to improve the lot of their patients. [Of course, not all psychologists and economists care about their patients; they study behavior for the models, not the patients.]

If the goal is to increase WB, my goal as an environmental welfare economist should be to manage the environment to achieve more WB, not necessarily preserve or clean it up. Trashing the environment can be fun, but I have to consider that trashing it now will make the future unhappy.[31] If better is defined explicitly as happier (greater emotional WB), the goal of all economic policy should be to make the members of society happier. Achieving it by implementing policies encouraging encephalin, anandamide, and other happiness neurotransmitters to flow.

Welfare economists who accept Assumption 9a are WB doctors but not necessarily emotional WB doctors.

This chapter considered "What is happiness?" and outlined ways to reduce unhappiness but didn't consider whether more happiness is morally superior to less. That conversation started in Chapter 3 and continues in Part III. Next, Chapter 6 looks at the evidence, pro and con, for whether consuming more increases or decreases WB.

[31] I used to own a snowmobile (we did not plow the road to the cabin); it emitted more pollution than a fleet of cars. Zooming through the snow was bliss.

References

Adolphs, Ralph, et al. 2005. "A mechanism for impaired fear recognition after amygdala damage." *Nature* 433 (7021): 68–72. https://doi.org/10.1038/nature03086. https://www.webofscience.com/wos/woscc/full-record/WOS:000226117100037.

Barrett, Lisa. 2006. "Solving the emotion paradox: Categorization and the experience of emotion." *Personality and Social Psychology Review* 10 (1): 20–46. http://www.affective-science.org/pubs/2006/Barrett2006paradox.pdf.

Bear, Mark, Barry Connors, and Michael Paradiso. 2020. *Neuroscience: Exploring the brain, enhanced edition: Exploring the brain*. Jones & Bartlett Learning.

Benjamin, Daniel, Ori Heffetz, Miles Kimball, and Alex Rees-Jones. 2012. "What do you think would make you happier? What do you think you would choose?" *American Economic Review* 102 (5): 2083–2110. https://doi.org/10.1257/aer.102.5.2083. https://www.aeaweb.org/articles?id=https://doi.org/10.1257/aer.102.5.2083.

Bernheim, Douglas, and Rangel. 2004. "Addiction and cue-triggered decision processes." *American Economic Review* 94 (5): 1558–1590. https://doi.org/10.1257/0002828043052222. https://www.webofscience.com/wos/woscc/full-record/WOS:000227099600014.

Berridge, Kent, and John O'Doherty. 2013. "Chapter 18: From experienced utility to decision utility." In *Neuroeconomics: Decision making and the brain*, edited by Paul Glimcher and Ernest Fehr. Academic Press.

Bordalo, Pedro, Nicola Gennaioli, and Andrei Shleifer. 2012a. "Salience theory of choice under risk." *The Quarterly Journal of Economics* 127 (3): 1243–1285. https://www.jstor.org/stable/23251985.

———. 2012b. "Salience in experimental tests of the endowment effect." *American Economic Review* 102 (3): 47–52. https://www.jstor.org/stable/23245503#metadata_info_tab_contents.

———. 2013. "Salience and consumer choice." *Journal of Political Economy* 121 (5): 803–843. https://www.journals.uchicago.edu/doi/https://doi.org/10.1086/673885.

———. 2020. "Memory, attention, and choice." *The Quarterly Journal of Economics* 135 (3): 1399–1442. https://doi.org/10.1093/qje/qjaa007. https://academic.oup.com/qje/article/135/3/1399/5824669?login=true.

———. 2022. "Salience." *Annual Review of Economics* 14: 521–544.

De Neve, Jan-Emmanuel, Nicholas Christakis, James Fowler, and Bruno Frey. 2012. "Genes, economics, and happiness." *Journal of Neuroscience Psychology and Economics* 5 (4): 193–211. https://doi.org/10.1037/a0030292. https://www.webofscience.com/wos/woscc/full-record/WOS:000209180800001.

Dietrich, Franz, and Christian List. 2016. "Reason-based choice and context dependence: An explanatory framework." *Economics and Philosophy* 32

(2): 175–229. https://doi.org/10.1017/s0266267115000474. https://www.webofscience.com/wos/woscc/full-record/WOS:000378589900002.

Dincheva, Iva, et al. 2015. "FAAH genetic variation enhances fronto-amygdala function in mouse and human." *Nature Communications* 6. https://doi.org/10.1038/ncomms7395. https://www.webofscience.com/wos/woscc/full-record/WOS:000352633400008.

Fiorillo, Christopher, Philippe Tobler, and Wolfram Schultz. 2003. "Discrete coding of reward probability and uncertainty by dopamine neurons." *Science* 299 (5614): 1898–1902. https://doi.org/10.1126/science.1077349. https://www.webofscience.com/wos/woscc/full-record/WOS:000181669700048.

Friedman, Richard. 2015. "The feel-good gene." *The New York Times*, March 6, 2015, Times Sunday Review. https://www.nytimes.com/2015/03/08/opinion/sunday/the-feel-good-gene.html.

Gazziniga, Michael, Richard Ivry, and George Mangun. 2014. *Cognitive neuroscience: The biology of the mind*. 4th ed. New York: W. W. Norton.

Gusnard, Debra and Marcus Raichle. 2001. "Searching for a baseline: Functional Imaging and resting human brain." *Nature Reviews Neuroscience* 2: 685–694.

Haybron, Dan. (2020) "Happiness." Stanford Encyclopedia of Philosophy. Stanford University. https://plato.stanford.edu/.

Heeger, David. 2022. "Lecture notes and slides on the brain." http://www.cns.nyu.edu/~david/courses/perception/lecturenotes/brain/brain.html.

Herculano-Houzel, Suzana. 2016. *Human advantage: A new understanding of how our brain became remarkable*. Cambridge, MA: MIT Press.

Ho, Chao-Yi, and Kent Berridge. 2014. "Excessive disgust caused by brain lesions or temporary inactivations: Mapping hotspots of the nucleus accumbens and ventral pallidum." *European Journal of Neuroscience* 40 (10): 3556–3572. https://doi.org/10.1111/ejn.12720.

Holt, Jim. 2006. "Oh, joy." *The New York Times*, February 12, 2006. https://www.nytimes.com/2006/02/12/books/review/oh-joy.html.

Jha, Amishi. 2021. *Peak mind*. HarperCollins.

Kirk, Robert. 2023. "Zombies." Stanford Encyclopedia of Philosophy. Stanford University. https://plato.stanford.edu/.

Kringelbach, Morten L., and Kent C. Berridge. 2017. "The affective core of emotion: Linking pleasure, subjective well-being, and optimal metastability in the brain." *Emotion Review* 9 (3): 191–199. https://doi.org/10.1177/1754073916684558. https://journals.sagepub.com/doi/abs/https://doi.org/10.1177/1754073916684558.

Kringelbach, Morten L., and Kent C. Berridge. 2012. "The joyful mind." *Scientific America* 307 (2): 5.

Leyton, Marco, et al. 2005. "Cocaine craving, euphoria, and self-administration: A preliminary study of the effect of catecholamine precursor depletion." *Behavioral Neuroscience* 119 (6): 1619–1627. https://doi.org/10.1037/0735-7044.119.6.1619. https://www.webofscience.com/wos/woscc/full-record/WOS:000234758700018.

Matsumoto, Masayuki, and Okihide Hikosaka. 2009. "Two types of dopamine neurons distinctly convey positive and negative motivational signals." *Nature* 459 (7248): 837–841. https://doi.org/10.1038/nature08028. https://www.nature.com/articles/nature08028.

McMahon, Darrin. 2006. *Happiness: A history*. Grove Press.

Morales, Ileana, and Kent Berridge. 2020. "'Liking' and 'wanting' in eating and food reward: Brain mechanisms and clinical implications." *Physiology & Behavior* 227. https://doi.org/10.1016/j.physbeh.2020.113152. https://www.webofscience.com/wos/woscc/full-record/WOS:000588306800022.

Nagel, Thomas. 1974. "What is it like to be a bat?" *The Philosophical Review* 83 (4): 435–450. https://www.jstor.org/stable/2183914#metadata_info_tab_contents.

Nguyen, D., E. E. Naffziger, and Kent Berridge. 2021. "Positive affect: Nature and brain bases of liking and wanting." *Current Opinion in Behavioral Sciences* 39: 72–78. https://doi.org/10.1016/j.cobeha.2021.02.013. https://www.webofscience.com/wos/woscc/full-record/WOS:000664653700012.

Pecina, Susana, and Kent Berridge. 2005. "Hedonic hot spot in nucleus accumbens shell: Where do mu-opioids cause increased hedonic impact of sweetness?" *Journal of Neuroscience* 25 (50): 11777–11786. https://doi.org/10.1523/jneurosci.2329-05.2005. https://www.webofscience.com/wos/woscc/full-record/WOS:000233942200032.

Pessiglione, Mathias, et al. 2006. "Dopamine-dependent prediction errors underpin reward-seeking behaviour in humans." *Nature* 442 (7106): 1042–1045.

Proust, Marcel. 1913. *Swann's way: In search of lost time*. Vol. 1. Translated by Lydia Davis.

Quenqua, Douglas. 2006. "Where personal memories take root." *The New York Times*, June 23, 2006. https://www.webofscience.com/wos/woscc/full-record/WOS:000282571000032.

Schachter, Stanley, and Jerome Singer. 1962. "Cognitive, social, and physiological determinants of emotional state." *Psychological Review* 69 (5): 379–399. https://doi.org/10.1037/h0046234. https://www.webofscience.com/wos/woscc/full-record/WOS:A1962WN80300001.

Shields, Christopher. 2014. "Aristotle." Stanford Encyclopedia of Philosophy. Stanford University. https://plato.stanford.edu/.

Stark, Eloise A., Peter Vuust, and Morten L. Kringelbach. 2018. "Music, dance, and other art forms: New insights into the links between hedonia (pleasure) and eudaimonia (well-being)." *Progress in Brain Research* 237: 129–152. https://www.sciencedirect.com/science/article/pii/S0079612318300190?via%3Dihub.

Todorov, Tzvetan. 2010. "Tzvetan Todorov and the Enlightenment today." *Philosophy Bites*. https://philosophybites.com/2010/01/tzvetan-todorov-on-the-enlightenment-today.html.

Wikipedia. 2015. "Romanticism." Wikipedia Foundation. https://en.wikipedia.org/wiki/Romanticism.

Wixted, John, et al. 2014. "Sparse and distributed coding of episodic memory in neurons of the human hippocampus." *Proceedings of the National Academy of Sciences of the United States of America* 111 (26): 9621–9626. https://doi.org/10.1073/pnas.1408365111. https://www.pnas.org/doi/full/https://doi.org/10.1073/pnas.1408365111.

Wyvell, Cindy, and Kent Berridge. 2000. "Intra-accumbens amphetamine increases the conditioned incentive salience of sucrose reward: Enhancement of reward 'wanting' without enhanced 'liking' or response reinforcement." *Journal of Neuroscience* 20 (21): 8122–8130. https://www.webofscience.com/wos/woscc/full-record/WOS:000090003600003.

Additional Readings

Aquinas, Thomas, and Fathers of the English Dominican Province. 1265–1274/1947. "The Summa Theologica." Benziger Bros. https://www.ccel.org/a/aquinas/summa/FS.html.

Berridge, Kent, and Jonath Aldridge. 2008. "Decision utility, the brain and the pursuit of hedonic goals." *Social Cognition* 26 (5): 621–646. https://doi.org/10.1521/soco.2008.26.5.621. https://www.webofscience.com/wos/woscc/full-record/WOS:000260639600008.

Berridge, Kent, and Morten Kringelbach. 2013. "Neuroscience of affect: Brain mechanisms of pleasure and displeasure." *Current Opinion in Neurobiology* 23 (3): 294–303. https://doi.org/10.1016/j.conb.2013.01.017. https://www.webofscience.com/wos/woscc/full-record/WOS:000354069800008.

Berridge, Kent, and Terry Robinson. 1998. "What is the role of dopamine in reward: Hedonic impact, reward learning, or incentive salience?" *Brain Research Reviews* 28 (3): 309–369. https://doi.org/10.1016/s0165-0173(98)00019-8. https://pubmed.ncbi.nlm.nih.gov/9858756/.

Bristow, William. 2011. "Enlightenment." Stanford Encyclopedia of Philosophy. Stanford University. https://plato.stanford.edu/.

Burnyeat, Myles. 2007. "Myles Burnyeat on Aristotle on happiness." *Philosophy Bites*. https://philosophybites.com/2007/11/miles-burnyeat.html.

Burton, John. 1746. *Life and correspondence of David Hume*. Vol. 2. Edinburgh: William Tait. https://books.google.com/books?id=Gvg5AAAAcAAJ.

Carlye, Thomas. 1843/1963. *Past and present*. Boston: Estes and Lauriat Publishers. https://books.google.com/books?id=QqoPAAAAYAAJ&printsec=frontcover&source=gbs_ge_summary_r&cad=0#v=onepage&q&f=false.

Colombo, Matteo. 2014. "Deep and beautiful. The reward prediction error hypothesis of dopamine." *Studies in History and Philosophy of Science Part C-Studies in History and Philosophy of Biological and Biomedical Sciences* 45: 57–67. https://doi.org/10.1016/j.shpsc.2013.10.006. https://www.webofscience.com/wos/woscc/full-record/WOS:000320712700015.

Crane, Tim. 2007. "Mind and body." *Philosophy Bites*. https://philosophybites.com/2007/09/tim-crane-on-mi.html.

Crisp, Roger. 2015a. "Desire theory." Stanford Encyclopedia of Philosophy. Stanford University. https://plato.stanford.edu/.

———. 2015b. "Well-being." Stanford Encyclopedia of Philosophy. Stanford University. https://plato.stanford.edu/.

Daw, Nathaniel, and Philippe Tobler. 2013. "Value learning through reinforcement." In *Neuroeconomics: Decision making and the brain*, edited by Paul Glimcher and Ernst Fehr, 4th ed. Boston: Elsevier Academic Press.

Dolan, Paul, and K. Laffan. 2016. "Bad air days: The effects of air quality on different measures of subjective well-being." *Journal of Benefit-Cost Analysis* 7 (1): 147–195. https://doi.org/10.1017/bca.2016.7. https://www.webofscience.com/wos/woscc/full-record/WOS:000378203100007.

Dolan, Paul, Tessa Peasgood, and Matthew White. 2008. "Do we really know what makes us happy? A review of the economic literature on the factors associated with subjective well-being." *Journal of Economic Psychology* 29 (1): 94–122. https://doi.org/10.1016/j.joep.2007.09.001. https://www.webofscience.com/wos/woscc/full-record/WOS:000221072000005.

Dolan, Paul, L. Kudrna, and A. Stone. 2017. "The measure matters: An investigation of evaluative and experience-based measures of well-being in time use data." *Social Indicators Research* 134 (1): 57–73. https://doi.org/10.1007/s11205-016-1429-8. https://www.webofscience.com/wos/woscc/full-record/WOS:000410864500003.

Dolan, Paul, et al. 2019. "Quantifying the intangible impact of the Olympics using subjective well-being data." *Journal of Public Economics* 177. https://doi.org/10.1016/j.jpubeco.2019.07.002. https://www.webofscience.com/wos/woscc/full-record/WOS:000487167300005.

Dolan, Paul, Chloe Foy, Giorgios Kavetsos, and Laura Kudrna. 2021. "Faster, higher, stronger... And happier? Relative achievement and marginal rank effects." *Journal of Behavioral and Experimental Economics* 95. https://doi.org/10.1016/j.socec.2021.101761. https://www.webofscience.com/wos/woscc/full-record/WOS:000701264400008.

Duke University. 2012. "With altered brain chemistry, fear is more easily overcome." *Science Daily*, June 12, 2012. Science News. https://www.sciencedaily.com/releases/2012/06/120612101328.htm.

Frank, Robert. 1997. "The frame of reference as a public good." *Economic Journal* 107 (445): 1832–1847. https://doi.org/10.1111/1468-0297.00261. https://www.webofscience.com/wos/woscc/full-record/WOS:000071086300014.

Glimcher, Paul W., and Ernst Fehr, eds. 2013. *Neuroeconomics: Decision making and the brain*. 2nd ed. Edited by Paul W Glimcher and Ernst Fehr: Elsevier Academic Press.

Gunduz-Cinar, Ozge, Mathew Hill, Bruce McEwen, and Andrew Holmes. 2013a. "Amygdala FAAH and anandamide: Mediating protection and recovery from stress." *Trends in Pharmacological Sciences* 34 (11): 637–644. https://doi.org/10.1016/j.tips.2013.08.008. https://www.webofscience.com/wos/woscc/full-record/WOS:000327581000009.

Gunduz-Cinar, Ozge, et al. 2013b. "Convergent translational evidence of a role for anandamide in amygdala-mediated fear extinction, threat processing, and stress-reactivity." *Molecular Psychiatry* 18 (7): 813–823. https://doi.org/10.1038/mp.2012.72. https://www.webofscience.com/wos/woscc/full-record/WOS:000320712700015.

Konstan, David. 2014. "Epicurus." Stanford Encyclopedia of Philosophy. Stanford University. https://www.webofscience.com/wos/woscc/full-record/WOS:000437276600007.

Kraut, Richard. 2014. "Aristotle's ethics." Stanford Encyclopedia of Philosophy. Stanford University. https://plato.stanford.edu/.

Kreeft, Peter. 1990. *A summa of the summa: The essential philosophical passages of St. Thomas Aquinas' Summa Theologica*. Edited and explained for beginners. Ignatius Press.

McInerny, Ralph, and John O'Callaghan. 2015. "Thomas Aquinas (moral doctrine)." Stanford Encyclopedia of Philosophy. Stanford University. https://plato.stanford.edu/.

McMahon, Darrin. 2005. "The pursuit of unhappiness." *New York Times*, December 29, 2005. http://www.nytimes.com/2005/12/29/opinion/29McMahon.html.

Nussbaum, Martha. 2012. "Who is the happy warrior? Philosophy, happiness research, and public policy." *International Review of Economics* 59 (4): 335–361.

Parfit, Derek. 1984. *Reasons and persons*. Oxford: Clarendon Press.

Robinson, Dan. 2012. "Dualism." Stanford Encyclopedia of Philosophy. Stanford University. https://plato.stanford.edu/.

Rousseau, Jean Jacques. 1754. "A discourse on a subject proposed by the academy of Dijon: What is the origin of inequality among men, and is it authorised by natural law?" In *The social contract and discourses*.

Schultz, Wolfram. 1998. "Predictive reward signal of dopamine neurons." *Journal of Neurophysiology* 80 (1): 1–27. https://doi.org/10.1152/jn.1998.80.1.1. https://www.webofscience.com/wos/woscc/full-record/WOS:000074750800003.

Schultz, Wolfram, Peter Dayan, and Read Montague. 1997. "A neural substrate of prediction and reward." *Science* 275 (5306): 1593–1599. https://doi.org/10.1126/science.275.5306.1593. https://www.science.org/doi/https://doi.org/10.1126/science.275.5306.1593.

Solderpalm, Anna, and Kent Berridge. 2000. "Food intake after diazepam, morphine or muscimol: Microinjections in the nucleus accumbens shell." *Pharmacology, Biochemistry, and Behavior* 66 (2): 429–434. https://doi.org/https://doi.org/10.1016/S0091-3057(00)00220-3.

Stoljar, Daniel. 2015. "Physicalism." Stanford Encyclopedia of Philosophy. Stanford University. https://plato.stanford.edu/.

Svendsen, Lars. 1999/2005. *A philosophy of boredom (in English)*. Oslo: Universitetsforlaget (1999 (Norwegian) and Realtion Books 2005.

The Internet Encyclopedia of Philosophy. 2021. "Epicurus." In *The Internet Encyclopedia of Philosophy*.

CHAPTER 6

Does Consuming More Increase Well-Being? Is Getting Rich the Path to Happiness?

> Money is better than poverty, if only for financial reasons. (Woody Allen, Without Feathers 1975)

> Those who say that money can't buy happiness don't know where to shop. (Anonymous)

Does consuming more goods and services increase your WB? Does expanding your set of available paths?. Your available paths vary in the amounts of goods consumed; some, for example, have lots of leisure, but little is spent on goods and services. While in others, you work more, have more income, and buy more stuff. One's income limits expenditures, so newly available paths with more income make more consumption possible. This does not imply you will choose to consume more. For example, MacKenzie Scott could consume more goods and services than she does.[1] However, many spend all they make, so they need to switch to a path with more income if they want to consume more.

This chapter begins by reviewing the data and research on the influence of income on WB. Complicating is that some surveys ask about happiness, others about emotional WB or life-satisfaction WB. Or they ask about the emotion the subject is currently experiencing. Finally, some ask about

[1] She did not buy Twitter for fun and is not building a super yacht like her ex, Jeff.

E. R. Morey, *Deconstructing Behavior, Choice, and Well-being*, https://doi.org/10.1007/978-3-031-36712-0_6

something that isn't quite any of these. So, keeping track of what is asked in each survey is crucial. Of course, this would be less of an issue if income had the same effect on emotional WB and life-satisfaction WB, but this does not seem to be the case.

My read of the evidence on WB is that you will be better off if expanding your set of available paths allows you to go from a path that does not meet your basic needs to one that does: feeding the hungry increases their WB, so does giving those without shelter a roof, and so does giving those who face dangers a haven. However, once your basic needs are met, the evidence is mixed on whether more income will increase your long-run emotional WB—there will be a short-term happiness bump. And what you do with more income is important.

But the research also indicates that, at every time and place, the poor are less happy than the rich (report lower levels of emotional WB), even if their basic needs are met. This seems, at first, a quandary: more does not make most of us happier, at least not for long, but, at a point in time, more income relative to others does. The evidence suggests that over time a group's average emotional WB does not increase substantially as its average income increases. But, among group members at a point in time, those with less are less happy. How can both be true, and why?

The Evidence on the Relationship Between Income and Happiness: The Big Picture

The data, at first blush, can be confusing. In a 2008 article in the *Journal of Economic Literature*, Andrew Clark, Paul Frijters, and Michael Shields put the findings of studies in four categories (they use the word "happiness" to summarize the findings):

1. Country-level data shows average happiness remaining flat over time despite large increases in average income per capita.

But, when one looks at data on the individual level, the results indicate that

2. Across individuals at a point in time, reported happiness is higher for individuals with higher incomes. This effect is strongest in developing countries.

3. Panel data (data on income and reported happiness for the same individuals at different points in time) finds that an increase in an individual's income increases that individual's happiness, at least in the short run, but, again, more so in developing countries.
4. And, when one looks at large samples of aggregate data across countries and time, and one corrects for country fixed-effects (idiosyncrasies across countries), the higher a country's per-capita GDP, the happier it tends to be. Average happiness in a country is also positively related to how fast its per-capita GDP is growing relative to like countries.

I add two additional findings to their list:

5. The effect of income on life-satisfaction WB differs from its effect on emotional WB/happiness.
6. And both average emotional WB and average life-satisfaction WB are more sensitive to a decrease in national income than an increase.

Research on the relationship between income and WB is ongoing, so these six findings might not summarize what we know in five years. My goal is to discuss the fundamental issues and questions concerning the data, including (A) how to measure emotional WB/happiness and life-satisfaction WB and how to measure changes in their levels, (B) absolute income versus relative income, (C) that the data are diverse and not always comparable, and (D) WB is determined by many factors, making it challenging to identify their specific influence.

In sections "A Hypothesis: Your WB Is Determined More by Your Relative Position Than by Your Absolute Level of Consumption" and "Differences in Happiness, by Income, in the Same Society at a Point in Time Could, in Part, Be the Result of Expectations and Aspirations" of this chapter, I look at different theories of what determines WB and ask how well they explain the six categories of findings—but for now, consider just the data.

Data and Studies on the Relationship Between Income and WB

A Bit of History: The Easterlin Effect/Paradox

In 1974, Richard Easterlin pioneered the economic study of happiness, publishing "Does economic growth improve the human lot? Some empirical evidence." Its notable finding, now known as the *Easterlin Paradox*, is that while US aggregate income increased significantly between WWII and the early 1970s, reported happiness remained relatively flat—the Easterlin data is self-reported "happiness". This trend has continued: while real per-capita income increased nearly 100% between 1970 and 2004, there was no corresponding increase in average happiness. This finding upset a few economists: it suggests that economic growth isn't the path to increased WB. The Paradox is reflected in two figures in Clark et al. (2008) (https://www.researchgate.net/publication/4981498_Relative_Income_Happiness_and_Utility_An_Explanation_for_the_Easterlin_Paradox_and_Other_Puzzles). Their Fig. 1. Happiness and Real Income Per Capital in the United States, 1973–2004 has time on the horizontal axis (1973–2004) and on the vertical scale both average happiness and real income per capita in 2000 US$.[2] Average happiness fluctuated slightly but was almost the same in 2004 as in 1973.

Their Fig. 2: Life Satisfaction in Five European Countries, 1973–2004 has time on the horizontal axis and "Average Life Satisfaction" for each country on the vertical axis.[3] Like average happiness, life satisfaction remains flat: highest for the Netherlands and lowest for France and Italy, with the UK and Germany in the middle. Both average emotional WB and average life-satisfaction WB have remained flat as incomes have risen.

Psychologists and sociologists get the same result, and the Paradox holds for Japan.[4] In 1974, Easterlin concluded that average happiness

[2] "Happiness is the average reply to the following question: Taken all together, how would you say things are these days? (3) Very happy, (2) Pretty happy, and (1) Not too happy."

[3] "On the whole how satisfied are you with the life you lead. (4) Very satisfied, (3) Fairly satisfied, (2) Not very satisfied, and (1) Not at all satisfied."

[4] This growth-without-happiness paradox has been replicated in other countries and time periods by economists (e.g., David Blanchflower and Oswald 2004), psychologists (e.g., Edward Diener and Shigehiro Oishi 2000), political scientists

does not vary between rich and developing countries, and economic growth isn't the path to greater happiness. He recently moderated this conclusion.

While Easterlin found no temporal relationship between per-capita income and average happiness, he found a positive relationship between one's happiness and one's relative income at each point in time. This relative-position effect has since been seen in numerous contexts. For example, based on Eurobarometer data from 1975–1986 on 109 thousand Europeans, the economist Andrew Oswald (1997) reports that individuals in the lowest income quartile are less happy than those in the top quartile ("Very happy" 19% vs. 28% and "Not very happy" 27% vs. 13%).[5] More recent studies, using different reference groups and different measures of relative position, continue to find that relativeness matters for emotional WB/happiness.[6]

John Helliwell (2003) at the University of British Columbia has analyzed data on life-satisfaction WB, finding the relative-income effect different in OECD countries versus developing countries. In developing countries, the effect remains strong through all 10 deciles (each 10% income category from the lowest to the highest). For example, moving from the 80th income percentile to the 90th still significantly improves life-satisfaction WB. But in OECD countries, increasing relative income does not significantly improve life-satisfaction WB once one reaches the 40th percentile—surprising. Moving from the 40th percentile (top 60%) to the 99th (top 1%) requires a vast increase in income in OECD countries.

Measuring WB

Most measures of WB are self-reported ("What is your level of happiness on a scale of 1 to 5"). In 1974 (and still), economists dismissed Easterlin's findings because the data is not observed behavior but self-reported feelings—economists dismiss stated feelings and views. So, what

(e.g., Ronald Englehart and Hans-Dieter Klingemann 2000) and sociologists (e.g., Ruut Veenhoven 1993).

[5] For an Oswald talk on the economics of happiness see https://www.youtube.com/watch?v=Ggcexz4ZNLE.

[6] See Paul Dolan et al. (2008), David Dorn et al. (2007), Ada Ferrer-i-Carbonell (2005), and Erzo Luttmer (2005).

observed behaviors could be used to determine WB—facial expression? Body language? While neuroscientists use facial expressions to assess liking, can you imagine an economist measuring WB this way? Charles Darwin suggested both as windows into the emotions of animals. After winning an Oscar, Anne Hathaway's expression was described in *The New Yorker* as joy as only a child can express. Still, her expression pales compared to Alexander Gamme's reaction when he discovered a candy bar he had stowed on the way out on the 86th day of his solo trek to and from the South Pole. Emotional WB is not always so expressive. At the other extreme, one can observe behaviors indicative of extreme unhappiness, such as crying, frowning, shaking, lethargy, and suicide attempts, but unhappiness, like happiness, is often unexpressed. Blanchflower and Oswald (2008) find, using country-level data, a negative relationship between average happiness and the proportion with hypertension.[7] Hypertension and the hormone cortisol correlate with stress, making happiness less likely.

A researcher could use the assessments of friends and family (which happen to be significantly correlated with self-reported happiness), but many economists would reject these as unobjective.

Brain activity is objective in that it can be externally observed, at least in theory. And a specific pattern could be deemed a measure of emotional WB if most subjects report they are happy when this pattern is observed. Then, we would not have to ask if you're happy; instead, we would monitor your brain patterns in real time. In the future?[8]

Instead of directly asking about happiness, a few researchers have asked about the frequency and intensity of sensations and emotions experienced in the last hour or day, experiences such as joy, laughter, smiling, sadness, stress, and anger. The researchers then convert the answers into a level of happiness (emotional WB).[9] How to do this is now a research question,

[7] Countries with high hypertension happen to be countries where people are overweight. This raises the question of how happiness and being overweight are related. I know of no studies that look at this relationship, but many of us imagine we would be happier if we lost a few.

[8] See the discussion of hedonic hotspots in Chapter 4.

[9] Taking a middle approach to measuring emotional WB, the Health and Retirement Study at the U. of Michigan asks, "Please tell me if each of the following was true for you much of the time this past week: a) You felt you were happy b) You felt sad c) You enjoyed life d) You felt depressed."

motivated more by policymakers than economists: policymakers are asking for direct estimates of WB.[10]

NBT assumes that the individual chooses their highest-ranked available path, so economists are in a circular quandary when assessing WB. For example, when I buy a giant TV, it must increase my WB. Otherwise, I would not have bought it; if I say, "Buying it did not increase my WB." I must be wrong?

Admittedly, there are issues with comparing self-reported WB across individuals and even for the same individual at different points in time. Our short-term memories of sensations and emotions can be faulty. Culture, language, and expectations differ across individuals, so they complicate comparisons. For example, Italians report lower happiness than Germans, but this may be due to a cultural difference in how feelings are expressed. How happy you report to be may be a function of how happy you think you have the right to be or whether happiness is viewed as societally desirable.[11] Statistical models estimated with panel datasets are starting to be used to control for such idiosyncrasies (see categories 3 and 4 above), clarifying the picture.[12] But first, let's look at the time-series data.

Time-Series Data and the Difficulties in Determining the Influence of Income

To identify the influence of a change in aggregate income on either average emotional WB or life-satisfaction WB, one must control for all the changes that could affect WB. These include age composition, health, social institutions, and gender and racial equality. This isn't easy. For example, studies suggest that an individual's happiness is U-shaped by

[10] Daniel Benjamin et al. (2014) proposed an index for calculating your WB. It is a weighted average of your answers to questions that ask you to trade off different aspects of WB; for example, would you prefer to be less anxious or somewhat happier? Such questions differ from the standard, "How happy are you?" Or "How happy would this make you?" The weights in the index are estimated using the answers to such questions by many people. The estimated index is therefore a WB index for an average individual, not for a specific individual. The authors conservatively pitch their model as an initial step in the long process of building a WB index.

[11] For more on the measurement of happiness, see Diener (2000).

[12] Data on income, self-reported happiness, and other explanatory variables, for the same individuals at multiple points in time.

age, decreasing in one's twenties but increasing for old farts—like me. So, since many populations are aging, one must also determine how the changing age composition affects happiness to assess the influence of aggregate income on happiness.

Occasionally situations arise where an exogenous shock causes a large change in a country or region's GDP. For example, in east Germany, during the decade after reunification, both life-satisfaction WB and real income jumped, raising the question of whether the income increase caused the happiness increase. Part, but not all, of the jump can be attributed to more individuals fulfilling their basic needs. Explaining the rest requires separating the influences of increased income from increased freedoms and expectations. One must also factor in that incomes in east Germany rose relative to their neighbors: average income in Poland and west Germany did not rise.

At Each Point in Time, the Unemployed Are, on Average, Not as Happy as the Rest of Us

But this might not be because they have less to spend.

Nineteen percent of the individuals in the Eurobarometer data reported being "Not very happy"; but 33% of the unemployed are in this category. The unemployed are anxious and distressed. Interestingly, the highly educated unemployed are more unhappy than the lowly educated unemployed—a disconnect between expectations and outcome? The poorly educated are less surprised by unemployment, so they experience less distress when it occurs? Oswald suggests that most unemployment distress isn't caused by the loss of income but by a loss of self-esteem, a sense of failure, and embarrassment; being unemployed reduces one's status. Helliwell finds that the negative effect of unemployment on life-satisfaction WB is on par with a one-unit drop in one's health (health measured on a five-point scale).

One Study in Detail: The Happiness Bump

Seven-thousand eight-hundred and seventy-one Germans were followed from 1985 to 2000, with data collected yearly on their income and happiness. The sample consists of randomly selected individuals living in the Western part of Germany for whom there were at least five years of data. This is panel data, the beauty of which is that it is the same people, year after year, rather than sampling different people yearly. So one can rule out the possibility that answers are changing because this year's respondents differ from last year's.[13] The data has been analyzed by Rafael Di Tella, John Haisken-DeNew, and Robert MacCulloch (2010); nothing contradicts the Easterlin Paradox: income rose substantially while average reported happiness (on a 10-point scale) remained flat. See the graph at https://www.sciencedirect.com/science/article/abs/pii/S0167268110001952.

They also estimate a statistical model(s) of everyone's reported happiness as a function of their current income and job status; job status and income in prior years; socioeconomic characteristics including marital, employment, and educational level in each year; plus, gender and political orientation. The model includes individual-specific constants (individual "fixed effects") and year-specific constants, so it controls for the fact that some people are just naturally happier and that things change from year to year in ways the researcher can't always observe.

The results are summarized with two of their graphs. A permanent 50% increase in an individual's income is estimated to cause a temporary bump in their happiness, but after three years, most of it has been lost. In contrast, for most individuals, the increase that results from a permeant increase in status (an increase in relative position) persists for at least six years.

Summarizing their findings, most people get used to (adapt to) having more income and consumption, but the happiness increase from an increase in their status persists. There is minimal adaptation to increased status.[14]

When One Looks at Large Data Sets Across Countries and Corrects for Idiosyncrasies Across Them, Average Happiness Increases with Per-Capita Income but Only Slightly

This is the fourth category of finding. The higher the per-capita GDP in a country relative to other countries, the higher its average happiness tends to be—people in more affluent countries tend, on average, to be

[13] It does not control for age; the sample is necessarily aging.

[14] There are fascinating exceptions; those on the political right grow accustomed to an increase in their status, but the effect on their happiness of an increase in absolute income persists. Why?

somewhat happier. Still, the differences in income do not explain much of the variation in happiness across countries.

And, if two countries have similar per-capita incomes, the one where per capita is growing faster tends to be happier—high growth rates relative to others increase happiness.

These category four findings need to be squared with the Easterlin paradox—that increased aggregate income does not significantly increase a country's average happiness. Keep in mind: (1) Richer countries tend to be more democratic, tend to have more stable institutions, and individuals tend to have more rights and freedoms. All of these could increase both emotional and life-satisfaction WB. And (2) the fourth category of findings can be explained by relative position.

The Fifth Finding: Life-Satisfaction WB Increases (and Decreases) with Income

Kahneman and Deaton (2010) investigated a Gallup panel of Americans; each individual was repeatedly asked to separate their emotional WB from their life-satisfaction WB. Increases in yearly income increased emotional and life-satisfaction WB, but only for incomes less than $75K (2010 dollars). Beyond that, additional income grows life satisfaction but not emotional WB. Kahneman and Deaton define emotional WB as the "frequency and intensity of experiences of joy, stress, sadness, anger, and affection that makes one's life pleasant or unpleasant." Whereas they define life-satisfaction WB as "the thoughts people have about their life when they think about it."[15]

And Finally, the Sixth Finding: Both Emotional WB and Life-Satisfaction WB Are More Sensitive to a Decrease in National Income Than to an Increase

Using the same data as Kahneman and Deaton, De Neve and his coauthors find that an individual's emotional and life-satisfaction WB are more sensitive to a decrease in national income than an increase. A decrease of X will lower WB more than an increase of X will increase it. This can explain why, in the long run, average happiness did not increase even

[15] They use "WB" to refer to what I am calling life-satisfaction WB.

though real per-capita income rose substantially. Over the business cycle, the average individual's WB drops more when aggregate income declines than it rose when income grew. In the authors' words, "...recessions can rapidly undo the WB gains from longer expansionary periods and lead to an insignificant relationship between national income and average WB when considered in the long run."

Complementing their primary finding, they find that self-reported unhappiness (stress, worry, reduced joy) increases when aggregate income declines, but it does not wholly abate when income rebounds. Chapter 9 details a 2013 study by Christopher Boyce and coauthors that supports these conclusions.

A Hypothesis: Your WB Is Determined More by Your Relative Position Than by Your Absolute Level of Consumption

"Relative position" can be your position relative to others or your current position relative to your former self. For individuals whose basic needs are met, relative position can explain (1) why a permanent income increase does not cause a permanent increase in WB (emotional or life satisfaction) and (2) why an increase in relative income (status) can cause a long-term increase in both emotional and life-satisfaction WB. And (3) relative-position effects could explain why a loss of income decreases emotional WB more than an equal income increases it.[16]

The Relative-Income (Status) Hypothesis

> We all have strength enough to endure the misfortunes of others. (Francois de La Rochefoucauld, French essayist 1613–1680). I would add *and the rich have the most endurance*

[16] Looking ahead, Chapter 9 discusses the *endowment* effect: a loss of income decreases WB more than an income increase of the same magnitude increases WB. The typical economic explanation for the endowment effect is loss aversion—we are averse to losses. The endowment effect explains, in part, why an increase in average National income over the long-run does not necessarily cause an increase in average emotional WB: economic contractions decrease emotional WB more than expansions increase emotional WB. To re-acquire the level of emotional WB you had before the great recession, the subsequent expansion will need to raise your income substantially above what it was pre-recession.

> What everyone most aims at in ordinary contact with his fellows is to prove them inferior to himself. (Arthur Schopenhauer, German philosopher 1788–1860)

You would be happier if you continue to consume the same path of goods and services, but your neighbors and peers come to consume less, making you relatively better off. And you would be less happy if your consumption remains constant and they increase their consumption: you are relatively worse off.[17]

The relative-income hypothesis is consistent with the finding that, at a point in time, people at the bottom of the scale are less happy than those at the top—those at the bottom are, by definition, "poor." Data indicates that the poor perceive the world as largely beyond their control, controlled by those higher up the socioeconomic ladder. This perceived lack of control—a correct perception—causes stress. We all experience stress, but those higher up the ladder have more control over their stressors and more resources to deal with them. One result is that the poor don't live long, suffering more from diabetes and hypertension. Their quality of life is further depressed because the rest of us have little empathy. Research by Dacher Keltner, Kraus, and others shows that we pay less attention to those lower down the scale and more to those higher up. Those at the scale's bottom are invisible to those at the top—an interpersonal empathy-gap. When individuals of different statuses meet, the higher-status individual signals disregard for the other person by talking

[17] One could hypothesize the opposite. One might be happier if there are people consuming paths with more consumption than yours because their existence makes you believe you will eventually be consuming more: observing others with more fuels the American Dream? This alternative could explain why many poor Americans do not want the rich taxed more because they hope to be rich one day.

Recent research indicates that Americans seriously overestimate the potential for upward mobility. For the rich, the overestimation justifies their wealth, and for the poor, it gives them more hope than there is. Subjects in one study were asked to estimate the probability that a randomly selected individual currently in the bottom 20% income category (the poorest quintile [1/5]) would move up. For moving from the bottom quintile into the top three (top 60% of incomes), the average estimate was that 45% would move up, but just 30% do. Conservatives overestimate more than liberals. In another study, respondents overestimated the probability by five-fold that a college student came from the bottom quintile. Michael Kraus, Shai Davidai, and David Nussbaum conclude that "Taken together, these sets of results suggest that belief in the American dream is woefully misguided when compared to objective reality" (*New York Times* 2009).

at them, not listening to them, and looking past them. A 2013 *NY Times* article sums it up, "Rich people just care less." When we do pay attention, we higher up the scale tend to believe those lower are lower for a good reason, that "social class has an underlying, inherent or natural foundation" (Kraus and Keltner 2013). We feel our higher rank is justified. People at the bottom, in contrast, think that relative position is the luck of the draw.[18]

The influence of relative position and status harps back to Rousseau. He blamed property rights, markets, commerce, and the Enlightenment—beyond what you would find in a village—for creating an unnatural desire to want more than others. The result is unhappiness. The institutions that allow us to consume more lead to misery because we acquire a desire (an unnatural desire) for a higher relative position.[19]

[18] Covering four studies (Paul Piff et al. 2010), found lower-class individuals to be more generous, charitable, trusting, and helpful because "of a greater commitment to egalitarian values and feelings of compassion."

[19] Rousseau did not believe the desire genetic; for him, it started when a man first enclosed a field and claimed "Ceci est a moi." It's an interesting conjecture: property rights, the institution that has made it possible for us to consume great amounts of goods and services, make us unsatisfied; they bring inequality because with them comes the potential to concentrate them. Paraphrasing the philosopher Melissa Lane, the Enlightenment propelled the idea that we all could have a higher standard of living (progress) if we commercialized society (more buying, selling, profits and property rights, more competition). Hume, Smith, and Rousseau all believed commercialization would increase consumption. Rousseau argued that it would not bring happiness because it creates a system based on desires (Assumption 9b), including the desire to have more than others. Paraphrasing Rousseau, commercialization changes a man from a virtuous independent (a noble farmer in a small village) to a pursuer of desires who competes with others for self-esteem in the eyes of others. Commercialization is driven by pride, vanity, and esteem-seeking; it creates a world where you can never be satisfied, an unnatural world. He argues that the market system makes us unhappy because it causes inequality and neighbor-lusting. Long before Marx and Hegel, Rousseau was criticizing the market system. Economists tend to dismiss Rousseau's economic views, but it is the case that once basic needs are met, increased consumption does not always increase emotional WB.

[An aside: Rousseau was an early environmentalist arguing that commercialization would cause significant environmental degradation (large, polluted cities and the destruction of nature). He harped for a return to nature, not a return to "acorn grubbing": a return to a simple agricultural society organized around the family and the village.]

Rousseau was emotional and passionate[20]—a bit kinky—and felt emotions should play a larger role. He distinguished between desires and needs, finding desires evil. Echoing Rousseau, the American economist, sociologist, and critic of capitalism, Thorsten Veblen (1857–1929), in his famous 1899 book *The Theory of the Leisure Class*, harangued relative consumption, calling it "pecuniary emulation". Veblen is responsible for the term "conspicuous consumption"—showing off with goods—arguing that demonstrating superiority with goods replaces showing off with excess leisure (a leisure class) as an economy matures.

Who Do We Compare with? And Do We Compare Only in Terms of Income?

Why do we compare? Social psychologists have *social-comparison theory*: we use other people to gather information about ourselves (Leon Festinger 1954). Comparison is part of our quest to make ourselves feel better.[21] Social comparison theory and the data indicate that you compare with those like you, those you know: neighbors, relatives, friends, co-workers, your ethnic group, and your age cohort. For example, data from the National Survey of Families and Households find your happiness negatively correlates with your neighbors' incomes, and the effect is stronger the more you socialize with them.

As noted, a jump in personal income temporarily increases happiness (emotional WB). While part of the happiness bump is attributable to consuming more new stuff, part is because we have improved our position relative to others, including our past selves. And like the effect of

[20] Hume referred to Rousseau as the "wild philosopher" noting he "is plainly mad after long having been maddish." Rousseau thought a lot of people, including Hume, were out to get him—a few were. He was paranoid and had visions. And he dropped his five children off, one by one, at the foundling asylum. In the 1890 *American J. of Psychology*, there is an article titled "The insanity of Jean-Jacque Rousseau": it is an early example of psychological profiling, stating "that Rousseau was insane is generally, but not universally, admitted." The article presents the evidence.

[21] Quoting Morey and David Kritzberg (2012), "Motives for the drive include self-enhancement, perceptions of relative standing, maintaining a positive self-image, and closure…Studies indicate that the inclination to socially compare is positively correlated with (1) low self-esteem and neuroticism, (2) a strong interest in others and what they feel, and (3) having a 'high chronic activation of the self'…".

consuming new stuff, this self-effect must be temporary because our new self will become our old self.

Residents of a region or country also compare their per-capita GDP and its growth rate with these measures in other places. This affects happiness; another country can be part of one's reference group. We get a happiness bump from living in a more affluent and faster-growing country, and this bump persists if our country's relative advantage persists. Although US, European, and Canadian residents are affected by each other's per-capita income, we are not affected ours relative to the per-capita income of Liberia.

While Our Happiness Is Influenced by Our Relative Income, It Is Also Influenced by Our Relative Position on Other Scales

This has not gotten enough attention. Tim Wadsworth, a sociologist at the University of Colorado, finds that happiness increases in how often you have sex relative to the average for your age/gender cohort.[22] Besides sex and money, people compare based on commodities (e.g., cars, houses), athletic accomplishments, the accomplishments of one's children, and the attractiveness of one's partner.[23]

Loss of White Privilege

> You see a common pattern in the Capital insurrections. They are mainly middle-class to upper-middle-class whites who are worried that, as social changes occur around them, they will see a decline in their status in the future. (Robert Pape, as quoted in *The Washington Post*, April 6, 2021)
>
> In the aftermath of the Capital attack, the polling firm Echelon Insights decided to ask voters a simple question: Do they think the goal of politics is more about "enacting good policy" or "ensuring the country's survival as we know it?"… nearly half [of Republicans] said it's about survival. (Brooks 2021)
>
> A February [2021] Economist-YouGov poll asked Americans which statement is closest to their view: "It's a big, beautiful world, mostly full of

[22] A positive correlation between sex and happiness does not imply that more sex results in more happiness: maybe happy people are more inclined.

[23] I spend a great deal of time training, so I can bike faster and longer than my biker friends, or at least not be too far behind. My comparison group used to be all Boulder bikers; then I reduced it to females and older males; now it is limited to senior citizens.

> good people, and we must find a way to embrace each other and not allow ourselves to become isolated" or "Our lives are threatened by terrorists, criminals and illegal immigrants, and our priority should be to protect ourselves."...Over 75% of Biden voters chose "a big beautiful world." Two-thirds of Trump voters chose "our lives are threatened."

The University of *Chicago Project on Security and Threats* (CPOST) analyzed the home-county demographics of the 337 (to date) Americans arrested or charged in the January 6th Capital siege. Ninety-five percent are white, and 85% are male. Only 10% have ties to right-wing groups, and approximately half are from Blue counties. Their significant finding: "Counties with the most significant declines in the non-Hispanic white population are the most likely to produce insurrectionists who now face charges" (*Washington Post*, April 6, 2021).[24] That is, from counties where the proportion of non-whites is growing the fastest. CPOST (February and March 2021) found that a primary motivator is *The Great Replacement*: the fear that minorities and immigrants will take over the country.[25]

The loss of privilege does not need to be realized; its perception is enough to cause anguish. Hopefully, a realized loss of white privilege will increase the WB of non-whites.

If We Compare on Multiple Dimensions, the Rate at Which You Will Substitute Higher Status on One Scale for a Reduction on Another Is Critical

I can spend more time publishing research papers to increase my professional status, but that would leave less time for training to maintain my position in my cycling gruppo. So, what's my rate of exchange? Parents sacrifice the McMansion to send their children to a prestigious college—a few have risked jail by bribing a USC rowing coach. Capital insurrectionists risked jail to support white privilege. [A few rioters advertised

24 "... the [U.S.] counties that saw the greatest decline in White population had an 18% chance of sending an insurrectionist to D.C.; while the counties that saw the least decline had only a 3% chance."

25 Some in White America are experiencing an "actual or potential loss of dominance, a sense of resentment at this loss which is bound up with issues of entitlement—the undeserving are taking what we deserve"—"dominant group victimhood" (Stephen Reicher and Yasemin Ulusahin 2020).

their crimes on social media.] Alternatively, could those who suffer racial discrimination be made whole with money (e.g., payments to Black Americans to offset discrimination or reparations for native Americans sent to residential schools)?

Differences in Happiness, by Income, in the Same Society at a Point in Time Could, in Part, Be the Result of Expectations and Aspirations

Comparing to Your Past and Future Self

You are unhappy because you feel underpaid relative to your peers and ability. You are disappointed because your pay does not meet your expectations, expectations driven by your assessments of your ability, relative ability, and sense of what is fair.

Aspirations (what you aspire to and want to achieve) are influenced by what others have. For example, a peer with a higher income can make you believe a raise is plausible. Research by the Swiss economist Alois Stutzer and others indicates that high-income aspirations and expectations reduce happiness. Aspirations are often thwarted, more so for the poor. A few are poor because they lack aspirations (the happy poor?), but most of us, even the poor, aspire. Thwarted expectations cause frustration; frustration leads to discouragement—not a pretty picture. In animals, stress that can't be controlled leads to *learned helplessness*.[26] The picture is quite unpleasant if you expect that your aspirations will come true, and they don't. Danes appear happier than other Europeans. It is suggested that this is because Demark has, relatively speaking, more income equality, making it unrealistic for Danes to aspire to a higher relative income.

[26] An animal repeatedly subjected to an unpleasant stimulus they can't control learns to stop trying to avoid the stimulus, even when avoidance becomes possible.

If Emotional or Life-Satisfaction WB Is Determined by Relative Status, What Would Increase Aggregate WB?

This section is about what policies would increase aggregate WB if relative-status effects exist. It isn't about whether invoking such policies is the right thing to do. And while people care about their WB, it isn't clear they care much about increasing the WB of most others.

If relative position in society is more important than absolute income in determining WB, increasing aggregate income will not necessarily increase aggregate WB. Depending on how the increase is distributed, it may even decrease. When my income increases but not yours, it reduces your WB: your relative income has declined. So, unconstrained in pursuing a higher income, I will strive too much from your perspective. I inefficiently work too much from society's perspective—so do you; Robert Frank discussed this in 1997.

If earning more increases your WB but reduces the WB of others, what WB-increasing policies might be pursued? A standard economic solution would be to raise marginal income-tax rates at the high end (make the tax more progressive) to encourage you to work less and earn less. [Like taxing cigarettes to discourage too much smoking: using the tax to increase the private cost of smoking (or working) so it equals the societal cost.]

At the high end, after-tax income will decline because taxes have increased and possibly also decline because those at the high end may choose to work less: they would keep less of every additional dollar. There is scant evidence that more progressive tax rates would cause the rich in the United States to work less or earn less. Given the current marginal tax rates, increasing progressiveness would not decrease the amount we work. Moreover, US tax rates are historically low and low compared to other countries. Detailed analysis by the French economist Thomas Piketty (author of Capital in the Twenty-First Century) and the Berkeley economist Emmanuel Saez indicates that higher marginal tax rates would not retard economic growth.

Consistent with their conclusion, the Scandinavian countries and Nederland have higher marginal and effective tax rates than the United States and higher labor-force participation rates (more women work). See A big safety net and strong job market can coexist, *NY Times*, December 17, 2014.

The United States has one of the lowest effective tax rates and one of the lowest labor-force participation rates. [Denmark, with one of the world's highest labor-force participation rates, ranks near the top on measures of happiness and life satisfaction. This suggests work may even increase happiness if the stress of working and raising a family is reduced by a safety net for childcare and health services.]

So, what would happen to relative-income positions in the United States if taxes were made more progressive without affecting total tax revenues?[27] The rich would pay more and the poor less, but no one's income rank (first, second, ..., last) would change. The income distribution would squish—we would move closer to our richer and poorer peers.

Whether this squishing would increase or decrease WB depends on how it affects perceived status and expectations: the rich would not be as rich as they were compared to you, but the poor would not be as poor, and the number of people with incomes similar to yours would increase. How this would affect average WB is difficult to nail down. For example, Scandinavian countries rank high in happiness rankings, but why? Is it because of their progressive tax rates or robust safety nets, or because their populations are ethically and racially more homogenous?[28] Or maybe all three.

Another critical but unanswered question is how average WB is affected by wealth distribution compared to income distribution. Ways to squish the wealth distribution (as compared to the income distribution) include wealth and inheritance taxes.

Numerous developed countries restrict hours of work (35-hour workweeks, 6 weeks of mandatory vacation). Increasing the cost of working more makes sense on efficiency grounds if people gain status by working more than their peers, so reduce the status of those who don't—picture new associates at a high-powered law firm.

Relative consumption is influenced by public commodities (those consumed by all[29]) and government services such as education and

[27] More progressive taxes do not mean that tax revenues will necessarily increase; they might even decrease. If tax revenues are affected, what happens to emotional WB will also depend on what is cut from or added to the budget.

[28] When I was a professor in Norway, my marginal tax rate was 90%.

[29] A public commodity is a commodity that once produced is consumed/experienced by all, whether they like it or not. A standard example is national defense. Fighting the

healthcare. For example, resources allocated to building a McMansion benefit primarily its inhabitants in absolute and relative terms, but resources allocated to increasing national security make us all more secure. Government-provided healthcare increases the real income of the poor more than the rich. In a market economy, allocating more resources to produce private goods will typically lead to more consumption disparity than allocating those resources to producing public goods or government-provided services.

To be clear, I am not claiming that increased income equality and spending more on public goods will, for sure, increase WB. Rather, I am pointing out that relative-income/status effects should not be ignored if the intent is to increase WB. Income inequality is rising. In the United States, 60% of the increase in US national income between 1977 and 2007 went to just the top 1% of earners. While, among white Americans who do not have a college degree, despair and deaths of despair (e.g., suicides and overdoses) are rising alarmingly (Ann Case and Deaton 2020, 2021; Carol Graham 2021).[30]

In summary, relative effects are critical and complicated. Despite this, most modern economists ignore them, and all economists ignore relative effects on dimensions other than income/consumption. NBT can accommodate relative effects if my ordering of paths depends on what I consume and what those in my reference groups are consuming.

Other Data and Theories Suggest Income and Wealth Are Not Major Determinants of Happiness, Nor WB

This section relates four different perspectives on the causes of WB, starting with genetics and what happened when you were a baby.

war in Iraq was a public commodity, a public good for some, a bad for others. Polar bears saved from extinction is a public commodity: if they are saved for you, they are saved for me, whether I like it or not.

[30] Quoting Case and Deaton (2021), "Deaths of despair, morbidity, and emotional distress continue to rise in the United States. The increases are largely borne by those without a four-year college degree—the majority of American adults. For many less-educated Americans, the economy and society are no longer providing the basis for a good life."

One's Happiness Has a Set Point from Which It Is, Long Run, Difficult to Deviate?

Adam Smith, a former Chair of Moral Philosophy at Glasgow University, thought so:

> The mind of every man, in a longer or shorter time, returns to it natural and usual state of tranquility. In prosperity, after a certain time, it falls back to that state; in adversity, after a certain time, it rises up to it.—The Theory of Moral Sentiments (1759/2022)

If we each have our own fixed baseline happiness, our *fixed point*, and our basic needs are met, market outcomes, government policies, and making more money can't make you happier, at least not for long. Nothing can—they also can't permanently decrease your WB.[31]

Even the death of a loved one only affects WB for a while. Kimball et al. (2015) investigated. See Fig. 1 at https://www.nber.org/papers/w21365: Emotional WB is on the vertical axis. It takes, on average, six months for an adult to rebound from the loss of their mother but five years if they lose a child.

The early set-point research suggested a lifetime baseline of happiness determined by genetics and one's infancy. However, more recent research by the same researchers suggests the point is quasi-fixed rather than a hard fix: something that can, with effort, be modified. And not necessarily with more goods.

In a seminal 1996 study, David Lykken and Auke Tellegen, then psychology professors at the U. of Minnesota, interviewed thousands of reared-apart identical twins. They found that 44% to 52% of the variation in reported happiness across individuals could be attributed to genetics. Having resampled those twins for years, they concluded that 80% of an individual's stated happiness was inherited. Differences in income,

[31] Forty years ago, Philip Brickman, a young and rising psychologist, was the first to investigate the fixed-point hypothesis. He interviewed lottery winners ($50K to $1M), and individuals paralyzed in accidents (Brickman , Dan Coates, and Ronnie Janoff-Bulman 1978). The interviews were within a year of the event. The victims were less happy than they were before their accidents, but not as much as one would expect, and the winner assessed their current level of happiness as the same as it was before their winning. A few years later, Brickman jumped off a ten-story building—after years of depression. He accepted that his fixed point was depression, and there was no long-run escape (Jennifer Senior 2020).

marital status, education, and other observed socioeconomic characteristics explain a few percent of the variation. They concluded that how happy you are, compared to me, is primarily determined by your genes. Their paper ends with the quote,

> It may be trying to be happier is as futile as trying to be taller and therefore counterproductive.

In 2000, after more research, Lykken tempered his conclusion, stating that while a lot of happiness is determined by genes, the environment is also influential. He concludes you can increase your fixed point by changing your attitude and developing solid relationships. Both require conscious effort.

In 2005, Frank Fujita and Diener addressed whether one's life satisfaction is predetermined. By following 2,336 men and 2,873 women over 17 years, they found that while there is a "soft baseline" for life satisfaction, "some individuals do change significantly," and small fluctuations in happiness are common, some lasting for years.

Personality

One hypothesis to explain a quasi-fixed baseline happiness is through personality: assume personality is a prime determinant of one's WB and that personality is quasi-fixed.

In the Big Five model of personality, a dominant model in psychology, personality has five dimensions: openness to experience, conscientiousness, extroversion, agreeableness, and neuroticism, and one's position on these dimensions can be determined using standard tests.

Numerous studies indicate that neuroticism and extroversion are strong predictors of WB. The more neurotic one is (the extent to which one reacts to setbacks, risks, and ignorance with negative emotions), the less happy. Extroverts tend to spend more time socializing, which is why some researchers hypothesize that extroverts report more life-satisfaction WB. Being an introvert, I don't buy this! The other three dimensions influence whether an individual is likely to put himself in WB-enhancing situations. One study estimated that at least 35% of the variation across individuals in life-satisfaction WB is due to personality variation (Alex Wood, Steven Joseph, and John Maltby 2008).[32]

[32] Boyce, Wood, and Nattavudh Powdthavee et al. (2013) survey this literature.

The historical view was that personality is effectively fixed by adulthood. If personality is fixed and affects life satisfaction, it is accounted for in WB studies with *fixed effects*. These individual-specific constant terms capture all the reasons why individuals differ, including, but not limited to, their personality differences. Fixed effects are how individual idiosyncrasies are typically accounted for in statistical models.

More recent research shows that personality is malleable, but change takes time. An Australian panel data set follows the same households over time, asking the respondent Big Five personality questions and a life-satisfaction question ("How satisfied are you with your life, all things considered? a 10-pt. scale"). The data set also includes household income, job status, and other possible determinants of life satisfaction. Based on this data from over eight-thousand individuals, Boyce, Wood, and Powdthavee find that personality variation across individuals explains more of the variation in life satisfaction than does variation in income and job status—confirming previous findings. And, for an individual, more of the changes in life satisfaction over time is explained by personality changes than income and job-status changes.

* * *

What are the implications if WB is quasi-fixed for whether consuming more increases WB? While one can tell a story consistent with more consumption results in more short-run WB, if WB is quasi-fixed, increasing consumption will not permanently increase WB—if WB is quasi-fixed, Adam Smith was mostly correct. The quasi-fixed research suggests it isn't more consumption that increases long-term WB, but more and better relationships and conscious efforts to improve how you experience your life: actions such as meditation, exercise, therapy, and religion.[33] SSRIs, and other depression and anxiety-reducing drugs, can also make life more enjoyable for long periods. At this point, I expect you might conclude, "Morey has lived in Boulder, a rich, liberal enclave, for too long, so he thinks the road to salvation is to give up one's worldly pursuits for a yoga mat." In my defense, I don't do real yoga, but rather

[33] People actively involved with religion are, on average, happier than those who are not; one reason is social involvement and support. Therapies such as cognitive behavioral therapy can be effective in reducing anxiety, and so can exercise and meditation.

geezer (Kaiut) yoga, and while I don't own a mat, my wife owns a booster.

Economists implicitly reject the hypothesis that WB is quasi-fixed. One possible reconciliation is that an increase in income beyond what is needed to fulfill basic needs does not increase long-run emotional WB but does increase long-run life satisfaction. Note that economicus can have a quasi-fixed WB: NBT does not preclude it.

Chapter 8 will review psychological studies on how and why we adapt to good and bad events. Again, the findings are consistent with a soft happiness baseline. For example, a recent study found that patients on dialysis were no less happy after getting used to dialysis than a control group.

WB Is Created by Doing, Not by Acquiring?

Picture a New Yorker cartoon from Jun. 23, 2014: a dog, having climbed the mountain, attentively waits on the words of wisdom from the monk sitting cross-legged in front of his cave. The caption: *The bone isn't the reward—digging for the bone is the reward.* My first thought was that the monk does not understand dogs, but he does.

Bertrand Russell's gardener:

> When I was a boy, I knew a man bursting with happiness whose business was digging wells. He was of enormous height and of incredible muscles, he could neither read nor write, and when in 1885 he got a vote for Parliament, he learnt for the first time that such an institution existed. His happiness did not depend on intellectual sources; it was not based upon belief in natural law, or the perfectibility of the species, or the public ownership of public utilities, or the ultimate triumph of the Seventh Day Adventists, or .... It was based on physical vigor, a sufficiency for work, and the overcoming of not insuperable obstacles in the shape of rock. The happiness of my gardener is of the same species; he wages a perennial war against rabbits, of which he speaks exactly as Scotland Yard speaks of Bolsheviks; he considers them dark, designing and ferocious, and is of the opinion that they can only be met by means of a cunning equal to their own. Like the heroes of Valhalla who spend every day hunting a certain wild boar, which they killed every evening but which miraculously came to life again in the morning, my gardener can slay the enemy one day without any fear that the enemy will have disappeared the next day. Although well

over seventy, he works all day and bicycles sixteen hilly miles to and from his work, but the fount of joy is inexhaustible, and it is "they rabbits" that supply it—Russell, 1930, The Conquest of Happiness

Increasing their incomes would have decreased their emotional and life-satisfaction WB if it relieved them from their battles with rabbits and rocks. In contrast to income, health and vigor allowed them to battle longer. NB Russell's choice of the word "conquest". Work, not consumption, produced their WB.

US job satisfaction isn't increasing; in 2013, fewer than half of American workers were satisfied with their jobs; in 1987, when the Conference Board's survey started, it was 61%.

Mihály Csíkszentmihályi's Flow

The psychologist Mihály Csíkszentmihályi pioneered the survey technique of contacting people randomly during the day to ask what they are doing and how they feel (*experience sampling*). Based on his findings, in 1990, he published *Flow: The Psychology of Optimal Experience*. A president of the American Psychological Association, Martin Seligman, has called him the world's leading researcher in "positive psychology."

Flow is an experience, the experience of being so involved in an activity that one loses one's sense of time and oneself. One is motivated and engaged with no desire to be elsewhere—one is "in the zone", focused, and goal-directed. There is neither anxiety nor depression. The experience is enjoyable and rewarding, but unconsciously rather than self-reflectively. While flowing, you would never say, "Boy, Am I having fun!"; it would not cross your mind; you're too busy doing what you are doing. Russell's gardener and well-digger achieved flow daily.

Csíkszentmihályi introduced flow to modern Western science, but he isn't the originator; it, and the benefits of achieving it, is foundational in Taoism, Hinduism, and Buddhism.

Flow is achieved by performing activities with the right amount of challenge: too little, and one becomes bored; too much and frustration results. Appropriate challenges match your intelligence, education, and skill set. Ideally, one's work is a flow experience: one faces problems and tasks that are challenging but doable. Social interactions can, but often don't, produce flow. And, unless one is pretty dull, watching TV will not generate flow, but playing a suitable video game will. Flow requires the perception of control: one must perceive influence and a prospect of success. Individuals who are self-motivated and curious are more inclined to experience flow.

From a Western perspective, flow activities are non-traditional happiness. The experience can be fleeting, but it can also last for extended periods (artists and scientists can spend hours or days engrossed in a project that produces flow). It can be repeated if one chooses suitable activities. Playing games, playing a musical instrument, and sports can be flow activities, and so can hobbies. For me, writing this book produced flow. Flow isn't sensual pleasure (like sex, scratching, or a great taste), nor does it necessarily involve doing anything meaningful. One can get flow from doing crossword puzzles but doing them does not give one's life meaning or contribute to the greater good. While, after the fact, people describe flow experience as enjoyable, the enjoyment isn't conscious during flow.

The pursuit of flow is consistent with the NBT if paths that generate flow are high in one's ordering. Flow WB does not depend on one's income if one has enough income to meet one's basic needs; it typically does not require acquiring more possessions. Flow WB is inconsistent with a job numbing in its boredom or far beyond one's ability. Flow outside of work requires time to peruse flow activities. Interestingly, we do not pursue flow experiences but seek distractions like watching TV.

Buddhist Flow: It's the Job, Not What the Wages Allow You to Consume

Economists typically consider working a necessary evil. The Buddhist view is that an ideal job, ***Right Livelihood***, not consumption, makes us better off (ends our suffering and awakens us). Right Livelihood is part of the Buddhist Eight-fold path. E.F. Schumacher, in his often reprinted "Buddhist Economics," referring to the modern economist, says,

> His fundamental criteria for success is simply the total quantity of goods produced during a given period of time.... From a Buddhist point of view, this is standing the truth on its head by considering goods more important than people and consumption as important as creative activity....For the modern economist, this is difficult to understand. He is used to measuring the 'standard of living' by the amount of annual consumption, assuming... a man who consumes more is 'better off...

Quoting from earlier,

> The Buddhist point of view takes the function of work to be at least threefold: to give man a chance to utilise and develop his faculties; to enable him to overcome his ego-centredness by joining with other people in a common task, and to bring forth goods and services needed for a becoming existence. To organise work in such a manner that it becomes meaningless, boring, stultifying, or nerve-racking for the worker would be little short of criminal;...Equally, to strive for leisure as an alternative to work would be considered a complete misunderstanding of one of the basic truths of human existence, namely that work and leisure are complementary parts of the same living process and cannot be separated without destroying the joy of work and the bliss of leisure.

Consider Adam Smith's famous pin factory (it produces straight pins). Smith compares the number manufactured if each pin is manufactured by one worker (he cuts the wire, sharpens one end, etc.) to specialization, where each worker does one of eighteen steps. Smith convincingly shows that specialization will lead to more pins per day (it's more efficient—increased output with no input increase).[34]

[34] "To take an example, therefore, from a very trifling manufacture; but one in which the division of labour has been very often taken notice of, the trade of the pin-maker; a workman not educated to this business (which the division of labour has rendered a distinct trade), nor acquainted with the use of the machinery employed in it (to the invention of which the same division of labour has probably given occasion), could scarce, perhaps, with his utmost industry, make one pin in a day, and certainly could not make twenty. But in the way in which this business is now carried on, not only the whole work is a peculiar trade, but it is divided into a number of branches, of which the greater part are likewise peculiar trades. One man draws out the wire, another straights it, a third cuts it, a fourth points it, a fifth grinds it at the top for receiving the head; to make the head requires two or three distinct operations; to put it on, is a peculiar business, to whiten the pins is another; it is even a trade by itself to put them into the paper; and the important business of making a pin is, in this manner, divided into about eighteen distinct operations, which, in some manufactories, are all performed by distinct hands, though in others the same man will sometimes perform two or three of them. I have seen a small manufactory of this kind where ten men only were employed, and where some of them consequently performed two or three distinct operations. But though they were very poor, and therefore but indifferently accommodated with the necessary machinery, they could, when they exerted themselves, make among them about twelve pounds of pins in a day. There are in a pound upwards of four thousand pins of a middling size. Those ten persons, therefore, could make among them upwards of forty-eight thousand pins in a day. Each person, therefore, making a tenth part of forty-eight thousand pins, might

For a Buddhist, this conclusion, while correct, misses the point. With specialization, the work is tedious and stultifying, so, quoting Schumacher, "little short of criminal." At this point, an economist would say that specialization will lead to higher wages, which will compensate for the tedium. They would be correct if unfulfilling work and goods are WB-commensurable. Buddhists reject this.

Buddhism rejects the belief that increased income leads to increase happiness. Economicus could have an ordering based on Buddhist principles: there isn't anything in NBT that implies that more WB requires more consumption or possessions.

One critical factor for work satisfaction is workplace trust (trust in management and co-workers), and work satisfaction is strongly and positively linked to life-satisfaction WB. A 2009 Helliwell study finds that moving up one place on a 10-point scale of workplace trust has the same effect on life-satisfaction WB as a forty-percent bump in income—Wow! Unfortunately, there is little research on how WB varies by job and profession. The evidence on whether the self-employed are happier is mixed. One study finds a self-employment happiness bump but only for the self-employed that are rich.

Decreasing Your Ill-Being by Being Less Reactive

In this Buddhist perspective, a typical life includes a lot of ill-being (unhappiness). And most of it is unnecessary but challenging to avoid because evolution has predisposed us to react in ways that cause ill-being—*dukkha* (Pāli).[35] Dukkha is often translated as "suffering" and not

be considered as making four thousand eight hundred pins in a day. But if they had all wrought separately and independently, and without any of them having been educated to this peculiar business, they certainly could not each of them have made twenty, perhaps not one pin in a day; that is, certainly, not the two hundred and fortieth, perhaps not the four thousand eight hundredth part of what they are at present capable of performing, in consequence of a proper division and combination of their different operations" (Smith 1791/2022).

[35] This is one view, my view, of how Buddhism would describe the Buddhist process of decreasing your personal ill-being. [Buddhism as an ethic is considered in Chapter 11.] While I am not a Buddhist, I am interested in it from ethics, WB, and choice perspectives. Some Buddhists would assess my view as a wrong view. There are different schools with different canons, and statements within them can conflict. There is debate as to which are the Buddha's original words. Nothing was written down until hundreds of years after he died (c.480–c.400 BCE), and was first written in Pāli, now extinct—a language he did

just physical suffering. It includes existential gloom and unsatisfactoriness. So, the way to increase your WB is to reduce unnecessary ill-being.

I discuss this Buddhist perspective because while it rejects increased wealth and status as ways to greater WB, an economicus could be on a Buddhist path. What modern psychology and behavioral economics say about behavioral quirks can be discovered in historical Buddhism—see Chapters 8 and 9. [And, looking ahead, WC and Buddhist ethics have a lot in common.]

Dukkha comes with the bad and the good; it is the way of life:

> Birth is duhhka, aging is duhhka, sickness is duhhka, death is duhhka, encountering what is not dear is duhhka, separation from what is dear is duhhka, not getting what one wants is duhhka. (Bhikkhu Bodhi 2000, p. 1844)

While dukkha has multiple sources, one cause is not accepting that life and its components are impermanent. Impermanence is what makes a life a life. All relationships will end; all possessions will be lost. Pleasures, such as sex, drugs, and rock-n-roll, are tainted: one knows the sensations will soon be over, the act can be illicit, and it is often regretted the next morning. [Giacomo, my dog, unlike humans, does not suffer from knowing all is impermanent—lucky him, but he suffers in other ways.]

The first step in reducing dukkha is to understand that, typically, life is dukkha (worse case: life is shit, and then you die).

A cause is t*aṇhā* (Pāli: craving, thirsting, desiring, reacting). Buddhism teaches that humans naturally order paths based on wants and desires (Assumption 9b), and this is misguided: it is negatively correlated with an ordering based on WB (9a). As I noted in Chapter 2, "craving" is a synonym for "wanting and desiring" but with a negative edge, chosen to draw the critical Buddhist distinction between want fulfillment and WB.

> If we understand dukkha as shorthand for 'life', we can think of taṇhā as shorthand for the myriad reactions that life provokes in us. (Batchelor 2015)

not speak. In summary, there are diverse takes on historical and modern Buddhism—as with Christianity.

Through years of meditation and study, a select few can reach a state where they no longer crave. But, unfortunately, most will never attain that state: we will continue to want and desire. And with effort, we can become less responsive/reactive to our wants and desires—the itch does not always need to be scratched.

Being sentient and the product of evolution, I interpret what is happening as "it is happening to me"—there is a me being bombarded by sensations. This me interprets them from an "I" perspective: "I am hungry," "I thought of you." "My arm hurt after I got vaccinated." "He insulted me." "I will go to Italy next year." This "I" becomes attached to wants and desires.

When I say "I," I am referring to my *self*; when I say "you," I am referring to your *self*.

Buddhism teaches there is no self in the person I think of as me: *no-self* (*anata* in Pāli). It is a convenient fiction: a way to identify the object you refer to, a "convenient designator".

And my false belief that there is a me causes unnecessary ill-being: with "me" comes "mine" (no me implies no mine). This leads to attachments "in the form of desires and aversions, and the strengthening of ignorance concerning the true nature of sentient existence" (Mark Siderits 2019). Saying "mine" comes early in life.

You are reasonably asking, "If there is no me, who is experiencing this ill-being?" Consider your cat and dog. While they experience pain, excitement, and hunger, they do not associate the feeling with their self—they do not have one. Likewise, spiders feel pain, but no one argues that spiders have a self. A Buddhist would say that part of the difficulty of understanding no-self is the limitations of language and the multiple meaning of pronouns and proper names.

"The Buddha's 'middle path' strategy first argues there is nothing that the word 'I' genuinely denotes and then explains that our erroneous sense of an 'I' stems from our employment of the useful fiction represented by the concept of the person."

Searching for what makes me me and not finding it is not unique to Buddhism. In lockstep with Buddhism, Hume could not find the self.[36]

[36] Descartes believed that one's self existed and was one's enduring mind: "Cogito ergo sum" (I think therefore I am). In explanation, the mind is the source of one's thoughts which it produces in a continuous stream. [Recollect that Descartes believed the mind transcends the brain: he was a dualist.] Hume and Buddhism reject this, arguing that

[The Berkeley psychologist Alison Gopnik speculates that Hume might have known of Buddhism.] [And see the section in Chapter 8 on the future-self empathy-gap.] A person is a collection of components that are changing over time, and no one component is the self: not their thoughts nor sensations, nor their heart, left arm, or temporal lobe: are all impermanent.[37] One sense of self is your one-and-only lifelong control center (the enduring executive in charge). Buddhism rejects this assertion that various and varying processes take charge; there is no one controller nor even one for a particular function. The processes that caused you, one day, to buy donuts and marry Mary are not necessarily the same processes that drove you yesterday to go skiing, start with a Green Run, and have wine with lunch. In defense of this view, neurobiologists can't find your executive.

I sense that somewhere inside my container, something constitutes the real me. Despite this, since the container is the result of a process to enhance the passing along of its genes, one would expect me to have a sense of self even if it's just an illusion—the *illusion-of-self*—it motivates me to pass along my genes.[38] To foster the fantasy, one "learns to think of life as a kind of narrative" (Siderits 2007), with the story revolving around you, so you strive too much for importance and significance.

My intent is not to convince you that there is no you in you. Instead, it's to point out that the Buddhist view is that most of us suffer from an illusion-of-self, which causes unnecessary ill-being—you are free to disagree. Thinking about no-self makes me think about self as a continuum: at one extreme is no-self; at the other extreme, there is a definite me in me—what most of us believe. Midway is a fluid self. Thinking about whether one has a self causes one to take a more nuanced view of one's desires and cravings.

one's thoughts are brief, distinct, and impermanent, so they do not imply the existence of a mind. One's thoughts could be the product of an impermanent brain. And since thoughts are ubiquitous, we have the illusion of a mind, and then wrongly define this illusion as the me in me.

[37] Echoing this view, the philosopher Norman O. Brown (1966) defined a person as a corporation of persons, "a corporate body". "The unity of a person is as real, or unreal, as the unity of a corporation." Like Apple, it is a collection of ever-changing people.

[38] My sense of self motivates me to keep living and to have kids. Chapters 9 and 10 consider the *illusion of choice*.

So, the Buddhist view is that most people don't understand that life is suffering, all is impermanent, and there is no me, so no mine. If we accept this, our ill-being will lessen—cease—objects and experiences will have less "mine" attached to them. We will no longer expect permanence, so we react more appropriately to the sensations (good and bad) that life throws at us—our attachments to these sensations will have waned.

In lockstep, trying to fulfill your wants and desires will be counterproductive if the goal is to reduce your ill-being. As noted above, the Buddhist view is that our default ordering of paths is based on cravings (wants and desires) rather than WB, and the two orderings are negatively correlated. Fulfilling desires brings pleasures, but, like everything else, these pleasures are impermeant and cause more cravings: giving Ralph, the rat, a chunk of cheddar for pushing the bar causes him to crave and push more.

You need enough resources to fulfill your and your family's need for food, shelter, and safety, but more could be counterproductive if the goal is less ill-being (more WB). I recently read, "Here is how bored rich are spending their extra cash" (Berstein 2021). The pandemic has been great for rich guys who spend their quarantine hours online perusing and buying vintage Rolexes, Porsches, and Pokémon cards.

> "All I do is go through watch porn," he said. "I'm selling watches. I'm buying watches. It's crazy. I have no reason right now to buy a watch. I'm at home all day at a computer. Time is staring me right in the face. What reason do I have to look at my wrist? But I want a tangible sign of something, so I'm looking at watches."
>
> [Prices are rising, so it's "investing."]

How to get liberated from suffering is beyond my scope, but, in summary, the Buddhist view is it is possible but challenging, and one gets gradually closer by adhering to the eight-fold path:

> And this is the path: the path with eight branches: complete view, complete thought, complete speech, complete action, complete Livelihood, complete effort, complete mindfulness, complete concentration. (Bodhi 2000, p. 1844)

Meditating is necessary because liberation from one's thoughts and sensations is otherwise unattainable. It teaches you to look at your thoughts and sensations in new ways, encouraging you to understand and accept no-self and impermanence.

Earlier, I suggested that an economicus could be a Buddhist, a *Buddhist-economicus*. Examples of economici that are not Buddhists prove that they don't have to be.[39] An economicus could be at a point in life where their ordering of paths is based on understanding suffering, impermanence, and no-self. Their wants and desires line up with reducing ill-being. Assumptions 9a and b both hold. And the individual is liberated. [The goal, in words, is minimizing ill-being (paths ordered from least to most ill-being), not maximizing WB. The difference is the perspective: Buddhists think dukkha is pervasive, and neoclassical economists have a more optimistic view of the human condition. For Buddhists, framing the goal as maximizing WB is folly. Minimizing suffering has, at least for me, more appeal as an ethic than maximizing aggregate WB.]

But can a Buddhist be an economicus? Buddhists believe that most humans order paths based on their wants and desires, and this ordering does not line up with the individual's WB, which is consistent with NBT. However, they also believe that humans, with difficulty, can choose a path that is not one of their highest-ranked available paths, which violates Assumption 7: *At every point in time, economicus takes one of their HRAPs*. So, as envisioned by Buddhism, a human cannot be an economicus. What about enlightened individuals? Assumptions 9a and b hold, and they experience their HRAP, but they will have chosen to: they were not required to, so while Assumption 7 is violated, they behave as if it is not.

The next chapter returns to comparability and commensurability and their implications for NBT.

References and Sources

Batchelor, Stephen. 2015. *After Buddhism: Rethinking the dharma for a secular age*. Yale University Press.

Benjamin, Daniel, Ori Heffetz, Miles Kimball, and Nichole Szembrot. 2014. "Beyond happiness and satisfaction: Toward well-being indices based on stated preference." *American Economic Review* 104 (9): 2698–2735. https://doi.org/10.1257/aer.104.9.2698. https://www.webofscience.com/wos/woscc/full-record/WOS:000341588200004.

[39] My Roomba vacuum cleaner being one example, worms another.

Berstein, Jacob. 2021. "Here's how bored rich people are spending their extra cash." *The New York Times*, March 30, Style. https://www.nytimes.com/2021/03/20/style/spending-rich-people.html.

Blanchflower, David, and Andrew Oswald. 2004. "Well-being over time in Britain and the USA." *Journal of Public Economics* 88 (7–8): 1359–1386. https://doi.org/10.1016/s0047-2727(02)00168-8. https://www.webofscience.com/wos/woscc/full-record/WOS:000220417600007.

———. 2008. "Hypertension and happiness across nations." *Journal of Health Economics* 27 (2): 218–233. https://doi.org/10.1016/j.jhealeco.2007.06.002. https://www.webofscience.com/wos/woscc/full-record/WOS:000255138900003.

Bodhi, Bhikkhu. 2000. *The connected discourses of the Buddha: A new translation of the Samyutta Nikaya*. Somerville, MA: Wisdom Publications.

Boyce, Christopher, Alex Wood, and Nattavudh Powdthavee. 2013. "Is personality fixed? Personality changes as much as 'variable' economic factors and more strongly predicts changes in life satisfaction." *Social Indicators Research* 111 (1): 18. https://doi.org/10.1007/s11205-012-0006-z.

Brickman, P., D. Coates, and R. Janoff-Bulman. 1978. "Lottery winners and accident victims: Is happiness relative?" *Journal of Personality and Social Psychology* 36 (8): 917–927. https://doi.org/10.1037/0022-3514.36.8.917. https://www.webofscience.com/wos/woscc/full-record/WOS:A1978FM23000013.

Brooks, David. 2021. "The GOP is getting even worse." *The New York Times*. https://www.nytimes.com/2021/04/22/opinion/trump-gop.html.

Brown, Norman. 1966. *In love's body*. Random House.

Case, Anne, and Angus Deaton. 2020. *Deaths of despair and the future of capitalism*. Princeton, NJ: Princeton University Press. https://press.princeton.edu/books/hardcover/9780691190785/deaths-of-despair-and-the-future-of-capitalism.

———. 2021. "Title." NBER Working Paper Series.

Clark, Andrew, Paul Frijters, and M. A. Shields. 2008. "Relative income, happiness, and utility: An explanation for the Easterlin paradox and other puzzles." *Journal of Economic Literature* 46 (1): 95–144. https://doi.org/10.1257/jel.46.1.95. https://www.webofscience.com/wos/woscc/full-record/WOS:000254586800004.

Csíkszentmihályi, Mihály. 1990. *Flow: The psychology of optimal experience*. New York: Harper and Row.

De Neve, Jan-Emmanuel, et al. 2018. "The asymmetric experience of positive and negative economic growth: Global evidence using subjective well-being data." *Review of Economics and Statistics* 100 (2): 362–375. https://doi.org/10.1162/REST_a_00697. https://www.webofscience.com/wos/woscc/full-record/WOS:000431420600013.

Di Tella, Rafael, John Haisken-De New, and Robert MacCulloch. 2010. "Happiness adaptation to income and to status in an individual panel." *Journal of Economic Behavior & Organization* 76 (3): 834–852.

Diener, Ed. 2000. "Subjective well-being—The science of happiness and a proposal for a national index." *American Psychologist* 55 (1): 34–43. https://doi.org/10.1037/0003-066x.55.1.3.4. https://www.webofscience.com/wos/woscc/full-record/WOS:000085290800004.

Diener, Edward, and Shigehiro Oishi. 2000. "Money and happiness." In *Culture and subjective well-being*, edited by Edward Diener and E. Suh. Cambridge, MA: MIT Press.

Dolan, Paul, Tessa Peasgood, and Matthew White. 2008. "Do we really know what makes us happy? A review of the economic literature on the factors associated with subjective well-being." *Journal of Economic Psychology* 29 (1): 94–122. https://doi.org/10.1016/j.joep.2007.09.001. https://www.webofscience.com/wos/woscc/full-record/WOS:000221072000005.

Dorn, D., J. A. V. Fischer, G. Kirchgassner, and A. Sousa-Poza. 2007. "Is it culture or democracy? The impact of democracy and culture on happiness." *Social Indicators Research* 82 (3): 505–526. https://doi.org/10.1007/s11205-006-9048-4. https://www.webofscience.com/wos/woscc/full-record/WOS:000246758500007.

Easterlin, Richard. 1974. "Does economic growth improve the human lot? Some empirical evidence." In *Nations and households in economic growth: Essays in honour of Moses Abramowitz*, edited by P. A. David and M. W. Reder. New York and London: Academic Press. https://www.webofscience.com/wos/woscc/full-record/WOS:A1978FM23000013.

———. 1995. "Will raising the incomes of all increase the happiness of all?" *Journal of Economic Behavior and Organization* 27: 13.

Englehart, Ronald, and Hans-Dieter Klingemann. 2000. "Genes, culture, democracy and happiness." In *Culture and subjective well-being*, edited by Edward Diener and E. Suh. Cambridge, MA: MIT University Press.

Ferrer-I-Carbonell, A. 2005. "Income and well-being: An empirical analysis of the comparison income effect." *Journal of Public Economics* 89 (5–6): 997–1019. https://doi.org/10.1016/j.jpubeco.2004.06.003. https://www.webofscience.com/wos/woscc/full-record/WOS:000229162300011.

Festinger, Leon. 1954. "A theory of social comparison processes." *Human relations* 7 (2): 117–140. www.humanscience.org/docs/Festinger%20%281954%29%20A%20Theory%20of%20Social%20Comparison%20Processes.pdf.

Frank, Robert. 1997. "The frame of reference as a public good." *Economic Journal* 107 (445): 1832–1847. https://doi.org/10.1111/1468-0297.00261. https://www.webofscience.com/wos/woscc/full-record/WOS:000071086300014.

Fujita, F., and Ed Diener. 2005. "Life satisfaction set point: Stability and change." *Journal of Personality and Social Psychology* 88 (1): 158–164. https://doi.org/10.1037/0022-3514.88.1.158. https://www.webofscience.com/wos/woscc/full-record/WOS:000226178400011.

Gopnik, Alison. 2009. "Could David Hume have known about Buddhism? Charles Francois Dolu, the Royal College of la Fleche, and the global Jesuit intellectual network." *Hume Studies* 35 (1–2): 22.

———. 2015. "How an 18th century philosopher helped solve my midlife crisis: David Hume, the buddha, and the search for eastern roots of the western Enlightenment." *The Atlantic*, October.

Graham, Carol. 2021. America's crisis of despair: A federal task force for economic recovery and societal well-being.

Helliwell, John. 2003. "How's life? Combining individual and national variables to explain subjective well-being." *Economic Modelling* 20 (2): 331–360. https://doi.org/10.1016/s0264-9993(02)00057-3. https://www.webofscience.com/wos/woscc/full-record/WOS:000181674000005.

Helliwell, John, Haifang Huang, and Robert Putman. 2009. "How's the job? Are trust and social capital neglected workplace investments?" In *Social capital reaching out, reaching in*, edited by Viv Ona and James Davis. Edward Elgar.

Hume, David. 1954. *New letters of David Hume*. Edited by Raymond Klibansky and Ernest Mossne. Oxford: Oxford University Press.

Kahneman, Dan and Angus Deaton. 2010. "High income improves evaluation of life but not emotional well-being." *Proceeding of the National Academy of Sciences of the United States of America* 107 (38). http://doi.org/10.10.1073/pnas.1011492107.

Kimball, Miles, Ryan Nunn, and Dan Silverman. 2015. *Accounting for adaptation in the economics of happiness*. National Bureau of Economic Research. http://www.nber.org/papers/w21365.pdf.

Kraus, Michael, and Dacher Keltner. 2009. "Signs of socioeconomic status: A thin-slicing approach." *Psychological Science* 20 (1): 99–106. https://doi.org/10.1111/j.1467-9280.2008.02251.x. https://www.webofscience.com/wos/woscc/full-record/WOS:000262285200016.

———. 2013. "Social class rank, essentialism, and punitive judgment." *Journal of Personality and Social Psychology* 105 (2): 247–261. https://doi.org/10.1037/a0032895. https://www.webofscience.com/wos/wohscc/full-record/WOS:000322430200005.

Kraus, Michael, and Jacinth Tan. 2015. "Americans overestimate social class mobility." *Journal of Experimental Social Psychology* 58: 101–111. https://doi.org/10.1016/j.jesp.2015.01.005. https://www.webofscience.com/wos/woscc/full-record/WOS:000352251800012.

Krauss, Michael, Shai Davidai, and David Nussbaum. 2009. "American dream? Or mirage." *The New York Times*, May 1. https://www.nytimes.com/2015/05/03/opinion/sunday/american-dream-or-mirage.html.

Lane, Melissa. 2008. "Melissa Lane on Rousseau on modern society." *Philosophy Bites*. https://philosophybites.com/2008/07/melissa-lane-on.html.

Luttmer, E. F. P. 2005. "Neighbors as negatives: Relative earnings and well-being." *Quarterly Journal of Economics* 120 (3): 963–1002. https://doi.org/10.1162/003355305774268255. https://www.webofscience.com/wos/woscc/full-record/WOS:000232224500005.

Lykken, David. 2000. *The nature and nurture of joy and contentment*. New York: St. Martin's Press.

Lykken, David, and Auke Tellegen. 1996. "Happiness is a stochastic phenomenon." *Psychological Science* 7 (3): 186–189. https://doi.org/10.1111/j.1467-9280.1996.tb00355.x. https://www.webofscience.com/wos/woscc/full-record/WOS:A1996UM14800012.

Morey, Edward, and David Kritzberg. 2012. "It's not where you do it; it's who you do it with?" *Journal of Choice Modelling* 5 (3): 176–191. https://doi.org/10.1016/j.jocm.2013.03.004. https://www.sciencedirect.com/science/article/pii/S1755534513000055.

Noyes, William. 1890. "The insanity of Jean-Jacques Rousseau." *The American Journal of Psychiatry* 3 (3): 23. https://www.jstor.org/stable/1411748?seq=1#page_scan_tab_contents.

Oswald, Andrew. 1997. "Happiness and economic performance." *Economic Journal* 107 (445): 1815–1831. https://doi.org/10.1111/1468-0297.00260. https://www.webofscience.com/wos/woscc/full-record/WOS:000071086300013.

Oswald, Andrew J., and Nattavudh Powdthavee. 2008. "Does happiness adapt? A longitudinal study of disability with implications for economists and judges." *Journal of Public Economics* 92 (5–6): 1061–1077.

Pape, Robert. 2021. "Opinion: What an analysis of 377 Americans arrested or charged in the capital insurrection tells us." *Washington Post*, April 6. https://www.washingtonpost.com/opinions/2021/04/06/capitol-insurrection-arrests-cpost-analysis/.

Piff, Paul, et al. 2010. "Having less, giving more: The influence of social class on prosocial behavior." *Journal of Personality and Social Psychology* 99 (5): 771–784. https://doi.org/10.1037/a0020092. https://www.webofscience.com/wos/woscc/full-record/WOS:000284191700004.

Processes, Organizational Behavior and Human Decision. 2007. "Special issue on social comparison processes." *Organizational Behavior and Human Decision Processes* Special issue.

Reicher, Stephen, and Yasemin Ulusahin. 2020. "Chapter 13: Resentment and redemption: On the mobilisation of dominant group victimhood." In *The social psychology of collective victimhood*, edited by Vollhardt and Johanna. Oxford: Oxford University Press.

Russell, Bertrand. 1930. *The conquest of happiness*. London: Allen and Unwin. http://books.google.com/books/about/The_Conquest_of_Happiness.html?id=--lefVQ_MYYC.

Saez, Emmanuel. 2013. "Income inequality: Evidence and policy implications." The Arrow Lecture, Stanford. http://eml.berkeley.edu/~saez/lecture_saez_arrow.pdf.

Schumacher, E. F. 1966. "Buddhist economics." *Resurgence*.

Senior, Jennifer. 2020. "Opinion: Happiness won't save you." *The New York Times*, November 24. https://www.nytimes.com/2020/11/24/opinion/happiness-depression-suicide-psychology.html.

Siderits, Mark. 2007. *Buddhism as philosophy: An introduction*. Indianapolis and Cambridge: Hackett.

———. 2019. "Buddha." Stanford Encyclopedia of Philosophy. Stanford University. https://plato.stanford.edu/.

Smith, Adam. 1759/2022. *The theory of moral sentiments*. Vol. 1. Ireland: J. Beatty and C. Jackson and The Gutenberg Project. https://www.webofscience.com/wos/woscc/full-record/WOS:000283912100003.

———. 1791/2022. *An inquiry into the nature and causes of the wealth of nations: By Adam Smith*. Vol. 4. JJ Tourneisen; and JL Legrand. https://www.gutenberg.org/ebooks/3300.

Stutzer, Alois. 2004. "The role of income aspirations in individual happiness." *Journal of Economic Behavior & Organization* 54 (1): 89–109. https://doi.org/10.1016/j.jebo.2003.04.003. https://www.webofscience.com/wos/woscc/full-record/WOS:000255138900003.

The Conference Board. 2014. "Job satisfaction." https://www.conference-board.org/research/job-satisfaction/job-satisfaction-2014.

University of Michigan. "Hrs: Health and retirement study: A public resource for data on aging in America since 1990." Accessed 2021. https://hrsonline.isr.umich.edu/.

Veblen, Thorstein. 1899. *The theory of the leisure class*. The Gutenberg Project. http://www.gutenberg.org/etext/833.

Veenhoven, Rutt. 1993. *Happiness in nations: Subjective appreciation of life in 56 nations, 1946–1992*. Rotterdam: Risbo Press.

Wadsworth, Tim. 2014. "Sex and the pursuit of happiness: How other people's sex lives are related to our sense of well-being." *Social Indicators Research* 116 (1): 115–135. https://doi.org/10.1007/s11205-013-0267-1. https://www.webofscience.com/wos/woscc/full-record/WOS:000331644000005.

Wood, Alex, Stephen Joseph, and John Maltby. 2008. "Gratitude uniquely predicts satisfaction with life: Incremental validity above the domains and facets of the five-factor model." *Personality and Individual Differences* 45 (1): 49–54. https://doi.org/10.1016/j.paid.2008.02.019. http://www.nber.org/papers/w21365.pdf.

Additional Readings

Asessina, Alberto, Rafael Di Tella, and Robert MacCulloch. 2004. "Inequality and happiness: Are Europeans and Americans different?" *Journal of Public Economics* 88 (9–10): 2009–2042. https://doi.org/10.1016/j.jpubeco.2003.07.006. https://www.webofscience.com/wos/woscc/full-record/WOS:000222185300016.

Asessina, Alberto, Edward Glaeser, and Bruce Sacerdote. 2006. "Work and leisure in the United States and Europe: Why so different?" *NBER Macroeconomics Annual 2005* 20: 1–64. http://www.nber.org/chapters/c0073.pdf.

Brown, Claire. 2017. *Buddhist economics: An enlightened approach to the dismal science*. New York: Bloomsbury Press.

Christensen, K., A. M. Herskind, and J. W. Vaupel. 2006. "Why Danes are smug: Comparative study of life satisfaction in the European Union." *British Medical Journal* 333 (7582): 1289–1291. https://doi.org/10.1136/bmj.39028.665602.55. https://www.webofscience.com/wos/woscc/full-record/WOS:000243160700008.

Damrosch, Leo. 2005. *Jean-Jacques Rousseau: Restless genius*. Boston: Houghton Mifflin Company.

Davidai, Shai, and Thomas Gilovich. 2015. "Building a more mobile America—One income quintile at a time." *Perspectives on Psychological Science* 10 (1): 60–71. https://doi.org/10.1177/1745691614562005. https://www.webofscience.com/wos/woscc/full-record/WOS:000348054400004.

Feuer, Alan. 2021. "Fears of white people losing out permeate capital rioters' town, study finds." *The New York Times*, April 4. https://archive.nytimes.com/opinionator.blogs.nytimes.com/2013/10/05/rich-people-just-care-less/.

Gethin, Rupert. 1998. *The foundation of Buddhism*. Oxford: Oxford University Press.

———. 2008. *Sayings of the Buddha*. Oxford: Oxford University Press.

Goleman, Daniel. 2013. "Rich people just care less." *The New York Times*, October 5. https://archive.nytimes.com/opinionator.blogs.nytimes.com/2013/10/05/rich-people-just-care-less/.

Irwin, Neil. 2014. "A big safety net and a strong job market can coexist. Just ask Scandinavia." *The New York Times*, December 17. https://www.webofscience.com/wos/woscc/full-record/WOS:A1978FM23000013.

Krugman, Paul. 2005. "French family values." *The New York Times*. https://www.nytimes.com/2005/07/29/opinion/french-family-values.html.

Lowrey, Annie. 2012. "For two economists, the Buffett rule is just a start." *The New York Times*, April 16. https://www.nytimes.com/2012/04/17/business/for-economists-saez-and-piketty-the-buffett-rule-is-just-a-start.html.

———. 2013. "The rich get richer through the recovery." *The New York Times*, September 10. https://archive.nytimes.com/economix.blogs.nytimes.com/2013/09/10/the-rich-get-richer-through-the-recovery/.

Magnuson, Joel. 2022. *The dharma and the socially engaged Buddhist economics*. Palgrave Macmillan.

Peterson, Christopher, Nansook Park, and Martin Seligman. 2005. "Orientation to happiness and life satisfaction: The full versus the empty life." *Journal of Happiness Studies* 6: 16.

Rahula, Walpola. 1959. *What the Buddha taught*. New York: Grove Press.

Tellegen, Auke, et al. 1988. "Personality similarity in twins reared apart and together." *Journal of Personality and Social Psychology* 54 (6): 1031–1039. https://doi.org/10.1037/0022-3514.54.6.1031. https://www.webofscience.com/wos/woscc/full-record/WOS:A1988N666500012.

Weber, Lauren. 2014. "US Workers can't get no (job) satisfaction." *Wall Street Journal*, June 18. https://www.wsj.com/articles/BL-ATWORKB-1852.

Wright, Robert. 2017. *Why Buddhism is true: The science and philosophy of meditation and enlightenment*. Simon and Shuster.

CHAPTER 7

Returning to Whether All the Different Kinds of Well-Being Are Commensurable and Whether All the Different Bearers of WB Are Comparable

> It is the incommensurability that is the crux of the problem. It is this incommensurability of 'plural; values' that provides perhaps the main challenge to Utilitarianism, as well as to any attempts to present a unique system of moral theory. (Wilfred Beckerman 2017)

Many believe they're not always. Chapter 2 pointed out that Assumptions 2 and 9a.

Assumption 2: *At every point in time, an economicus has one ordering of all paths—1st, 2nd, ... An economicus has an ordering if, for all paths j and k, either Path j is ranked higher than Path k, Path k is ranked higher than Path j, or paths j and k have the same rank.*

Assumption 9a: *An economicus's ordering of paths is based on its WB (well-being), WB, accounting for uncertainties. The more WB economicus associates with a path, the higher its rank...*

Imply that an economicus has a complete WB ordering of all paths. Chapter 2 also demonstrated that Assumption 2 is violated if any paths are WB-incomparable. And, if any kinds of WB are incommensurable, there will be WB-incomparable paths. Recollect from Chapter 2:

E. R. Morey, *Deconstructing Behavior, Choice, and Well-being*, https://doi.org/10.1007/978-3-031-36712-0_7

Paths h and k are WB-incomparable if **none** of the following statements are correct: h is ranked higher than k, k is ranked higher than h, or h and k have the same rank. They are WB-comparable if one, and only one, of these statements, is correct.

And

WB-commensurability: WB kind A and WB kind B are incommensurable if you are incapable of comparing them in terms of overall WB

This chapter discusses the arguments for and against complete WB-comparability and complete WB-commensurability.

Before jumping in, here are a few things to recollect from Chapter 2: Even if paths *h* and *k* are incomparable in terms of overall WB, they still could be comparable in terms of a specific kind of WB (e.g., Path *k* generates more happiness than *h*, but less life satisfaction). And Paths *h* and *k* being comparable does not imply that either is comparable with any other paths.

The existence of bearer-of-WB-incomparabilities doesn't mean you can never WB-compare paths. For example, paths with more chocolate cake and fewer rats than the current path, all else the same, are ranked higher even if cake and rats are WB-incomparable. Also, be mindful that rats and cake could be WB-comparable at a few levels but not all. For example, I can conclude that a path with 75% fewer rats and one less cake is WB preferred to my current path, but I cannot compare if the alternative path has 15% fewer rats.

More on Why Complete WB-Incommensurability Is Important

Complete WB-comparability requires complete WB-commensurability. So, if there is not complete WB-commensurability, the individual's ordering of paths will not be complete. And this has significant implications for behavior: choice theory becomes less specific in its predictions.[1]

[1] Recollect from Chapter 2, that WB-incompatibility is sufficient, although not necessary for incompleteness to occur.

The Impact of Incompleteness on Behavior and Choice

If the ordering is incomplete (Assumption 2 is violated), the theory predicts the individual will choose a path not ranked lower than any other available path ("maximizing," not "optimizing").[2] And there can be many (Sen 1997, Hsieh 2007, and Hsieh and Andersson 2021). And, we can't say which the individual will select—we can only determine which available paths will not be chosen.[3] Consider again Fig. 2.5, but now suppose the three commodities are market goods, *m*, less global warming, *lgw*, and third, instead of relationships, saved souls, *s*. Suppose *m* and *s* are WB-comparable, but neither is with *lgw*. Finally, assume the origin path is available. For convenience, I repeat the figure, now Fig. 7.1 with *r* replaced by *s*.

Repeating a bit from Chapter 2: all paths with the same level of *gw* as the origin path are ranked relative to each other; Paths in Quadrant A (front top left) are ranked higher than the origin path; those in G (back bottom-right) are ranked lower. Paths inside Quadrants B-F and H are not ranked relative to the origin path.

To predict behavior, the budget set must be specified. Suppose the individual has a fixed income, *y*, and the prices p_m and p_s are exogenous. [The Church posts the cost of saving a soul and accepts PayPal.] The level of *gw* is exogenous at the level represented by the horizontal plane through the origin path. And the origin path exhausts her budget. The *available set* of paths is the horizontal *gw* plane on and to the right of the *m/s* budget line through the origin (budget line not shown). The budget line's slope reflects the relative prices of *m* and *s*. It goes from right front to back left (as her consumption increases, the number of souls she saves must decrease).

The individual takes *gw* as given and selects the highest-ranked path on her budget line (she optimizes): her income will be exhausted, and her chosen path may not be the origin path. She has a complete ordering of all available paths, even though she can't order all conceivable paths.

In the 1920s and 1930s, WB-commensurability was debated in the context of the functionality of socialism (the ability to compare values in the absence of market prices). See Ludwig von Mises (1920/1935) and Otto Neurath (1928/1973) on the functionality of socialism (the ability to compare values in the absence of prices).

[2] Maximizing and optimizing are equivalent when the ordering is complete.

[3] Maximizing when the ordering is incomplete is akin to *satisficing* (Simon 1982): The individual concludes, "I'm satisfied, and I know I could have done worse."

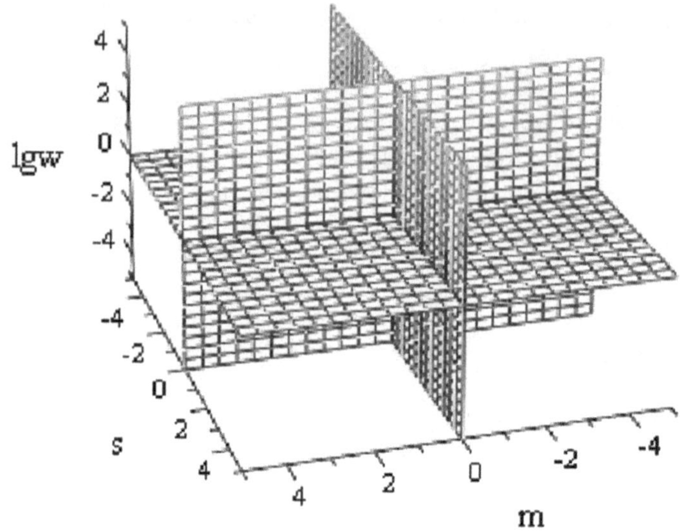

Fig. 7.1 m-*s*-*lgw* paths (Fig. 2.5 with *r* replaced by *s*)

The Impact of Incompleteness on Transitivity

Recollect from Chapter 2 that a complete ordering—meaning all paths are WB-comparable—is, by definition, transitive. As noted there, transitive means that for all paths *i*, *j*, *k*, and *l*, if Path *i* is ranked at least as high as *j* and *j* as least as high as *k*, and *k* at least as high as *l*, then *i* is ranked at least as high as *l*. Transitivity no longer holds for all sets of paths if the ordering is incomplete.

Intransitivity is worrisome because it can produce incoherent behavior called *money pumps* (Walter Bossert and Kotaro Suzumura 2010; Sven Hansson 2018). For example, you voluntarily exchange Path *i* for *j*, then *j* for *k*, then *k* for *l*, and then pay to get back to *i*—you end up back where you started but with less money—so you pumped money down the drain. This led many to infer that coherent behavior must be transitive. They are wrong.

In explanation, while with incompleteness, there is no longer transitivity, there still can be a restrictive property on the relationships between paths called *Suzumura consistency* (*S-consistency*) (Suzumura 1983; Bossert and Suzumura 2010; Bossert 2018; Sen 2018): if Paths *i*, *j*, *k*, and *l* have the relationships *j* is ranked at least as high as *i*, *i* is ranked at least as high as *k*, and *k* at least as high as *l*, then S-consistency means *l* will not be ranked strictly higher than *j*.[4]

S-consistency is both necessary and sufficient to make money pumps impossible. Incomplete orderings don't necessarily imply incoherent behavior, even though incompleteness negates transitivity.

Transitivity implies S-consistency, but S-consistency does not imply transitivity. If the ordering is complete, transitivity and S-consistency amount to the same.[5]

Individuals sometimes behave as if their ordering of paths is intransitive. Incompleteness would explain. If your ordering is incomplete, it will sometimes seem intransitive. Despite this, if you are S-consistent, you are coherent and won't money pump.

The Impact of Incompleteness on Valuing, in Money, a Shift from Path i *to Path* t

Consider the implications of a complete ordering vs. an incomplete one on my life's work: defining and estimating how an individual values,

[4] An example of S-consistency but not transitivity: Returning to Fig. 7.1 with market goods, *m*, saved souls, *s*, and less global warming, *lgw*, consider four paths, *i*, *j*, *k*, and *l*. Let *i* be the path at the origin. Define Path *j* to have the same amounts of *m* and *s* as Path *i* but less *gw*. In Fig. 7.1, it is vertically right above Path *i*. Therefore, Path *j* is ranked strictly higher than *i* (so ranked at least as high). Let Path *k* be on the horizontal indifference curve that passes through *i* but with more *s* and less *m* than Path *i*. The individual is indifferent between Paths *i* and *k*, so *i* is ranked at least as high as *k*. Finally, let Paths *l* and *k* have identical amounts of *m* and *s*, but Path *l* has more *gw*, so Path *l* is vertically right below Path *k*. So, Path *k* is ranked strictly higher than *l* (so ranked at least as high as *l*). Summarizing: *j* is ranked at least as high as *i*, *i* at least as high as *k*, and *k* at least as high as *l*.

But now examine paths *j* and *l*; *j* has less *gw* than *l* but also less *s*. Since in this example, *lgw* and *s* are WB-incomparable, Paths *j* and *l* are not comparable, so not ranked relative to each other, and the ordering is incomplete. Transitivity is violated: Path *j* is not ranked at least as high as *l*, but S-consistency holds: *l* is not ranked strictly higher than *j*.

[5] Note that S-consistency is different from quasi-transitivity, a different weakening of transitivity that was defined in Chapter 1. S-consistency is also different from another weakening of transitivity called *acyclivity*: if Paths *i*, *j*, and *k* have the relationships *j* is ranked higher than *i*, and *i* is ranked higher than *k*, then acyclivity means *j* is ranked at least as high as *k*. Acyclivity is less restrictive than S-consistency. Neither S-consistency nor quasi-transitivity imply the other.

in money, a shift from Path *i* to *t*. For example, the enactment of a government policy that will reduce the rate of global warming.

The most common money measure is the *compensating variation*, *CV*, for a shift from Path *i* to *t*, where paths are expressed in terms of what is exogenous to the individual on that path. Typically, these exogenous variables are in three categories: the individual's income on that path, the prices of market commodities (quantities consumed endogenous), and fixed components (those whose quantities/levels are exogenous).

If the individual has a complete ordering—the neoclassical assumption—the *CV* for a change from the origin path to any other path exists. A *CV* exists if either (I) or (II) holds.

(I): There exists a finite amount of money (positive or negative) that, when subtracted from income on the proposed path, causes the individual, after the subtraction, to be indifferent between the two paths. With compensation, the two paths have the same rank. If such an amount exists, it is a finite amount of money and is the *CV*. If the shift from *i* to *t* improves WB, this finite *CV* is a positive number and willingness-to-pay, WTP, to enact the shift. If the shift from *i* to *t* would decrease WB, this finite *CV* is a negative number and, in absolute terms, willingness-to-accept, WTA, the shift.

Or (II): No matter how much is subtracted or added to income on the proposed path, the initially ranked higher path remains higher (the same rank can't be achieved). For Case II, if the shift from Path *i* to *t* would improve WB, the *CV* is positive infinity and indicates that the individual would be WTP all the money they have, no matter how much they have, to enact the shift. Conversely, suppose the shift from Path i to t would decrease WB. In that case, the *CV* is negative infinity indicating that for no amount of money would the individual voluntarily accept Path *t*. [NB, II implies the ordering, while complete, has a lexicographic aspect. Lexicographic was defined in Chapter 2. Unfortunately, some economists who value amenities in terms of money do not understand the distinction between a complete but lexicographic ordering and an incomplete ordering.]

For both Cases I and II, money is a meaningful comparison metric. It says a lot about you and me if you would pay $1000 to half the rate of global warming, and I would pay $10. It also says a lot if you would pay your entire income, no matter its magnitude, to half the rate.

If the individual has a complete ordering of paths, the *CV* for every path shift is defined. And if the ordering of paths is incomplete, the *CV* is undefined for some shifts. In my example, commodities *m* and *s* are WB-comparable, but neither is WB-comparable with global warming, so the ordering of paths is incomplete, as noted above.

Consider a shift from Path *i* to *t*, where *i* is the origin path in Fig. 7.1 If paths *t* and *i* are not WB-comparable, a *CV* for the shift is meaningless because there is no answer to whether paths *i* or *t* would produce more WB. For example, if Path *t* has more *m* or *s* than Path *i* and more *gw*, there is no *CV*. There is also no *CV* if Path *t* has less *m* or *s* and less *gw*.

If the ordering is incomplete, the *CV* can be meaningless even when Paths *i* and *t* are WB- comparable. Continuing with our example, assume Path *t* is identical to Path *i* (the origin path) except that it has less *gw* (in Fig. 7.1, Path *t* is now directly above *i*, like Path *j*). Path *t* is WB preferred to *i*, but a *CV* remains meaningless because the kinds of WB produced by less global warming are not comparable to those produced by *m* and *s*.

Think about this in terms of a budget set where y, p_m, p_s, and *gw* are exogenous to the individual. A *CV* for a shift from Path *i* to *t* exists only if it does not change the exogenous level of *gw*. Otherwise, the paths can't be compared in terms of money, making it meaningless to talk about this individual's WTP to reduce global warming or her WTA an increase in global warming. [One could still collect data, estimate a model, and incorrectly call the result an estimate of WTP to reduce global warming: it is impossible to produce an estimate of something that does not exist.] The *CV* for a change in p_m or p_s is also meaningless if the price change causes *gw* to change, which is likely.[6]

* * *

WB-comparability and commensurability are also critical to tort law (e.g., can you be compensated with money for losing an arm, cognitive ability, or a loved one?).[7] WB-comparability is also critical to assessing whether a system or economy is WB-sustainable, and it is critical to hedonic wage and price studies.[8]

[6] Market goods and saving souls are not carbon equivalent.

[7] See, for example, the *University of Pennsylvania Law Review* symposium on commensurability (Matthew Adler 1997; Sunstein 1993).

[8] If the objective is the sustainability of overall WB, the objective is meaningful only if it is possible to convert all packets of WB into overall WB. Hedonic wage and

Modeling Behavior When the Ordering Is Incomplete

Whether you believe an incomplete ordering of paths makes for a more realistic and better behavior theory is your call. Sen (2018) thinks it would: quoting him, "I explore the need for allowing–and incorporating—incompleteness of preference in choice theory...."[9] I agree. Above I noted incompleteness as an explanation for coherent intransitivities.

An incomplete ordering can exhibit as an endowment effect (Chapter 9) and, more generally, as a *status-quo effect* (staying on the current path even though additional paths have become available). For example, why switch if another path becomes available but is not WB-comparable with the current path? Only switch if it is ranked strictly higher than the current path—incompleteness due to WB-incompatibilities encourages you to remain on your current path (Michael Mandler 2004).

property-value studies are a method of estimating the *CV* for amenities such as cleaner air, lower crime rates, better schools, and distance to parks. They are dependent on the assumption that in equilibrium everyone is indifferent to where they work and live. Does the existence of this equilibrium requires complete WB-commensurability?

[9] Interestingly, Sen asserts that WB-incomparabilities are a "much-hyped issue" and a "mundane occurrence". I have stated that WB-incomparabilities cause the ordering of paths to be incomplete making complete WB-comparability is a necessary condition for a complete ordering. Sen questions this: his argument is that one can, often, order paths even if they contain components that are WB-incomparable and neither path Pareto dominates the other. He finds incomparability ubiquitous, but that it does not stop us from ranking most pairs of paths.

My difference with Sen comes down to how one defines "incomparable". Consider two of his examples. "If I love bananas much more than apples, I would not be deterred from going for a banana by the peculiar worry that apples cannot be measured in the same unit, which is what commensurability is concerned with." I'm confused, "loving bananas much more" seems to say they are comparable, at least in terms of love. And what is the same unit in "same unit". Then he considers the choice between a fine mango that provides nutrition, "as well as some palatal or olfactory pleasure, and a vinyl record of a song that would offer a different reward (not immediately reducible in the dimensions of the other). But, given a budget constraint, we could quite possibly face the choice of having one or the other. This involves choosing between non-commensurable results. And yet we might have no great difficulty in opting for the mango when hungry and starved and going for the song when well-endowed with tasty food but short of melodious entertainment. The choice need not be hard to make in many situations, despite the incommensurability involved. The distinct dimensions of value might not be reducible into one another and yet there might be no problem whatsoever in deciding what one should do ...".

Maybe our different takes come down to commensurability vs. WB-commensurability.

Consider the 1989 Jack Knetsch experiment with coffee mugs, chocolate bars, and college students. Half got a mug and half a chocolate bar. Then they could trade. Ten percent did. In contrast, when students were offered a choice between a mug or a chocolate bar, approximately half chose each, "suggesting half preferred the mug and half the bar." So why did only 10% endowed with a mug or bar trade for the other item? Knetsch, and most everyone else, reports this as evidence of an endowment effect (see Chapter 9). However, it could, instead, be an example of WB-incomparability.[10] The student knows that getting the chocolate or the mug is WB-wise better than getting neither. Still, if the student cannot WB-compare the chocolate with the mug, there is no reason to trade for the other once you acquire either. This is a status-quo effect caused by an incomplete ordering.

* * *

So, precisely what is required for WB-commensurability?

WB-Commensurability Requires That All the Kinds of WB Generated by a Bearer Can Be Separated from the Bearer

The pleasure from eating chocolate must be separable from the eating, and your pride in your children must be separable from what they did to make you proud. If not, different kinds of WB couldn't be aggregated independently of their bearers. This necessary condition is called *WB/bearer separability*—think of it as a type of consequentialism (the act's consequences matter, not the bearer of those consequences).

But complete WB/bearer separability is not sufficient for WB-commensurability—an example demonstrates: the separation of happiness from the bearers of happiness and the separation of life-satisfaction from its bearers doesn't imply happiness and life-satisfaction are WB-commensurable.

[10] That half chose the chocolate and half the mug when given a choice does not imply half like the chocolate more and half like the mug more. An inability to compare them would generate the same result: you select by mentally flipping a coin if you can't compare chocolate and mugs. I am not claiming that chocolate and mugs are WB-incomparable; instead, I am pointing out that an incomplete ordering can produce behavior that looks like what an endowment effect would cause.

Rejecting WB/bearer separability goes back to Aristotle. M. Nussbaum (2012):

> Throughout his [Aristotle's] work, he insists on the tremendous importance of qualitative distinctions among the diverse constituent parts of human life;... pleasure is something that comes along with, supervenes on, activity, "like the bloom on the cheek of a young person." it is so closely linked to the relevant activities that it cannot be pursued on its own, any more than bloom can be adequately cultivated by cosmetics... what Aristotle has in mind is that pleasure is a kind of awareness of one's own activity,...

She argues that J. S. Mill rejected WB/bearer separability, and so do contemporary philosophers (2012, p. 338).

Consider your ability to separate a sensation, such as pain, from the activity or circumstance that produced it. For example, the same chest pain could be because you just ran your best marathon, found your partner in bed with someone else, or you are having a heart attack. Whether a sensation increases or decreases different kinds of WB depends on whether you chose it, whether you think it will be gone soon, what you imagine is causing it, and whether experiencing it helped you achieve an important goal. Humans think about the causes of their sensations: this suggests difficulty in separating the feeling from its cause.

The WB/bearer separability issue is whether everyone can separate every kind of WB from its bearer. Maybe you can, but Sunstein (1993) says most of us can't. According to him, the *awe* (an emotion) produced by viewing a mountain differs from the awe produced by viewing a skyscraper, which differs from the awe produced by a remarkable musical or athletic performance. Since these awes can't, in his view, be separated from their bearers, they are WB-incommensurable. And besides, they are incommensurable with the kinds of WB produced by consuming conventional goods and services. He is asserting WB/bearer inseparability, not proving it.

Many bearers of WB are public goods in that everyone experiences their existence (e.g., if global warming is reduced for you, it's reduced for everyone, same for saving a species from extinction). An issue is whether it is easier or harder to separate the kinds of WB produced by a bearer from the bearer if the bearer is a public good. I don't have an answer.

I have sympathy for WB/bearer inseparability. Still, I suspect it depends a lot on the specific bearer and the specific kind of WB, and on the extent to which that kind of WB has a significant cognitive component.

Non-Humans vs. Humans

I imagine that the extent to which kinds of WB can be separated from their bearers varies across species: becoming more difficult the greater the species' ability to cogitate. All animals experience sensations, but only humans consciously think about them in light of their past experiences, knowledge, and the big picture. And the world and your reactions to it produce new sensations, perceptions, thoughts, and emotions. Contrast this with animals who experience positive and negative sensations but have less cognitive capacity to assess and evaluate them. I conjecture that it is easier for my dog than for me to separate pleasure from the activity that produced it and easier for a worm than for my dog.

Related to the above conjecture is my conjecture that there are fewer kinds of dog WB and ill-being than human kinds, and there are still fewer for worms. Why? Humans experience more thoughts and emotions than other primates, primates more than dogs, and worms none. And, the more thoughts and emotions one can experience, the more kinds of WB and ill-being there are.

For humans, the ultimate existentialist fear is their death, but most other living things are incapable of experiencing this fear. So we don't need to be told, "You and I were born to die" (Lana Del Ray, the sadcore album *Born to Die*, 2012). As Schopenhauer (1788–1860) put it, "The brute first knows death when it dies, but man draws consciously nearer to it every hour he lives" (Schopenhauer 1818/2011).

A Flawed Argument for Complete WB-Comparability: It's Circular

In common economic vernacular, the argument goes as follows: everyone makes choices involving tradeoffs over different kinds of WB, so everyone must be able to compare them. What makes this circular is saying everyone makes tradeoffs over different kinds of WB requires that, for everyone, all paths are WB-comparable, which requires that, for everyone, there is complete WB-commensurability. Put another way, the argument assumes what it hopes to demonstrate. [*circulus in probando*: quoting

Wikipedia, "the reasoner begins with what they are trying to end up with. Circular reasoning is not a formal logical fallacy but a pragmatic defect in an argument where the premise (in this case, everyone makes tradeoffs over different kinds of WB) needs proof or evidence…"].

One way to prove the premise that all paths are WB-comparable would be to prove what? That everyone constantly experiences their highest WB-ranked available path? If so, no one has proven it, and some psychologists believe they have disproven it. For example, see the studies cited and discussed in this chapter and Chapter 8.

You may find it helpful to consider, again, the distinction between *behaviors* and *chosen behaviors*—we all do things (behave in specific ways), but this does not imply that all of our behaviors are chosen behaviors.[11] I hope everyone agrees that if there are N alternatives and the individual must experience only one, the individual will experience one. Behavior is required. So, what is the best word to neutrally describe the alternative experienced? I am inclined to go with the *alternative experienced*; the term *alternative chosen* implies what one is trying to demonstrate.

A weak defense of the premise that all paths are WB-comparable is that people will tell you that they chose the alternative they are experiencing by consciously trading off all the kinds of WB that would have been generated by the different alternatives. And we believe we do this. This is more comforting than, "I have no clue as to why I do what I do." But saying something does not make it true. Hundreds of psychological studies indicate that our reasons for doing what we do are often made up, post hoc, to justify what we are doing. See Chapter 11.

You're mistaken if you think you can WB-compare apples and oranges simply because you ate the orange rather than the apple. Eating the orange doesn't imply you "chose" the orange: you had to eat something.[12] More generally, just because you believe you can compare two bearers of WB or two kinds of WB does not mean you can.

Don't use circular reasoning to defend WB-comparability and commensurability.

[11] Chapter 9 distinguishes between behaviors and choices (chosen behaviors).

[12] Sen (1979) calls this *decision inescapability*: you have to start another path no matter what.

Two Kinds of WB Are WB-Incommensurable If an Ability to Compare Them Is Incompatible with Experiencing Them

Experiencing some kinds of WB is inconsistent with comparing them with other kinds. Quoting Philip Tetlock (2003), "...incommensurability arises when values are treated as commensurable subverts one of the values in the tradeoff calculus." Consider, for example, the kinds of WB produced by a meaningful and symmetric relationship (Raz 1986). Raz argues you can't compare a loving relationship with market goods because it isn't a loving relationship if you or your partner can. [People do compare, but they are not in love, or so the argument goes.] Feeling love and friendship, feeling trusted, and the safety in knowing trusted others have your back are all produced by personal relationships. It is difficult to argue that these kinds of WB are comparable to those produced by market goods.[13] Consider one's relationship with God. You can't experience the grace of God if you can compare his grace with the taste of chocolate cake.

What about personal relationships between members of different species, such as Giacomo and me? Or if I feel a personal bond with nature. Starting with the dog, I think it is fair to say that "I love him", that he is bonded to me, and that we enjoy most of our interactions. Of course, one day, I will have to put him to "sleep" or delay his death with vet bills, but that does not imply I can compare my love for him with the kinds of WB produced by market goods. If I could, I question whether I am capable of loving him. Could the same be said about a love of nature?[14]

Consider the inconsistency argument for resources that you believe to be sacred: when one experiences a feature that they believe to be sacred

[13] Sunstein (1993): "Suppose that [Adam] Smith has arranged to have lunch with a friend today, but that he has become very busy and perhaps would like to cancel. Suppose Smith thinks in this way: if he cancels, his friend will be disappointed, because he would like Smith's company, and also a bit insulted, because it is cavalier and disrespectful to cancel lunch at the last minute. Maybe Smith should make it up to him, or provide compensation, by offering a nontrivial cash payment...[but] A cash payment would be inconsistent with *the way* that someone values a friend. Even if the friend would prefer $1, or $10, or $100, or $100 to lunch with Smith—the offer of cash would be perceived as an insult rather than a compensation. In this context, the difference in kinds of valuation means that a financial exchange would be inappropriate."

[14] For many, our relationship with living things is fundamentally different from our relationship with goods and services. Unlike golf balls, animals suffer when they are struck, and much animal suffering is caused by humans.

(e.g., a geographical feature, historical site, religious shrine), spiritual and religious thoughts and emotions are produced. There are corresponding negative thoughts and emotions if something sacred is lost or denigrated. Tetlock (2003) defines "sacred values as those a moral community treats as possessing a transcendental significance that precludes comparisons, tradeoffs, or any mingling with secular values." A synonym for "sacred" is "inviolable"—"secure from assault or trespass"—Merriam-Webster. Sacred is a belief; if one believes a feature is sacred, its existence evokes reverential awe, a kind of WB. For indigenous populations, natural environments generate the kinds of WB associated with culture and religion, including the experience of sacredness. Such experiences are not limited to indigenous populations.[15]

Experiencing sacredness is inconsistent with comparing it with the kinds of WB that money can buy, so a sacred resource is incompatible with it being WB-comparable with market goods. Remember that observing a profane individual consuming market goods does not imply honoring the sacred is WB-comparable with market goods. The individual had to do something. [See the flawed circular argument outlined above.]

If an economist argues every kind of WB is commensurable with the kinds produced by market goods, they must argue that nothing is sacred. Maybe so—I don't know. [For some individuals, nothing is sacred. I won't mention names.]

Most of us prosper from having a cultural identity: belonging to a group, being supported by that group, and sharing its values—belonging to the tribe. And we would feel a significant loss if we were exiled. Or if the group and its values were threatened. Related to cultural identity is one's way of life: what one does, friends and family, and occupation. It, like one's cultural identity, bears kinds of WB. These bearers are WB-incompatible with market goods if an ability to compare them is inconsistent with a capacity to experience the kinds of WB unique to one's cultural identity and way of life. Maybe culture and goods are WB-comparable for people who believe they are, but not for people who don't? For many people, shopping and consumption is their culture.

[15] There is a long, and continuing, history of humans believing some environmental resources are sacred (e.g., specific species and certain geographical features and places). Secular Westerners poo-poo sacredness, although it is common elsewhere and in other groups. Even among Westerners, there are individuals who believe nature has sacred components.

I think about whether experiencing certain emotions is possible if their effects on your WB are commensurable with the kinds produced by market goods. For example, consider your ability to experience grief due to losing a loved one. It is painful, but you would want to feel grief, given your loss. Can one experience grief if one can compare it with the pleasures of market goods? Can I grieve for the dead wife I bumped off for the insurance money? I miss her chocolate cake, but grieve? Could I have truly loved her?

Consider depression (a kind of ill-being). It affects most people and severely affects the WB of millions. [Remember that a primary way to increase WB is to reduce ill-being.] A characteristic of severe depression is that you are incapable of experiencing WB—the pleasures of an ice-cream cone on a hot day can't be experienced—often, you can't even get out of bed. Given the nature of depression, how could you compare the ill-being of depression with the kinds of WB produced by market goods?[16]

Consider *inclinations*: on your current path, you are, in your view, a woman of integrity, whereas, on my current path, I'm selfish and lacking in empathy (a bit of a sociopath). Consider paths that vary by one's inclinations and consumption levels. A complete ranking of paths in terms of WB requires that you can WB-compare the kinds of WB associated with different inclinations with the kinds produced by market goods. For example, can you experience honesty if you can WB-compare it with a path that keeps your kid out of jail because you are dishonest? Can I WB-compare two paths if I am a sociopath with lots of toys on the current path, and on the other, I am empathetic but toyless? Can I know what empathy would feel like if I have never experienced it?

[16] In some past research I have assumed you can. In hypothetical choice experiments, I have asked depressed subjects to choose between treatment programs, programs that varied by dollar cost and effectiveness. See Jennifer Thacher, Edward Morey, and Edward Craighead (2005) and Morey et al. (2007). Some of the subjects might have been incapable of such WB comparisons.

The WB Produced by Learning (Acquiring Knowledge) Is WB-Incommensurable with the Kinds of WB Produced by What You Learned About?

Consider the WB effects of acquiring knowledge about the process of global warming (its causes, effects, man's role, etc.) compared to the WB effects of a change in its rate. I chose global warming for this example because it's a global public process that will cause a lot of ill-being, and many are ignorant and want to stay ignorant.

Education leads to knowledge acquisition, and the acquiring produces different kinds of WB.[17] Education (reading, studying, and listening) is the bearer. When unsuccessful, it generates ill-being (confusion, frustration, and a sense of failure). Then there is the issue of how you are affected by the new knowledge. New knowledge about processes directly affects WB. For example, acquiring knowledge about global warming and cancers can affect different kinds of WB in different ways.

The question is whether knowledge WB is WB-commensurable with the kinds of WB that would be produced by a change in the level of what you have acquired knowledge of. Knowledge, once acquired, can't be traded away. You can sell your house and car, but you can't unlearn things, even if what you learned decreases your WB.[18] Another aspect of knowledge about a process is that before you acquire it, you are ignorant. You don't always know whether its acquisition will increase or decrease your overall WB. These two aspects of knowledge suggest that it is challenging to compare education with other bearers of WB.

Consider my knowledge of global warming. Suppose paths vary only in my understanding of it and its expected rate. Can I compare these two bearers of WB? I'm not sure; there are inherent difficulties. To keep

[17] One subset in the list of emotions is *epistemic emotions*: emotions that have a knowledge component (Scarantino and de Sousa 2018). Examples include curiosity, surprise, validation, feelings of doubt or certainty, the feeling of knowing, and the bliss of ignorance. So, learning for learning's sake can directly increase or decrease WB.

[18] Note the earlier mentioned findings (Chapter 1) that 16% of the university students sampled were willing to forego a payment of $10 to avoid learning whether they had genital herpes, and people will pay to not learn about their IQ or how attractive others find them.

things simple, assume everyone agrees that a lower expected rate would increase their WB, and I am uneducated about global warming.

Further, imagine that my uneducated prior is that while global warming will be bad, it will not be terrible.[19] How would I determine whether I would have more WB in a world where I'm more educated about the effects of global warming and there is a different expected rate? I don't know if I could make such comparisons.

Now flip the example, and imagine I'm already educated about global warming (so I know how it works and its effects). Then I'm asked whether I would experience more WB if I knew less and there was a different global warming rate. So how do I assess not knowing what I already know?

In summary, people are ignorant about physics, chemistry, and biology, particularly the environmental sciences, ecosystem dynamics, and the health effects of chemicals. And the kinds of WB we experience when our environment changes (species go extinct, the expected rate-of-global warming changes, there is less [or more] PCB contamination) are a function of our level of knowledge—ignorance can be bliss. But once knowledge is acquired, it is not freely disposable. Comparing environmental kinds of WB with knowledge about the environment is difficult, causing me to suspect I'm incapable of ordering paths in terms of their environmental effects and my understanding of those effects.

While my example has been global warming, this comparability conundrum arises whenever paths vary by the levels of different processes and the individual's understanding of those processes. For example, compare a medical test that will inform you whether the black mole on your toe is cancer with being treated for that cancer. Compare educating yourself on the research on the benefits and costs of immunizing your children vs. immunization rates. Compare learning the actual probability of being killed in a terrorist attack vs. how much is spent on fighting terrorism.

[19] Also think through the example imagining that in my ignorance I imagine global warming is worse than it actually is.

You Cannot Compare Certain Kinds of WB Because It Is Morally Unacceptable to Even Imagine Such Comparisons?

How much money would you need to push the button that would extinct elephants or dump a gigaton of PCBs in Lake Michigan? How much would you need to eliminate equal rights? Many regular people, but not neoclassical economists, would find it unimaginable to compare these bearers with market goods or WB-compare the existence of elephants with equal rights. Suppose you can't WB-compare elephant extinction with ending Biden's Presidency. That means you can't WB-rank elephants and no Biden vs. Biden and no elephants. Or, if you like both elephants and Biden, it means you can't WB-rank elephants and no Biden vs. Biden and no elephants. [Remember my caution: an inability to compare for moral reasons is different from comparing and concluding there is no amount of money you could be paid to be willing to give up your morals.]

The inability to compare because of moral or cultural sanctions varies drastically across cultures and religions. Research indicates that secular Westerners with high-socioeconomic status (Europeans and North Americans) are willing to make comparisons that non-Westerners and Western religious conservatives will not make (Haidt and Graham 2007; Graham et al. 2009). The two latter groups, but not the first group, morally require ingroup/loyalty, authority/respect, and purity/sanctity. This makes it difficult for them to compare sanction violations with money. [Loyalty, respect, and purity are not something one compares with chocolate cake.] For American First Peoples, the kinds of WB born by their culture and natural surrounding are likely WB-incommensurable, on moral grounds, with the kinds of WB resulting from market goods and services.[20]

For Western religious conservatives, WB-comparability requires that the kinds of WB reduced by disloyalty are commensurable with those reduced by impure and sacrilegious acts. Complete WB-comparability

[20] Tribes are often trustees in NRDA cases. To cite an extreme example, consider the "water pollution, soil contamination, deforestation, and cultural upheaval" (Wikipedia: Lago Agrio oil field) resulting from oil exploration and extraction in the Sucumbíos Province of Ecuador caused by Texaco (now owned by Chevron) and its effect on the indigenous tribes who, arguably, lost their culture and way of life. Chevron and Ecuador battled over damages in both the U.S. and Ecuadorian courts. If their culture and money are, in fact, WB-incomparable, monetary damages are undefined.

requires that one can WB-compare, for example, desecrating a cross, disrespecting the President, religious freedom, a ban on abortion, income (in)equality, global warming, animal extinctions, and market goods.

Some secular Westerners believe we have a moral obligation to the environment, a preservation ethic. Consider the famous quote by Aldo Leopold in his 1940s essay "The Land Ethic,"[21]

> A thing is right when it tends to preserve the integrity, stability, and beauty of the biotic community. It is wrong when it tends otherwise.

Summarizing his ethic, humans don't stand alone. They are part of the community of plants, animals, lands, and waters (collectively, the "land"), and, as members of that community, we must respect its other members. They have the "right" to exist and prosper (e.g., animal rights), and it is our moral responsibility to see that they flourish—we play the role of parents. And parental responsibility is inconsistent with sacrificing one's children for money.[22] Accepting the right of others to exist and prosper is, arguably, inconsistent with their demise being WB-comparable with market goods.

Ecological Economists Accept as Gospel That Complete WB-Commensurability Does Not Exist

This is what distinguishes ecological economists from environmental economists: environmental economists take complete WB-commensurability as gospel. To start.

[21] Leopold's *Sand County Almanac* was published by his son in 1949 (shortly after Leopold's death). It is a collection of essays: essays about the land in Wisconsin where he had a farm (the part of Wisconsin with sandy soil), essays about other regions, essays about his personal experiences in nature, and essays that sketch an environmental ethic. The "Land Ethic" is the last essay in the book. The book was unknown until the 1970s. It, along with Rachel Carson's *Silent Spring* (1962) are foundations of the environmental movement in the U.S.

[22] There are differing views on how Leopold might have applied his land ethic in specific situations, I suspect there would be disagreement among environmental ethicists as to whether he believed the WB humans get from the land are incommensurable with other kinds of WB. And environmentalists say they are incommensurable and view Leopold as a source.

Ecological Economists Believe That There Are Kinds of WB That Only the Environment Can Produce

Are there? I'm not sure, but many believe it. If people do, more wilderness, less global warming, and saving a species from extinction are bearers.

Kinds of WB unique to natural environments include the freedom and self-reliance that can only be experienced in the wilderness. They include experiencing the joys of in-situ learning about plants and animals. They include experiencing the awe produced by seeing majestic mountains and rivers. They may include the kinds of WB produced by nature-based recreational activities (hiking, skiing, biking, swimming, diving, fishing, hunting, and camping).[23] Also, the kinds of WB natural environments produce for indigenous populations (these were discussed earlier). And, the argument that an understanding of the significant relationships that natural environments create (e.g., human to human, human to animal, animal to human, animal to animal, animal to plants, and plants to animal) contributes, in a unique way, to a "worthwhile life" (see Alan Holland 2006; Dan Firth 2008). Many of us aspire to a worthwhile life.[24] [You may find nothing unique about the types of sensations, perceptions, thoughts, and emotions nature can produce, but that does not prove others don't.]

[23] In contrast, there are kinds of WB that are experienced in natural settings such as the thrill of going fast on skis, a bike, or a snowmobile that are, arguably, not environmental-specific kinds of WB. For example, when I was young, I got similar thrills from going fast in cars.

[24] Quoting Firth, "A meaningful relationship occurs when the interactions between two entities have significance in their past history and its anticipated continuation." Examples include our historical relationships, as humans, with nature, animal parent/child relationships, historical relationships between land and human communities, the relationships between humans and the plants and animals they eat, the relationship between a rancher and his herd, the relationship between two wolves in a pack, and the relationship between a wolf pack and its potential prey. This last example is discussed in detail by Leopold (1949/1987). In summary, an understanding and appreciation of nature-based relationships is an important component of a worthwhile life, according to this perspective.

Ecological Economists Value Ecological Systems (ES), and ES Are Prime Suspects When It Comes to Incommensurabilities

Ecological systems (ES) such as wetlands, forests, coral reefs, estuaries, bays, and rivers integrate biological, hydrological, physical, and human processes providing services to plants, animals, and humans. An ES can be viewed as a bearer of WB or a vector of bearers of WB, these bearers are inputs that produce recreation, animal and plant preservation, a way of life, water purification, and flood control. And they produce overlapping vectors of different kinds of WB. For example, for an indigenous population, a reef fishery maintains the WB associated with the continuation of their way of life. And produces recreational benefits for the non-indigenous and knowledge of preservation for distant populations, all while making coastline residents worry less about global warming sea rise.[25]

One has to question whether these different kinds of WB are commensurable with the kinds of WB produced by other goods and activities. There is a ton of ecological literature on ES. Most articles include variations on the word "incommensurable," taking incommensurability as a given. Paraphrasing Joan Martinez-Alier et al. (1998), WB-incomparabilities and WB-incommensurabilities are the "foundation

[25] These kinds of WB effects vary drastically in their magnitudes: the loss of a sport-fishing opportunity has a small effect on our WB, whereas the loss of one's culture, community, and way-of-life are life-shattering. Cynthia Burke (2010) reports on how the loss of subsistence fishing activities has affected the way of life of the Nuxall First Nation of British Columbia. Quoting from K. Chan, Terre Satterfield, and Joshua Goldstein (2012), "A Kyuquot–Checleset elder (of the northwest coast of Vancouver Island, B.C.), described (pers. comm.) the loss of fishing opportunities as causing a loss of knowledge and cultural identity in the community's youth, which she seemed to attribute to a lack of transformative experiences, all of which were entangled with both self- and other oriented, group and individual values… a Kyuquot–Checleset fisherman (pers. comm.) suggested the decline of local Chinook … as triggering loss of inspiration and spiritual benefits…".

of ecological economics".[26,27] Typically what ecological economists are evaluating have more interconnected bearers than what environmental economists value: most of my (neoclassical) valuation studies have been limited to a component of an ES such as a catch rate, a fish-consumption advisory, or a ski or mountain-bike trail.

While this aside has been about the environment, my applied field in economics, similar arguments could be made by those who study bearers of WB such as families, public institutions, and political processes. For example, childcare is produced by families, firms, and the government, each producing different kinds of WB and ill-being. Parents worry about

[26] This article has been cited a thousand times by ecologists and ecological economists—environmental economists don't cite it. The article starts from the premise that environmental amenities are WB-incomparable with market goods—the authors don't provide arguments for their premise. The literature citing this article typically cites it as proof of the premise. Unlike the philosophical literature on incommensurability, this literature does not adopt the distinction between kinds of WB and bearers of WB, which is unfortunate.

Martinez-Alier is a past president of the International Society of Ecological Economics. His title "foundation of ecological economics" asserts that all that separates ecological economist from neoclassical environmental economists is ecological economists believe the kinds of WB produced by environmental resources are incommensurable with the kinds produced by market goods. K. William Kapp (1983) might be the first modern economist to state this position. He said, referring to the kinds of WB produced by environmental resources, "they are heterogenous and cannot be compared quantitatively among themselves and with each other, not even in principle." Two publications that cite Martinez-Alier, Munda, and O'Neill and assume incomplete WB-comparability are Spash et al. (2008) and Munda (2016). Many of the citing articles are in *Ecological Economics* or *Environmental Valuation*.

[27] Because of incommensurabilities, ecological economists choose environmental projects based on multiple criteria: "Incommensurability means that there is not a common unit of measurement, but it does *not* mean that we cannot compare alternative decisions on a rational basis, on *different* scales of values, as in multi-criteria evaluation" (Martinez-Alier 1995). Another example is Berta Martin-Lopez, Erik Gomez-Baggethun, Marina Garcia-Llorent, and Carlos Montes (2014).

If an individual's WB-comparability is not complete, his ordering of paths will be incomplete, so, for example, he might rank environmental projects *A* and *B* both higher than the status quo, even though *A* and *B* are not ranked relative to each other, so additional criteria are needed for him to decide between them. That is, multiple-criteria are often needed to decide between environmental projects when the kinds of WB produced by each is incommensurable with the kinds produced by the other and incommensurable with the kinds produced by market goods. For example, one might select B over A if B helps poor people more. There is much debate as to what the additional criteria should be. Besides Martinez-Alier (1995) and Martinez-Alier et al. (1998), see, for example, Munda (2016) and Espen Stabell (2021).

whether the kinds produced inside and outside the family are child WB-commensurable. Some kinds of WB produced by the criminal/justice system are also produced by the market (e.g., a sense of safety from a lock or alarm system), but some aren't, such as the sense that justice was served and your rights are protected.

If You Have No Control over How Much of a Bearer You Experience, You Don't Compare It with Other Bearers

Don't sweat what you cannot influence. Elizabeth Anderson (1997) articulates this argument. If you cannot control a bearer's level, there is no reason to think about how to compare it with another bearer. And besides it being a waste of your time, it would be something to avoid. Economists, in contrast, assume that when you wake up, you have a complete ordering over all conceivable paths, so they reject that the two paths are first compared when the individual has to choose between them. Economists like me, who value in dollars environmental resources, assume you have a well-defined *CV* for less global warming, even if you cannot affect its rate. You have it even before the surveyor asks you what it is. Economists of my ilk would say that a contingent-valuation survey is simply a way for the researcher to find your *CV* to reduce global warming (less global warming is a bearer).

In contrast, Anderson would say that you don't show up at the survey center with a *CV* for panda preservation because it never crossed your mind that you would ever be comparing panda preservation with beer and chocolate cake. And, you won't during the survey unless you are convinced by the survey that panda preservation is something you can influence. Those of us creating and using contingent-valuation surveys to value environmental resources have sympathy for her point, but not enough to reject the WB-comparability of market goods with environmental commodities whose levels you have no control over.

Historically, most of us could not control pollution levels or amounts of environmental preservation. However, this is starting to change, at least probabilistically, particularly if one is extremely rich and/or politically active. [Jeff Bezos recently pledged $10 billion to address climate change.]

Evolution and WB Comparison

The ability to WB-compare is a skill one inherits or learns. In evolutionary terms, the survival of humans and prehumans had nothing to do with the sorts of health, environmental and long-term choices we now face. Cancer risks vs. diet and exercise were not issues. Evolution was not driven by benefits now vs. distant ones. As a result, humans did not evolve to WB-compare modern-world alternatives. We see this also in our inability to WB-compare when small probabilities are in play.

Inadequate Processing Skills

Imagine I have complete information about two paths in that I know the specifics of each, including probabilities, so my ignorance (lack of knowledge) is not an issue. The paths, however, have more moving parts than I can cognitively process, making it impossible for me to WB-order them. I think this is a possible cause of WB-incommensurability. Still, I don't want to make too much of it because it causes issues for choice theory beyond WB-incommensurability.

You could counter that this is an example of inability to compare because of ignorance, not an example of WB-incommensurability. It is ignorance in that I'm ignorant of the WB effects of each path, but I'm not ignorant of the properties of each path, so it isn't lack-of-knowledge ignorance.

The lack of processing skills argument is if too many kinds of WB differ between the two paths, one's ability to WB-compare breaks down, even if one could WB-rank the two paths if fewer kinds of WB were changing.

Saying "Paths *i* and *j* Are WB-Incomparable" Does Not Make It So

Earlier, I noted that asserting that, for you, *i* and *j* are WB-comparable does make it so. Asserting the opposite ("I can't WB-compare i and j") also does make it so (Posner 1998). It is a flawed argument either way. There are many reasons for saying, "I can't—even if I can. We may not want to do the cognitive work, or we don't want to convey that we are the sort who can compare the WB from saving polar bears with the WB from beer, even if we are. Admitting to your spouse that their love is WB-commensurable with the pleasure from extra-marital sex would reduce their love for you, so you lie.

Path Incomparability Is Sometimes Mandated by Law

The US *Endangered Species Act* says species aren't comparable: extincting one to save three is illegal. The Delaney Clause forbids carcinogenic substances which implies cancers are not comparable with market goods (Sunstein 1993). And the US Federal Courts have ruled that even if the damage from degrading an environmental resource is less than the cost of restoring it, the destroyer is responsible for the higher restoration cost; suggesting that, environmental damages are not comparable with market goods.

The issue for WB-comparability is whether a legal mandate that things are not comparable makes it more difficult for an individual to WB-compare them.

A Few Other Qualms About WB-Commensurability

(I) A lot of what we consume are *public commodities*: commodities that are non-congestible and non-excludable. Some increase WB (*public goods*), and others decrease WB (*public bads*). This makes comparing the WB produced by public commodities with those produced by market goods awkward: how do you compare consuming a good that will only increase your WB with consuming a good that will increase everyone's WB? Or compare your consumption of a market good with providing a public commodity that would increase your WB but decreases everyone else's. People who lack empathy for others make such comparisons, but that does not mean everyone can. Not everyone can compare the personal WB they would get from private goods with the WB losses everyone would get from dirtier air or more global warming—they feel they don't have the right to make such comparisons, so they don't.

(II) Imagine comparing the WB relief from less global warming with being less anxious. Making such comparisons is complicated because being more anxious will influence how much relief you get from less global warming. [One could lab test this by invoking anxiety before a contingent-valuation question or choice experiment. The design would vary the amount of the change in global warming and the amount of anxiety invoked.[28]]

(III) Personal responsibilities and personal commitments can complicate WB-commensurability. [Contrast personal responsibilities and obligations with those placed on everyone by religious or cultural mores.] Consider a Western rancher whose family has had the ranch for generations. Typically, ranches provide wildlife habitat, a bearer of environmental WB for the rancher and others.[29] Ranchers are committed to and feel responsible for maintaining the ranch in its current state and keeping it in the family (both of these responsibilities motivate conservation easements). It wouldn't be surprising if ranchers would have difficulty comparing the WB associated with maintaining the ranch habitat with the WB obtained by selling it and retiring to a condo in Florida.

One final qualm about a world of complete WB-commensurability and complete comparability: most of the richness and variety of life would be beside the point. At the end of the day, no one would care what caused their WB. Of course, people hope they don't live in such a world, but this does not prove they do or don't.

[28] Anxiety levels can be manipulated with, for example, computer simulations and by varying the environment. Rajagopal Raghunathan and Michel Pham (1999) is an example of a study that evoked anxiety. For examples of modeling choices as a function of personality and emotions see Mario Solinõ and Begona Farizo (2014), and Morey and Thiene (2017).

[29] Ranches, near where I lived north of Steamboat CO, besides grazing cattle and sheep, provide habitat for elk, deer, moose, mountain lions, trout, and other animals. There are conservation easements on properties, even though obtaining the easement reduce a ranch's market value.

OK, Maybe Some People Cannot WB-Rank All Conceivable Paths, but Who Cares If Most People Can WB-Rank Their Current Available Paths

Choice does not require complete WB-comparability, only the ability to WB-compare the available paths. If one could demonstrate that most people can do this, the cost of ignoring WB-incomparability would be negligible. However, I don't know how one would determine, case by case, what proportion of the population could WB-compare a specific pair of paths. [And, as I noted earlier, asserting "I can" does not prove you can.]

Neurological Evidence in Support of Comparability and WB-Commensurability

Recent findings on the neurobiology of choice oppose the above philosophical arguments against complete WB-commensurability. These findings are consistent with complete comparability (don't contradict it). Quoting Dino Levy and Glimcher (2012),

> Indeed, there is now broad consensus in the neuroscience of the decision-making community that reward magnitude is represented in a small number of well-identified areas. Here we conduct a meta-analysis using evidence from human functional magnetic resonance imaging (fMRI) studies conducted over just the past few years that suggest that one of these reward magnitude encoding areas, the ventromedial prefrontal cortex/orbital frontal cortex (vmPFC/OFC), can be thought of as representing the value of nearly all reward types on a common scale that predicts behaviorally observe comparison and choice.

They claim that the research demonstrates that we all have complete WB-comparability. They claim too much.

The striatum and the ventromedial prefrontal cortex are your *valuation circuit* (Glimcher 2013). Picture a two-dimensional topographical map of neurons, where each alternative is represented by a different point on the neuron map (Fig. 7.2: 2 alternatives).[30] The third dimension is the firing rates of the neurons. The alternative whose neuron achieves the highest peak (firing rate) will be selected. Initially, the firing rates for the different alternatives fluctuate. If a neuron's firing rate increases, it increases the firing rates of nearby neurons while inhibiting the firing rates of distant neurons, including those associated with the other peaks. Eventually, one peak dominates, and you go with that alternative.

(I) The final selection of an alternative (at least for the sorts of sets of alternatives studied in neuroscience labs) takes place in the valuation circuit. (II) The variation in firing rates across the neurons determines/ predicts which alternative will be selected—firing rates are all that matter. This is consistent with complete WB-comparability.

In the studies D. Levy and Glimcher review, some male subjects were asked to choose between alternatives; others only viewed the alternatives. fMRI measured firing rates. Alternatives were presented with different amounts of the same reward, different reward types, and both different types and magnitudes. Alternatives included money (magnitude and when it would be delivered), college trinkets, pain, pictures of females that varied in attractiveness, and snack foods. In all the studies that involved choosing—not all did—money was one alternative.

Fig. 7.2 Cartoon of the valuation circuit with two alternatives (Courtesy of Ryan Webb)

[30] "... most classes of information recorded in the cerebral cortex are topographically encoded on anatomically two-dimensional 'maps'." "The cortex is made of dozens of these small topographical maps" (Glimcher 2013).

No matter the alternatives presented, the valuation circuit was activated, suggesting the selection process always includes the valuation circuit. And the firing-rate findings are consistent with which alternative the individual says they would prefer (see, in particular, D. V. Smith et al. 2010; Levy and Glimcher 2011, 2012).

However, these findings do not imply that relative firing rates reflect how each alternative would be ranked by a well-defined monotonic index of overall WB. They don't even imply that a WB index exists. So, they do not imply complete WB-comparability. The authors use the word "value" but define it in terms of firing rates: the alternative with the highest firing rate is defined as the one with the highest value, so the rest have lower values. It's simply a measure of electrical activity in a particular place in your head.

These findings are consistent with all bundles being comparable in terms of something different from WB, even something inconsistent with WB. For example, they are consistent with selecting the alternative you most desire, the one that makes you least anxious, most proud, or even different criteria on different selection occasions.[31]

Recollect the incorrect circular argument. First, you assume a complete WB ordering of alternatives and that the individual chooses their highest-ranked available path. Then you observe the individual selecting the alternative with the highest firing rate. It, by assumption, is the one with the highest value. The argument does not demonstrate complete WB-comparability: you started by assuming it.

To summarize, the neurological evidence is consistent with WB-commensurability and bearer-of-WB-comparability but doesn't demonstrate either.

Those who reject complete WB-commensurability wouldn't be surprised by the neurological findings nor disagree with them. Instead, they would say that comparability between money and snacks doesn't imply complete comparability.

Levy and Glimcher were looking for a spot in the brain where WB-commensurability occurs, and they found a candidate.

[31] See Chapter 4 for more on desires/wants vs. likes.

Summing Up and Looking Forward

A pillar of NBT is the complete WB-comparability of paths, which requires complete WB-commensurability. This chapter reviewed the issues and arguments and presented relevant theories and research.

While NCT was formulated initially to explain and estimate the demand functions for market goods, its scope has been leaping and creeping wider—which is why I define an ordering over paths rather than bundles of market goods. Economists working in labor, urban, public, development, and family economics have widened the span. It now includes bearers of WB such as school quality, public services, roads, air-pollution levels, water quality, parks, wilderness, global warming, crime rates, job security, human rights, number of bathrooms, commuting time, and national defense, plus a lot more.

When NCT was only about market goods, arguably, advocates only needed to worry about the comparability of bundles of market goods. This required commensurability of the kinds of WB produced by market goods. Now paths have more components, and more kinds of WB need to be modeled.

Pushing back against the neoclassical assumption that everything is WB-comparable are ethicists, and many others, who believe many things we care about cannot be compared with market goods.

If there is not complete WB-commensurability, there will not be a complete ordering of paths. And this has implications. Predictions become less specific: all we can predict is that the individual will not experience a path ranked lower than another available path (maximizing rather than optimizing). Adding to this, I have shown that if there is not complete WB-comparability for many path shifts (Path i to j), there is no compensating variation, CV, corresponding to that shift—the CV concept is not defined. For example, a CV for a policy that reduced the rate of global warming does not exist if any changes in any kind of WB (or ill-being) affected by the policy are incommensurable with each other or with anything else whose level the individual can influence. Or if it is associated with changes in path components that he cares about but can't influence. To make these issues disappear, one has to believe that the kinds of WB produced by national defense, friends and family, lovers, freedoms, fairness, and all else are WB-commensurable.

My intent in this chapter was not to tell you that there is or isn't complete WB-comparability. My goal was to express the implications of incomplete WB-comparability and outline arguments one must defend against if one wants to argue for complete WB-comparability. Of course, if you only have to deal with people who are OK with complete WB-comparability, your road ahead is smooth. [I wonder why the issue of WB-incomparability has not been raised by lawyers and economists representing the defendant in NRDA litigations (e.g., the BP Gulf of Mexico spill). I suspect it is because all the economic-valuation experts on both sides are neoclassical economists, so they accept, without thought, complete WB-comparability.[32]]

Economists can reject all the arguments against complete WB-comparability and complete WB-commensurability, but they should be able to articulate why these arguments are wrong. Also, economists should know the neurological evidence.

This brings us to the end of Part II. Parts I and II presented NCT along with evidence and arguments supporting and contradicting its Assumptions. Rather than calling it neoclassical choice theory, NCT, I called my presentation neoclassical behavior theory, NBT. I did this for two reasons, I did not want to quibble about what exactly is and isn't NCT, and I wanted to draw a vital distinction between behaviors and chosen behaviors (choices). Economists believe most behaviors are chosen; therefore, the adjective "choice" in choice theory. In contrast, many philosophers and psychologists argue, with evidence, that behaviors are often not chosen.

Bringing us to Part III: Behavioral quirks.

[32] If I had been working for British Petroleum on the legal case to assess the dollar damages from the 2010 oil spill in the Gulf of Mexico [I worked for the other side], and if my intent had been to reduce, or eliminate, their liability, I would have introduced the argument that environmental kinds of WB are incommensurable with the kinds of WB generated by spending on private goods, making it impossible for many to trade-off environmental injuries for money. Arguing this would, at a minimum, have forced both sides to hire some philosophers and neuroscientists to defend or attack WB- commensurability. Philosophers could use the extra income.

References and Sources

Adler, Matthew. 1997. "Incommensurability and cost-benefit analysis." *University of Pennsylvania Law Review* 146: 1371.

Anderson, Elizabeth. 1997. "Practical reason and incommensurable goods." In *Incommensurability, incomparability, and practical reason*, edited by Ruth Chang. Cambridge, MA: Harvard University Press.

Beckerman, Wilfred. 2017. *Economics as applied ethics: Fact and value in economic policy*. 2nd edition. Palgrave Macmillan.

Bossert, Walter. 2018. "Suzumura-consistent relations: An overview." *International Journal of Economic Theory* 14 (1): 21–34.

Bossert, Walter, and Kōtarō Suzumura. 2010. *Consistency, choice, and rationality*. Harvard University Press.

Burke, Cynthia. 2010. "When the fishing's gone: Understanding how fisheries management affects the informal economy and social capital in the Nuxalk nation." Resource Management and Environmental Studies, University of British Columbia.

Carson, Racheal. 1962. *Silent spring*. Houghton Mifflin Harcourt.

Chan, K. M. A., T. Satterfield, and J. Goldstein. 2012. "Rethinking ecosystem services to better address and navigate cultural values." *Ecological Economics* 74: 8–18. https://doi.org/10.1016/j.ecolecon.2011.11.011. https://www.webofscience.com/wos/woscc/full-record/WOS:000301277000003.

Firth, D. 2008. "Do meaningful relationships with nature contribute to a worthwhile life?" *Environmental Values* 17 (2): 145–164. https://doi.org/10.3197/096327108x303828. https://www.webofscience.com/wos/woscc/full-record/WOS:000256321100003.

Glimcher, Paul. 2013. Chapter 20: Value-based decision making. In *Neuroscience second edition: Decision making and the brain*, edited by Paul Glimcher and Ernst Fehr. Elsevier.

Graham, Jesse, Jonathan Haidt, and Brian Nosek. 2009. "Liberals and conservatives rely on different sets of moral foundations." *Journal of Personality and Social Psychology* 96 (5): 1029–1046. https://doi.org/10.1037/a0015141. https://www.webofscience.com/wos/woscc/full-record/WOS:000265305100007.

Haidt, Jonathan, and Jesse Graham. 2007. "When morality opposes justice: Conservatives have moral intuitions liberals may not recognize." *Social Justice Research* 20: 18.

Hansson, Sven. 2018. "Money pumps." In *Introduction to formal philosophy: Springer undergraduate texts in philosophy*, edited by Sven Hansson and V Hendricks. Springer. https://doi.org/10.1007/978-3-319-77434-3_31.

———. 2006. "Must we give up environmental ethics?" In *Environmental ethics and international policy*, edited by H. Have. Paris: UNESCO.

Hsieh, Nien-He. 2007. "Is incomparability a problem for anyone." *Economics and Philosophy* 23 (1): 65–80.

Hsieh, Nien-He, and Hendrik Andersson. 2021. "Incommensurable values." *Stanford Encyclopedia of Philosophy*. http://plato.standford.edu.

Kapp, William K. 1983. *Social costs, economic development, and environmental disruption*. Introduction by J. E. Ullmann. Lanham, MD: University Press of America.

Knetsch, Jack. 1989. "The endowment effect and evidence of non-reversible indifference curves." *American Economic Review* 79 (5): 1277–1284. https://www.webofscience.com/wos/woscc/full-record/WOS:A1989CD48800024.

Leopold, Aldo. 1949. *A sand country almanac*. Oxford: Oxford University Press.

Levy, Dino, and Paul Glimcher. 2011. "Comparing apples and oranges: Using reward-specific and reward-general subjective value representation in the brain." *Journal of Neuroscience* 31 (41): 14693–14707. https://doi.org/10.1523/jneurosci.2218-11.2011. https://www.webofscience.com/wos/woscc/full-record/WOS:000312470900016.

———. 2012. "The root of all value: A neural common currency for choice." *Current Opinion in Neurobiology* 22 (6): 1027–1038. https://doi.org/10.1016/j.conb.2012.06.001. https://www.webofscience.com/wos/woscc/full-record/WOS:000312470900016.

Mandler, Michael. 2004. "Status quo maintenance reconsidered: Changing or incomplete preferences?" *The Economic Journal* 114 (499): F518–F535.

Martinez-Alier, Joan. 1995. "Political ecology, distributional conflicts, and economic incommensurability." *New Left Review*, May 1.

Martinez-Alier, J., G. Munda, and J. O'Neill. 1998. "Weak comparability of values as a foundation for ecological economics." *Ecological Economics* 26 (3): 277–286. https://doi.org/10.1016/s0921-8009(97)00120-1. https://www.webofscience.com/wos/woscc/full-record/WOS:000076181000004.

Martin-Lopez, Beta, Erik Gomez-Baggethun, Marina Garcia-Llorente, and Carlos Montes. 2014. "Tradeoffs across value-domains in ecosystem services assessment." *Ecological Indicators* 37: 220–228. https://doi.org/10.1016/j.ecolind.2013.03.003. https://www.webofscience.com/wos/woscc/full-record/WOS:000329385300023.

Morey, Edward, Jennifer Thacher, and Edward Craighead. 2007. "Patient preferences for depression treatment programs and willingness to pay for treatment." *Journal of Mental Health Policy and Economics* 10 (2): 73–85. https://pubmed.ncbi.nlm.nih.gov/17603148/.

Morey, Edward, and Mara Thiene. 2017. "Can personality traits explain where and when you recreate? A latent-class site-choice model informed by estimates from mixed-mode lc cluster models with latent-personality traits." *Ecological Economics* 138: 223–237. https://doi.org/j.ecolecon.2017.03.038.

Munda, G. 2016. "Beyond welfare economics: Some methodological issues." *Journal of Economic Methodology* 23 (2): 185–202. https://doi.org/10.1080/1350178x.2016.1157199. https://www.webofscience.com/wos/woscc/full-record/WOS:000377038500007.

Neurath, Otto. 1973. "Personal life and class struggle." In *Empiricism and sociology*, 249–298. Springer.

Nussbaum, Martha. 2012. "Who is a happy warrior? Philosophy, happiness research, and public policy." *International Review of Economics* 59 (4): 335–361.

Posner, Eric A. 1998. "The strategic basis of principled behavior: A critique of the incommensurability thesis." *The University of Pennsylvania Law Review* 146 (5): 1185–1214.

Raghunathan, R., and M. T. Pham. 1999. "All negative moods are not equal: Motivational influences of anxiety and sadness on decision making." *Organizational Behavior and Human Decision Processes* 79 (1): 56–77. https://doi.org/10.1006/obhd.1999.2838. https://www.webofscience.com/wos/woscc/full-record/WOS:000081328200003.

Raz, Joseph. 1986. *The morality of freedom*. Clarendon Press.

Scarantino, Andrea, and Ronald De Soursa. Winter 2018. "Emotion." Stanford Encyclopedia of Philosophy. Stanford University. https://plato.stanford.edu/.

Schopenhauer, Arthur. 1818/2011. *The world as will and idea*: The Project Gutenberg. www.gutenberg.org/files/38427/38427-pdf.

Sen, Amartya. 1979. "The welfare basis of real income comparisons: A survey." *Journal of Economic Literature* 17 (1): 1–45.

———. 1997. *Maximization and the act of choice*. Econometrica.

———. 2018. "The importance of incompleteness." *International Journal of Economic Theory*. https://doi.org/10.1111/ijet.12145.

Simon, Herbert. 1982. *Models of bounded rationality*. Vols. I and II. New York: Wiley.

Smith, David, et al. 2010. "Distinct value signals in the anterior and posterior ventromedial prefrontal cortex." *Journal of Neuroscience* 30 (7): 2490–2495. https://doi.org/10.1523/jneurosci.3319-09.2010. https://www.webofscience.com/wos/woscc/full-record/WOS:000274599600011.

Solino, Mario, and Bengona Farizo. 2014. "Personal traits underlying environmental preferences: A discrete choice experiment." *Plos One* 9 (2). https://doi.org/10.1371/journal.pone.0089603. https://www.webofscience.com/wos/woscc/full-record/WOS:000331714700132.

Spash, Clive. 2008. "How much is that ecosystem in the window? The one with the bio-diverse trail." *Environmental Values* 17 (2): 25.

Stabell, Espen. 2021. "Hard environmental choices: Comparability, justification and the argument from moral identity." *Environmental Values* 30 (1): 111–130. https://doi.org/10.3197/096327119x15678473651009. https://www.webofscience.com/wos/woscc/full-record/WOS:000608033000006.

Sunstein, Cass. 1993. "Incommensurability and valuation in law." *Michigan Law Review* (92): 779.

Suzumura, Kotaro. 1983. *Rational choice, collective decisions, and social welfare.* Cambridge University Press.

Tetlock, Philip. 2003. "Thinking the unthinkable: Sacred values and taboo cognitions." *Trends in Cognitive Sciences* 7 (7): 320–324. https://doi.org/10.1016/s1364-6613(03)00135-9. https://www.webofscience.com/wos/woscc/full-record/WOS:000184366800011.

Thacher, Jennifer, Edward Morey, and Edward Craighead. 2005. "Using patient characteristics and attitudinal data to identify depression treatment preference groups: A latent-class model." *Depression and Anxiety* 21 (2): 47–54. https://doi.org/10.1002/da.20057. https://www.webofscience.com/wos/woscc/full-record/WOS:000229157100001.

Von Mises, Ludwig. 1920/1935. "Economic calculation in the socialist commonwealth." In *Collectivist economic planning*, edited by F. Hayek. London: Routledge and Kegan Paul LTD.

Additional Readings

Bargh, John, et al. 2010. "From the physical to the psychological: Mundane experiences influence social judgment and interpersonal behavior." *Behavioral and Brain Sciences* 33 (4): 267-+. https://doi.org/10.1017/s0140525x10000993. https://www.webofscience.com/wos/woscc/full-record/WOS:000284381100003.

Broome, John. 2001. "Are intentions reasons? And how should we cope with incommensurable values." *Practical Rationality and Preference: Essays for David Gauthier*: 98–120.

Flemming, Timothy, et al. 2012. "The endowment effect in orangutans." *International Journal of Comparative Psychology* 25: 285–298.

Glimcher, Paul W., and Ernst Fehr, eds. 2013. *Neuroeconomics: Decision making and the brain.* 2nd ed. Edited by Paul W Glimcher and Ernst Fehr: Elsevier Academic Press.

Griffin, James. 1986. *Well-being: Its meaning, measurement, and moral importance.* Clarendon Press.

———. 1997. "Incommensurability: What's the problem?" In *Incommensurability, incomparability, and practical reason*, edited by Ruth Chang. Cambridge, MA: Harvard University Press.

———. 2000. "Replies." In *Essays in honor of James Griffin*, edited by R. Crisp and B. Hooker. Oxford: Oxford: Clarendon Press.

Griffin, James, Roger Crisp, and Brad Hooker. 2000. *Well-being and morality: Essays in honour of James Griffin*. Oxford University Press.

Hayek, Friedrich A. 1935. *The present state of the debate*. London.

Holland, Alan. 2002. "Are choices tradeoffs." In *Contested choices*, edited by D. Bromley and J. Paavola. Oxford: Oxford University Press.

Locke, John. 1700/1975. "On modes of pleasure and pain." In *4th edition, An essay concerning human understanding Book II: Ideas*. Oxford: Oxford University Press. https://www.earlymoderntexts.com/assets/pdfs/locke1690book2.pdf.

Morey, Edward. 2020. "Can economic choose? Can homo sapiens?" Working Paper. Boulder, CO: University of Colorado. https://edwardmorey.org/discuss.html.

O'Neill, J., A. Holland, and A. Light. 2008. *Environmental values*. London: Routledge.

Posner, Richard. 1983. *The economics of justice*. Harvard University Press.

Schroeder, Mark. 2012. "Value theory." Stanford Encyclopedia of Philosophy (Summer). Stanford University. https://plato.stanford.edu/.

Von Hayek, Friedrich. 1937. *The nature and history of the problem*. Routledge.

Williams, Lawrence, and John Bargh. 2008. "Experiencing physical warmth promotes interpersonal warmth." *Science* 322 (5901): 606–607. https://doi.org/10.1126/science.1162548. https://www.webofscience.com/wos/woscc/full-record/WOS:000260299100048.

PART III

Behavioral Quirks

CHAPTER 8

Common Quirks, Incorrect Beliefs, and Flawed Choosing

Psychologists, neuroscientists, and behavioral economists study quirks (behavioral regularities). A *quirk* is a peculiar cognitive habit, "peculiar" as in "strange and surprising." The adjective "common" because all humans, or at least most, share these cognitive habits—they are part of our built-in cognitive makeup.[1] We share them with non-human primates. They need to be contrasted with quirks shared by some, but not most humans, including your unique quirks. Examples include an aversion to purple foods and not stepping on sidewalk cracks.

In contrast, the common quirk duration bias is the cognitive habit of overestimating the durations of WB shifts: up and down shifts. Most of us do this. Psychologists and behavioral economists have spent their careers identifying and studying common quirks—there are thousands of published articles—I list a few.

[1] Terms in the literature include "biases" and "anomalies." They are not all "biases," and an "anomaly" is a deviation from what is common. But they are common.

E. R. Morey, *Deconstructing Behavior, Choice, and Well-being*, https://doi.org/10.1007/978-3-031-36712-0_8

Distinguish Between NBT Violations, Common Quirks, Incorrect Beliefs, Flawed Choosing, and a Wrong Choice

While a few common quirks violate at least one NBT Assumption, not all do. A common quirk might or might not imply that I fail to experience my highest-ranked available path: "common quirk" isn't a synonym for violating an NBT Assumption.

And while the common quirk duration bias is a type of *incorrect belief*, not all common quirks are incorrect beliefs, and not all incorrect beliefs are common quirks.

Individuals hold *beliefs*: how they think the world works and what they think will happen if event *A* happens. Beliefs include the subjective probabilities associated with different possible outcomes. For example, I believe there is a 40% chance it will be sunny tomorrow and a 20% chance that humans cause global warming.[2] These probabilities are personal beliefs, a function of how I believe the world works. Another set of beliefs is subjective beliefs about how different events will affect WB. Before tenure, I believed denial would make me miserable for years.

I define an *incorrect belief* as a divergence between what the individual believes is true and the best estimate of truth based on science and the available data. For example, suppose on the next flip of a coin, I believe with certainty that it will be heads, but it's a new penny, and there isn't anything unusual about the flipper, so the best estimate is 50%, even though it was tails on the first three flips. That I believe my depression will last forever is duration bias, an incorrect belief because all the data and science indicate a mean duration of three months for people of my ilk.[3]

NBT does not rule out incorrect beliefs.

[2] Many people agree—Actually, I don't.

[3] As someone who developed surveys to estimate how much an impacted group is damaged by an environmental injury, I am acutely aware that the beliefs respondents hold affect how they answer questions designed to estimate damages. People typically come to the interview with varying ones, often incorrect. (Consider an oil spill: people hold incorrect beliefs on how much oil was spilled, the physics and chemistry of how oil is dispersed in water, and the biological mechanisms by which oil affects plants and animals.) My hope was that after the respondents had read the description of the injury, they had a common and correct understanding (held correct beliefs). If not, I was estimating the damages for something other than the actual injury.

Assumption 9a: *An economicus's ordering of paths is based on its WB (well-being), WB, accounting for the uncertainties* and

Assumption 9b: *An economicus's ordering of paths is based on its wants and desires.*

Both 9a and b are consistent with incorrect beliefs. Assumption 9b puts no restrictions on the origins of wants and desires, and 9a admits beliefs and subjective probabilities that are not based on the best science and data.

Consider my most recent disaster: I Gorilla-glued duck feathers to my arms, and, flapping frantically, I leapt off my roof. Before the leap, I told my friend Neil that I would fly to France and alight atop the Arc de Triomphe. Neither before nor after my crash could Neil conclude I had violated an assumption of NBT. My subjective probability of success was 97%, and I knew if I made Paris, I would be joyous. And I have always hoped to fly like a bird. I chose the most-WB available path in terms of my subjective-probabilistic WB. And most people, including Neil and my therapist, would say I made a wrong choice in an abnormal-psychology sense. Psychologists assess selections not by what was selected but by whether the selection process was flawed. In my defense as an economist, my choosing was flawed but consistent with me being an economicus. There is always a story about a bizarre ordering, awful constraints, or weird beliefs that would make almost any behavior consistent with NBT. So, I won't try to identify a choice inconsistent with NBT. Instead, I ask whether the behavioral quirks discussed are inconsistent with what NBT assumes about *the process of choosing*.

Individuals can, all else constant, rank a path where their beliefs are mostly incorrect higher than one where their beliefs are mostly correct. Beliefs directly affect WB. I prefer to believe that I will last to 120. Believing that I am going to heaven would also be comforting.

Flawed choosing is choosing in a faulty manner: using a process or set of beliefs that are not expected—based on best estimates—to achieve the maximum available WB. Flawed choosing is an abbreviation for *flawed choosing in terms of WB*. Distinguish between the alternative selected (the choice) and the process of choosing, noting that even if your choosing is flawed, you could still end up experiencing the available path that produces the most WB. Some, but not all, common quirks cause flawed choosing. For example, quirks based on incorrect beliefs cause flawed choosing. Duration bias is an example. My confident expectation that

Trump would make America great again was incorrect. Your choosing is flawed if your subjective probabilities differ from the best estimates. Incorrect beliefs are often, but not always, the cause of flawed choosing.

While flawed choosing does not imply that every specific choice reduces WB, I suspect it reduces aggregate WB over time; there would be more if there was no flawed choosing. I am not sure; it is an untested hypothesis that would be difficult to test. However, I am not alone in believing that flawed choosing reduces overall WB.

Like common quirks, flawed choosing may result from violating an NBT Assumption, but flawed choosing does not imply a violation: NBT admits flawed choosing.

Please note that I have not defined a *wrong choice*. It is difficult to define (wrong relative to what?). One could define a choice as "wrong" if the choosing was flawed, but I reject that: what I flawfully chose could increase my WB.

Three + Common Quirks (Duration Bias, Our Emotional Empathy-Gap, Salience Effects, and a Possible 4th, Lack of Empathy for One's Future Self). What Does Each Mean for NBT?

First, I discuss *duration bias*: it's straightforward, and understanding it will help us understand the other. Duration bias does not violate any of the NBT Assumptions: it is an incorrect belief, a systematic and persistent bias in our subjective beliefs about the durations of WB shifts.

Table 8.1 summarizes the relationships between NBT and duration bias. Duration bias violates none of the NBT Assumptions but causes flawed choosing in terms of WB. It includes the relationships between NBT and the five quirks (the emotional empathy-gap, the future-self empathy-gap, incentive salience, and the endowment effect). For now, consider Column 2 (duration bias).

Previewing, the emotional empathy-gap and incentive salience violate only Assumption 4. The endowment effect violates 4 and 6a. Table 8.1 has a lot of blank cells: assumptions not violated. Three quirks cause flawed choosing. Whether the endowment effect causes it depends on whether the anticipated WB drop is realized. The endowment effect is an incorrect belief only if the anticipated WB drop is unrealized. Incentive

Table 8.1 Which NBT Assumptions are violated by each common quirk

	Duration bias	*Emotional empathy-gap*	*Endowment effect*	*Future-self empathy-gap*	*Incentive salience*
	No assumptions violated			No assumptions violated	
Assum1: at every pt. in time, only one path					
Assum2: at every pt. in time, only 1 ordering					
Assum3: ranking of two Paths can't depend on what else is imaginable					
Assum4: order. does not change in SR		Violated	Violated		Violated
Assum5 must be on an avail. path					
Assum6a: ordering can't depend on which Paths are avail.			Violated		
Assum6b: which Paths are avail. can't depend on ordering					
Assum7 chooses HRAP					
Assum 8 sensations					
Assum9a: ordering WB Or					Violated

(continued)

Table 8.1 (continued)

	Duration bias	*Emotional empathy-gap*	*Endowment effect*	*Future-self empathy-gap*	*Incentive salience*
Assum9b: ordering on wants/desires					Specifically assumed
Incorrect belief	Yes	Yes	It depends	Yes	No
Flawed choosing (wrt WB)	Yes	Yes	No, if WB drop realized. Yes, if not realized	Yes	Yes, but...

salience assumes Assumption 9b, so it can't be faulted for causing flawed choosing in terms of WB.

Duration Bias

It is the habit of systematically over-predicting the duration of WB shifts. Things you imagine will enhance your emotional WB (new car, new spouse, polar bears saved) will, but not for as long as you imagine. And symmetrically, things you believe will make you unhappy (getting dumped, cancer) will, but not for as long as you imagine.[4] Dan Gilbert et al. (1998) find that we suffer from it but are unaware that we do.

> People are generally unaware of the operation of the system of cognitive mechanisms that ameliorate their experience of negative affect (the psychological immune system), and thus they tend to overestimate the duration of their affective reactions to negative events. This tendency was demonstrated in 6 studies in which participants overestimated the duration of their affective reactions to the dissolution of a romantic relationship, the failure to achieve tenure, an electoral defeat, negative personality feedback, an account of a child's death, and rejection by a prospective employer.

[4] While the observed bias, on average, is people believe the WB shift will last longer than it will, some people believe the WB shift will not last as long as it will.

Related to duration bias is magnitude bias. It is a bias in the magnitude of the immediate shift in emotional WB. Magnitude bias is less studied than duration bias and can also cause one's ordering of paths to be out of sync with realized WB.

> Participants failed to distinguish between situations in which their psychological immune systems would and would not be likely to operate and mistakenly predicted overly and equally enduring affective reactions in both instances. The present experiments suggest that people neglect the psychological immune system when making effective forecasts.

While duration bias is an incorrect belief, the subjective probability that event *A* will occur is not biased. Instead, it's overestimating the duration of the WB shift that *A* would cause. Biases in anticipated WB shifts could cause Path *j* to be ranked higher than Path *d*, even though Path *d* would be higher if the durations were more accurately anticipated.

Duration bias is one source of flawed choosing, and flawed choosing will eventually cause realized WB to be lower than it could have been: our ordering is based on an incorrect belief. Because of duration bias, we spend too much time and money acquiring new items and situations that produce constant streams of positive attributes (e.g., clearer TV picture, Modigliani over the mantle, saved rain forest). And we spend too much money and time trying to avoid or eliminate items and situations that will produce constant streams of negative attributes. We spend too much effort trying to stay healthy, too much on eliminating ugly stuff from our new house, and too much time complaining to the HOA about our neighbor's new landscaping and house paint. Why? Because we overestimate the long-term WB implications of these long-lasting changes. Imagine you become incontinent or, worse, paralyzed from the waist down. I believe paralysis would guarantee misery until the day I die. And I am incorrect. I don't understand that I will adapt, not entirely, but way more than I could now imagine. Duration bias is an assault on the economic assertion that we typically choose, given our constraints, our highest-ranked path. Still, it does not violate any of the NBT Assumptions.

More Examples of Duration Bias

Thinking back to before I got tenure (all universities make mistakes), I thought being denied would ruin my life; getting it would permanently increase my WB (both emotional and life-satisfaction). Unfortunately, tenure didn't permanently increase my emotional WB—I am still the same-old, anxious pessimist. I don't know whether a denial would have ruined my life but probably not. A survey (mentioned earlier) of academics a year after their tenure decision shows no significant difference in average happiness between those that did and did not get tenure.

I spent the better part of my young adulthood working night and day to get tenure because I thought I would be devastated if denied—was it all a big mistake? Assistant professors correctly predict how they will feel when they learn they didn't get tenure—that their emotional and life-satisfaction WB will plunge. But are incorrect about how long their WB will be diminished. I am unsure whether getting tenure increased my long-term life-satisfaction WB, but I would like to think it did.

We believe that if we become disabled or are diagnosed with a long-term illness, our WB will decrease, so we get physicals and avoid bacon, which tastes great. Are we trying too much if our beliefs about the extent of the decrease in WB are incorrect? Quoting from a University of Michigan press release about a 2005 paper by Jason Riis and others:

> A Study of dialysis patients yields surprising findings. Despite what able-bodied healthy people might think, people with severe illnesses and disabilities don't wallow in misery and self-pity all the time. In fact, a new study finds, such patients, on the whole, may be just as happy as those without major medical conditions. The finding adds to the growing body of evidence that ill and disabled people adapt to their condition and show a resilience of spirit that many healthy people can't imagine.

This isn't to say people prefer being sick or that you will return to your state of WB before the illness.[5] While adaptation is typical, it can be incomplete, even after years. E.g., Oswald and Powdthavee (2008) present evidence of partial adaptation to a disability three years after onset.

While most of the research on duration bias has been for private goods, duration bias also applies to public goods and bads. As President of the United States, Barak Obama was a public commodity. Once he became the President of the U.S. for me, he became that for everyone, including French people and Afghan terrorists. We were all forced to consume the results of his actions; for some, the Obama Presidency was a public good, and for others, a public bad. Before he was first elected President, many thought his election would bring them tremendous and long-lasting joy; others expected tremendous and long-lasting misery. Short run, both groups were mostly correct. But now that Obama's Presidency is long

[5] Duration bias does not imply you can't shift to a new quasi-fixed WB.

over, we realize we weren't as affected by it as we imagined we would be—the good and bad did not last as long as we imagined they would. The same is likely true of our love, or hatred, of Trump and Biden

Reducing the rate of global warming is, for most, a public good (if it does not get as hot for me, it does not get as hot for you). However, if we underestimate our ability to mentally adjust to global warming, we could allocate too many resources to reducing it.[6] A trite example: as an avid skier, I now dread a future without snow. But, as temperatures increase, I will find myself biking more and skiing less—my interest in skiing will decay, but now I can't imagine it. God forbid, I might even start playing golf—again.

Less trite, global warming will disrupt cultivation zones causing large-scale poverty and migration. E.g., coffee will no longer come from Central America; coffee will cost more, and less will be drunk. Poverty in Central America will increase, causing even more northward migration pressure. Those affected will suffer (many catastrophically), but they won't suffer as much as they imagine if they suffer from duration bias.

I will get a flash of pleasure when I hear that wolves have been reintroduced into Colorado, my adopted State.[7] But after reading the literature on my psychological immune system and my tendency to suffer from duration bias, I now suspect my happiness would adjust to the news in a matter of hours. Liberal environmentalists over-predict the long-term pleasure produced by Obamas and wolves, and conservatives and ranchers over-predict the duration of their displeasure. The ladder has led states like Montana, Idaho, and Wyoming to recently legalize the slaughter of wolves—they have become victims of the culture wars.[8] Duration bias suggests that the pleasure from their slaughter will not last as long as imagined. I get sad and upset whenever I read about wolves dying because they wandered out of Yellowstone, but it's of short duration.

[6] We are currently allocating too few resources. My point is that how much should be allocated should depend on how much our WB will affected in the long run, not on an overestimate.

[7] In November 2020, Colorado passed a statewide amendment mandating the reintroduction of wolves. This, by itself, gave me a flash of pleasure.

[8] Recently, driving and listening to a religious segment on a Coleville WA radio station, I heard a local pastor say the Bible calls for the killing of all wolves. He thought we should keep a few in zoos.

I almost made a mistake. A few years ago, the State of Colorado passed a law that expanded where you could carry a concealed weapon. Based on the law, in 2012, the Colorado Supreme Court struck down the University of Colorado's campus ban on guns. This ruling meant that any of my three hundred Principles students could start packing. I got stressed (an emotional state), worrying that I could get shot if I failed or offended the wrong student. Retiring crossed my mind. If I had retired because I was worried about guns on campus, it would have been flawed choosing. I got used to the idea of guns in class and stopped worrying about it. I misinterpreted how long my anxiety would last and came close to making a poor choice. [Anxious people typically over-predict how long a bout of anxiety will last, especially those who medicate as soon as they become anxious. By circumventing the anxiety with a drug, they never experience the anxiety naturally subsiding, so they do not realize it will subside.]

Duration bias should be suspected whenever a choice involves long-term changes. For example, with environmental policies, there are long-run implications. Consider the extinction of a species or the PCB contamination of a water body. When an environmental injury occurs, people get upset (are damaged), but duration bias implies that even if the injury remains, the upset will not last as long as they imagine. This raises questions about estimating how much society was damaged, in dollars, by an oil spill—one of my sidelines for years. Suppose that soon after the injury, while you were bummed, you were asked whether you would be willing to have your taxes increased by $25 a year to ensure there wouldn't be another extinction, spill, or pollution event. Suppose further that you said yes because (1) it is worth $25 to not experience, for a year, the bad feeling you are experiencing, and (2) you believe the bad feeling will persist for years. If the bad-feeling duration turns out to be shorter than you are predicting, the value you place on prevention is less than your answer indicates.[9]

[9] Some economists argue that answers to hypothetical questions about willingness-to-pay are biased upwards because you answer knowing you will not have to pay. Whether this is true or false is a different from people having an actual WTP that is more than it would be if they did not suffer from duration bias.

So, Why Do We Suffer from Duration Bias?
Is there an advantage? In his 2002 book, *Strangers to ourselves: discovering the adaptive unconscious*, Timothy Wilson, a social psychologist, discusses reasons why this quirk is common (this is his list with my explanations):

- *Focalism*: When something great happens, or the shit hits the fan, it captures all our attention (conscious and unconscious)—it is all we can think about—we focus—the happening has salience. When we think about how it will make us feel in the future, we don't realize that it will no longer be the be-all-and-end-all, so we overestimate its long-run impact on our WB. It is good that our focus wains: we would get in big trouble if our attention was wholly occupied by past events: survival requires paying attention to the present. If B.B. Wolf is at the door and you're still cranked about something that happened last year, you will get eaten.
- We fail to adequately foresee how we can and will adjust. Economics preaches that when a negative occurs (price increase, loss of job, global warming), we, over time, minimize the cost to us (substitute to cheaper substitute, find a new job, etc.) Duration bias occurs because we don't realize how much we can and will adjust to the new reality. Two friends recently lost their older dog. They were overly sad because they did not foresee her death bringing them closer to the other dog. When your house floods, you, at first, fail to realize that the hated purple-paisley drapes are history, and you no longer need to fret about what basement junk to keep.
- There is the aforementioned *quasi-fixed WB* that we forget we have (Chapter 6).
- *Misconstrual* (perception errors): We don't know how we will react to a change because it is difficult to predict the WB impact of events we haven't previously experienced. And, even if the experience isn't new, we still have trouble predicting how it will affect our WB: memories of past emotions, distress, and pain are often flawed. When we remember a pain, we don't re-experience it, so mothers forget how much childbirth hurts. And marathon runners forget how they felt at the eighteen-mile point, making it easy to make duration errors.
- Overestimating how long the happiness will last increases current happiness and contentment. Or you overestimate the duration of your unhappiness because doing so makes you feel better prepared.

This is ***motivated distortion***: thinking your stomach pain is cancer makes you think that you will be better able to handle the diagnosis when it comes. Or you convince yourself you did poorly on the final exam, so you will be better prepared for the long-term WB drop when you get your grade.

- *Spin*: Failure to realize how adept our minds are at spinning things to our emotional advantage. We spin/interpret things to uncover the silver lining: when the shit hits the fan, we figure out a way to spin it, so it does not seem as shitty. Duration bias occurs partly because we fail to realize that we spin. When my students fail an exam, they don't feel as bad after they spin to blaming someone else, me. Initially, they don't realize they will blame me.

* * *

There are a lot of unanswered questions about the duration of WB shifts. We adapt to different things at different rates, and some events are difficult to adapt to. There is limited research on the duration of various WB shifts as a function of the event that caused the shift, which emotions were affected (love, fear, hate, anxiety), and the affected individual's age, gender, personality type, etc.[10] And, one first needs the best estimation of the shift's duration to estimate the bias based on the best science and

[10] Di Tella et al. (2010) find that duration of a WB shift resulting from an income shift is less than a shift caused by a change in status. Recollect that an adult's WB drop associated with the death of a parent lasts, on average, 6 months, whereas the loss of a child lasts five years. See the section on a happiness set point in Chapter 5.

Wilson and Gilbert (2008) survey the literature on what we do and don't adapt to. One study finds that "people adapt more easily to incarceration than to unpleasant noises."—Really! We don't adapt to unpredictable noise (consider traffic noises and overheard cell phone conversations) although adapt to clocks ticking. And, as noted in Chapter 5, while we adapt to consuming more and better things, the happiness lift from being rich relative to others endures. Losing your job "is particularly difficult to adapt to and has a long-term impact on life satisfaction."

It seems that the WB loss associated with commuting endures. "You can't adapt to commuting because it's entirely unpredictable. Driving in traffic is a different kind of hell every day" (Daniel Gilbert as quoted in Traffic: Why we drive the way we do by Tom Vanderbilt). The happiness researchers Alois Stutzer and Bruno Frey (2008) have identified the ***paradox of commuting***: you go for the bigger house and yard in exchange for a longer commute, not realizing that you will adapt to the house and yard, but not to the commute. So, if you commute, your house is too big.

data. Then there is the issue of how WB is defined: a shift in emotional WB or a shift in life-satisfaction WB: the durations differ.[11]

I am unaware of research on whether the bias varies with the actual length of the WB shift—it is complicated. I can't imagine that the bias is always a fixed length (e.g., one month or one year) or a constant multiple of the actual length, but I don't know this. Other unanswered questions include the length of the duration bias for emotional WB vs. life-satisfaction WB. And, if emotional WB, does the bias depend on the specific emotion (e.g., fear vs. anger)?

Duration bias shows that WB forecasts are based on common and systematic incorrect beliefs. Choices with long-term implications are made based on our perception of how they will make us feel in the long run, but with duration bias, beliefs are systematically biased. One can still use NBT to model behavior (as one can with any incorrect belief); the challenge is to model it and the extent to which it affects behavior—including how much behavior is based on this incorrect belief.

You and I can increase our WB simply by being aware that we suffer from duration bias. When a choice has long-run implications, consider the possibility that you are overestimating the durations of the WB effects. I learned about duration bias when guns were first allowed in my classroom.

The Emotional Empathy-Gap

When we select a path, we do not fully appreciate that our selection is based on our current emotional state and the ordering associated with that emotional state. We are limited in our ability to empathize with our other emotional selves. This common quirk is what George Loewenstein, the Herbert A. Simon, Professor of Economics and Psychology at Carnegie Mellon University, calls the *empathy-gap*. People have emotion-specific orderings. My ordering of paths depends on my emotional/chemical state. The emotional empathy-gap is that we are limited in our ability to realize this, so we do things now when we are in one emotional state that we will have to live with after that emotion subsides and is replaced by another. You cut me off in traffic, my anger flairs, and I shoot you with the Glock I keep under the seat. My anger is quickly replaced by fear, anxiety, and guilt since I am now the deserving subject of the

[11] Kahneman and Deaton (2010) find that an income increase has an enduring effect on life-satisfaction WB but not emotional WB.

all-points bulletin, "Armed and dangerous old white guy driving south on I-25 in a red Buick." My empathy-gap is that while livid, I chose my highest-ranked available path, HRAP, incorrectly, imagining that I would have the same ordering tomorrow.

Separate in your mind the issue of whether you have multiple ordering from whether you fail to empathize with your other emotional selves, thinking about what each implies for the NBT Assumptions.

Multiple Orderings?

> A hot temper leaps o'er a cold decree.—The Merchant of Venice, CCT 1, scene 2

Behavioral research, primarily by psychologists, demonstrates that we have different orderings of paths for different emotional states—you are not of one mind and don't have one ordering. In summary, in my words, not theirs, your ordering depends on your emotional state of mind. Assuming S possible states, in *State of mind s*, you use the ordering coughed-up for State s. These S different orderings determine choice in that in State s, you will select the highest s-ranked path from those available. For example, Jordan, sexually aroused, does not have the same ordering as Jordan, who wakes up with a stranger; so, the selection that increased Saturday-night Jordan's WB might make Sunday-morning Jordan miserable or even happier.

> As she melted small and wonderful in his arms, she became infinitely desirable to him; all his blood vessels seemed to scald with intense yet tender desire, for her; for her softness, for the penetrating beauty of her in his arms, passing into his blood. And softly, with that marvelous swoon-like caress of his hand in pure soft desire, softly he stroked the silky slope of her loins… And she felt him like a flame of desire. (*Lady Chatterley's Lover*, D.H. Lawrence, quoted and discussed by Robert Sapolsky in Why Zebras Don't Get Ulcers)

Depending on your literary and erotic tastes, this quote may be causing your pancreas to secrete hormones, changing your visceral state. Economists don't talk or think like D. H. Lawrence. While emotions affect choice, emotions have been purged from NBT and welfare economics. Economists should be pitied: ordinary people have passions, lusts, and rages, while modern economists have an ordering of paths.

There are states induced by psychoactive drugs such as tobacco, alcohol, and caffeine—most of us start our day by altering our mind with coffee, tea, or a Diet Coke, blocking the receptors for the neurotransmitter adenosine.[12] Even the bacteria in your gut affect your emotional state.[13] Ordering-altering emotions and moods include anxious, depressed, scared, exhausted, bored, sad, grieving, curious, joyful, feeling alienated, embarrassed, and, my favorite mood, grumpy.[14] We experience these states in ourselves and others, affecting how we behave and experience the world. But we are not always aware of our state.

Loewenstein and coauthors provide examples of how choice differs across emotional states; for example, the planned turn-back time for a Himalayan Mountain ascent is ignored during the stress and exhaustion of the climb. The result can be tomorrow's self is dead, the ultimate *negative external effect*.

Sexual arousal, induced by erotic pictures, films, and self-stimulation, changes your propensity to take risks, be aggressive on a date, and what is appropriate behavior. Loewenstein et al. (1997) had

> Sexually aroused and non-aroused males predict their own behavior in a date-rape scenario. Aroused and non-aroused participants were asked a

[12] Caffeine also affects dopamine, acetylcholine, and serotonin.

[13] Your body contains six to ten pounds of bacteria, much in your gut. They produce dozens of chemicals, including some that in the brain act as neurotransmitters (e.g., dopamine, serotonin, and GABA). Recent research indicates that their production stimulates nerves in the gut which synapse with neurons in the brain, influencing emotional state (Peter Smith 2015 and the research of Mark Lyte). In a path-breaking study (Javier Bravo et al. 2011), mice were divided into two groups: a control and a group that was fed a broth containing the common bacteria *Lactobacillus*. Human babies ingest it as they pass through the birth canal. It, in the gut, produces GABA, and GABA inhibits nervous activity. Both sets of mice were subject to the same stressful environment (a forced swim where the rat can neither touch the bottom nor climb out). The mice fed the broth exhibited less stress. For more on bacteria and emotions see the 2014 TEDMED talk by John Cryan.

[14] Examples include Loewenstein and Frederick (1997), Loewenstein (1999, 2000), Loewenstein, Drazen Prelec, and Catherine Shatto (1998), Loewenstein, Daniel Nagin, and Raymond Paternoster (1997), Jennifer Lerner, Deborah Small, and George Loewenstein (2004). Ariely and Loewenstein (2006), Michael Kosfeld et al. (2005), Peter Ditto et al. (2006), Lerner et al. (2013), and Nitka Garg and Lerner (2013). For a neurological discussion of the effects of emotions on choice see Antonio Damasio (1994) and Jon Elster (1998).

> battery of questions designed to measure their perceptions of the costs and benefits of acting in a sexually aggressive manner, their level of arousal, and a probabilistic prediction as to how aggressively they would act in the conditions described in the scenario… Sexual arousal increases the "subjects' expectations of their own sexual aggressiveness and that this impact isn't mediated by perceptions of the costs or benefits of such aggression.

Ditto and colleagues have researched the effects arousal has on choice. Males not in a relationship and who typically use condoms either watched a video or read a description of the following situation.

> The written text: *Imagine that you are single and that you run into an attractive acquaintance, Rebecca, at a bar. You continue to spend time together throughout the night and end up at her apartment at the end of the evening. After talking and kissing on the couch, it is clear that you are both very interested in having sex with each other. However, neither of you has a condom. You discuss the possibility of going to a store, but there isn't one nearby. She tells you that she is on the pill and has not slept with anyone since her last boyfriend.*
>
> The video: *In the video, two attractive students, Pierre and Rebecca, talk after class and arrange to meet at a bar later that night. After an evening of dancing, they go to Rebecca's apartment where they kiss on her couch. Eventually, Rebecca takes off her shirt and indicates that she is interested in having sex (alleviating the threat of a potential date-rape situation). Pierre then discloses that he did not bring any condoms. Rebecca tells him that she also does not have any condoms but is on the pill (alleviating the threat of pregnancy). The two discuss the idea of obtaining condoms from a local store but conclude that it isn't available. They discuss their sexual history (e.g., Pierre states that he is "clean," and Rebecca states that she does not "sleep around"). The video ends with Pierre asking Rebecca, "What do you want to do?" and Rebecca replying, "I don't know. What do you want to do?".*

The video watchers were more inclined to say they would take the risk and have unprotected sex.

Switching to other emotions, when depressed, you have a depression ordering, including paths with suicide. Invoking curiosity changes behavior—it killed the cat. When curious, you are more inclined toward a reward now vs. later. [It can be invoked by asking an interesting question to which the respondent does not know the answer.]

Sadness does not have the effect you would expect. Some negative emotions (e.g., disgust) cause you to value everything less. While sadness causes us to value what we have less, it causes us to value new things more. In a 2004 experiment by Loewenstein and Small (Professor of Marketing and Psychology at the U. of Penn.), disgust was invoked with a video clip from the movie Trainspotting and sadness with one from The Champ. They used a neutral clip from National Geographic as the control. Subjects were divided into two groups: potential buyers and potential sellers. The potential sellers were given a set of highlighters. Potential sellers who got the disgust or sad treatment were willing to sell them for less than those in the control group. Potential buyers who got the disgust treatment were willing to pay less than those in the control group, but potential buyers who got the sad treatment were willing to pay more. Lerner (Director, Harvard Laboratory for Decision Sciences) interprets this to mean that when you are sad, you will pay more to get new stuff, hoping it will perk you up.

In a 2012 Lerner study, subjects were offered either $85 paid in three months or a lesser amount immediately. The median respondent in her control group needed $56 now to pass up the $85, but for those who got her sad treatment, the median was $37: sadness invokes impatience. However, when both were future payments, the difference between the sad and control disappeared, suggesting sadness causes us to want the reward now, not simply sooner. [She has found that subjects who got the sad treatment ate more free M&Ms.]

Boredom makes most other situations look good—my students long to be anywhere else. On the other hand, it turns teenage boys into vandals—it provokes wild and crazy behavior. For a review of philosophical takes on boredom, see *A Philosophy of Boredom* by the Norwegian philosopher Lars Svendsen. For extreme reactions to boredom, he considers the 1996 David Cronenberg movie, Crash and the book and movie American Psycho (nothing un-bores Patrick Bateman, a rich 80s investment banker and party boy, not even torture and murder).

Market transactions require trust. Kosfeld, Paul Zak, Urs Fischbacher, Fehr (economists), and Markus Heinrichs (a psychologist) have shown that nasally administering the neurotransmitter oxytocin increases the probability you will enter into a financial contract requiring trust it makes us more trusting. (For mammals, oxytocin helps mom and baby bond, also dogs and their owners.)

Happiness is an emotional state and, like other emotional states, affects your ordering of paths.[15] This is crazy-making for NBT: you choose the available path that will bring you the most WB, but being happy (high emotional WB) affects which path you choose—a confounding circularity.

An aside: Multiple orderings share properties with dissociative personality disorders (Dr. Jekyll and Mr. Hyde and the actress Joanne Woodward in, The Three Faces of Eve) (Fig. 8.1).[16]

Consider: as Edwina, I wear dresses, heels, and bar flirt. When Edward, I sit in my office doing research, unable to walk in heels. Edward would be shocked to learn Edwina hit the bars last night. My third persona, Edalandra, the ballerina, finds Edward tedious and hates that Edwina is

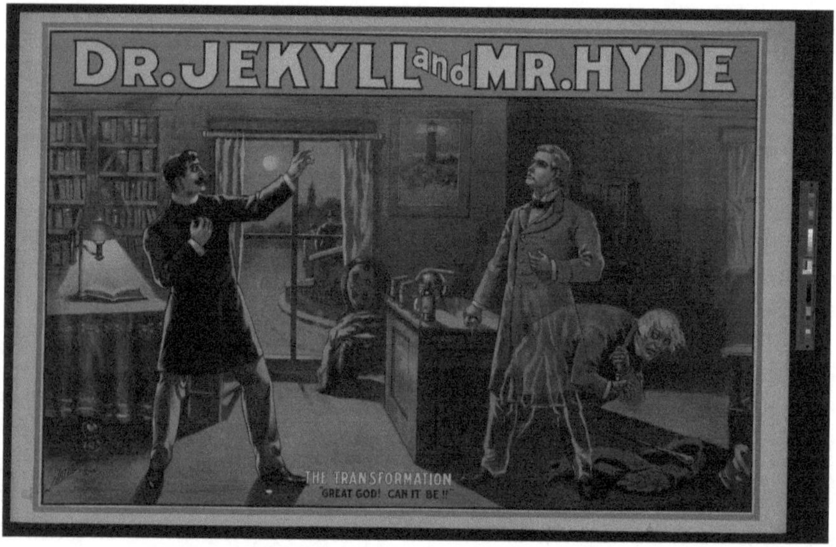

Fig. 8.1 Dr. Jekyll and Mr. Hyde

[15] See Cassie Mogilner et al. (2012) and Aparna Labroo and Vanessa Patrick (2009); the latter find that happiness affects choice because when one is happy one's perspective is broader, more future-looking, and more analytical.

[16] DPD was previously called a multiple-personality disorder. While the disorder fascinates, it isn't clear it exists: one hypothesis proclaims it a product of the therapist's suggestions.

always borrowing and ruining her tutus. Each personality does things that affect the other two (how could they not, they have the same body), but none consider these external effects when deciding how to live their lives. Edward and Edalandra hate cigarettes and cigarette smoke, but Edwina has smoked Camels for years—unfortunately, when Edwina dies of lung cancer, Edward and Edalandra will pass as well. People with dissociative personality disorder have multiple orderings; they consist of more than one self. The same holds for all of us living with varying emotions.

The Emotional Empathy-Gap

You suffer from an empathy-gap (you lack empathy for your other emotional selves) if you select your HRAP based on the WB ordering associated with your current emotional state. And do this at each point in time. While multiple orderings are necessary for this gap, it isn't sufficient. You must be unaware that your ordering will differ after you morph into another emotional state. [Or be aware that it will change, but you are unable to act contrary to your current ordering.]

Why Is There an Emotional Empathy-Gap?

It isn't because we have no experience with different states of mind; we have all been angry, scared, hungry, tired, sexually aroused, curious, and bored. So is there an evolutionary reason we do not empathize with our other selves, or is it simply a kluge?

Loewenstein and David Schkade point out that emotional memories are "qualitatively different" from other types of memories, making it difficult to project how we will feel and assess in a different emotional state. We are adept at recovering visual images, also the sum of 2 + 2 but not adept at recovering feelings. When you picture mom, you experience/see an image; when you remember a song, you hear it. However, when you remember being in pain, you don't experience pain, and when you remember a time when you were hungry, you don't feel hungry. The forward reflection of this inability is that it is difficult to correctly comprehend the emotional salience of future hunger unless you are hungry. [Remembering the circumstances that made you mad can make you mad, but that's different.] When you remember being in a visceral state, you recover the circumstances but don't experience the emotion. It is as if you store the events around the emotion but not the emotion, so don't experience the compulsions it would engender. When I decide to go to the grocery store after work, I am aware that I will be hungry when I get to the store, but I don't experience the buying compulsions that that hunger will engender. When my neighbor puts a gun in her glove compartment to feel safer during her nightly rural commute, she can't appreciate the compulsion that her anger will engender when another driver cuts her off and then flips her off. We underestimate because we can't retrieve the compulsive feeling from memory.

An inability to recover old feelings has its evolutionary advantages—it is evolutionary rational. For example, if remembering a good time recovered the excellent feeling (made you feel great), you could feel great simply by lying around and remembering pleasurable times. And this would increase the probability of you becoming lion food. And it would decrease your incentive to eat and have sex; you could feel satiated by simply remembering past liaisons and meals. The inability to experience a future emotion is merely the flip side of our inability to recover old feelings, so while not necessarily evolutionary adaptive, a side effect of a trait that is.

The gap may exist because empathizing with a different self diminishes your current sense of self and the legitimacy of your current feelings.

What Does the Emotional Empathy-Gap Imply About Behavior and Choice?

Are the NBT Assumptions violated? First, recollect that the gap rests on two components: having emotion-specific orderings and behaving as if you don't.

Assumption 2: *At every point in time, an economicus has one ordering of all paths—1st, 2nd, …*

Emotion-specific orderings and varying emotions will lead to behaviors that appear to violate Assumption 2: at one moment, you rank Path *m* above Path *k*; later, the ranking is flipped.[17] But, emotion-specific orderings and varying emotions don't strictly violate Assumption 2. They are consistent with, at each moment, a unique, effective ordering: there are multiple orderings in your brain, but at this moment, one is in charge.

[17] Early in the day you are angry so rank path *m* higher than path *k*; later when your anger turns to anxiety, path *k* is ranked higher than path *m*.

Consider Assumption 4: *An economicus's ordering does not change in the time-span behavior is modeled.* It is violated if emotions vary during the span for which behavior is modeled. Since most people have varying emotions, this is problematic.

Like duration bias, the emotional empathy-gap does not violate

Assumption 9a: *An economicus's ordering of paths is based on its WB (well-being), WB, accounting for uncertainties. The more WB economicus associates with a path, the higher its rank. And WB is determined, in part, by sensations.*

Because higher-ranked paths are better given the incorrect belief that one's ordering will not change. Besides 4, no Assumptions are violated.

The emotional empathy-gap is having emotion-specific orderings and, at that moment, the incorrect belief that you don't. This leads to flawed choosing. Given our state of mind, we won't momentarily reduce our WB even though it would increase our overall WB. When Homer Simpson is depressed and can't imagine the depression lifting (a characteristic of depression), his WB is maximized by not going to work, not socializing, and spending night and day on the couch watching Simpson reruns, given his beliefs. If he knew that on antidepressants, he would be able to empathize with his future self, he would have instead stopped at the pharmacy, picked up an SSRI, and continued on his way to work.

The emotional empathy-gap, like duration bias, is an assault on the economic assertion that we typically choose, given our constraints, our highest-ranked WB-path in terms of realized WB.[18] But, strictly speaking, it is consistent with the NBT Assumptions.

How Might Knowing You Have an Emotional Empathy-Gap Make You Better Off?

First, understand your natural inclination to not empathize with your other emotional selves. Instead, try to empathize with them. Next, learn to recognize and acknowledge your emotions and what triggers them.

[18] The emotional empathy-gap will not generate flawed choosing if the individual cares not at all about the future: if you live in the moment, you care nothing about your future WB. If I shoot you in anger after you insult my dog, it's not flawed choosing if I don't care about the future. Most of us discount the future, although not fully, so the emotional empathy-gap typically leads to flawed choosing.

And finally, think about how you can influence how and when different emotional states will occur. All are tall tasks. Simply understanding that you have an empathy-gap is the place to start.

If you can speculate on how your ordering of paths may differ across emotional states, you might choose now not to keep a loaded gun under your bed.[19] And, you might take an Uber to the bar rather than driving—and not bring the gun. How should I react when a guy at the bar successfully hits on my wife? If I can empathize with my future selves, I won't start shooting or hitting the guy—or my wife. Most males regret hitting people, but an estimated 22% of women have been physically assaulted by an intimate partner.

The emotional empathy-gap suggests that if an objective is to train an individual to behave when they are mad, scared, or aroused, the training will be more effective if it occurs in that state. So train soldiers and police officers when they are afraid and angry how to avoid shooting civilians when they are afraid and angry. Training males to practice safe, consensual sex when they are sexually aroused will be more effective if the training occurs when they are aroused.

Complicating Even Further: Your Assessment of Your Emotions Can Be Incorrect, an Incorrect Belief

The psychologists Don Dutton and Arthur Aron (1974) had an attractive female approach males in a Vancouver, B.C. Park and ask them to fill out a short survey about the park. At the survey's end, she provided the respondents with her phone number "in case they had further comments or questions." Half the males were approached on a scary foot-path suspension bridge over a deep ravine, half after crossing the bridge. Dutton and Aron speculated that a few subjects would call and ask her out. They hypothesized the ask rate varied by where she interviewed them. She got numerous date requests from those interviewed on the bridge. Their propensity to call was greater because they mistook fear for arousal, an incorrect belief, resulting in flawed choosing. Even an unconscious emotional state can affect behavior.[20]

[19] Oscar Pistorius (the double amputee, "Blade Runner"), shot his girlfriend four times through the bathroom door, either in anger, or, as his lawyer argued, because he was in a vulnerable and fearful state. He is in prison until at least 2023.

[20] In a lovely study, the psychologists Lawrence Williams and John Bargh (2008) had each subject met by a greeter who accompanied them to the lab. The greeter was juggling

Incentive-Salience Effects

Recollect the incentive-salience hypothesis of Chapter 5. This common quirk is associated with Berridge and his lab at the U. of Michigan.[21] Summarizing the discussion of *Incentive salience* in Chapter 5, it is a fancy term for serious wanting (a strong urge—conscious or not) compared to run-of-the-mill wanting. The *incentive* is to choose the most *salient* (striking, attention-grabbing). Incentive salience assumes you choose the alternative you most want/desire. Often, it is the alternative you will like the most (generate the most WB). But wanting can deviate from liking. This happens when you have a physiological or emotional need (you are hungry, aroused, tired, etc.), more than one alternative fulfills that need, and one alternative is cued. For example, you are thirsty and notice an attractive person enjoying a Pepsi (a cue), so you choose Pepsi over Coke even though you would have enjoyed the Coke more. The root of this common quirk is evolution's separation of wanting from liking.

So, how should one think about incentive salience in terms of NBT? It is inconsistent with Assumption 9a but consistent with Assumption 9b: *Paths that are more desired/wanted are ranked higher.* Physiological states are like emotional states. While incentive-salience affects behavior, it doesn't produce incorrect beliefs—you desire the item more. The incentive-salience quirk can momentarily change an ordering of paths based on desires/wants, so they can violate Assumption 4: *An economicus's ordering does not change in the time-span behavior is modeled.* They make it challenging to model and predict behaviors: behavior depends on one's need state, along with any cues. If the objective is desire fulfillment, the incentive-salience quirk does not cause flawed choosing—you still end up experiencing the most desired available path. Incentive salience does

a pile of papers and a drink. She asked the subject to hold the drink; sometimes it was hot, sometimes cold. When they got to the lab, the greeter left, taking her drink. The researcher described a person, and then the subject was asked to describe that person in their own words. The subjects who carried a hot drink more often judged the person as having a warm personality. [I always carry around a Diet Coke with ice; this could explain why students found me cold and unapproachable.]

[21] See Berridge and Terry Robinson (1998), Wyvell and Berridge (2000, 2001), Kringelbach and Berridge (2012), and Berridge and Kringelbach (2013), also the textbooks: Bear et al. (2020) and Gazziniga et al. (2014).

cause flawed WB-choosing, but *So What?* if NBT adopts Assumption 9b but not Assumption 9a.

Imagine a top-level ordering unaffected by cues and a ground-level ordering that is. Your ground-level ordering deviates from your top-level ordering when you are in a need state, and one alternative is cued. If the 9a and 9b ordering are identical when there are no incentive-salience effects, their presence will cause them to diverge, and there will be some flawed WB-choosing.

The Future-Self Empathy-Gap

The *future-self empathy-gap* is a lack of empathy for one's future selves. It violates no NBT Assumptions. Does it cause flawed choosing? The word *gap* suggests it.

Animals discount the future, including humans. Cuttlefish, for example, pass their equivalent of the marshmallow test.[22] When ordering

[22] "Cephalopods resisted eating a piece of prawn for as long as two minutes to get a better snack (a live shrimp)" (Alexandra Schnell et al. 2021; Elizabeth Preston 2002). Most animals with backbones will wait a few seconds for a larger reward: birds and rodents will wait a few seconds more for a reward three times larger; if the wait is around 10 seconds, they go with the immediate smaller reward (Laurie Santos and Alexandra Rosati 2015). Non-human primates are more patient, though not as much as humans. Lesser primates will wait longer than birds and rodents, but still less than a minute. However, great apes will wait minutes for a larger reward. Macaques become indifferent between the immediate smaller reward and the three-times larger reward at approximately 40 seconds (Henry Tobin et al. 1996). Tamarins and marmosets (new-world monkeys) hold out for 10–20 seconds (Jeffrey Stevens, Elizabeth Hallinan, and Mark Hauser 2005). Michael Beran and his colleagues (Beran, Sue Savage-Rumbaugh, Joy Pate, and Duane Rumbaugh 1999; Beran and Theodore Evans 2006; Evans and Beran 2007) conducted experiments with chimps where the size of the reward visually grew over time if the chimp did not touch the reward. The chimps would hold off for about 10 minutes, about the same as a small child, using the same sort of distracting tactics (e.g., not looking at the reward and playing with toys as a distraction [Evans and Beran 2007]). Quoting Santos and Rosati, "Further converging evidence that apes are capable of thinking about their future selves comes from planning studies in which apes must anticipate that saving a tool now will allow them to use it in the future." Indeed, some apes successfully plan to use a tool as long as 14 hours in advance (Nicholas Mulcahy and Josep Call 2006; Mathias Osvath and Helena Osvath 2008). Overall, these results suggest that humans and other great apes may share similar capacities to overcome immediate temptation and to act in ways that benefit their future-selves as well as similar strategies for doing so. That animals lack patience should not surprise; most animals have no conception of their future selves. It's remarkable is that some great apes will wait longer than small children and seem to have longer planning horizons.

paths, everything else is constant, most humans order paths lower (higher) the farther in the future each WB bump (dip) occurs. I will rank a path higher if its bump comes earlier. And if three paths only differ by when the same WB dip occurs, I will rank a path higher if its dip is farther in the future. Put simply, humans would rather experience the good stuff sooner and the bad stuff later and order paths accordingly. Researchers and policymakers who consider discounting a human flaw describe discounting as *impatience*.

There isn't anything about discounting the future inherently inconsistent with NBT. And—there are good reasons we discount the future; these include an uncertain future, everyone having a limited life span, and most animals lack the cognitive ability to imagine their future selves. In our world of scarcity, predators, and prey, discounting the future increases the probability that your genes will survive until tomorrow. Worrying about old age when one is young is a trait unique to humans. Evolutionary biology also suggests that, within a species, there will be genetic variation in the degree of discounting.

How much a human discounts the future depends on how much they empathize with their future selves (cares about them). And this depends on the extent to which you will remain the same person (identity as the same person). Your identity depends on *connectedness*, and your empathy for your future self increases with your connectedness to them (Parfit 1984; Daniel Bartels and Oleg Urminsky 2011; Christine Tappolet 2010).[23] My current choices and behavior will affect my future selves,

[23] This issue of what makes a person the same person they were yesterday can quickly become speculative. You are free to suppose a person is the thing that inhabits the same body over time. *Materialistic* identity, however, does not solve the problem of how you should behave if your body's ordering of paths changes unexpectedly.

Two bookends in the evolution of identity are Locke and Parfit. Paraphrasing Gottlieb (2016), what makes someone the same person over time was a hot topic among English pastors in Locke's time: on Judgement Day, what part(s) of you will God need to resurrect you? Body parts? Not a problem if you are still buried in the parish cemetery, a problem if you were burned at the stake or eaten by cannibals?

Locke concluded that if you now remember doing something, you are now the same person who did it—implying that if I don't remember that last night the drunken me robbed a 7–11, I am not that guy. His definition implies that the teenage you and young adult you are the same person if the latter remembers high school. And the young adult you and the old you are the same person if the latter remembers the behavior of the former. However, even if both are true, the teenage you and the old you are not the same person if the old you does not remember high school.

generating external effects on others (future me-s) whose ordering could differ from mine in ways I can't predict.

Bartels and Urminsky, marketing professors at the U. of Chicago, hypothesize that a reason we discount the future is a disconnect between our current and future selves. I don't save for old age, partly because I don't comprehend or relate to the old guy spending my money, my future-self empathy-gap.[24] Quoting them,

> We will argue that our understanding of what constitutes a 'reasonable' discount rate ...has been limited by the implicit assumption that people should maximize the utility of a constant self over one's lifetime. An alternative position, proposed by the philosopher Derek Parfit (1984), is that a decision about consuming now or later should depend not only on the temporal distance between events but also on the perceived continuity between one's present and future selves. This implies that the degree of concern one has for one's future self should be scaled by the degree of 'psychological connectedness'—overlap in personality, temperament, major likes and dislikes, beliefs, values, ambitions, life goals, ideals, and so on—held between one's current and future self...Economists assume a constant self.

In five separate experiments, the results are consistent with decreased connectedness causing increased impatience. [In the lab, connectedness is

Parfit gets around this, arguing that what is important for survival and responsibility is psychological connectedness: remaining the same person is unnecessary. Person X at time t_1 is psychologically continuous with person Y at t_2 if and only if X is psychologically continuous with Y, "where psychological continuity consists in overlapping chains of strong psychological connections like memories, intentions, beliefs/goals/desires, and similarity characteristics" (David Shoemaker 2019).

As noted, Buddhists consider the "persisting person" a useful fiction, arguing that there is no me in the me (*no-self*). Parfit's conclusion is similar, a conclusion he has described as liberating and consoling.

A common view, not shared by philosophers though preached from pulpits, is that your identity is your eternal soul.

Then there is the "Beam-me-up Scotty" transporter where the you in you is converted into an energy pattern—destroying you. And you are resurrected on Vulcan when you are converted back. Sometimes Scotty screws up, and duplicates appear, problematic for personal identity.

[24] Imagine how you would act if you expected your future self to be a Franz Kafka insect or a 155-pound Phillip Roth breast.

manipulated by citing evidence that significant future events (e.g., graduation, marriage) will change the subject's core identity. Or citing evidence that core identity is fixed early in life.]

In *Procrastination and Personal Identify*, the U. of Montreal philosopher and ethicist Christine Tappolet attributes procrastination to an inability to connect with your future selves. [In Latin, *pro* means "for," and *crastinus* means "of the morrow".] I put off what I should be doing because I don't connect and emphasize with the person who will suffer from my procrastinating. She speculates that this is why the Russian nobleman Itia Ilitch Oblomov (the main character in an Ivan Goncharov novel) stays in bed rather than doing what has to be done to keep his estate afloat.

Empathy for one's future selves, or its absence, is, conceptually, no different from empathy for other human and non-human animals (caring about others).[25] The NBT Assumptions are consistent with any degree of empathy for one's future self or others.

But—a lack of empathy for one's future selves causes flawed choosing if modern humans are programmed by biological or cultural evolution to have less future-self empathy than is warranted, given the recent and dramatic jump in human life spans. We are quirked to not save for our sixties and beyond. Why? Because until the last few centuries, few lived that long. If you fail to empathize with your future self because you incorrectly believe that you won't live that long, the gap is caused by an incorrect belief.[26] Believing now that you will not care about your future self when you are him is also an incorrect belief but of a different sort.

[25] It is notable that economists do not balk at modeling what is WB-best, overall, for a sequence of individuals who all inhabit the same, changing, body, but balk at modeling what is WB-best, overall, for a group of individuals who inhabit separate bodies. It is also notable that psychologists find lack of empathy for one's future self a flaw but not lack of empathy for others.

[26] Imagine that you believe you will die soon, and it is based on ignorance and a misreading of the longevity statistics for people like you. So, you blow the retirement account driving your new Mercedes to Grateful Dead reunions. You survive longer than you expected and end up eating cat food in your twilight years, cheap cat food. You would have been better off in your old age if you had forgone the car and concerts, though you did what was best, given your knowledge and ignorance at the time. But it was flawed choosing.

But not all life spans have jumped dramatically: most animals have not experienced it, and neither have the millions of humans that live in violence and poverty. So, while the future-self empathy-gap causes rich Western me to suffer flawed choosing, it does not cause everyone to.

References and Sources

Ariely, Dan, and George Loewenstein. 2006. "The heat of the moment: The effect of sexual arousal on sexual decision making." *Journal of Behavioral Decision Making* 19 (2): 87–98.

Bartels, Daniel M., and Oleg Urminsky. 2011. "On intertemporal selfishness: How the perceived instability of identity underlies impatient consumption." *Journal of Consumer Research* 38 (1): 182–198. http://home.uchicago.edu/bartels/papers/Bartels-Urminsky-2011-JCR.PDF.

Bear, Mark, Barry Connors, and Michael Paradiso. 2020. *Neuroscience: Exploring the brain, enhanced edition: Exploring the brain*. Jones & Bartlett Learning.

Beran, Michael, and Theodore Evans. 2006. "Maintenance of delay of gratification by four chimpanzees (pan troglodytes): The effects of delayed reward visibility, experimenter presence, and extended delay intervals." *Behavioural Processes* 73 (3): 315–324. https://doi.org/10.1016/j.beproc.2006.07.005. https://pubmed.ncbi.nlm.nih.gov/12038494/.

Beran, Michael, Sue Savage-Rumbaugh, Joy Pate, and Duane Rumbaugh. 1999. "Delay of gratification in chimpanzees (pan troglodytes)." *Developmental Psychobiology* 34 (2): 119–127. https://www.webofscience.com/wos/woscc/full-record/WOS:000078995500005.

Berridge, Kent, and Jonath Aldridge. 2008. "Decision utility, the brain and the pursuit of hedonic goals." *Social Cognition* 26 (5): 621–646. https://doi.org/10.1521/soco.2008.26.5.621. https://www.webofscience.com/wos/woscc/full-record/WOS:000260639600008.

Berridge, Kent, and Morten Kringelbach. 2013. "Neuroscience of affect: Brain mechanisms of pleasure and displeasure." *Current Opinion in Neurobiology* 23 (3): 294–303. https://doi.org/10.1016/j.conb.2013.01.017. https://www.webofscience.com/wos/woscc/full-record/WOS:000354069800008.

Berridge, Kent, and Terry Robinson. 1998. "What is the role of dopamine in reward: Hedonic impact, reward learning, or incentive salience?" *Brain Research Reviews* 28 (3): 309–369. https://doi.org/10.1016/s0165-0173(98)00019-8. https://pubmed.ncbi.nlm.nih.gov/9858756/.

Bravo, Javier, et al. 2011. "Ingestion of lactobacillus strain regulates emotional behavior and central GABA receptor expression in a mouse via the vagus nerve." *Proceedings of the National Academy of Sciences* 108 (38): 16050–16055. https://doi.org/10.1073/pnas.1102999108.

Damasio, Antonio. 1994. *Descartes' error: Emotion, reason, and the human brain.* New York: Putman.

Di Tella, Rafael, John Haisken-De New, and Robert MacCulloch. 2010. "Happiness adaptation to income and to status in an individual panel." *Journal of Economic Behavior & Organization* 76 (3): 834–852.

Ditto, Peter, Pizarro David, Eden Epstein, Jill Jacobson, and Tara Macdonald. 2006. "Visceral influences on risk-taking behavior." *Journal of Behavioral Decision Making* 19 (2): 99–113.

Dutton, Donald, and Arthur Aron. 1974. "Some evidence for heightened sexual attraction under conditions of high anxiety." *Journal of Personality and Social Psychology* 30 (4): 510.

Elster, Jon. 1998. "Emotions and economic theory." *Journal of Economic Literature* 38: 47–74.

Evans, Theodore, and Michael Beran. 2007. "Delay of gratification and delay maintenance by rhesus macaques (Macaca Mulatta)." *Journal of General Psychology* 134 (2): 199–216. https://doi.org/10.3200/genp.134.2.199-216. https://www.webofscience.com/wos/woscc/full-record/WOS:000078995500005.

Garg, Nitika, and Jennifer Lerner. 2013. "Sadness and consumption." *Journal of Consumer Psychology* 23 (1): 106–113.

Gazziniga, Michael, Richard Ivry, and George Mangun. 2014. *Cognitive neuroscience: The biology of the mind.* 4th ed. W.W. Norton.

Gilbert, Dan, et al. 1998. "Immune neglect: A source of durability bias in affective forecasting." *Journal of Personality and Social Psychology* 75 (3): 617.

Gottlieb, Anthony. 2016. *The dream of enlightenment: The rise of modern philosophy.* WW Norton & Company.

Kahneman, Dan, and Angus Deaton. 2010. "High income improves evaluation of like but not emotional well-being." *Proceedings of the National Academy of the United States of America* 107 (38): 16489–16493. https://doi.org/10.1073/pnas.1011492107.

Kosfeld, Michael, et al. 2005. "Oxytocin increases trust in humans." *Nature* 435 (7042): 673–676.

Kringelbach, Morton, and Kent Berridge. 2012. "The joyful mind." *Scientific American* 307 (2): 40–45.

Labroo, Aparna, and Vanessa Patrick. 2009. "Psychological distancing: Why happiness helps you see the big picture." *Journal of Consumer Research* 35 (5): 800–809.

Lerner, Jennifer, Deborah Small, and George Loewenstein. 2004. "Heart strings and purse strings: Carryover effects of emotions on economic decisions." *Psychological Science* 15 (5): 337–341.

Lerner, Jennifer, Ye Li, and Elke Weber. 2013. "The financial costs of sadness." *Psychological science* 24 (1): 72–79.

Loewenstein, George. 1999. "Because it is there: The challenge of mountaineering ...For utility theory." *Kyklos* 52 (3): 29.

———. 2000. "Emotions in economic theory and economic behavior." *American economic review* 90 (2): 426–432.

———. 2004. *Out of control: Visceral influences on behavior*. Edited by Colin Camerer et al. *Advances in behavioral economics*. Princeton: Princeton University Press. https://www.webofscience.com/wos/woscc/full-record/WOS:000287441800027.

Loewenstein, George, and Shane Frederick. 1997. "Predicting reactions to environmental change." *Environment, Ethics, and Behavior*: 52–72.

Loewenstein, George, and David Schkade. 1999. "Wouldn't it be nice? Predicting future feelings." *Well-Being: The Foundations of Hedonic Psychology*: 85–105.

Loewenstein, George, Daniel Nagin, and Raymond Paternoster. 1997. "The effect of sexual arousal on expectations of sexual forcefulness." *Journal of Research in Crime and Delinquency* 34 (4): 443–473.

Loewenstein, George, Drazen Prelec, and Catherine Shatto. 1998. "Hot/cold intrapersonal empathy gaps and the under-prediction of curiosity." Unpublished manuscript, Carnegie-Mellon University, Pittsburgh, PA.

Mogilner, Cassie, Jennifer Aaker, and Sepandar Kamvar. 2012. "How happiness affects choice." *Journal of Consumer Research* 39 (2): 429–443.

Mulcahy, Nicholas J., and Josep Call. 2006. "Apes save tools for future use." *Science* 312 (5776): 1038–1040. https://www.webofscience.com/wos/woscc/full-record/WOS:000287441800027.

Osvath, Mathias, and Helena Osvath. 2008. "Chimpanzee (pan troglodytes) and orangutan (pongo abelii) forethought: Self-control and pre-experience in the face of future tool use." *Animal Cognition* 11 (4): 661–674.

Oswald, Andrew J., and Nattavudh Powdthavee. 2008. "Does happiness adapt? A longitudinal study of disability with implications for economists and judges." *Journal of Public Economics* 92 (5–6): 1061–1077.

Parfit, Derek. 1984. *Reasons and persons*. Oxford: Clarendon Press.

Preston, Elizabeth. 2002. *Octopuses don't have backbones—or rights*. New York Times.

Riis, Jason, et al. 2005. "Ignorance of hedonic adaptation to hemodialysis: A study using ecological momentary assessment." *Journal of Experimental Psychology: General* 134 (1): 3.

Santos, Laurie, and Alexandra Rosati. 2015. "The evolutionary roots of human decision making." *Annual Review of Psychology* 66: 321–347. https://doi.org/10.1146/annurev-psych-010814-015310. https://doi.org/10.1146/annurev-psych-010814-015310.

Sapolsky, Robert. 2014. *Why zebras don't get ulcers*. New York: Henry Holt and Company.

Schnell, Alexandra, Markus Boeckle, Micaela Rivera, Nicola Clayton, and Roger Hanlon. 2021. "Cuttlefish exert self-control in a delay gratification task." *Proceeding of the Royal Academy B.* https://doi.org/10.1098/rspb.2022.3161.

Shoemaker, David. 2019. "Personal identity and ethics." Stanford Encyclopedia of Philosophy. Stanford University. https://www.webofscience.com/wos/woscc/full-record/WOS:000823346300001.

Smith, Peter. 2015. "Can the bacteria in your gut explain your mood?" *New York Times*, June 28.

Stevens, Jeffrey, Elizabeth Hallinan, and Marc Hauser. 2005. "The ecology and evolution of patience in two new world monkeys." *Biology Letters* 1 (2): 223–226. https://doi.org/10.1098/rsbl.2004.0285. https://www.ncbi.nlm.nih.gov/pmc/articles/PMC1626214/.

Stutzer, Alois, and Bruno Frey. 2008. "Stress that doesn't pay: The commuting paradox." *Scandinavian Journal of Economics* 110 (2): 339–366.

Svendsen, Lars. 1999/2005. *A philosophy of boredom (in English).* Oslo: Universitetsforlaget (1999 (Norwegian) and Realtion Books 2005.

Tappolet, Christine. 2010. "Procrastination and personal identity." *The Thief of Time: Philosophical Essays on Procrastination*: 115–129.

Tobin, Henry, et al. 1996. "Self-control in the monkey Macaca fascicularis." *Animal Learning & Behavior* 24 (2): 168–174. https://www.webofscience.com/wos/woscc/full-record/WOS:000242063600013.

Vanderbilt, Tom. 2009. *Traffic: Why we drive the way we do.* New York: Vintage Books.

Williams, Lawrence, and John Bargh. 2008. "Experiencing physical warmth promotes interpersonal warmth." *Science* 322 (5901): 606–607. https://doi.org/10.1126/science.1162548. https://www.webofscience.com/wos/woscc/full-record/WOS:000260299100048.

Wilson, Timothy. 2002. *Strangers to ourselves: Discovering the adaptive unconscious.* Cambridge, MA: The Belknap Press of Harvard University Press.

Wilson, Timothy, and Dan Gilbert. 2008. "Explaining away: A model of affective adaptation." *Perspectives on Psychological Science* 3 (5): 370–386.

Wilson, Timothy, et al. 2000. "Focalism: A source of durability bias in affective forecasting." *Journal of Personality and Social Psychology* 78 (5): 821.

Wyvell, Cindy, and Kent Berridge. 2000. "Intra-accumbens amphetamine increases the conditioned incentive salience of sucrose reward: Enhancement of reward "wanting" without enhanced "liking" or response reinforcement." *Journal of Neuroscience* 20 (21): 8122–8130. https://www.webofscience.com/wos/woscc/full-record/WOS:000090003600032.

———. 2001. "Incentive sensitization by previous amphetamine exposure: Increased cue-triggered "wanting" for sucrose reward." *Journal of Neuroscience* 21 (19): 7831–7840.

Additional Readings

Apicella, Coren, Eduardo Azevedo, Nicholas Christakis, and James Fowler. 2014. "Evolutionary origins of the endowment effect: Evidence from hunter-gatherers." *American Economic Review* 104 (6): 1793–1805. https://doi.org/10.1257/aer.104.6.1793. https://www.jstor.org/stable/42920866.

Cesarini, David, Magnus Johannesson, Patrik Magnusson, and Bjorn Wallace. 2012. "The behavioral genetics of behavioral anomalies." *Management Science* 58 (1): 21–34. https://doi.org/10.1287/mnsc.1110.1329. https://doi.org/10.1287/mnsc.1110.1329.

Flemming, Timothy, et al. 2012. "The endowment effect in orangutans." *International Journal of Comparative Psychology* 25: 285–298.

Goleman, Daniel. 2013. "Rich people just care less." *The New York Times*, October 5. https://archive.nytimes.com/opinionator.blogs.nytimes.com/2013/10/05/rich-people-just-care-less/.

Huck, Steffen, Georg Kirchsteiger, and Jorg Oechssler. 2005. "Learning to like what you have—Explaining the endowment effect." *Economic Journal* 115 (505): 689–702. https://doi.org/10.1111/j.1468-0297.2005.01015.x. https://academic.oup.com/ej/article-abstract/115/505/689/5085713?redirectedFrom=fulltext.

Kimball, Miles, Ryan Nunn, and Dan Silverman. 2015. *Accounting for adaptation in the economics of happiness.* National Bureau of Economic Research. http://www.nber.org/papers/w21365.pdf.

Krauss, Michael, Shai Davidai, and David Nussbaum. 2009. "American dream? Or mirage." *The New York Times*, May 1. https://www.nytimes.com/2015/05/03/opinion/sunday/american-dream-or-mirage.html.

Levy, Moshe. 2015. "An evolutionary explanation for risk aversion." *Journal of Economic Psychology* 46: 51–61. https://doi.org/10.1016/j.joep.2014.12.001. https://www.sciencedirect.com/science/article/pii/S0167487014001044?via%3Dihub.

CHAPTER 9

The Endowment Effect

Picture a gorilla given a choice between a grape and a carrot (they prefer grapes); he grabs for the grape but is given the carrot. Even though he chose the grape over the carrot, he is now unwilling to give up the carrot to get the grape. He would give up the carrot to get a fig: they are much preferred to grapes and carrots (Fig. 9.1).

The Knetsch experiment with coffee mugs, chocolate bars, and college students discussed in Chapter 7 is viewed as demonstrating the endowment effect. Other famous empirical studies include Kahneman et al. (1990) and Zvi Carmon and Dan Ariely (2000).

The endowment effect has even been observed with humans and other species when the item was acquired minutes earlier, even with M&Ms—people value the bag in their hand more than the bag in the researcher's hand. If standing in the store, the individual has to be paid more than they just paid to return the item.[1] The endowment effect has been observed with different goods, populations, children, and primate species. In econ-speak, what you were willing-to-pay, WTP, to acquire an item (what you were willing to sacrifice to acquire it) is less than what you would have

[1] If the store offers them another bag plus some change to give up the bag they are holding, many individuals won't do it. Of course, it depends on how much money is offered, everyone would return their bag of M&Ms for $10 and a new bag, though that isn't the issue. And you would not sell it for what you paid for it if re-purchasing required too much time and effort (driving back to the store, etc.).

E. R. Morey, *Deconstructing Behavior, Choice, and Well-being*,
https://doi.org/10.1007/978-3-031-36712-0_9

Fig. 9.1 Gorilla chomping a carrot

to be paid to voluntarily give it up—your WTA, willingness-to-accept its loss.

As mentioned above, the endowment effect is typically described as your WTP to obtain an item is less than your WTA its loss after it is acquired. However, NBT is specified in terms of paths, not WTP nor WTA. So, it is crucial to understand it in terms of ordering paths.

Imagine two paths: an initial path, Path i, and a proposed path, Path i^{+A}, where A is one unit of good A. Path i has no A; otherwise, the two paths are identical in terms of what is exogenous to the individual (same income (y), prices, and other exogenous factors). [A could be a durable good or a public good.] Path i^{+A} is ranked higher than Path i because of that unit of A. Now imagine a third path, Path i^{+B}, identical to Path i, except it has one unit of good B. Assume Path i^{+B} is ranked higher than Path i^{+A}. Initially, there are no available paths with A or B.

The individual is initially on Path i, where neither A nor B is sold or provided. The individual is then given the option of acquiring A at her wtp for A, $wtp(A)$. This is the amount of money that would have to be subtracted from her income, y, after A is acquired, so she would rank Path i^{+A} with that subtraction the same as the initial path, Path i. Call this path, Path $i^{+A-wtp(A)}$: by definition of $wtp(A)$, the individual is indifferent between Path $i^{+A-wtp(A)}$ and Path i: they share the same rank. Because acquiring A would increase her WB, $wtp(A)$ is positive but less than $wtp(B)$. The above holds whether or not there is an endowment effect: an endowment effect only kicks in if A is acquired.

Now assume the individual pays her $wtp(A)$ and acquires A, so she is now on Path $i^{+A-wtp(A)}$.[2] Now consider her $wta(-A)$ the loss of A: it is how much money would have to be added to her current income, $(y - wtp(A))$, after A is lost, so she would rank Path $i^{wta(-A)-wtp(A)}$ and Path $i^{+A-wtp(A)}$ the same. By definition, $wta(-A) > 0$, and she is indifferent between these two paths.

If there is no endowment effect, $wta(-A) = wtp(A)$, making Path $i^{wta(-A)-wtp(A)=0}$ identical to Path i. And the individual is indifferent between them and Path $i^{+A-wtp(A)}$ all three have the same rank in their ordering, her ordering before A is acquired and her ordering after it is acquired. This is because the two orderings are the same: the acquisition and loss of A have not affected her ordering: the ordering was unaffected by Path i^{+A-wtp} becoming available and her taking it.

But, if the acquisition of A creates an endowment effect, by definition, $wta(-A) > wtp(A)$, and Path $i^{wta(-A)-wtp(A)}$ is not identical to Path i: it has $wta(-A) - wtp(A)$ more income.

And because of this endowment effect, there is a different ordering of paths: before A was acquired, Path i and Path $i^{+A-wtp(A)}$ had the same rank. But after A is acquired, Path $i^{+A-wtp(A)}$ is ranked higher than Path i. Why? Because after A is acquired, the individual ranks Path $i^{+A-wtp(A)}$ the same as Path $i^{wta(-A)-wta(A)>0}$, but the latter is ranked higher than Path i because it is identical to Path i but with more income.

And recollect that before the individual acquired A, she ranked Path i^{+B} above Path i^{+A}. Their ranking can flip after A is acquired. The probability it flips increases with the strength of A's endowment effect and increases the smaller the initial $wtp(B) - wtp(A)$.

In summary, if acquiring A changes the individual's ordering of paths, A has an endowment effect.[3]

[2] Path i^{-wtp} is ranked below Path i because it is identical to i but has *wtp* less income.

[3] While acquiring a good with an endowment effect is sufficient to change your ordering of paths, it is not necessary: other things can change your ordering—for example, a knock on the head.

Which, if any, NBT Assumptions are violated by the endowment effect? It violates Assumption 6A: *An economicus's ordering of paths can't depend on which are currently available.* It also violates the spirit of Assumption 4: *An economicus's ordering does not change in the time-span behavior is modeled.* If the endowment effect kicks in immediately when Good *A* is acquired, Assumption 4 is violated. How long it takes to kick in is an empirical question.[4]

NBT is typically presented as separating one's ordering of paths (Assumption 2) from which are available (Assumption 5). However, the endowment effect destroys this separation: the ordering often changes when a path is taken. [In Fig. 2.4: if there is an endowment effect, the ordering isn't in set A:6a.]

But pause! While the ordering of paths is changed, does the change persist, or is it only a blip? Imagine you have two orderings: a *top-level ordering*, unaffected by endowment effects, and *ground-level ordering*, which is. Imagine that top-level ordering is how you would order paths if you were not on a path. And your ground-level ordering is your ordering given that you are currently experiencing a specific path. After you relinquish a good that generated an endowment effect and before you replace it with a new good, your ordering reverts to your top-level ordering? I don't know.

Does the Endowment Effect Cause Flawed Choosing?

Maybe Yes. Maybe No. It's Yes—but only if the effect is based on an incorrect belief. You incorrectly believe that losing the item will decrease WB by more than the WB loss associated with the item's services.

No! It does not cause flawed choosing if you would experience a WB decrease above and beyond the decrease associated with losing the item's services. I will call the former an *anticipated but unrealized endowment effect*, the latter *anticipated and realized*. Mostly, the distinction isn't made.

[4] The endowment effect leads to behavior that appears to violate **Assumption 2:** ***At every point in time, an economicus has one ordering of all paths—1st, 2nd, …*** Yet, Assumption 2 isn't violated: at both points in time there is one ordering, the new one is just different.

Table 9.1 Realized vs. unrealized endowment effects

	Realized WB drop from losing exceeds the amount acquiring increased WB	*Realized WB drop from losing equals the amount acquiring increased WB*
Anticipated WB drop from losing exceeds the amount acquiring increased WB	1. Anticipated and realized endowment effect: belief correct, so choosing not flawed	2. Anticipated but unrealized endowment effect: incorrect belief, so flawed choosing
Anticipated WB drop from losing equals the amount acquiring increased WB	3. Incorrect belief, so flawed choosing	4. No endowment effect: no incorrect belief, so choosing not flawed

Table 9.1 outlines four possibilities.[5]

Boxes 1 and 2 are endowment effects. Box 3 is a realized endowment effect that was not anticipated. My sense is many economists define the endowment effect as Box 2. Whether the WB drop is realized and for how long are empirical questions.

If the anticipated loss is experienced, it explains why an increase over the long run in average National income may not cause an increase in emotional WB: economic contractions decrease emotional WB more than expansions increase it. To re-acquire the same emotional WB you had before the last recession, the subsequent expansion will need to raise your income substantially above its pre-recession level.

Is the anticipated loss realized?

> ...it is unclear whether losses are actually experienced more intensely than comparable gains, or whether people simply behave as if they were. Some have argued that loss aversion isn't anything more than an affective forecasting error, while others have argued that there are many situations in which losses are actually more impactful than comparable gains. (Rick 2011)

Boyce et al. (2013), looking at income gains and losses, conclude the anticipated WB drop is realized and enduring. They estimated that an

[5] There are three more possibilities: cases where the anticipated WB drop from losing is less than the amount acquiring it increased WB—a reverse endowment effect.

income decrease of 10K euros will decrease realized WB twice as much as a 10K increase. They analyzed a German data set of 28K households. For each household, there is data for multiple years, including yearly income, yearly answers to "How satisfied are you with your life, all things considered?" (0 = totally unhappy, 10 = totally happy), plus age, gender, etc. There are 63K household/year observations. The authors estimated each respondent's WB in year t as a function of their reported WB in the previous year ($t - 1$) and whether income increased or decreased from the last year.[6] WB increased (decreased) when income increased (decreased).

They then expanded their regression, allowing the effect on WB of an income increase to be different from an income decrease. They found that realized losses affected WB more than realized gains. A second British data set of 120K observations supports their finding.[7]

William Gehring and Adrian Willoughby (2002) provide additional support that the anticipated WB drop is realized. They recorded neural activity while subjects gambled. The gambles were designed such that the financial gain (or loss) varied independently from whether the subject won the gamble. E.g., on some, you could win the bet and lose financially—you would have lost more if you had bet on the other alternative.[8] They found that whether the individual won the gamble is recorded in a different brain region than financial gains and losses. Financial gains and

[6] The log of the ratio of current income divided by last year's income. This transformation adjusts for the fact that a 10,000 euro increase in income has a smaller effect on WB the higher one's initial income.

[7] Instead of asking directly about WB, it asked standard psychological questions (extent respondent feels worthless, unhappy, and depressed).

[8] Neural activity was recorded while the subjects gambled. Each subject was repeatedly presented with two squares, each containing a number; they choose a square. Then each square turned green or red (green for a gain, red for a loss). The number indicated gain or loss in cents (e.g., red 25 would indicate a loss of 25 cents if you had chosen that square). The colors and amounts appearing in each square were determined randomly, so both squares could be green or red. E.g., if the two numbers were 5 and 25, and the subject picked 5, and 5 turned green and 25 red, they won 5 cents and found out they would have lost 25 cents if they had chosen the other square. The beauty of this design is that it separates financial losses and gains from correct and incorrect choices. E.g., if both the 5 and 25 boxes turn red and you choose the 5, you experience a financial loss, though you chose correctly in that you would have lost more if you had chosen the 25 square. And, if they both turned green, you experience a financial gain but chose incorrectly in that you would have gained more if you had chosen the 25.

losses are recorded in the anterior cingulate cortex. And realized financial losses generate more activity than realized financial gains.[9]

In an fMRI study, Robb Rutledge and Glimcher (2009) compared realized dollar gains and losses of equal magnitude. The losses generated more neural activity.

Complicating, Deborah Kermer et al. (2006) find, also with a gambling experiment, that subjects overestimate the WB impacts of losses (the authors call it an *affective forecasting error*). The authors note that their

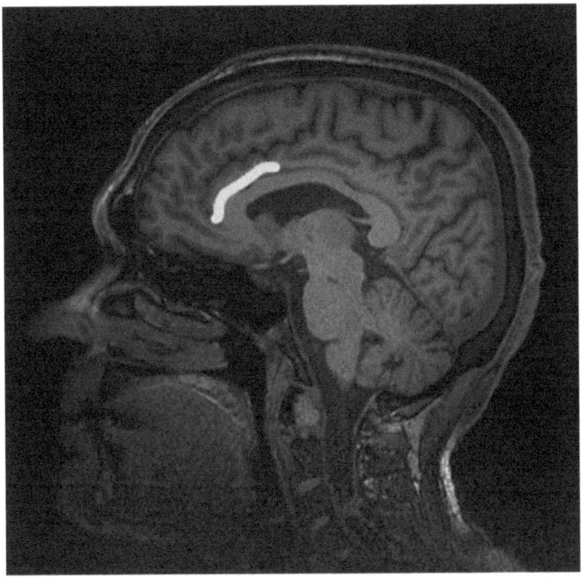

Fig. 9.2 The anterior cingulate cortex (yellow in file formats)

[9] Approximately 1/5 of a second after the colors appear, neural activity indicates, in terms of both location and intensity, whether the subject gained or lost financially: there was more activity for losses than gains at the electrode located at the medial frontal scalp (the anterior cingulate cortex). And this activity was independent of whether the individual chose correctly or incorrectly, so the increased activity (in yellow) is reflecting the loss, not an incorrect choice (Fig. 9.2).

finding is consistent with a WB loss greater than the initial gain. It only implies that subjects overestimate the WB loss.[10]

In a second experiment, they give each subject \$5 and then tell them they will flip a coin. And if it's heads, the subject will get an additional \$5, but if it is tails, she will lose \$3 and end up with \$2. Subjects anticipated that the \$3 loss would hurt more than the \$5 gain would feel good. After the flip, they rated the two outcomes as having the same effect on their WB. As Rick (2011) points out, since a \$3 loss is less than a \$5 loss, this result is consistent with a realized loss of \$5 affecting WB more than a realized gain of \$5. "The [Kermer] data provide only equivocal support for their title, "Loss aversion is an affective forecasting error" (Rich 2011). I agree.

The three studies just discussed investigated the WB effects of monetary gains and losses, not the gain or loss of a good.

* * *

One unanswered empirical question is, "When do you first anticipate that selling something will decrease your WB more than its acquisition increased it?" Is it immediately when you acquire it? Or only after you have possessed it for a while? Or only when you first consider relinquishing it? Then there is the issue of the endowment effect's magnitude. Is it an enduring constant, or does it wax or wane? If it wanes, the new ordering of paths will revert to the initial ordering, even though there is still an endowment effect in terms of WB.

Another complication is that if you sell Good *A* and use the money to buy Good *B* (e.g., sell the ski house to buy the beach house), Good *B* is now subject to the endowment effect. Is this anticipated? I sense the literature assumes no.

[10] For example, my WTP for good *G* is *\$X*, and my anticipated WTA its loss is *\$(X + 2)*. But I would only need *\$(X + 1)* to be whole.

Explanations for the Endowment Effect

There are at least two competing explanations for the endowment effect: *loss aversion* and *ownership/self*.[11,12] Loss aversion was the textbook explanation until recently, but it is being supplanted, at least

[11] Two also-rans are the *wealth-effect explanation* and the *cognitive-dissonance explanation*. The wealth-effect explanation (Michael Hanemann 1991a, b): if your real wealth is increased when you acquire something, the now wealthier you would have to get more to give it up than you would have originally paid for it. An example would be the Monet the previous owner forgot in the basement when he sold you your house. Another is your WTP for a protocol that would drive your nasty brain cancer into remission vs. what you would have to be paid to voluntarily abandon the protocol and have the cancer return. Your WTP was limited by your income, your WTA isn't. The wealth-effect explanation violates no NBT Assumptions. However, it does not explain most examples of the endowment effect: most don't include major wealth shifts.

Cognitive dissonance (Festinger 1962, 1964) is the negative feeling (stress) you experience when you hold conflicting beliefs and attitudes. A typical reaction to cognitive dissonance is to change your beliefs (reject some, modify some, or add some new ones). You chose *A* over *B*; but now that you have *A*, the fact that on some dimensions *B* is better than *A* causes dissonance. You eliminate the dissonance by suppressing your positive thoughts about *B* and finding more reasons why *A* is great. And, the result is your WTA the loss of *A* is now greater than what you were willing to pay for it (Brehm 1956; Frey 1986). This reaction to cognitive dissonance is "the spreading of alternatives effect," as in, you reassess to make the difference between the chosen alternative and the rejected alternatives greater. For example, you buy the Fiat 500 rather than the Dodge Ram Truck. After the Cinque Cento is in your driveway, you start stressing about your choice. The Fiat is fun to drive around town, easy to park, and you get lots of compliments. BUT! It is lousy in the snow, and there isn't enough room for your dogs and toys. Everything fits in Ram trucks, and they blast through the snow. While you chose the Fiat over the truck, some characteristics of the truck are better. You are conflicted and second-guessing your choice (experiencing cognitive dissonance). You reduce your stress by suppressing your positive thoughts about the Ram Truck and by finding more reasons why the Fiat 500 is great. You justify your choice by changing your assessments, which increases what you would have to be paid to give up the Fiat.

But—If the endowment effect is solely caused by cognitive dissonance there wouldn't be one if the item was not chosen. For example, if you inherited the Fiat from your aunt—rather than choosing it over the truck—acquiring it would not cause cognitive dissonance, and there would be no endowment effect. But the effect is observed when *A* is endowed rather than chosen, and cognitive dissonance can't explain this. And, if the endowment effect is solely caused by cognitive dissonance, it's hard to imagine why some non-human animals experience it.

[12] I just discovered a salience explanation for the endowment effect (Bordalo, Gennaioli, and Shleifer 2012): what's salient shifts after the good, *e*, is obtained. Before *e* is obtained, he values it in terms of its "best attributes" (relative to the status quo of not having it). When given the option of trading it away, what's salient are the "new goods disadvantages relative to the endowment" (*e* is now part of the status quo).

among psychologists, by the ownership/self explanation. Recent research supporting the ownership/self explanation includes Bertram Gawronski, Galen Bodenhausen, and Andrew Becker (2007), Carey Morewedge et al. (2009), and William Maddux et al. (2010).

A third possible explanation is that the behavior called the endowment effect is caused by the fact an individual does not have a complete ordering of paths. Instead, she has an incomplete ordering caused by WB-incomparabilities (some pairs of paths are not comparable in the amount of WB they generate). WB-comparability was briefly discussed in Chapter 2. Chapter 7 considers WB-incomparability and WB-incommensurability in detail. There, I consider whether an incomplete ordering can generate behaviors that look like endowment effects.

Loss Aversion

Loss aversion is that you are averse to relinquishing items you possess—the emphasis is on the adjective *loss*. Losing causes unpleasant emotions, or you anticipate it will—losing what you own is painful, even if the relinquishing is voluntary. Sometimes, I spend hours looking for junk: I look in the drawer for stamps and notice the worthless watch I have not worn for years isn't there. I then search for it. If I find it, I put it back in the drawer. I spend hours looking for something I have no use for. Why? I do not like to lose stuff. You may not waste your time this way, but psychologists say I have company.

There Is a Growing Empirical and Theoretical Literature on Whether Loss Aversion Is Genetic

Steffen Huck, Georg Kirchsteiger, and Jorg Oechssler (2005) argue that if the potential seller in a one-on-one barter is loss averse, he will drive a harder bargain. Therefore, potential sellers with loss aversion make better deals (end up better off); thus, increasing the genetic fitness (survival and reproduction) of loss-averse people.

In support, Moshe Levy (2015) argues that loss aversion minimizes the probability that your line of descendants will go extinct (maximizes the likelihood of having descendants forever). He provides evidence that for thousands of years, most exchanges were one-on-one barters (first between groups and then between individuals within a group). [His critical assumption is that bartered exchanges are *Nash-bargaining solutions*: both parties get their best outcome, given the other's outcome. So, how well a seller does depends on their bargaining skills relative to other potential sellers.]

Studying 11K Swedish twins, David Cesarini et al. (2012) find that loss aversion is "moderately heritable"—with identical twins, if one twin is loss averse, the other twin is more likely to be.

But in opposition to loss aversion being genetic, Coren Apicella et al. (2014) found a group of humans who do not experience the endowment effect, suggesting the effect is cultural rather than genetic.

> We experimentally test for the endowment effect in an isolated and evolutionarily relevant population of hunter-gatherers, the Hadza Bushmen of Northern Tanzania. We find that Hadza living in isolated regions do not display the endowment effect, while Hadza living in a geographic region with increased exposure to modern society and markets do display the endowment effect. (Apicella et al. 2014)

The isolated group is one of the few remaining hunter-gather populations. "All food brought to camp is equally shared, among all camp members, regardless of kinship." And "While the Hadza do own a few things, such as knives, bows and arrows, and animal skins, ownership is limited to what can be carried." Unlike the rest of us, they lack a culture of ownership and property rights. Their lack of the endowment effect suggests that the endowment effect is a cultural phenomenon, a widespread one, and one, by evolutionary standards, recent and universal in cultures with ownership.

* * *

Tversky, Kahneman, Knetsch, and Thaler are big-name supporters of the loss aversion explanation because it does not depend on how you came to own the item (a gift, a find, or you choose it over other alternatives). And according to them, sellers in research studies typically don't rate the item higher than the potential buyers—suggesting that owning it does not increase an item's value.[13]

The loss aversion literature is typically vague on whether or not the endowment effect is realized. Nevertheless, much of this literature must

[13] See Kahneman and Tversky (1979), Kahneman et al. (1990, 1991) and Tversky and Kahneman (1991). Some psychologists argue that loss aversion, without an underlying theory as to why we are loss aversion, isn't much of an explanation.

implicitly believe it isn't because it suggests that loss aversion causes flawed choosing.[14]

The Ownership/Self Explanation for the Endowment Effect

It is based on the following assumptions: (1) Everyone implicitly views themselves somewhere on a continuum that goes from an extremely negative assessment to extremely positive. E.g., considering yourself a terrible person and a failure is an extremely negative self-assessment (self-image). (2) When you acquire an item, you form an implicit association between yourself and the item: it becomes part of who you are. You transfer your self-assessment to it: it gets assessed, in part, as you assess yourself. If I imagine myself as worthless, acquiring new skis will decrease their value because they now belong to worthless me. If I imagine myself as a great guy, I value my new skis more because they are my skis.

Since most people positively self-assess, people need more money to sell the item than they were willing to pay to acquire it, which is the endowment effect. In contrast, the loss aversion explanation argues that I don't like my ski more because they are my skis but because I hate losing stuff, and selling them is a form of losing them.

Evidence for the Ownership/Self Explanation

Experiments by Gawronski, Bodenhausen, and Becker support the ownership/self explanation. Their goal was to see how your implicit valuation of an item is affected separately by whether you own it, whether you chose it, and your implicit self-assessment. The ownership/self explanation predicts that if you negatively self-assess, ownership implies a smaller rather than a larger WTA for the item's loss, so the opposite of what is typically observed.

According to the authors, two processes determine how we value ourselves, another person, or an item. One explicit and one implicit. For example, my explicit valuation of a pair of skis is based on how they look and ski: their actual characteristics and how they work for me. In contrast,

[14] The endowment effect as flawed choosing is common in the literature on financial investing (e.g. Haigh and List 2005: the argument is that you would make a higher rate-of-return on your stock portfolio if you were not averse to cutting your losses (selling at a loss). This isn't flawed choosing if he anticipated WB loss would be realized. The financial literature assumes it is not realized.

my implicit valuation is based on implicit attitudes. For example, Mikaela Shiffrin is famous and a skier beyond compare. And she endorses the skis, so I implicitly associate her greatness with them, independent of how they work for me.

In addition, the authors hypothesize an association between one's implicit self-assessment and one's implicit assessment of the owned item. And this was observed.

To test, over four experiments, they measured the subject's implicit self-assessment, their implicit values of two photos, and the their implicit association between themselves and each photo.[15] Experiment 1 estimated the implicit value of each photo before and after the individual choose which one they wanted to be gifted. The implicit value of the chosen (rejected) photo increased (decreased)—the standard result.

Experiment 2 found that after a photo was selected (rejected), the implicit association between it and the self-increased (decreased). Experiment 3 investigated how the subject's implicit self-assessment relates to the implicit value of their chosen photo. The implicit value of the chosen photo is positively correlated with their implicit self-assessment. The more you like yourself the more you value what you choose. So, for those who negatively self-assess (most people positively self-assess), WTA the loss of an item is less than was their WTP to obtain the item.

[15] The items were two scenic photographs. After the computer screen was blank for one second, one of the photos appeared for 1/5 of a second followed by either a positive or negative word for 1/5 of a second. The subject's task was to identify whether the word was a positive or negative word. Each photo appeared 40 times, 20 times followed by a positive word and 20 times by a negative word. Positive words included *paradise*, *health*, and *vacation*; negative words included *evil*, *vomit*, and *virus*. The more often and more quickly the subject answers correctly when the word is positive is a measure of the implicit value of the photo. The opposite for negative words. Corrects and incorrects are tabulated along with the time to respond. The result is a measure of the implicit value of each photo. [This is an *affective priming task*: it is widely used and has variants.]

Implicit self-assessment is measured by randomly presenting letters of the alphabet and having the respondent rate the likeability of each letter. How much more the respondent likes letters that are in their initials (my name letters are *e*, *r*, and *m*) is a measure of implicit self-esteem. [This method is common practice. For a critique of this method see Carl Falk and Steven Heine (2015).]

The test for association between the self and an item used a priming task like the item implicit-valuation task. But after a photo was presented, it was followed with either a "self" word (e.g., *me*, *my*, *I*) or an "other" word (e.g., *other*, *them*, *it*), and the individual had to indicate whether the word was a "self" word or an "other" word. This measure of association is increasing in how often and how quickly the subject correctly responds "self," and decreasing in how often and how quickly they correctly respond "other."

Their 4th experiment was designed to rule out cognitive dissonance as an explanation for the first three experiments. Experiment 4 was identical to Experiment 3, except which photo was gifted was determined by a roll of a die, so not chosen. With no choice, there should be no cognitive dissonance. However, one still gets the result that the photo's implicit value is positively correlated with your implicit self-assessment, implying that cognitive dissonance isn't driving the results in the first three experiments.

Adding independent support to the ownership/self explanation, Morewedge et al. (2009) compare it with the loss aversion explanation. They argue that most endowment-effect studies conflate loss aversion and the ownership/self effect. They describe the results of their Experiment 1 as follows, "In short, ownership without loss aversion caused the endowment effect, but loss aversion without ownership did not."

Explaining: In their first experiment, they experimentally created *ownership without loss aversion* by separating buyers into two treatments: buyers who already owned an identical mug to the one they were buying (*buyer-owner*) and buyers who did not (*buyer-nonowner*). In their first experiment, all sellers owned the mug (seller-owner). They found an endowment effect when the buyers are nonowners (the standard experiment).[16] However, they found no endowment effect when the buyers are owners (buyer-owners).

Their interpretation requires that buyer-nonowners are the *loss aversion without ownership group* and buyer-owners are the *ownership without loss aversion group*. Their quoted conclusion follows from these two assumptions and their two empirical results.[17]

[16] Their maximum buying price is significantly less than the minimum selling price of the owner-sellers. A subject's minimum selling price is determined by asking them whether they would sell at different prices: the lowest price for which they agreed to sell. A subject's maximum buying price is the highest at which they agreed they would buy the mug.

[17] One should ask what additional assumptions, or empirical findings, would justify their assumption that a buyer-nonowner must experience loss aversion. The authors implicitly assume (see their footnote 2) that people are loss averse when it comes to the gains and losses of others. When an individual makes a choice that directly affects only other people (e.g., the selling price of another's mug or the price to buy it for someone else, or which World Bank vaccination project to implement), the individual weighs a potential loss to the others of X dollars or X lives more than a gain of X dollars or X lives. [Taken on its own, it seems reasonable that if I am loss averse, others are as well, so I would take this into account if I were choosing based on what I think is best for them.] In addition,

In their second experiment, there are only seller and buyer agents: sellers do not own the mug they sell. Sellers typically own what they are selling; in contrast, a seller's agent (seller-nonowner) determines at what price they are willing to sell the mug but do not suffer its loss.

There were four treatments: buyer and seller agents who owned an identical mug to the one they bought or sold and those that did not. The findings: there was no endowment effect when both agents personally owned an identical mug. However, owning an identical mug increased both the maximum buying price and minimum selling price; that is, prices were higher when both agents owned their own mug. The authors argue that these results are what one would expect if the endowment effect was driven by ownership/self effects and not be expected if the endowment effect was driven by loss aversion. In addition, they argue that the loss aversion explanation should cause the agent seller's minimum selling price to be higher than the agent buyer's maximum purchase price "because sellers' brokers should think of the transaction as a loss and buyers' brokers should think of it as a gain."

Maddux et al. (2010) provide further evidence supporting the ownership/self explanation. If the endowment effect is driven by ownership/self, its magnitude depends on how individuals think about themselves (their self-construal). Some assess themselves by their abilities, values, wants, and likes (independent self-construal). Others by their relationships with others (interdependent self-construal). The authors reasonably hypothesize that the endowment effect should be weaker for those with interdependent self-construal. And this is what they found.

> Thus, if the endowment effect is at least partly a function of the tendency to value the self—and by extension the tendency to value objects that are owned [by the self] and thus part of the self relative to non-owned objects—then one should expect the effect ...to differ due to self-construals.

Explaining: Westerners lean towards independent self-construal and self-enhancement, and East Asians towards interdependent self-construal and less self-enhancement. This suggests that East Asians will exhibit weaker

the authors assume that if people are loss averse when it comes to the gains and losses of others, it somehow causes the buyer-nonowners to be loss averse.

endowment effects, and this is what the authors observe with coffee mugs and boxes of chocolates.[18]

To test whether the observed difference is caused by a difference in self-construal, the authors manipulated self-construal in a sample of 97 undergraduates at Yunnan Normal University in China. Each subject valued a coffee mug as either a buyer or seller after the subjects were divided into three treatments. The first treatment wrote a brief essay "about their friendships and camaraderie with other people and how they could foster these relationships." This treatment enhances interdependent self-construal. In the second treatment, subjects wrote about "their unique character and skills and how they stand out compared to other people"—thus enhancing independent self-construal. The third treatment (the control group) had no priming task. The observed endowment effect was strongest for the first treatment and weakest for the second, supporting the assumption that the difference in its strength is driven, in part, by independent vs. interdependent self-construal.

Adding additional support, the ownership/self explanation suggests that we increase our implicit assessments of what we own to protect our implicit self-assessment from a threat to that assessment. For example, I must be ok despite the threat to my self-image because my house and car are valuable. So, the ownership/self explanation suggests that the value of an owned good should increase when the self has been threatened. Sarah Dommer and Vanitha Swaminathan (2013) find this.

In summary, loss aversion was the standard explanation of the endowment effect for years, cognitive dissonance was a distant second, and the ownership/self explanation was either rejected or not considered. However, over the last fifteen years, the ownership/self explanation has emerged as the forerunner, at least in psychology. I find both loss aversion and ownership/self-intriguing explanations, and they can coexist—I don't like to lose things. Think of a sense-of-loss as a feeling/emotion, an unpleasant, specific emotion, like sadness and anger. Imagine its intensity depends on how much WB increased when the item was acquired. That

[18] The study of coffee mugs included 116 Northwestern students (59 identified as White or European U.S. citizens, 57 identified their ethnic background as Asian or East Asian). The chocolate study included 105 students at the University of Waterloo in Canada (34 identified as White or European Canadian citizens, 60 identified as Asian or East Asian).

said, my new gravel bike (coming soon) will increase in value when it's mine, which will improve my self-image, but first, I need to sell a bike.[19]

So, What Does the Ownership/Self Explanation Imply About Whether the Endowment Effect Loss Is or Isn't Realized?
The loss is realized.

Because my assessment of the item—which was, in part, a reflection of my self-assessment—transfers back to further reinforce my self-assessment. I value my new skis more because I transfer my positive self-image to the skis, which then feeds back, enhancing my self-image. If so, I experience more WB because the skis are mine, so my WB will drop when they are no longer mine: the endowment-effect loss is realized. My hesitancy to sell the skis isn't flawed. When I sell my ski, my WB drops more than the drop caused by the loss of the skis' services.

The Endowment Effect: Summing Up

It violates Assumption 6A: *An economicus's ordering can't depend on which paths are currently available*, and the spirit of Assumption 4: *An economicus's ordering does not change in the time-span behavior is modeled.* It causes flawed choosing only if the WB drop is unrealized. If the ownership/self explanation is correct, there is no flawed choosing because the anticipated loss is realized. Whether it is realized is an open empirical question.

The endowment effect is complicated, and unanswered questions abound. It is typically applied to the loss of something that provided WB, but what about the loss of items that are currently reducing your WB: the pain in your knee from an old sports injury or the old toaster that randomly burns the toast? They are also part of your self-assessment.

[19] The rule in my house and in my friends' homes is, "You can't buy another bike until you get rid of at least one of your current bikes." While I know of no specific study of the endowment effect and bicycles, I am sure how it would turn out. Bikes have characteristics that make them prime candidates for the endowment effect: bicycles are objects you experience; in action, your body and bike become integrated, they are long-lived, they are one of the few objects you also experienced as a child; you compete with yourself and others on a bike; you socialize on a bike, and they are highly customizable, so one of a kind. See Karly Coleman's thesis (2015) on cyclists' emotional attachment to their bikes.

Does the endowment effect imply that tossing the toaster will increase your WB more than you anticipate?

And how does its magnitude vary with what is lost? For example, chimps exhibit the endowment effect with food but not toys. Little is known about how the endowment effect in humans varies by what is lost (a relationship, an activity, a commodity, income) and what type of WB was lost (happiness, love, life satisfaction, etc.).

An aside: Buddhism has, for thousands of years, preached the perils of loss aversion and ownership/self, arguing that they, combined with the fact that all is *impermanent* (possessions, relationships, life) are *impermanent* lead to ill-being. The road to a less unsatisfactory life is to avoid the experience of loss by enjoying what you have, limiting your possessions, and breaking the ownership/self link between your implicit self-esteem and your possessions. See Batchelor (2015).

* * *

Summarizing the effects of the common quirks on NBT: collectively, they cause systematic incorrect beliefs, flawed choosing, and fluctuating orderings. That your ordering changes isn't a new criticism. Incentive salience, the endowment effect, and the emotional empathy-gap are simply reasons why.

A Few Thoughts on Modeling the Common Quirks

The common quirks argue for a behavior model involving a sequence of decision points. Either your current path is no longer available, or new and attractive available paths are. Decision points occur when prices change, a pandemic arrives, you lose or gain a job, you get sick, a baby arrives, your partner leaves or a new one arrives, and whenever uncertainties become certain.

I would initially model the sequence by restrictively assuming that there are only a small number of available paths at each decision point, limiting them to feasible paths similar to the one you are leaving.

I would suppose a constant but different top-level ordering for a few emotional states (e.g., angry, aroused, tired, hungry, and other). For a utility function, picture different top-level parameters for each emotion, e. Absent a cue or endowment effects, the ground-level ordering for emotion *e* is the same as its top-level ordering. But it can temporarily deviate from its top-level ordering due to cues and endowment effects.

In empirical modeling, outside the lab, it is hard to imagine a researcher observing what cues an individual is experiencing and how they affect that individual's behavior.[20] So, one could model their influence with random parameters. Imagine a sequence of discrete-choice random-utility models with random parameters (a mean and variance parameter) on the different path components. The important thing to capture is that your choices tell us less about your top-level ordering than is typically assumed. One might argue that the behavioral effects of random cues are one reason random-parameter models are prevalent.

The endowment effect can be modeled and estimated. At every choice point, the researcher observes what you own. When the individual considers which path to take next, Path *j*'s utility parameters momentarily shift on owned items lost if one takes Path *j*. For example, imagine that Path *j* involves replacing the current car. At the decision point, the parameter on car ownership shifts down for all paths that include replacing it.[21] Later, the parameter on car ownership shifts back to its top-level value.

Emotions are observable and can be invoked. As suggested above, imagine a top-level ordering for each emotion, *e*. If the researcher observes an individual's choice and the emotion they were experiencing when they made that choice, the research can estimate emotion-specific top-level utility parameters. This would be a conditional model, conditional on emotion.[22] A tricky part is modeling the sequence of an individual's emotions, which would be required to model their sequential

[20] Cues are often registered unconsciously, and what might be a cue for me might not be for you. Cues can be manipulated in choice experiments. This is already happening, though the researcher is unaware they are doing it. For example, in studies to estimate environmental damages, the injury description often includes phrases or photos that act as cues.

[21] If the current path does not include a car, the parameter on utility from a car does not shift—you can't experience the endowment effect for something you don't own.

[22] One might imagine a discrete-choice latent-class model with class-membership probability as a function of emotional state. Morey and Thiene (2017) value choice as a function of personality—the same model would work for emotional states. If a researcher followed individuals over time, recording their purchases, they could also ask questions about their emotional state.

choices.[23] One place to start would be modeling the behavior of a group of individuals who are persistently in emotional state, *e* (e.g., the chronically depressed or chronically anxious).[24] I defined a persistent emotion as a *temperament*.

Alternatively, in the lab, one could invoke different groups with different emotions, and then ask hypothetical choice questions.[25]

Does NBT Survive the Common Quirks

NBT based on Assumption 9b: *Paths that are more desired are ranked higher* (but not 9a), survives quite well; desires are desires: it does not matter whether those desires were produced by an emotion, a physiological state, a cue, a lack of empathy, or what you will like. Flawed choosing in terms of WB is immaterial. What causes you to want Path *j* more that Path *k* is immaterial, so are fluctuations in your wants and desires. If today I want to leave Shirley for Wanda, but tomorrow I want to leave Wanda for Shirley, more of my wants are fulfilled if I am successful on both days.

NBT based on Assumption 9a: *An economicus's ordering of paths is based on WB...* does not survive the common quirks as well. NBT based on Assumption 9a survives duration bias and lack of empathy for one's

[23] If the emotional state can't be predicted, one could model emotional state as a latent variable, and identify variables that influence the probability that individual *i* is in emotional state *e*.

[24] Thacher et al. (2005) and Morey et al. (2007) estimated the preferences of depressed individuals for different treatment programs. In a review, the neuro-psychologists Catherine Hartley and Elizabeth Phelps (2012) "explore the role of anxiety in decision-making with a neuroeconomic approach." "... anxiety-induced alterations in the brain circuitry of fear result in predictable cognitive biases that may influence later choices."

[25] A large part of my life has been estimating recreational choices (how often you go skiing, fishing, or whatever, and where you go when you go). My ancient dissertation was a model of where and how often individuals ski. Consider how to estimate skiing choices when the WB effects of skiing depend on whether the individual is anxious, depressed, or curious. [I imagine skiing lacks interest when one is depressed, when anxious one ranks the familiar and safe ski areas higher. When one is curious one ranks the unknown higher.] Picture a laboratory experiment with skiers where an emotion is invoked (e.g., anxiety), and subjects are then presented with hypothetical ski choices that vary in difficulty and familiarity.

For some commodities and activities, choice is insensitive to one's emotional state, for others sensitive. For example, I suspect that an individual's demand for air conditioning depends on the outside temperature and does not vary much with their emotional state, while the demands for alcohol and sweets are quite sensitive.

future self—and neither is inconsistent with Assumption 4: *An economicus's ordering does not change in the time-span behavior is modeled.* The emotional empathy-gap, the endowment effect, and incentive saliences each assault NBT: each violates Assumption 4—a questionable and problematic assumption. The common quirks highlight that your ordering fluctuates. It is surprising this isn't more discussed. The common quirks reinforce why there is flawed choosing in terms of WB.

The Common Quirks, Ethics, and Welfare Economics

The ethical implications of quirks depend on whether the ethical goal is maximizing WB or fulfilling wants.[26] Welfare (well-faring) economics is built on the former. What is right (morally preferred) for the individual is choosing their highest-ranked available WB-path. For society, it is maximizing societal WB in an aggregate sense.[27]

In contrast, for others, the ethical goal is want fulfillment: what is right for the individual is choosing their highest-ranked path in terms of wants fulfilled; for society, it is maximizing, in an aggregate sense, the number of wants fulfilled. Peter Singer, the most famous living utilitarian, argues for want fulfillment. Economic ethicists who agree with him are not welfare economists: their objective isn't to increase WB. If one adopts 9b and the goal of want fulfillment, each individual left to their own devices will do what is right for them, no matter how their behavior is affected by the common quirks. And there is no ethical reason to interfere in anyone's behavior unless it impinges on the ability of others to fulfill their wants and desires.

In contrast, if the goal is WB (the goal of welfare economics), *false choosing* should be avoided. While NBT is consistent with false choosing,[28] the common quirks explain false choosing and its direction. For example, incorrect beliefs are a significant cause of false choosing,

[26] Economists who consider how to parse right from wrong behaviors are typically unclear on whether the objective is fulfilling wants or maximizing WB.

[27] If the objective is WB, is it maximizing realized WB, or is it choosing the path associated with more WB in some subjective-probability sense? I will not consider this complication for reasons of taste, clarity, and brevity.

[28] As long as full certainty is not assumed.

duration bias, the emotional empathy-gap, and the future-self empathy-gap. All involve incorrect beliefs.

Incentive salience also causes flawed choosing by pushing desiring further from liking.[29]

More nuanced, the endowment effect only causes flawed choosing if the anticipated loss is not realized. Flawed choosing caused by the common quirks is flawed in terms of increasing WB but not flawed in terms of want fulfillment. So, for welfare economists, the common quirks motivate paternalism: you are not doing what is best for you. For example, you are not saving enough for your old self. So, nudging you to save more is warranted.[30]

If one hopes to argue that less government interference is ethically preferred, claiming so is easier if you believe in NBT based on Assumption 9b and believe the ethical objective is the fulfillment of wants and desires.

The argument for less government is more challenging if you adopt Assumption 9a and believe the ethical objective is more WB. While they violate only a few NBT Assumptions, the common quirks pile havoc on the notion that an individual left to his own devices will choose his highest-ranked available path, ordered in terms of realized WB. [Arguing for no governmental controls requires, in addition, that one imagines individual behavior has no effect on others, either their WB or wants. See the discussion of welfare effects in Chapter 13.]

This ends our conversation about the common quirks, making it an excellent time to take another general look at critical terms in Chapters 7 and 8.

Knowledge, Beliefs, Incorrect Beliefs, Subjective Probabilities, and Best Estimates

These concepts play an important role in behavior, choice, and WB. They are both distinct and overlapping. For example, a subjective probability is a belief based on knowledge or the lack of it. And if you believe something, can you know it is an incorrect belief? Again, probably not—if you knew it was incorrect, wouldn't you not believe it?

[29] It would be confusing to say that increased desiring is an incorrect belief: its intensity increases.

[30] See, for example, Thaler and Sunstein (2008) and Thaler and Benartzi (2004).

While our beliefs affect what we buy, who we marry, and who we vote for, they also directly affect our WB. An incorrect belief may enhance WB, while a correct one causes hopelessness. So, an incorrect belief may lead to greater WB even though it causes choices that, assessed alone, reduce WB. For example, my disbelief in global warming may increase my overall WB, even though it caused me to buy a Swiss ski chalet where snow will soon be a thing of the past.

Alternatively, an incorrect belief can directly increase WB and lead to choices that further increase WB. For example, suppose God and heaven don't exist, but I believe they do. As a result, I spend a lot of time attending church, reading the scriptures, and being nice. All is a waste of time because these activities will not increase my probability of making it to heaven. But! I am a happy camper, happier than if I were an atheist. And studying scripture reinforces my incorrect belief, leading me to choose future paths with even more scripture time.[31]

The WB associated with a path depends on the set of beliefs associated with that path. And one's ordering of paths depends on one's beliefs. Your beliefs will differ depending on whether you experience path m or *t*. This looks like a circular conundrum: A causes B, and B causes A, so one's beliefs and ordering are not separable concepts, a conclusion troubling for NBT and for explaining behaviors. I leave it at that.

Conscious and Unconscious Mental Processes: Whose Ordering Is It?

As noted in Chapter 2, while most believe humans have conscious thoughts and consciously choose, Assumptions 1–9 don't imply this: NBT does not require consciousness. Assumption 11 (self-awareness) implies consciousness but not conscious choosing. Finally, assumption 12 (the choosing axiom) adds it; it makes you consciously in charge—you choose,

[31] The influence of beliefs is further complicated by the fact that some are unconscious and these sometimes conflict with your conscious ones: you can have dueling beliefs. For example, many white people hold the consciously believe that they are not prejudiced against non-whites, while, in fact, are. To check out your racial prejudices, conscious and unconscious, take the test at Harvard's Project Implicit. Quoting from the web page, "It is well known that people don't always 'speak their minds,' and it is suspected that people don't always 'know their minds.' Understanding such divergences is important to scientific psychology. The website presents a method that demonstrates the conscious-unconscious divergences much more convincingly than has been possible with previous methods."

and this determines the path you experience. Part III started our discussion of conscious thought and unconscious processes in behavior and choice. Part IV continues it.

In 1782 Rousseau reflected on the unconscious when he realized why he had been avoiding a corner: a boy on that corner would always ask him for money.

> That is what I discovered on reflection, for until then none of it was distinctly in my thoughts. This observation has made me recall a multitude of others that convince me that the true and original motives of most of my acts are not as clear to me as I long supposed.

In the path of a bus, you jump back rather than staying put, making a "choice". This happens even before the situation registers as electrical activity in the parts of your brain that embed conscious thought. Alternatively, sometimes you experience cogitating for weeks on whether you should choose option *A* or *B*.

Economists do not distinguish between conscious and unconscious cognition. However, in psychology and neurobiology, the distinction is central to explaining behavior, beliefs, and how we make our way. Our brain consists of separate processing centers: some for conscious thought (ruminating about when I should retire) and others unconscious but instrumental in determining what I do, including when I retire.

The unconscious was once viewed as limited to harboring our infantile Freudian traumas and coordinating physical activities (language, not falling over, and seeing—activities the conscious mind need not bother with). Now, it plays a leading role in most of our actions. For a persuasive and accessible presentation, see Wilson (2002).

Keep in mind that if we consciously consider and decide how to act before we act, this does not mean it causes us to act the way we did. For example, I thought hard and long about buying a vacation home before doing so, but both the thinking and the doing could have been caused by my unconscious reaction to a prior event. [Event B precedes C, but B does not necessarily cause C; instead, both are possibly caused by an unobserved event A.]

Research on the unconscious indicates that its contents are determined by genetics, culture, and experience. See David McClelland, Richard Koestner, and Joel Weinberger (1989) for an example of research on how unconscious motives are formed,

There are two strands of research on the conscious's role in perception formation and choice. One strand argues that actions are (all or mostly) initiated by the unconscious before the act occurs, and if there is time, the unconscious causes a conscious experience of choosing. This strand, *The Illusion of Choice*, is discussed in Part IV. The other strand assumes beliefs are formed and actions are initiated by both the conscious and unconscious. In this strand, decisions made by the unconscious are more instinctive/programmed/than those formed consciously:

> A hallmark of the adaptive unconscious is automaticity, whereby information is processed in rapid, unconscious, involuntary ways.—Wilson

Quick action is required when a bus is barreling down, when you lock eyes with an attractive passing stranger, and when the conversational pause gives you only an instant to say something funny or witty. And the action taken is determined by one of our unconscious processors: cogitation would take too long. According to the second strand, when there is leisure to cogitate, our conscious thoughts play a role in what we will do, but not always. The context also plays a significant role in whether a choice is made by our conscious or unconscious minds. Context includes your emotional state, your current self-image, and whether someone attractive asked you to do it.

Survey questions on which option you prefer are typically answered quickly, suggesting the unconscious might play a more prominent role than the conscious in determining whether you circle option A or B or whether you circle "mostly agree" or "somewhat disagree". The timelines for consumer purchases are more varied: sometimes, we agonize over a purchase for months; sometimes, we go to Costco for groceries and come home with a portable power generator.

And the different processing centers don't always agree on the course of action. Quoting Wilson (2002)

> There is little research on the consequences of having disparate conscious and nonconscious 'selves' that are out of sync. An exception is the work of Joachim Brunstein and Oliver Schultheiss... they found little correspondence, on average, between people's nonconscious and conscious motives. (see, for example, Schultheiss et al. 2010)

We are not of one mind, either at a point in time or over time. Questions arise. Who or what is in charge? It depends on what is being determined and the context—contextual orderings. Are we conscious that a decision was made? Not always. Are we aware/conscious of why we do what we do? No, but our conscious brain makes up a good story to explain what was determined by our unconscious, or so say many psychologists. And what happens when our conscious and unconscious disagree?

Economists typically imagine the brain as a single black box that embeds one stable ordering of paths. They also don't think about how or why this ordering arises, arguing the mechanics of its creation are unimportant because the only goal is to predict choices. We are not concerned with why you like what you like. [A camp in psychology called *behaviorists* ruled the psychology journals in the Twentieth Century's first half. Again, quoting Wilson, "The behaviorist onslaught in psychology was fueled by a rejection of mentalism; behaviorists argued there was no need to consider what occurred inside people's heads, consciously or unconsciously." Psychology has largely rejected behaviorism; economics has not.]

> The goal of both NBT (and NBT plus) isn't only to predict what is chosen but to deem it the best choice.

If I Have an Ordering of Paths, Am I Consciously Aware of It?

Am I conscious of this ordering and able to describe it, or are only parts of it revealed to me when I observe my choices? I could imagine having an ordering but not a conscious awareness of it. My dog prefers meat to milk, milk to bread, and meat to bread (yes, his ordering is transitive), but he isn't consciously aware of it. He isn't unique in my household; quoting Shakespeare, "I have much ado to know myself." Bertrand Russell agrees with Shakespeare:

> The discovery of our own motives can only be made by the same process by which we discover other peoples, namely, the process of observing our actions and inferring the desire which could prompt them.—Russell, *The Analysis of the Mind*

Does It Matter Whether I Am Aware of My Ordering?

If the researcher's intent is to estimate your ordering (your demand curves), and if she is doing this by observing your real-world choices, it does not matter whether you were, a prior, aware of your ordering. What if she, instead, asked the hypothetical question, "Would you prefer A or B?" Economists mistrust hypothetical choice questions asserting the responses don't reflect the respondent's ordering of paths, explaining the disconnect is caused by lying or a lack of introspection. "Ask a hypothetical question, get a hypothetical answer."[32] But the issue is more profound. If I am not conscious of my ordering, I can't recover it through conscious thought, no matter how hard I introspect. And my conscious mind will make up a story for why I prefer A. Research shows we rationalize our choice to maintain a positive, or at least consistent, self-image. I would be embarrassed to say, "I am clueless as to why I do what I do." So make something up and believe it? As Wilson and Julie Stone suggest, another person may be a better predictor than me of why I do what I do.

A way to learn about your ordering is to observe your behavior or ask your friends. And conclude that your willingness-to-pay for a flat-screen TV or environmental cleanup is what others would pay after adjusting for age, gender, and income. In summary, introspection may be a misguided tool for determining how you order a set of paths.

References and Sources

Apicella, Coren, Eduardo Azevedo, Nicholas Christakis, and James Fowler. 2014. "Evolutionary origins of the endowment effect: Evidence from hunter-gatherers." *American Economic Review* 104 (6): 1793–1805. https://doi.org/10.1257/aer.104.6.1793. https://www.jstor.org/stable/42920866.

Batchelor, Stephen. 2015. *After Buddhism: Rethinking the dharma for a secular age*. Yale University Press.

Bordalo, Pedro, Nicola Gennaioli, and Andrei Shleifer. 2012. "Salience in experimental tests of the endowment effect." *American Economic Review* 102 (3): 47–52. https://www.jstor.org/stable/23245503#metadata_info_tab_contents.

[32] See, for example, Peter Diamond, a Nobel laureate, and Jerry Hausman. Interestingly, economists who disparage stated-preference data believe we have a stable and unique ordering, and observed choices are a manifestation of that ordering.

Boyce, Christopher, et al. 2013. "Money, well-being, and loss aversion: Does an income loss have a greater effect on well-being than an equivalent income gain?" *Psychological Science* 24 (12): 2557–2562. https://doi.org/10.1177/0956797613496436. https://www.webofscience.com/wos/woscc/full-record/WOS:000336263000011.

Brehm, Jack. 1956. "Post-decision changes in the desirability of alternatives." *The Journal of Abnormal and Social Psychology* 52 (3): 384. https://www.semanticscholar.org/paper/Postdecision-changes-in-the-desirability-of-Brehm/aea32a2d5a76f2f7c9cab957a4ed160bc8648fb8?p2df.

Carmon, Ziv, and Dan Ariely. 2000. "Focusing on the forgone: How value can appear so different to buyers and sellers." *Journal of Consumer Research* 27 (3): 360–370. https://academic.oup.com/jcr/article/27/3/360/1796841.

Cesarini, David, Magnus Johannesson, Patrik Magnusson, and Bjorn Wallace. 2012. "The behavioral genetics of behavioral anomalies." *Management Science* 58 (1): 21–34. https://doi.org/10.1287/mnsc.1110.1329. https://pubsonline.informs.org/doi/10.1287/mnsc.1110.1329.

Coleman, Karly. 2015. "Bicycles as objects: Identity, attachment, and membership categorization devices." The University of Alberta. https://www.webofscience.com/wos/woscc/full-record/WOS:A1991FP88800017.

Dommer, Sara Loughran, and Vanitha Swaminathan. 2013. "Explaining the endowment effect through ownership: The role of identity, gender, and self-threat." *Journal of Consumer Research* 39 (5): 1034–1050. https://doi.org/10.1086/666737.

Falk, Carl, and Steven Heine. 2015. "What is implicit self-esteem, and does it vary across cultures?" *Personality and Social Psychology Review* 19 (2): 177–198. https://doi.org/10.1177/1088868314544693. https://www.webofscience.com/wos/woscc/full-record/WOS:000352534100005.

Festinger, Leon. 1962. *A theory of cognitive dissonance*. Vol. 2. Stanford: Stanford University Press.

———. 1964. Conflict, decision, and dissonance. Stanford: Stanford University Press

Frey, Dieter. 1986. "Recent research on selective exposure to information." In *Advances in experimental social psychology*, edited by L. Berkowitz, 41–80. New York: Academic Press. https://www.sciencedirect.com/science/article/pii/S0065260108602129.

Gawronski, Bertram, Galen Bodenhausen, and Andrew Becker. 2007. "I like it, because I like myself: Associative self-anchoring and post-decisional change of implicit evaluations." *Journal of Experimental Social Psychology* 43 (2): 221–232.

Gehring, William, and Adrian Willoughby. 2002. "The medial frontal cortex and the rapid processing of monetary gains and losses." *Science* 295 (5563): 2279–2282. https://doi.org/10.1126/science.1066893.

Haigh, Michael S., and John A. List. 2005. "Do professional traders exhibit myopic loss aversion? An experimental analysis." *The Journal of Finance* 60 (1): 523–534.

Hanemann, Michael. 1991a. "Willingness to pay and willingness to accept: How much can they differ?" *American Economic Review* 81 (3): 635–647. https://www.webofscience.com/wos/woscc/full-record/WOS:A1991.FP88800017.

———. 1991b. "Willingness to pay and willingness to accept: How much can they differ? Reply." *American Economic Review* 81 (3): 12. https://doi.org/10.1257/000282803321455449. https://www.webofscience.com/wos/woscc/full-record/WOS:A1990EN42900009.

Hartley, Catherine, and Elizabeth Phelps. 2012. "Anxiety and decision making." *Biological Psychiatry* 72 (2): 113–118. https://www.sciencedirect.com/science/article/pii/S0006322312000091.

Huck, Steffen, Georg Kirchsteiger, and Jorg Oechssler. 2005. "Learning to like what you have—Explaining the endowment effect." *Economic Journal* 115 (505): 689–702. https://doi.org/10.1111/j.1468-0297.2005.01015.x. https://academic.oup.com/ej/article-abstract/115/505/689/5085713?redirectedFrom=fulltext.

Kahneman, Dan, and Amos Tversky. 1979. "Prospect theory: An analysis of decision under risk." *Econometrica* 47: 237–251.

Kahneman, Dan, Jack Knetsch, and Richard Thaler. 1990. "Experimental tests of the endowment effect and the Coase theorem." *Journal of Political Economy* 98 (6): 1325–1348. https://doi.org/10.1086/261737. https://www.webofscience.com/wos/woscc/full-record/WOS:A1990EN42900009.

———. 1991. "Anomalies: The endowment effect, loss aversion, and status-quo bias." *Journal of Economic Perspectives* 5 (1): 193–206. https://doi.org/10.1257/jep.5.1.193. https://www.webofscience.com/wos/woscc/full-record/WOS:A1990EN42900009.

Kermer, Deborah, Erin Driver-Linn, Timothy Wilson, and Dan Gilbert. 2006. "Loss aversion is an affective forecasting error." *Psychological Science* 17 (8): 649–653. https://doi.org/10.1111/j.1467-9280.2006.01760.x. https://journals.sagepub.com/doi/10.1111/j.1467-9280.2006.01760.x.

Levy, Moshe. 2015. "An evolutionary explanation for risk aversion." *Journal of Economic Psychology* 46: 51–61. https://doi.org/10.1016/j.joep.2014.12.001.

Maddux, William, et al. 2010. "For whom is parting with possessions more painful? Cultural differences in the endowment effect." *Psychological Science* 21 (12): 1910–1917. https://doi.org/10.1177/0956797610388818. https://www.webofscience.com/wos/woscc/full-record/WOS:000285457200026.

McClelland, David C., Richard Koestner, and Joel Weinberger. 1989. "How do self-attributed and implicit motives differ?" *Psychological Review* 96 (4): 690.

Morewedge, Carey, Lisa Shu, Dan Gilbert, and Timothy Wilson. 2009. "Bad riddance or good rubbish? Ownership and not loss aversion causes the endowment effect." *Journal of Experimental Social Psychology* 45 (4): 947–951. https://doi.org/10.1016/j.jesp.2009.05.014. https://www.webofscience.com/wos/woscc/full-record/WOS:000269278800042.

Morey, Edward, and Mara Thiene. 2017. "Can personality traits explain where and when you recreate? A latent-class site-choice model informed by estimates from mixed-mode lc cluster models with latent-personality traits." *Ecological Economics* 138: 223–237. https://doi.org/10.1016/j.ecolecon.2017.03.038.

Morey, Edward, Jennifer Thacher, and Edward Craighead. 2007. "Patient preferences for depression treatment programs and willingness to pay for treatment." *Journal of Mental Health Policy and Economics* 10 (2): 73–85. https://pubmed.ncbi.nlm.nih.gov/17603148/.

Rick, Scott. 2011. "Losses, gains, and brains: Neuroeconomics can help to answer open questions about loss aversion." *Journal of Consumer Psychology* 21 (4): 453–463.

Rousseau, Jean-Jacques. 1782/1979. *Reveries of the solitary walker (Les reveries du promenur solitarie)*. London: Penguin Ltd. https://www.webofscience.com/wos/woscc/full-record/WOS:A1991GW04400003.

Russell, Bertrand. 1921/2013. *The analysis of the mind*. The Project Gutenberg. https://www.gutenberg.org/files/2529/2529-h/2529-h.htm.

Rutledge, Robb, and Paul Glimcher. 2009. "Asymmetric bold responses to positive and negative outcomes." Annual meeting of the Society for Neuroeconomics.

Schultheiss, Oliver, et al. 2010. "Implicit motives: Current topics and future directions." In *The decade ahead: Theoretical perspectives on motivation and achievement (advances in motivation and achievement)*, edited by Timothy Urdan and Stuart Karabenick. Emerald Group Publishing Limited. https://doi.org/10.1108/S0749-7423(2010)000016A009.

Thacher, Jennifer, Edward Morey, and Edward Craighead. 2005. "Using patient characteristics and attitudinal data to identify depression treatment preference groups: A latent-class model." *Depression and Anxiety* 21 (2): 47–54. https://doi.org/10.1002/da.20057. https://www.webofscience.com/wos/woscc/full-record/WOS:000229157100001.

Thaler, Richard, and Slomo Benartzi. 2004. "Save more tomorrow: Using behavioral economics to increase employee saving." *Journal of Political Economy* 112 (1): S164–S187. https://doi.org/10.1086/380085. https://www.webofscience.com/wos/woscc/full-record/WOS:000188954100006.

Thaler, Richard, and Cass Sunstein. 2008. *Nudge: Improving decisions about health, wealth, and happiness*. New Haven, CT: Yale University Press. https://www.webofscience.com/wos/woscc/full-record/WOS:000249349000005.

Tversky, Amos, and Daniel Kahneman. 1991. "Loss aversion in riskless choice: A reference-dependent model." *Quarterly Journal of Economics* 106 (4): 1039–1061. https://doi.org/10.2307/2937956. https://www.webofscience.com/wos/woscc/full-record/WOS:A1991GW04400003.

Wilson, Timothy. 2002. *Strangers to ourselves: Discovering the adaptive unconscious*. Cambridge, MA: The Belknap Press of Harvard University Press.

Additional Readings

Benartzi, Slomo, and Richard Thaler. 2007. "Heuristics and biases in retirement savings behavior." *Journal of Economic Perspectives* 21 (3): 81–104. https://doi.org/10.1257/jep.21.3.81. https://www.webofscience.com/wos/woscc/full-record/WOS:000249349000005.

Brosnan, Sarah 2011. "Property in nonhuman primates." *New Directions for Child and Adolescent Development* 2011 (132): 9–22.

Brunstein, Joachim, Oliver Schultheiss, and Ruth Grässman. 1998. "Personal goals and emotional well-being: The moderating role of motive dispositions." *Journal of Personality and Social Psychology* 75 (2): 494.

Di Tella, Rafael, John Haisken-De New, and Robert MacCulloch. 2010. "Happiness adaptation to income and to status in an individual panel." *Journal of Economic Behavior & Organization* 76 (3): 834–852.

Diamond, Peter, and Jerry Hausman. 1994. "Contingent valuation: Is some number better than no number?" *Journal of Economic Perspectives* 8 (4): 45–64.

Flemming, Timothy, et al. 2012. "The endowment effect in orangutans." *International Journal of Comparative Psychology* 25: 285–298.

Gazzaniga, Michael, and Joseph Ledoux. 2013. *The integrated mind*. New York: Springer Science & Business Media.

Gilbert, Dan, and Timothy Wilson. 2000. "Miswanting." In *Feeling and thinking: The role of affect in social cognition*, edited by J. Forgas, 178. Cambridge MA: Cambridge University Press. https://www.webofscience.com/wos/woscc/full-record/WOS:A1991EZ69400013.

Harbaugh, William, Kate Krause, and Lise Vesterlund. 2001. "Are adults better behaved than children? Age, experience, and the endowment effect." *Economics Letters* 70 (2): 175–181.

Knetsch, Jack. 1989. "The endowment effect and evidence of non reversible indifference curves." *American Economic Review* 79 (5): 1277–1284. https://www.webofscience.com/wos/woscc/full-record/WOS:A1989CD48800024.

Wegner, Daniel, and Thalia Wheatley. 1999. "Apparent mental causation: Sources of the experience of will." *American Psychologist* 54 (7): 480.

Wilson, Timothy, and Julie Stone. 1985. "Limitations of self-knowledge: More on telling more than we can know." *Review of Personality and Social Psychology* 6 (1): 167–183.

PART IV

Choice or the Illusion-Of-Choice?

CHAPTER 10

How Would You Define a *Choice*? And the Difference Between a Choice and the Experience/Sense of Making a Choice

Necessary Conditions for a Situation to Be a Choice?

(1) An entity is faced with N options (an integer $N \geq 2$). (2) The entity can and must experience only one. (3) It can influence which one is experienced. And (4), It is not constrained to experience a specific one. Many would elaborate on (4), adding, "There was only a choice if the entity was free to experience an option different from the one experienced." While most people would not, unprompted, list these requirements, they would, after reflection, agree. Still, not everyone would (including neoclassical economists), particularly if we get more specific about what (3) and (4) mean.

Note that these conditions do not imply or require that the entity have a conscious choice *experience* (experiencing conscious thoughts about which alternative to choose).

Imagine, or not, that these 4 conditions are sufficient for a situation to be a choice.

E. R. Morey, *Deconstructing Behavior, Choice, and Well-being*,
https://doi.org/10.1007/978-3-031-36712-0_10

But! Does Choice Require a Choosing Experience? Have You Made a Choice Only if You Feel You Did?

And, if so, what brings about the feeling that you influenced which alternative was realized? You experience the need to make a choice, consciously decide on an alternative, and then experience that alternative, giving you the sense that you made a choice. Can you make a choice without consciously feeling that you have made a choice? Alternatively, can you not make a choice and think you have? The evidence on these two questions illuminates why we perceive some actions as choices and others not.

Contrary to What Economists Preach, the NBT Assumptions Seem to Make Choice Impossible?

Economists Assert That Economici Make Choices

But we appear to contradict ourselves. In explanation, since an economicus is constrained to consume its HRAP, since the set of available paths is exogenous, and since the ranking of paths is exogenous, there seems to be no real choice.[1] Behavior is axiomatically determined:

Assumption 4: *An economicus's ordering does not change in the time-span behavior is modeled.*
Assumption 5: *Most paths are unavailable, and an economicus must experience an available path.*
Assumption 7: *At every point in time, economicus takes one of its HRAPs.*

Most people would say economici don't make choices. So, when economists say economici make choices, they must mean something different from what most think of as a choice.

Of course, whether there is choice in NBT comes down to how choice is defined; but if you were constrained to select the path you experience, the man on the street would say there was no choice. His definition—you could have selected a different alternative—is the folk definition of choice

[1] Maybe in the past an economicus could influence its future ranking, though it cannot influence its current ranking.

(what most people mean by choice). So, when economists say that people make choices, they must mean something different from what most think of as a choice.

Economists Need to Define Choice in a Way That Makes a Choice Compatible with Their Theory of Behavior (or Drop the Word "Choice")

Economists would say an economicus has no choice if there is only one available option ($N = 1$), implying more than one option is necessary for choice. However, is more than one option sufficient? Does an entity have an economic choice if external constraints don't limit it to a specific path? Economists must think so because it is called "CT" even though internal constraints (an exogenous ranking and the requirement to experience the HRAP) constrain it to experience a specific path.

Looking ahead, economists define choice as situations where external constraints do not limit the entity to a specific path.

This is similar to the definition compatibilist philosophers use to make choice (free will in a weak sense) possible in a deterministic world. By this definition, other animals (even worms and mollusks) make choices whenever their behavior is not entirely determined by external constraints. For example, Giacomo always eats the meat first when dry food and fresh meat are in his bowl. And most nights, he sleeps in two or three places, but no puppeteer drags him on a lease from room to room. None of these behaviors are dictated by external constraints, so he exhibits weak free will.

So, What Is *Free Will*, and How Does It Relate to Choosing?

Isabel Archer is on her way to Italy to pursue her destiny and explains to her suitor, Caspar Goodwood, her aversion to his suiting.

> *Isabel*: If there's a thing in the world I'm fond of it's my personal independence... [I want] To put as many hundred miles of sea between us as possible.
>
> *Casper*: One would think you were going to commit some atrocity!
>
> *Isabel*: Perhaps I am. I wish to be free even to do that if the fancy takes me. (*The Portrait of a Lady*, Henry James 1917)

Isabel wants to be free to choose to commit one or more atrocities, but only if she fancies. Is Isabel free to will and choose?

I have used *free will* without defining it, which has been convenient given the disagreement about what it means. The *Stanford Encyclopedia of Philosophy*, *SEP*, defines free will as a "capacity to choose a course of action from among various alternatives." NB the words "capacity" and "choice." If you have free will, spirits or networks of neurons give you the capacity to choose.[2]

Consider the word "will" and what it means to say, "I will that Event A happens." [This is an archaic use and makes me think of God's will.] This could be interpreted as I choose Event A over the other alternatives. Or, if A is a behavior, I am inclined to adopt it. It could also be interpreted as I prefer A, and because I prefer it, I choose it. *Choosing*, *willing*, and *preferring* are close but imperfect synonyms. Free will is philosophical-speak for *the capacity to freely choose*, and the capacity to freely choose is economic-speak for free will.

But what does *free* mean? Kant thought that if an entity must be rational, and rationality determines what it will do, it does not have free will. So he would agree with my argument that NBT is incompatible with choice. But add that NBT is compatible with choice if the entity can choose whether to follow the HRAP rule. If you adopt the HRAP rule but do not have to, you have free will. For Kant, an economicus does not have free will because it cannot reject the rule.

Doubts About Free Will Go Way Back

> Men are mistaken in thinking themselves free; their opinion is made up of consciousness of their own actions, and ignorance of the causes by which they are conditioned. Their idea of freedom, therefore, is simply their ignorance of any cause for their actions. As for saying that human actions depend on the will, this is a mere phrase without any idea to correspond thereto. (Spinoza, *The Ethics Part II: Of the Nature and Origin of the Mind* [partially quoted by Wegner])

[2] I recommend *Free Will: An Introduction* by the philosopher Helen Beebee (2013). My interest in free will is what it tells us about economic choice while she is concerned with its relationship to moral responsibility. We cover a lot of the same ground and discuss some of the same studies in neuroscience and experimental philosophy. She does not care about economici.

> All theory is against the freedom of the will; all experience is for it. (James Boswell 1791/1866, The Life of Samuel Johnson (as quoted by Wegner 2002)[3])

Spinoza, Thomas Hobbs (1588–1679), and Locke rejected free will. The philosopher Jennifer Uleman (2010) summarizes the different takes on free will. Quoting her, [Hobbs] "denies that will can be free at all, [Hobbs] arguing that only bodies can be free, or unfree, where free just means unimpeded." [*Unimpeded* means unconstrained, as rich peoples' bodies are less impeded than poor peoples', and prisoners and those with disabilities are more impeded.]

Locke "concluded the human will is never free but is always determined by nature or reason: for Locke, 'free will' is a nonsensical thing."

In contrast, Descartes understood free will as "a mental ability to endorse and set oneself on a course of action (or more simply, to assent to something, or not) rather than as a function of the grounds determining action or assent" (Uleman 2010). You can will (choose) whatever you want, but that does not mean you determined what you would will (would choose) or that what you willed (what you chose) will occur. In his view, no one can stop me from willing A to happen, but that I willed A rather than B was not determined by me. Descartes' free will is limited, at best.

Kant asserted that a will is not free if its possessor must behave rationally, as must economici. But Kant does not require that humans behave rationally. He makes a distinction between the will and whether the will is free. For Kant, the *will* (not necessarily free) is a real thing that resides in each adult human. It is the place or process in a human mind that chooses an alternative and then causes the human to do what it takes to experience that alternative; it is the "choosing center"—willing is choosing. Quoting Uleman,

> A will is free, for Kant, if it determines itself and isn't determined by anything else. A will will be free, in other words, if it chooses ends, and pursues courses of action aimed at realizing those ends, on grounds that

[3] Boswell is best known for his biography of his friend, the English man of letters, Samuel Johnson; it is considered the first great biography in English. Boswell knew and admired Rousseau; he had a brief affair with Rousseau's partner—one of Boswell's dalliances.

are its own, and not on grounds given to it by something or someone external to it.

For Kant, Kantian free will is a possibility—for humans—but it's not guaranteed.[4]

Definitions of Free Will Fall Along a Continuum

> One wants to be what tradition has it that Eve was when she bit the apple. Perfectly free to do otherwise. So perfectly free, in fact, that even God couldn't tell which way she'd jump. (Jerry Foder [2003] philosopher and cognitive scientist)

Fodor is providing a definition, not arguing for it. This is *extreme free will*. Economicus doesn't have it.

At the continuum's other end, an entity has free will if another agent is not controlling it, and other agents, excluding God, cannot predict with certainty what it will do before it does it. You only lack it if a mad scientist, puppeteer, or God pulls your strings. Economicus has *vacuous free will*: while its behavior can be predicted, no puppeteer is pulling its strings.

In between these two extremes, but closer to extreme free will, is the ability to have chosen a different alternative. You chose A but could have chosen B (you could have behaved differently). And you have this ability even if God—if you believe in God—knew which alternative you would choose. This is *strong free will*. Economici do not have it: in economic-speak, an economicus does not choose in this sense. Most homo sapiens believe they have strong free will.

Weak free will is between the two extremes but closer to vacuous *free will*. You lack free will if your behavior is wholly determined by external constraints: you must experience the one available alternative ($N = 1$). So, the will is free if $N \geq 2$. For example, prisoners cannot choose to

[4] Kant relied on *dualism* to argue that will can be free (Uleman). His argument is awkward. Kant viewed the body as a physical thing controlled by the laws of physics and believed that if what you will is determined by the laws of physics—what you will isn't freely willed. He also believed that if what you will is constrained by reason, you do not freely will. They argue against the existence of a will that is free. These arguments are materialist. Kant got his will freed by imagining that will isn't something subject to reason or the laws of physics; it is a magical thing.

spend the night in their cell ($N = 1$).[5] Economicus has weak free will: in economic-speak, choice, in this weak sense, exists whenever $N \geq 2$. Every economicus is constrained to do whatever it does, but two of its constraints (his ordering of paths and having to select his HRAP) are internal.

I have defined four variants of free will. Economicus has the weak form: it cannot behave differently. The widely published philosopher Daniel Dennett (2003) defines free will as I just defined weak free will. He argues that strong free will (so also extreme free will) is "bonkers" given the laws of physics.[6]

> People care deeply about having free will, but they also seem to have misguided ideas about what free will is or could be ...Our decisions are not little miracles in the brain that violate the physics and chemistry that account for the rest of our bodies' processes, even if many folk think this must be what happens if our decisions are to be truly free. We can't conclude from this, however, that then we don't have free will, because free will in this bonkers sense is not the only concept of free will.

Weak free will is close to the legal definition, as in you signed the contract of your "own free will" if you were not "under duress or the influence of hallucination or another mental derangement." He claims it

> ... is probably the consensus [view of free will] not only among philosophers but also among judges, lawyers, and others who have to make distinctions about who is responsible for what and who is excused because they do not free will when they acted.

Fodor's assessment of Dennett's definition of free will is

> There's the lurking sense that what you got isn't quite what you ordered, and half an hour later you're hungry again.

[5] I wonder if advocates of this view of free will (in this weak sense) believe rich people have more of it than poor people because the rich are often less constrained.

[6] This is also how Hume defined free will. He starts by noting that everything has a cause (an earthquake has a cause, and you buying vanilla ice cream instead of strawberry has a cause), so if free will is when behavior is not caused, it is impossible. Rejecting free will in this sense, he says you have it when your behavior is not "compelled," defining compelled behavior as behavior wholly determined by exogenous forces.

In Fodor's view, Dennett has defined all behavior as chosen behavior—a bait and switch because what he calls free will, most people would not. Dennett would say economici exhibit free will; Foder is still hungry.

Causal Determinism

The hypothesis is your behavior is wholly determined by the laws of nature and what has come before (the state of the world, including your genetics and history)—your actions are caused. It is taken as fact by most, but not all, scientists and philosophers. Most people reject it, especially if anyone suggests it applies to humans.

Thinking about causal determinism and its implications for NBT informs what it means to make a choice and whether people are responsible for their choices (both critical ethical issues). However, be warned that thinking about causal determinism and choice can be crazy-making, and most do not like determinism or its implications.

With full information and the ability to process it, I could predict everything you will do—all acts are causal and deterministic.[7,8] This follows from classical deterministic-physics. The opposite is *indeterminism*. Most neuroscientists and physicists who are indeterminists are so because they believe behavior has a random component. The rest are determinists. Modern physicists accept quantum mechanics, which includes randomness at the subatomic level, but no one knows whether it affects the behaviors of individuals.

Historically, many philosophers were determinists, including Locke, Spinoza, Gottfried Leibniz (1646–1716), and Hume. So was the mathematician Pierre-Simon Laplace (1749–1872). In 1814, he articulated determinism as an intellect/demon who could predict all future acts.

> In Laplace's story, a sufficiently bright demon who knew how things stood in the world 100 years before my birth could predict every action, every emotion, every belief in the course of my life. Were she then to watch me live through it, she might smile condescendingly, as one who watches

[7] Causal determinism is different from fate and predestination. Both, like causal determinism, imply something is going to happen, but the fate and predestination reasons are magical: inconsistent with physics.

[8] This does not imply everything can be predicted: currently there is not enough computing power, and many believe there never could be.

> a marionette dance to the tugs of strings that it knows nothing about. We can't stand the thought that we are marionettes. Nor does it matter whether any demon (or even God) can, or cares to, actually predict what we will do: the existence of the strings of physical necessity, linked to far-past states of the world and determining our current every move, is what alarms us. (Carl Hoefer 2010)

Notable historical indeterminists include George Berkeley (1685–1753), Descartes, Kant, and Rousseau.[9] For Berkeley, Descartes, and Kant, their arguments for indeterminism were all based on their belief in dualism (your mind is more than your brain: magic)—Rousseau's argument is not.

Economicus's behavior is deterministic and consistent with a deterministic world. But only deterministic worlds whose initial configuration of atoms would produce economici. Human behavior is also consistent with a deterministic world, but there is no requirement that the initial configuration of atoms would produce economici.

Most Humans Believe Causal Determinism Does Not Apply to Humans

William James, the father of American psychology, desperately wanted to not believe in casual determinism.

> But the whole feeling of reality, the whole sting and excitement of our voluntary life, depends on our sense that in it things are really being decided from one moment to another, and that it is not the dull rattling off of a chain that was forged innumerable ages ago. (James 1890, quoted by Wegner)

But he admitted it might be.[10]

[9] Berkeley is "the great eccentric of Anglophone philosophy, who infamously argued...that the notion of matter is nonsensical, and that," except for God, "minds and their perceptions are the sole contents of the universe" (Gottlieb 2016). A modern counterpoint is the cognitive psychologist Donald Hoffman who argue that while there is a reality, our perceptions (what we see, hear, and feel) are mere illusions: our minds and sensory organs evolved to foster the successful transmission of genes, not to correctly represent reality (Hoffman 2019).

[10] "As a young man he [James] passed through a profound and prolonged crisis, mental or emotional or spiritual, insofar as such distinctions can be thought of as meaningful to him. In retrospect, he laid his despair to his loss of belief in freedom of the will. His depression was disabling to him physically, and the cures he sought out in Europe did

Until recently, the conjecture was untested. Quoting the experimental philosopher Shaun Nichols (2004):

> In a set of experiments exploring the lay understanding of choice, both children and adults tended to treat moral choices as indeterminant. Participants were presented with cases of moral choice events (e.g., a girl steals a candy bar) and physical events (e.g., a pot of water comes to a boil), and they were asked whether, if everything in the world was the same right up until the event occurred, the event had to occur. Both children and adults were more likely to say that the physical event had to occur than that the moral choice event had to occur. This result seems to vindicate the traditional claim that ordinary people in our culture believe that at least some human decisions are not determined.

Why? Determinism conflicts with our sense of self—it is diminished if you think your behavior is set. We have two views of how the world works: a mechanical view that applies to the behaviors of rocks, dogs, and all other non-human plants and animals, and a magical view that applies to people—your mind is more than your brain—the dualist view. Rejecting determinism makes it easier to believe humans consciously set their course. People readily believe the behavior of lesser animals is deterministic (or random), believing lesser animals are driven by instinct and stimuli, so they do not make choices in the sense people do.

So, Is Choice Consistent with Causal Determinism? Compatibilists and Incompatibilists

There are numerous schools of thought, varying on whether you believe in determinism and whether choice is consistent with it. For example, behavior having a random component is a way to generate indeterminism, but adding a random component to an entity's behavior does not mean it is making choices—choosing freely isn't the same thing as behaving randomly.

nothing to relieve it. He struggled with thoughts of suicide. Then he read a book by the French philosopher Charles Bernard Renouvier, who argued that one was made free by acting as if he were free. So began his convalescence …" (the novelist and essayist Marilynne Robinson 2010). Renouvier argued that free will was the ability to influence one's thoughts, leading James to conclude that his belief he had this ability was not necessarily an illusion, which, for him, opened the door to possible choice (James 1890).

Most Neuroscientists and Physicists Are Incompatibilists, Rejecting Free Will and Choice

As previously mentioned, they are either determinists or indeterminists because they believe behavior has a random component. And most don't think free will is consistent with either if free will is the ability to behave differently. [Dennett, a champion of compatibilism, lists the following as distinguished members of the *choice-is-illusion* camp (incompatibilists): the physicists Albert Einstein and Stephen Hawking (1942–2018), the neuroscientists Wolf Singer, Chris Frith, and Patrick Haggard, and the psychologists Paul Bloom and Wegner.]

What Are Philosophers? Many Are Deterministic Compatibilists

According to the compatibilist Dennett and the incompatibilist Nichols, most philosophers are compatibilists, including the determinists Hobbes, Locke, Leibniz, and Hume. Hume even argued determinism is required for free will.[11] Most compatibilists are determinists, but a few determinist philosophers are not compatibilists.[12]

Why are there deterministic compatibilists? Cynically, according to Nichols (2006),

> Many of us incompatibilists think we know the answer to this: it's wishful thinking! Philosophers embrace compatibilism because they want it to be true. This view is, I think, common among incompatibilists. Famously, [William] James dubs compatibilism a "quagmire of evasion." Even more famously, Kant says it is a "wretched subterfuge." We can

[11] Hume's analogy: imagine a slope with rocks lined up in a row from the top to the bottom, with the bottom rock's shape and size representing you and what is in your head (your internal constraints). Determinism is a causal chain of events starting with the top rock rolling into the second, causing it to move and roll into the third, causing it to ..., until a rock rolls into you. If the size and speed of the rock that hits you are sufficient to fully determine where you will end up, your behavior is compelled, and you did not choose where to roll. However, if which way you roll is determined, in part, by your shape and size, you (the rock) have free will and some choice as to where to roll. If the path taken is not wholly determined by exogenous constraints—there is more than one externally available path, you have it and made a choice. Modern deterministic compatibilists, like Dennett, would agree. Hume's free will is weak free will.

[12] These include Spinoza, and the Enlightenment thinkers Diderot, Voltaire, and Paul-Henri D'Holbach (1723–1789). There are a few indeterminant philosophers who argue that free will could exist even if the world were deterministic.

> put the incompatibilists' motivational hypothesis somewhat more precisely as follows: philosophers embrace compatibilism despite its counter-intuitiveness because compatibilism is motivationally attractive.

In summary, many philosophers believe in determinism, and most believe determinism is compatible with free will in its weak sense.[13] Economists are implicit and unaware *compatibilists*.

Do Regular People Think Choice Is Consistent with Causal Determinism?

Nichols and Joshua Knobe (2007) asked college students to imagine two different universes.

> Imagine a universe (Universe A) in which everything that happens is completely caused by what happened before it. This is true from the very beginning of the universe, so what happened in the beginning of the universe caused what happened next, and so on right up until the present…
>
> Now imagine a universe (Universe B) in which almost everything that happens is completely caused by whatever happened before it. The one exception is human decision-making…

Ninety percent of the respondents thought our world was more like B, consistent with Nichols' (2004) finding: determinism except for humans.

Everyone was then asked either:

> In Universe A, is it possible for a person to be fully morally responsible for their actions? Yes or No?

[13] An exception is C. List (2014) who argues that determinism is compatible with strong free will. His argument turns on how one interprets "for someone's action to count as free is that the agent can do otherwise." He provides three possible interpretations: (1) "If the agent were to try (or choose) to do otherwise, he or she would succeed in doing otherwise," (2) "The agent has the disposition to do otherwise when, in appropriate circumstances (to be spelt out further), he or she tries to do otherwise," and (3) "It is possible (in a sense to be spelt out further) for the agent to do otherwise." He then argues that (1) and (2) are consistent with determinism. While I am somewhat confused, (1) seems consistent with determinism in that while you must choose as you choose given the moment's determinants, if you were to choose to do otherwise (because the world was different deterministically) you would be successful. To buy his conclusion, you have to agree that either (1) or (2) is the correct definition of being able to do otherwise.

Or

> In Universe A, a man named Bill has become attracted to his secretary, and he decides that the only way to be with her is to kill his wife and 3 children. He knows that it is impossible to escape from his house in the event of a fire. Before he leaves on a business trip, he sets up a device in his basement that burns down the house and kills his family. Is Bill fully morally responsible for killing his wife and children? Yes or No?

86% answered "No" (not responsible) to the first question, indicating that most respondents thought the person could not have acted differently. However, only 25% answered "No" (not responsible) to the second question. So, most believe Bill could have chosen not to kill the family, even though everything is caused in Universe A.

The Bill question can't determine whether the difference in "No" responses is because Universe A is abstract while B is concrete or because B has a visceral effect that A does not.

So, they did a second experiment. Again, there were two questions: half of the people who got each question were told to answer assuming Universe A, and half Universe B.

> As he has done many times in the past, Mark arranges to cheat on his taxes. Is it possible that Mark is fully responsible for cheating on his taxes? Yes or No?
>
> Or
>
> As he has done many times in the past, Mark stalks and rapes a stranger. Is it possible that Mark is fully responsible for raping the stranger? Yes or No?

Both actions are concretely described, but the second generates a negative visceral response. For those told to assume Universe B (the indeterminant universe), most concluded that the rapist and tax cheater did not have to do it, so they are responsible. Those instructed to assume Universe A (the determinant case) believed the tax evader had to cheat, but the rapist did not have to rape.

To summarize, humans believe a deterministic act is consistent with free will if it is explicitly harmful, is concretely described, was performed by a human, and viscerally upsets them. In such cases, they attribute moral responsibility to the actor. In contrast, they believe a determinist act is inconsistent with free will when the natures of the act and actor are unspecified.[14] This result has been replicated in non-Western populations. We are of two minds regarding whether free will is consistent with determinism: a logical mind that concludes the deterministic actor is not responsible and an emotional mind that often concludes they are.

Why Do We All Feel and Believe We Have Free Will and Make Choices?

While we understand that some of our actions are taken unconsciously—most of us feel that most of what we do happens because we consciously and freely decide to behave that way. This is because we believe we have free will—that we *will—freely*—most of our actions.

Two Reasons to Believe We Have Free Will and Make Choices

Reason 1: because we do have free will and do make choices. We believe this is the correct answer. We consciously chose ham and eggs for breakfast rather than dry granola, which is why we are now eating animal products rather than plants. We could be wrong. Another possible reason (Reason 2) is evolution has kluged us: left us with a flawed sense of causality, causing us to incorrectly believe that the conscious experience of making a choice is what led us to take a specific action.

A Bit on Causality and Logic

Consider two events (II and III) where Event III always happens soon after Event II, and Event III never occurs unless Event II precedes it. We conclude that Event II caused Event III—evolution has caused us to think this way. Its objective is not to produce perfectly rational and logical animals, only animals that get it right enough of the time. The sun rises in New York City (II) before it rises in Chicago (III), but that does mean the sunrise in NYC caused the sun to rise in Chicago. Each is caused by Event I, the sun's and earth's motions.

[14] "*Indeed, concrete cases of bad behavior lead people to attribute responsibility, even when the action is caused by a neurological disorder [like a brain tumor]*" (Nichols 2011).

The illogic is *necessary* is confused with *sufficient*. If Event III occurs only when Event II occurs first, then Event II is necessary for Event III (without II, there can be no III). Remember that Event II being necessary does not mean it is sufficient to cause Event III. [If it were sufficient, then the occurrence of Event II would guarantee that III happens.] Two examples: a necessary condition for being Bob the Bear is that you are a bear, but being one isn't sufficient to make you Bob the Bear. And the sun rising in NYC is necessary for it to rise in Chicago, but it does guarantee it.[15]

Events II and III—and Choice

The two events of interest are *having the conscious experience of deciding to do something* (Event II) and *doing what was consciously decided* (Event III). Examples of Event II are me consciously choosing to drink a Coke and Melvin consciously deciding to propose to Wilma. Event III is the actual drinking or proposing. That Event II precedes III does not mean it caused III. For example, Melvin proposed to Wilma after he had the experience of deciding to propose. Nevertheless, the cause of both II and II could be an earlier Event I involving a slinky red dress, an event he doesn't even remember. Or perhaps he forgot it was Wilma's idea.

The possibility that Event II did not cause Event III is a hard thing to get your head around when it seems apparent that it did, and you want to believe it did. You want to believe that consciously deciding to buy a new car caused you to buy it.

Another category (type IV Events) is behaviors not preceded by a choosing experience. We are all aware that many/most of our actions are not preceded by a conscious decision to take action: automatic behaviors/ involuntary actions. So, we know action does not require a prior choosing experience. Examples of *automatics* include the different components of physical activities such as walking, skiing, driving, and breathing—the mechanics are mostly produced unconsciously. [Imagine if, to breathe, you had to always consciously inhale and exhale.[16]] Other examples are habits, acts driven by emotions, and instinctive reactions. For example, if the spinal cord receives data that there will be bodily injury if immediate

[15] It's necessary as long as NYC continues to exist.

[16] Conscious breathing is the norm in endurance races, meditation, and scuba diving.

action is not taken, it will send instructions to the muscles to immediately act. This happens before you are consciously aware of any danger[17]—you register what happened after you dove out of the way. There is an evolutionary advantage to foregoing a choosing experience when delaying would get you run over. But danger is not required. You are more likely to win the tennis match if you don't consciously choose how to hit every ball flying your way. If an attractive other smiles as you pass on the street, you either react or lose the opportunity. And circumstances that require a quick response are not the only situations where we forego the choosing experience; more on this in Chapter 11.

Another category, a Type I event, is an unconscious neurological event before Events II and III, where II is a conscious choosing experience, and III is acquiring B rather than A. If Event I causes III, Event II is simply window dressing, the *illusion of choice* (an epiphenomenon) like the whistle on a steam locomotive that blows before the train crosses the road. It does not cause the train to cross the road.

The evidence suggests that most of our behavior is determined unconsciously. And later, but before the behavior occurs, we sometimes have a choosing experience. Our conscious brain tricks us into thinking it determines what we do. Note that this does not mean conscious thought plays no role: conscious thoughts can affect the unconscious, so influence future behaviors. Chapter 11 presents the evidence. [If we were created in God's image, we would not entertain such an illusion—God hopefully does not suffer from it.]

References and Sources

Bear, Mark, Barry Connors, and Michael Paradiso. 2020. *Neuroscience: Exploring the brain, enhanced edition: Exploring the brain*. Burlington, MA: Jones & Bartlett Learning.

Beebee, Helen. 2013. *Free will: An introduction*. Basingstoke: Springer.

Boswell, James. 1791/1866. *Boswell's life of Johnson: Life*. Vol. 3. London: Routledge. https://books.google.com/books/about/The_Life_of_Samuel_Johnson.html?id=Q0FXAAAAYAAJ.

[17] Stepping on a tack fires pain neurons in your foot; the message is transmitted to your spinal cord; from there one message goes to your brain and the other heads straight back down a motor neuron to your foot, causing a muscle contraction before you register the event. Bear et al. (2020) have a nice diagram.

De Spinoza, Benedict, and Rhm Elwes. 1883/2001. *Ethics part ii. Of the nature and origin of the mind*. Translated from the Latin with an introduction by R. H. M. Elwes. London: G. Bell (1883), Blackmask Online (2001).

Dennett, Daniel. 2003. *Intuition pumps and other tools for thinking*. Kindle edition. New York: W. W. Norton.

Foder, Jerry. 2003. "Why would mother nature bother? (review of freedom evolves by Daniel Dennett)." *London Review of Books*, 2.

Gottlieb, Anthony. 2016. *The dream of enlightenment: The rise of modern philosophy*. New York: W. W. Norton.

Hoefer, Carl. 2010. "Causal determinism." Stanford Encyclopedia of Philosophy. Stanford: Stanford University. https://plato.stanford.edu/.

Hoffman, Donald. 2019. *The case against reality: Why evolution hid the truth from our eyes*. New York: W. W. Norton.

James, Henry. 1917/2008. *Portrait of a lady (chap. xvi)*. 2 vols. Vol. 1. Project Gutenberg. https://www.gutenberg.org/files/2833/2833-h/2833-h.htm.

James, William. 1890/1983. *The principles of psychology*. Vol. 1 and 2. New York: Henry Hold and Company 1890, Harvard University Press 1983. https://en.wikipedia.org/wiki/The_Principles_of_Psychology.

List, Christian. 2014. "Free will, determinism, and the possibility of doing otherwise." *Nous* 48 (1): 156–178. https://doi.org/10.1111/nous.12019. https://www.webofscience.com/wos/woscc/full-record/WOS:000330872900007.

Nichols, Shaun. 2004. "The folk psychology of free will: Fits and starts." *Mind & Language* 19: 29. https://sites.google.com/view/shaunbnichols/publications/publications-by-date?pli=1.

———. 2006. "The rise of compatibilism: A case study in the quantitative history of philosophy." *Philosophy and the Empirical* 31: 260–270. https://www.webofscience.com/wos/woscc/full-record/WOS:000250202000013.

———. 2011. "Experimental philosophy and the problem of free will." *Science* 331 (6023): 1401–1403. https://doi.org/10.1126/science.1192931. https://www.webofscience.com/wos/woscc/full-record/WOS:000288504000031.

Nichols, Shaun, and Joshua Knobe. 2007. "Moral responsibility and determinism: The cognitive science of folk intuitions." *Nous* 41 (4): 663–685. https://doi.org/10.1111/j.1468-0068.2007.00666.x. https://www.webofscience.com/wos/woscc/full-record/WOS:000250773100004.

Robinson, Marilynne. 2010. *Risk the game: On William Games*. The Nation: Books and Art, December 31. https://www.thenation.com/article/archive/risk-game-william-james.

Uleman, Jennifer. 2010. *An introduction to Kant's moral philosophy*. Cambridge: Cambridge University Press.

Additional Readings

Clarke, Randolph, and Justin Capes. 2014. "Incompatibilist (nondeterministic) theories of free will." Stanford Encyclopedia of Philosophy. Stanford: Stanford University. https://plato.stanford.edu/.

Downing, Lisa. 2020. "George Berkeley." Stanford Encyclopedia of Philosophy. Stanford: Stanford University. https://plato.stanford.edu/.

Mckenna, Michael, and Justin Coates. 2015. "Compatibilism." Stanford Encyclopedia of Philosophy. Stanford: Stanford University. https://plato.stanford.edu/.

O'Connor, Timothy. 2014. "Free will." Stanford Encyclopedia of Philosophy. Stanford: Stanford University. https://plato.stanford.edu/.

Rohlf, Michael. 2010. "Immanuel Kant." Stanford Encyclopedia of Philosophy. Stanford: Stanford University. https://plato.stanford.edu/.

Shanks, David, et al. 2013. "Priming intelligent behavior: An elusive phenomenon." *Plos One* 8 (4). https://doi.org/10.1371/journal.pone.0056515. https://www.webofscience.com/wos/woscc/full-record/WOS:000318340400001.

CHAPTER 11

The Evidence on Conscious Choice

The Neurological Evidence:

Starting with the 1983 Benjamin Libet (1916–2007) experiment, an increasing number of neurological studies indicate that before you consciously decide what to do, neural activity can be observed that predicts what you will do—activity you are unaware of.[1] Event I (the neural activity) precedes Event III (a voluntary act). Event I is necessary and sufficient to cause the choosing experience (Event II). Event II occurs after Event I but before Event III. Event I is a *readiness potential*: your

[1] Neural activity is observed by observing electrical activity; initially, this was accomplished by attaching electrodes to the scalp. More recently with fMRI and now, sometimes, by directly implanting tiny electrodes in the brain that isolate on specific groups of neurons. Implants are uncommon: when its done, it is during surgery to treat severe epilepsy.

E. R. Morey, *Deconstructing Behavior, Choice, and Well-being*,
https://doi.org/10.1007/978-3-031-36712-0_11

unconscious is getting ready to cause the voluntary act.[2,3] Paraphrasing Wegner (2002), choosing is an experience, not a cause.[4]

* * *

The Libet Experiment

Imagine you are a subject. You enter a small room and sit at a desk, comfortably resting your left arm on the desk. On the wall is a giant 60-second stopwatch with an illuminated dot traveling around its circumference. The stopwatch has the seconds marked in five-second intervals (0, 5 sec., 10 sec., etc., up to 55 sec.). You notice it moves much faster than an ordinary stopwatch. While you don't know its exact speed, the dot covers 60 seconds in 2.6 standard seconds. It takes the dot 0.43 seconds (430 msec.) to go from 0 to 10 and 1.3 seconds (1300 msec.) to go from 0 to 30. So, if you tell someone where the dot was when an event occurs (e.g., when your hand is touched), they can determine when you think the event happened.[5]

A research assistant attaches two sets of electrodes. The first set attaches to your left wrist. It will record if and when you flick your wrist (when your wrist-flexing muscle contracts). The second set is attached to your scalp, recording if and when a certain negatively charged pulse occurs at the top of your brain. You are told to sit there for a few minutes and, if

[2] Quoting Libet, in 1965, Kornhuber and Deecke "found that a recordable electrical charge in brain activity regularly and specifically preceded a voluntary act... a slow rise in electrical negativity ... The electrical charge started at about 800 msec. or more before a subject performed an apparently voluntary act... the readiness potential (RP) or in German, the "bereitschaftspotential."

[3] A readiness potential does not precede every action; it only precedes voluntary actions. It does not precede reflex actions or other uncontrolled actions. For example, when people with Tourette's syndrome involuntarily swear, the swearing is not proceeded by a readiness potential, while their voluntary actions are preceded by readiness potentials. So, a readiness potential is not necessary for an action to occur because all actions are not preceded by readiness potentials, though they are necessary and sufficient for voluntary actions.

[4] "...conscious will is an experience, not a cause."

[5] Testing dot time: dot time for an unseen stimulus to a subject's hand (a light touch) is about 50 msec. after the touch, so the sensatory lag is small, measurable, and can be accounted for.

you want, sometimes flick your wrist. When is up to you. You are asked to remember the dot's position if and when you decide to flick.

This is a stylized description of the famous experiment conducted in 1983 at the University of San Francisco. The results: Approximately a half second (500 msec.) before your wrist muscle contracts, the electrode on your scalp records the start of a negatively charged pulse (a *readiness potential*). This neural activity, which you are unaware of, precedes and predicts you will flick your wrist a half second before you flick it. Your unconscious is getting ready to cause your wrist muscle to contract. [Note the experiment does not demonstrate that the RP causes your wrist to flick—an even earlier neurological event could have caused the RP—more on that later.]

The issue is, when do you have the conscious experience of choosing to flick your wrist? Based on where the dot was when you decided to flick, this happens, on average, approximately 200 msec. before the muscle contracts, indicating the flick is initiated by your unconscious at least 300 msec. before you consciously "decide" to flick. WOW, but with caution.

* * *

Interpret the Libet result carefully. It indicates that your unconscious determined (chose?) when you would flick your wrist and that your conscious experience of choosing to flick is not what caused it.

Questions since the experiment include: (1) Does it indicate your unconscious caused your wrist to flick and that your conscious decision was not the cause? It seems to. (2) If yes, does the result hold for more complex decisions (e.g., proposing to Wilma)? Complex decisions are hard to test (see Lady Ottoline Morrell, discussed below). If consciously choosing an action is not what caused it, this violates Assumption 12b: *That perception of choosing is what causes an economicus to take the path it took.*

Numerous neuroscientists and philosophers have questioned whether the experiment demonstrates what it suggests. Reasonable answers support the conclusions, but these answers are not bombproof. Nevertheless, the fundamental finding that an act can be predicted based on unconscious brain activity has been replicated multiple times. One example is Chun Siong Soon, Marcel Brass, Hans-Jochen Heinze, and John-Dylan Haynes (2008). Using fMRI imaging, they could predict, with 60% accuracy, whether you will push the left or right button as much as 7 seconds before you pushed it and 6 seconds before you "chose" which button to push. Quoting Kerri Smith, the Podcast Editor for the journal *Nature*, talking about a 2011 study:

> Some researchers have literally gone deeper into the brain. One of those is Itzhak Fried, a neuroscientist and surgeon at the University of California, Los Angeles, and the Tel Aviv Medical Center in Israel. He studied individuals with electrodes implanted in their brains as part of a surgical procedure to treat epilepsy. Recording from single neurons in this way gives scientists a much more precise picture of brain activity than fMRI or EEG. Fried's experiments showed that there was activity in individual neurons of particular brain areas about a second and a half before the subject made a conscious decision to press a button. With about 700 milliseconds to go, the researchers could predict the timing of that decision with more than 80% accuracy. 'At some point, things that are predetermined are admitted into consciousness,' says Fried. He suggests that the conscious will might be added to a decision at a later stage.

What are the concerns? Issue 1: While the Libet results are consistent with Event I (the RP) being both necessary and sufficient for Event III (the voluntary act),[6] his results are consistent with Event I being necessary but not sufficient for Event III. Or so argues Aaron Schurger and his coauthors in two separate papers (2012, 2016). They hypothesize an alternative explanation for the Libet finding. They distinguish between *intent* and *commitment*, arguing that the onset of the RP is not signaling a commitment to act but instead signals the start of an intent (an intent to flick the wrist or push the button).[7] [Remember that an RP is simply a slow build-up of neurological activity (electrical activity on the scalp or the firing rates of specific neurons)-a neurological pulse/wave.] Schurger and his coauthors assume intent is necessary for commitment but not sufficient. According to their hypothesis, commitment occurs when the RP wave reaches a neurological threshold. If correct, an RP will occur some percentage of the time without the act occurring, but the Libet experiment was not designed to identify this percentage. Everyone eventually flicked their wrist, making it impossible to observe a wave that did not end with a flick. This, according to Schurger, caused Libet and

[6] Libet's interpretation.

[7] "Commitment" is the point in time when the mind is made up. As in, I intend to learn Latin, but I have not committed to learning Latin.

others to mislabel *necessary* as *sufficient* because the studies limit their data collection to time periods that always end with the act occurring.

The Schurger hypothesis is consistent with the commitment occurring before or after Event II (the choosing experience). If it is after the choosing experience, it is inconsistent with the Libet interpretation that unconscious commitment always precedes the choosing experience. The Schurger hypothesis and results don't demonstrate that the choosing experience caused anything.

Issue 2 (clock time): In real life, you are rarely asked when you decided on A rather than B: you don't have to tell someone when you had the choosing experience. In these research studies, respondents have to. In the Libet experiment, if they flicked their wrist, they had to specify when they decided to. An issue is whether the requirement to monitor the clock affects the timing and amplitude of the RP wave.[8] In a 2011 experiment (Jeff Miller, Peter Shepherdson, and Judy Trevena compared the wave pattern of the electrical activity with and without clock monitoring. While the two graphs have similar shapes, clock monitoring shifted it downward (more negative than without the monitoring). Put simply, clock monitoring amplifies the RP. Miller and his coauthors interpret their findings to imply that the RP might not be sufficient to determine how you will behave. I don't understand. With clock monitoring, which is required to determine when the choosing experience occurs, it becomes difficult to determine which part of the wave is caused by the intent/commitment to act and which part is the result of monitoring the clock.

On a broader level of criticism, there is Ben Newell and David Shanks' (2014) review of "unconscious influences on decision making". They conclude

> Our critical analysis points to a surprising conclusion, that there is little convincing evidence of unconscious influences on decision making in the areas we review, and that, as a consequence, such influences should not be assigned a prominent role in theories of decision making and related behaviors. This conclusion is consistent with the view that conscious thoughts are by far the primary driver of behavior.

[8] As an aside, in experiments where respondents had to estimate clock time, some always report their decision occurring after they flicked or pressed a key. "This [a mistake?]seems to stem at least in part from difficulties in determining the spot's location at the decision time" (Miller et al. 2011). More interestingly, it could indicate that the choosing experience actually occurs after the individual has acted.

To be clear, they reject the entire literature on unconscious influences on behavior, not just the Libet-type studies. They are not convinced. They also reject all the priming and cueing studies that I will discuss. Their paper was published in *Behavioral and Brain Sciences*, along with 28 commentaries, some supportive, others not. Either way, the review makes important points, many around the awareness (consciously aware), measures of awareness, and determining when cognition becomes conscious. Their primary conclusion is that the literature demonstrating unconscious influences on behavior has not sufficiently demonstrated the absence of awareness. [The Libet experiment assumes a lack of awareness until the indicated decision time.]

As the commentaries to the review critically ask, does the evidence have to reject the null that there is awareness or reject a null of unawareness? Newell and Shanks' null is awareness. They then argue there is not sufficient evidence to reject it. Said another way, they start with the null that conscious thought influences behavior, then conclude there is insufficient evidence to reject this null.

They got me thinking about *unawareness* and how to measure it. Define it as unconscious cognition (unconscious thoughts), when you think about something but are not aware that you are.

Brain imaging has now been used to identify unconscious cognition (Creswell, James Bursley, and Ajay Satpute 2013). They presented 21 subjects with a complex decision task in an fMRI machine. Each subject spent 84 seconds (the processing phase) seeing how four different cars (or backpacks) varied by 16 attributes (e.g., good or bad gas mileage). Subjects were told they would quality-rate the four products. The four products were configured to vary objectively in quality (price was not an attribute). There were three treatments. After the processing phase, subjects in the first treatment immediately quality-rated each product.

There was a 120-second intermediate phase between the processing and decision phases in the other two treatments. In the second, the individual was asked to think about how they would rate the four products, so 120 seconds of conscious thought. In the third treatment, subjects spent the 120 seconds playing a game.[9] The game grabs your attention, making it difficult to consciously think about the alternatives. So if there

[9] A *2-back-n-back game*: a number appeared on the screen for .5 seconds, followed by an * for 2.5 seconds, then a new number. The subject had to click a button whenever the current number was the same as the second-back number.

is thinking about them in the third treatment, it is unconscious. For the third treatment, subjects played the game a second time after rating the four products. Remember, brain activity was continuously recorded. What happened subconsciously during the intermediate phase in treatment 3 is obtained by subtracting the brain images in the second game of treatment 3 from the first game's images. That is, the brain images from conscious cognition were removed, leaving the images for unconscious thought.

As previously shown in prior studies without the fMRI, the performance on the rating task was best for the group that played the game before they rated the alternatives and worse when they consciously considered them. This indicates that useful cogitating occurred unconsciously during the game. Notably, the brain regions activated unconsciously were the same ones activated during the processing phase. The results are consistent with the hypothesis that the unconscious makes the final decision. The study was the first to map unconscious thought with neuron activation.

* * *

My summary of the above neurological evidence: Most everyone agrees that the RP is necessary for a voluntary movement; whether it is sufficient is more contested. When you become aware of your commitment to act is debated. There are two issues: measurement of the awareness and whether the start of the RP indicates commitment (whether RP is sufficient). Suppose the time at which awareness occurs is measured without error, and the RP demonstrates unconscious commitment. In that case, awareness of commitment comes after the commitment.

Alternatively, if one assumes that the RP is necessary but not sufficient for commitment (the threshold model), then awareness might be concurrent with commitment (when the threshold is reached).

Both are consistent with the unconscious choice, so neither assumption implies that the choosing experience plays a role in what follows.

Additional support for the behavioral role of the unconscious is the finding that your brain can both formulate a goal (e.g., get you invited to a party) and cause you to take actions to achieve that goal without you being aware of why you are taking these actions. Distinguish between goals and actions/behavior. [A goal often motivates actions; choosing to lose weight is a goal, skipping dessert is an action.] In a 2010 *Science* article, Ruud Custers and Henk Aarts (2010) interpret recent research on unconscious goal-formation. The previous view, and what most of us want to believe, is that goals are consciously chosen. For example, my goal to write this book must have been consciously adopted?

To summarize, you can be subliminally motivated to adopt a goal and then unconsciously take actions to achieve it. In the lab, the goal is subliminally brought to the attention of your unconscious. Outside the lab, motivation is with environmental cues you are unaware of.[10] You then unconsciously evaluate the rewards associated with that goal. If the magnitude of the subliminal reward is sufficient, you adopt the goal and act.[11]

In the lab, motivation is either a subliminally cued reward or a subliminal cue that has previously been subliminally associated with a reward.

Despite such findings, most people believe consciously choosing causes them to perform an action or adopt a goal. While most people believe Assumption 12b is true, there is a good chance it is false.[12] NBT can

[10] People speak more softly when seeing a picture of a library, are more inclined to clean their table if there is a vague whiff of cleaner, and get more competitive when they enter an office if there is a leather briefcase on the desk (Henk Aarts and Ap Dijksterhuis 2003; Rob Holland et al. 2005; Aaron Kay et al. 2004).

[11] In one study they review, students were seated

> in front of a computer, allegedly to test their computer mouse skills. Before starting on this test, some participants were subliminally exposed to words on the computer screen related to the goal of socializing, whereas others were exposed to unrelated words. At the onset of the mouse-skill test, they were told that if there would be enough time left after the test, they could engage in a lottery in which they could win tickets to a popular student party. Thus, spending more effort (by working faster) on the mouse-skill test was instrumental in attaining the goal to socialize. The participants worked harder on the mouse-skill test when the socializing goal was first unconsciously primed. And this effect was stronger when socializing evoked a stronger positive reward signal in the minds of the participants (which was assessed in a separate implicit affective association task). Importantly, checks indicated that priming caused participants to pursue the goal independently of their reported motivation to attain it.

[12] Interestingly, Libet, in late life, raised the possibility that after the RP and the conscious deciding occurs, you still might be able to consciously veto the action (stop yourself) which would be *free won't* rather than free will.

get along without Assumption 12b, and an economicus absent a me—recollect that basic NBT is Assumptions 1–9.

So, Do the Libet and Related Findings Imply That Conscious Thought, Including the Choosing Experience, Does Not Affect Behavior?

No! Even if your unconscious is the determining step before an action is taken, it leaves the possibility that earlier (right before or much earlier) conscious thinking influenced what your unconscious now determines.[13] For example, the choosing experience—after your unconscious has decided, while not affecting whether you now go with A or B can influence what the unconscious will select in future choice sets. Supporting the conjecture that conscious thought has influence, Roy Braumeister, E.J. Masicampo, and Kathleen Vohs (2011) argue that "The evidence for conscious causation of behavior is …empirically strong. However, conscious causation is often indirect and delayed, and it depends on the interplay with unconscious processes."[14]

Imagine if One Never Has Choosing Experiences

The choosing experience informs the unconscious, blabber-mouthing ideas to the conscious you, and these can influence what you will do later. Imagine our brains evolved absent choosing experiences. We would not know what we would do until we did it. You would not be able to tell the kids you were taking them for cheeseburgers rather than to boarding school.[15] Bertrand Russell learned he loved Lady Ottoline Morrell when

[13] While consciously thinking about what to do is a conscious thought, most thoughts are not choosing experiences. For example, you consciously realize you are reading this footnote.

[14] They reviewed experiments where conscious thought was manipulated (e.g., asking you to imagine a future action), and subsequent behavior was then observed. They found studies where experimentally manipulating conscious thought influenced behavior (e.g., you are more likely to perform an action if you first imagine performing it). As Baumeister and Bargh (2014) note, none of these experiments contradict the Libet result that the immediate cause of the behavior is unconscious.

[15] Quoting Baumeister and Masicampo (2010), "we think that the evolutionarily decisive advantages of conscious thought are not to be found in private, solipsistic ratiocination but rather in its contribution to communication."

he heard himself saying, “I love you.”—a surprise to him.[16] Without choosing experiences, life would be a sequence of conscious surprises.

Without choosing experiences, your sense of self (conscious identity) would be lessened. Believing that consciously choosing determines what happens next conveys an evolutionary advantage, even if it is not true—evolution has programmed us to believe we consciously choose. We tend to think that the choosing experience is absent in worms and wolves—they go straight from I to III. Absent choosing experiences, it is difficult to coordinate your behaviors with your friends and colleagues—as Baumeister and his coauthors note, it is difficult to imagine unconscious talking. Consciousness improves our decision-making, even if the unconscious makes the final call.

Other Evidence on Choosing Experiences and Subsequent Actions

An issue complicating the study of the relationship between a choosing experience and the subsequent action is you cannot, by definition, consciously know whether your unconscious determined what you did—you cannot be conscious of your unconscious.

Consider how the perception of choosing to act, the action, and the outcome can all be distorted. Begin by deconstructing what Ralph told the bartender:

> Yesterday I decided to go duck hunting, saw a duck in the sky, chose to shoot, shot the duck, and my dog retrieved the now-dead duck that I shot.

The sequence as Ralph perceives it is (1) he had two choosing experiences: to hunt and to shoot; (2) shot in a duck’s direction; (3) these caused a shot duck; (4) he has a dead duck in his truck; and (5) he believes he committed premeditated duckicide. In Ralph’s mind, he chose to shoot, and this resulted in an outcome, a dead duck. To be correct, all five of these implicit conjectures must be valid. However, neurological research throws conjecture (3) in doubt, even if (1) and (2) are correct. What

[16] Morrell, a dramatic British socialite and arts patron, had an open marriage and was off and on with Russell for years; she had many lovers. D. H. Lawrence portrayed her in *Women in Love*, and some critics believe she inspired *Lady Chatterley*. http://www.theguardian.com/uk/2006/oct/10/books.booksnews.

about (1), (2), (4), and (5)? Much research in psychology indicates that they are often wrong.

To keep things simple, assume (4) is correct. (1) is incorrect if his recollection is false; maybe he shot reflexively, but, being a responsible gun owner, Ralph cannot imagine shooting without first deciding to, so he concludes he must have decided to shoot. Maybe (5) is incorrect: maybe another hunter shot at the same time as Ralph, or maybe the duck died in midflight of natural causes as Ralph shot his gun. Maybe (2) is incorrect: maybe he did not shoot in the duck's direction, and he believes he did because after he shot, the duck fell from the sky.

Humans are great at (A) imagining we had a choosing experience when we didn't; (B) believing the choosing experience caused what we did; (C) believing we caused an outcome to occur when we did not (or believing we did not cause an outcome when we did); and (D) believing the outcome is different from what it is. Also, remember that action does not require a choosing experience. This, plus these four inclinations, incline us to misinterpret the importance and influence of conscious choice—independent of (3).

Let's Start with Most of What We Do Isn't Preceded by Conscious Choosing

One way to think about the relationship between conscious choosing and the subsequent action is to contrast that relationship with actions not preceded by conscious choosing. [Economists do not explicitly consider whether a purchase (e.g., buying a TV or going to Chez Faux for dinner) first requires conscious choosing.]

We are all aware that many actions are not preceded by a conscious decision to act, so everyone knows action does not require prior conscious choosing. Above, I referred to these as Type IV Events.

A: Believing We Had a Choosing Experience When We Didn't

In a 1977 experiment by Nisbett and Wilson, subjects memorized lists of word pairs, and in one treatment, the list included the pair "ocean-moon".[17] Later they were asked to name a laundry detergent. Those

[17] The article has been cited seventeen-thousand times.

whose list included "ocean-moon" listed Tide significantly more often—not surprising. And when asked why, the subjects said things like "Tide was the detergent their mother used." Or "It has a cool box." No one said, "Because I memorized 'ocean moon'." They imagined consciously choosing to say Tide because afterward they felt compelled to rationalize their answer. I observe my behavior and then create an explanation that I find plausible and works for me—sometimes, it is even correct.

B: Believing the Choosing Experience Caused What We Did

We all want to believe we exert conscious control over our lives. So are compelled to attribute outcomes to our conscious reckonings. Still, choice experiments demonstrate that the probability of choosing a particular alternative can be manipulated by messing with your unconscious, independent of what you consciously reason. This supports the neurological results discussed above.

Recent studies with subliminal cues demonstrate that choice can be influenced by these cues (information that never reaches conscious awareness). Subjects are shown a piece of information for a few msec., followed by a random letter that masks the information. Behavior is influenced, demonstrating that the conscious is not always in charge, even when we think it is.[18]

[18] Subliminal research got a bad name in 1957: James Vicary claimed that inserting "Drink Coke" and "Eat Popcorn" in movie frames caused movie goers to buy more of each. He could not replicate the study and later claimed the whole thing was a gimmick. His initial claim caused a public uproar and made research on subliminal cues a dangerous endeavor. It led to subliminal advertising being banned in Australia, Britain, and the United States.

Earlier I note that Newell and Shanks (2014) reject the literature on unconscious influences on behavior including the literature I discuss on unconscious priming and cues. They argue that this literature's conclusion that the subject was not aware of the cue is based on an inadequate test of awareness. Someone telling you they were not aware of the snake in the room does not imply their unconscious was unaware. I might have seen a snake, but am not sure, so, to be safe, report no awareness, or so they argue. They also argue awareness is a continuous variable that does not jump from unconscious to conscious when awareness reaches a specific intensity, meaning conscious awareness is a continuous variable. Summarizing, they suspect there is conscious awareness when the researcher concludes there is none. And, if correct, this would call into question the subliminal priming support for unconscious choosing. For a rebuttal from the same issue of *Behavioral and Brain Sciences* see Dijksterhuis et al. (2014), also Samantha Brooks and

Subliminal persuasion is easily demonstrated when it addresses a conscious physical need (hunger, thirst, etc.). In 2006, the psychologists Johan Karremans, Wolfgang Stroebe, and Jasper Palmier-Claus demonstrated

> priming of a brand name for a drink [Lipton Iced Tea] will only affect choice behavior of people who are thirsty (i.e., have a goal to drink)

Supporting this finding, in a 2009 study, Christina Bermeitinger and her coauthors showed

> Subliminally presented brands of dextrose pills biased choices of tired (but not non-tired) participants.

More recently, Thijs Verwijmeren and colleagues investigated the influence of subliminal cues on the choice between two beverages when one is consumed more frequently. The two beverages were Lipton Iced Tea and Spa Rood (a popular Dutch mineral–water brand). The subliminal cue was either "Lipton Iced Tea" or a control. It influenced choice if the subject was thirsty, consistent with the two other studies. The Lipton cue had no influence if the subject habitually drank Lipton, even if he was thirsty. Alternatively, if he more often drank Spa Rood, the Lipton cue increased the probability he would choose Lipton. Respondents chose an alternative different from the beverage they typically chose because they were presented with information, unconsciously obtained—conscious processing did not determine their selection.[19] This research is consistent with the incentive-salience hypothesis discussed in Chapter 5. When one is in a drive state, alternatives that address that state become more salient and even more salient if that alternative is associated with a cue. The research on subliminal cues drives home the finding that one need not be conscious of the cue: it does have to be observing a pretty girl drinking a Pepsi.

Dan Stein (2014). They find that subliminal vs. conscious cues activate different brain regions.

[19] The subjects were not debriefed on why they made the selection they made. In a personal email, Thijs Verwijmeren speculated that if asked the subjects would have come up with an incorrect reason for their choice.

To summarize, subliminal cues affect choices when one is motivated to fulfill a physical need. But can choice be affected by subliminal information when the motivation is more implicit, such as a motivation to succeed? This conjecture was tested and found correct in 2012 by Maxim Milyavsky, Ran Hassin, and Yaacov Schul: information processed unconsciously can influence choice whenever there is a motivation for choosing, not just when it's a physical and conscious need.[20]

C: Believing You Caused It When You Didn't, and Believing You Didn't When You Did

The Denver Broncos football team lost the 2014 Super Bowl because I, stupidly, wasn't paying attention during the Bronco's disastrous first play from scrimmage.

Exotic examples of things we cause but don't think we cause are the voices people with schizophrenia hear, the things hypnotized people do, and the words we spell out on Ouija boards. Students who got a *D* on my first midterm believe they did not cause their *D*: It was caused by Edward's lousy grading. In contrast, *A* students believe their conscious efforts caused their grade. When we pray to God to give us the strength to act and then act, we attribute the act to God rather than ourselves—problematic if God does not exist or does not care what we do. It could not have been an operator error when I could not find this chapter on my computer.

[20] Motivation to achieve was manipulated: before a "separate" choice task, subjects played "find the words" in a square of letters. One set of subjects' letter-squares included words related to achievement; the other treatment (the control group) saw motivationally neutral words.

Then, before the choice task, each subject was subliminally cued with a word or non-word. There were 16 word-cues and 16 non-word cues, and each cue was related to just one of four categories (emotions, clothes, family, and fruits). E.g., the emotion words were love, joy, anxiety, and jealousy, and the emotion non-words were nadsach, sitam, dagma, and ragham.

Then the four categories came on the screen, and the subject had to guess the correct category (e.g., fruits if the subliminal cue was mango). Correct guesses were rewarded. The subjects in the control group guessed correctly no better than random; the subjects who were motivated to achieve guessed correctly significantly better than random. The critical point is that these subjects were not consciously aware that they had been motivated to achieve.

We have all heard of false confessions, even some where the confessor believes they did it. In 1996 Saul Kassin and Katherine Kiechel produced these in the laboratory. Each subject was falsely accused of crashing the experimenter's software, thus ruining the study. The subject typed a list of letters read off by a research assistant posing as a second subject. The assistant read them at 43 letters per min. or 72 *lpm*. Before the trial started, subjects were warned that the software would crash and data would be lost if they hit the ALT key. After sixty seconds of typing, the experimenter claimed the program crashed and accused the subject of hitting the ALT key. No one had, and everyone initially denied it. The experimenter then turned to the letter reader and asked if she saw anything. She claimed, "I did not see what happened," or "I saw the subject hit the ALT key." Of the subjects who heard 72 lpm and were witnessed against, 100% signed a confession, and 65% became convinced they were guilty. [When leaving, the following subject (another RA) privately asked, "What happened?").] Thirty-five percent confabulated details to support their false belief that they hit the Alt key. [They were asked in the debriefing to say when they hit the ALT key.]

Of the subjects who heard 43 lpm and were witnessed against, 89% signed the confession. Of those who got this slow pace and were not witnessed against, 35% signed the confession. In summary, it is not difficult to make you think you did something you didn't, even if it's a bad thing.

Billy Wayne Cope is in jail for raping and murdering his daughter. He confessed and provided gory details after the police told him the semen in her vagina matched his DNA—it did not—the DNA was much later matched to a rapist who had recently moved to the neighborhood.

My hard work, not my coauthors, is responsible for my published coauthored papers, but they believe it was their hard work. Correctly attributing an outcome that results from a complex interaction between people (work, social, sexual) is tricky—exactly who initiated that kiss? And, if we like the outcome, we tend to attribute it to our efforts but to others if we don't: *self-serving attribution*; it increases self-esteem.

We ascribe causation if physical action on our part immediately precedes an observed outcome. There is a bucket full of light-switch experiments: there is a light switch, and a light flashes on or not. These experiments demonstrate that subjects think they control the light, even when it is not attached to the switch. We believe we are causing things even when we are not.

As discussed in Chapter 9, there is the tendency to ascribe causation if physical action on our part immediately precedes an observed outcome. (I flicked the switch, and the light came on. I shot in the air, and a duck fell.) If *A* proceeds *B*, we tend to infer *A* caused *B*, particularly if *B* is desirable, so we take authorship for *A*. Man evolved to think in this second-best manner.

Consider an experiment where you choose whether to press a button or not every second or so, and then a light flashes. The light does not always flash after you push the button; sometimes it flashes even when you didn't push it. Treatments vary by the actual amount of control you and the other subjects have over the light (e.g., 25%, 50%, and 75%)—complete control (100%) means the light flashes every time you push the button and never flashes when you don't.[21] You can be tricked into thinking you have more control than you have by increasing the number (not the proportion) of times when the outcome is what you predict (the number of successes), independent of your actual amount of control. Successes are when you flick, and the light comes on, and when you don't, it doesn't.

In a different light experiment, Alloy and Abramson studied the perception of control using a sample that intentionally included both depressed and non-depressed subjects. The non-depressed subjects, but not the depressed subjects, overestimated how much control they had over whether a light came on. Like the study described above, subjects flicked a switch, and a light sometimes came on. Subjects suffering from depression accurately assessed their lack of control—which could have something to do with why they were depressed in the first place. A conjecture for why we suffer from an *illusion-of-control* is actual control is easier to recognize than no control (independence between our actions and what happens next).

In a simple 1983 experiment by Howard Tennen and Jeanette Sharp, the light came on a fixed proportion of the time, independent of whether the subject pushed the button. Hence, the subject had no control, but the subjects experienced the illusion of control. Before the trials, each subject was classified as either an *internal* or *external* type using an I-E scale of control orientation. [Externals tend toward believing what happens is out of their control, whereas internals tend to view their actions as having

[21] With 25% control, the light comes on 75% of the time when the button is pushed and 50% of the time when the button is not pushed. Whereas, with 50% control, the percentages are 75% and 25%. Control is the difference between the two percentages.

influence.] The hypothesis was that the internals would suffer the illusion of control, but not the externals. Both types suffered it, the internals just more so.

In 2008, Dijksterhuis, Jesse Preston, Daniel Wegner, and Henk Aarts showed that whether or not you take credit for an action can be influenced by subliminal cues that "direct attention to self".[22] Subjects looked at a sequence of strings of letters on a computer screen in a fast race with the computer to determine whether each string was a word. They were told the first response (theirs or the computer's) would blank the screen, after which another string appeared. However, the screen blanked half a second after each string appeared, independent of what the respondent did—the subject never caused the screen to blank. After each screen blank, the subject was asked if they answered before the computer. Before each trial, the subject was subliminally cued with either a personal pronoun ("I" or "me") or a neutral word. When the cue was a personal pronoun, the subject was likelier to say they beat the computer.

In another experiment, subjects subliminally cued with the word "God" were less likely to say they beat the computer if they were believers. [Believers attribute outcomes to God—God's will.] In another experiment, Aarts demonstrated that when causation is unclear, "feelings of control and self-causation" are enhanced if success is subliminally conveyed.

D: Believing the Outcome Is Different from What It Is

There is it, and what caused "it". This sub-section is about whether it is true, not what caused it. Was the duck even dead, or even a duck? My mother once called to report her sister died and told me she had called the funeral home to come for the body—the funeral home went to the hospital and reported that their services were not yet required. People make mistakes about the facts on the ground.

[22] In a 2013 paper David Shanks and his coauthors report that they could not replicate another Dijksterhuis finding, his finding that people who think about professors before they take an intelligence test do better than those who think about football hooligans. This, in part, has called into question the findings that "behavior can be influenced or 'primed' by thoughts or motives triggered unconsciously…" In a 2012 open letter to researchers in social priming, Daniel Kahneman said more replications were needed, but that he is a "general believer" in priming effects. See Allison Abbott (2013).

Truth, like beauty, is in the beholder's eye. The accused believes there was no rape because the accused believes the victim wanted to have sex. He believes the victim chose to have sex and sent signals indicating this. He is attributing the sex to a choice made by the other party when, in fact, the other party did not necessarily make that choice. And, if she didn't, the accused caused the sex. Most Americans believe that Barack Obama is a US citizen, but not all. Some think our planet is warming, others don't, and everyone can't be correct. We judge truth based on what is happening around us, filtered through personal perspective: our implicit biases, what our group/tribe believes, and "facts" reported to us by second-hand sources we trust.

That your actions are influenced by your unconscious does not imply you are not making choices—it is your unconscious. Unconscious choice is consistent with the NBT Assumptions Plus, except for 12b. What about the causal determinism discussed in Chapter 9? Causal determinism must be the case unless God, spirits, magic, or randomness intervenes. [Most of us subscribe to magic to some degree, often unconsciously.] Causal determinism is consistent with actions being initiated unconsciously. Whether you can make a choice—consciously or unconsciously—in a world of causal determinism comes down to how choice is defined.

Summarizing

This ends Part II, our discussion of what is a choice and do humans make choices. Neoclassical choice theory, NCT, assumes economici make choices: "choice" is in the theory's title. And saying that behavior (as explained by NCT) is chosen behavior is inconsistent with the street sense of *choice*, which is an economicus could have experienced a different path. NBT assumes it must experience its HRAP, and its ordering and what is available are given, so an economicus had to behave the way it did. Its behavior is deterministic in the restrictive sense that at the beginning of time, the configuration of atoms was such the species economicus would inhabit the earth.

Applying NCT to human behavior requires that humans are economici. Most humans don't believe this. They believe the behavior of animals and refrigerators is causally deterministic, but they are disinclined to believe it holds for humans.

The question is how to make a behavior a *choice* for you and economici. It is done by implicitly defining a choice as any situation with two or more available paths. Even though your ordering of paths and which are available are exogenous and you are constrained to experience the highest-ranked available path.

Physicists and neuroscientists tend to be *incompatibilists* (believe causal determinism is incompatible with free will and choice). Philosophers tend to be *compatibilists*, believing causal determinism is consistent with free will and choice. Economists tend to be implicit and unaware *compatibilists*: we implicitly define free will as "your will is free if external constraints do not limit you to one alternative."

Economists should be aware that physicists and neuroscientists reject that free will is compatible with causal determinism.

The issue is whether the choosing experience influences which alternative you select: While we believe it does, there is strong evidence that many choices (in the economic sense) are made unconsciously: at the final step, the unconscious selects the alternative and, sometimes, you then have a conscious experience of choosing what your unconscious decided on. [Of course, the evidence is debated.] While this isn't fatal for NBT (most axiomatic expressions of NCT say nothing about the conscious vs. the unconscious), it is an injury. I suspect most economists believe the choosing experience is why you did what you did (most other people believe this as well: unconscious choosing is not what most of us had in mind.

With questions about the ability to choose in mind, I now turn to *Part V: Most Moral Philosophers are not Welfare Consequentialists, so what are they?*

References and Sources

Aarts, Henk, and Ap Dijksterhuis. 2003. "The silence of the library: Environment, situational norm, and social behavior." *Journal of Personality and Social Psychology* 84 (1): 18–28. https://doi.org/10.1037/0022-3514.84.1.18. https://www.webofscience.com/wos/woscc/full-record/WOS:000180072500002.

Abbott, Alison. 2013. "Disputed results a fresh blow for social psychology." *Nature* 497 (7447): 16–16. https://doi.org/10.1038/497016a. https://www.nature.com/articles/497016a#/ref-link-1.

Baumeister, Roy, and E. J. Masicampo. 2010. "Conscious thought is for facilitating social and cultural interactions: How mental simulations serve the animal-culture interface." *Psychological Review* 117 (3): 945–971. https://doi.org/10.1037/a0019393. https://www.webofscience.com/wos/woscc/full-record/WOS:000280450400009.

Baumeister, Roy, E. J. Masicampo, and Kathleen Vohs. 2011. "Do conscious thoughts cause behavior?" *Annual Review of Psychology* 62: 331–361. https://doi.org/10.1146/annurev.psych.093008.131126. https://www.webofscience.com/wos/woscc/full-record/WOS:000287331200013.

Baumeister, Roy, Kathleen Vohs, and E. J. Masicampo. 2014. "Maybe it helps to be conscious, after all." *Behavioral and Brain Sciences* 37 (1): 20–21. https://doi.org/10.1017/s0140525x13000630. https://www.webofscience.com/wos/woscc/full-record/WOS:000332474000003.

Baumeister, Roy F., and John A. Bargh. 2014. "Conscious and unconscious." In *Dual-process theories of the social mind*, 35–49. New York: The Guilford Press.

Bermeitinger, Christiana, et al. 2009. "The hidden persuaders break into the tired brain." *Journal of Experimental Social Psychology* 45 (2): 320–326. https://doi.org/10.1016/j.jesp.2008.10.001. https://www.webofscience.com/wos/woscc/full-record/WOS:000266066000003.

Brooks, Samantha, and Dan Stein. 2014. "Unconscious influences on decision making: Neuroimaging and neuroevolutionary perspectives." *Behavioral and Brain Sciences* 37 (1): 23–24. https://doi.org/10.1017/s0140525x13000666. https://www.webofscience.com/wos/woscc/full-record/WOS:000332474000006.

Brooks, Samantha, et al. 2012. "Exposure to subliminal arousing stimuli induces robust activation in the amygdala, hippocampus, anterior cingulate, insular cortex, and primary visual cortex: A systematic meta-analysis of fMRI studies." *Neuroimage* 59 (3): 2962–2973. https://doi.org/10.1016/j.neuroimage.2011.09.077. https://www.webofscience.com/wos/woscc/full-record/WOS:000299494000094.

Creswell, John, James Bursley, and Ajay Satpute. 2013. "Neural reactivation links unconscious thought to decision-making performance." *Social Cognitive and Affective Neuroscience* 8 (8): 863–869. https://doi.org/10.1093/scan/nst004. https://www.webofscience.com/wos/woscc/full-record/WOS:000327549100004.

Custers, Ruud, and Henk Aarts. 2010. "The unconscious will: How the pursuit of goals operates outside of conscious awareness." *Science* 329 (5987): 47–50. https://doi.org/10.1126/science.1188595. https://www.webofscience.com/wos/woscc/full-record/WOS:000279402700026.

Dijksterhuis, Ap, Jesse Preston, Daniel Wegner, and Henk Aarts. 2008. "Effects of subliminal priming of self and god on self-attribution of authorship for events." *Journal of Experimental Social Psychology* 44 (1): 2–9. https://doi.org/10.1016/j.jesp.2007.01.003. https://www.webofscience.com/wos/woscc/full-record/WOS:000253282100001.

Dijksterhuis, Ap, Ad Van Knippenberg, Rob Holland, and Harm Veling. 2014. "Newell and shanks' approach to psychology is a dead end." *Behavioral and Brain Sciences* 37 (1): 25–26. https://doi.org/10.1017/s0140525x1300068x. https://www.webofscience.com/wos/woscc/full-record/WOS:000332474000008.

Holland, Rob, Merel Hendriks, and Henk Aarts. 2005. "Smells like clean spirit." *Psychological Science* 16 (9): 689–693. https://doi.org/10.1111/j.1467-9280.2005.01597.x. https://www.webofscience.com/wos/woscc/full-record/WOS:000231393000006.

James, William. 1890/1983. *The principles of psychology*. Vol. 1 and 2. New York: Henry Hold and Company 1890, Harvard University Press 1983. https://en.wikipedia.org/wiki/The_Principles_of_Psychology.

Kassin, Saul, and Katherine Kiechel. 1996. "The social psychology of false confessions: Compliance, internalization, and confabulation." *Psychological Science* 7 (3): 125–128.

Kay, Aaron, Christian Wheeler, John Bargh, and Lee Ross. 2004. "Material priming: The influence of mundane physical objects on situational construal and competitive behavioral choice." *Organizational Behavior and Human Decision Processes* 95 (1): 83–96. https://doi.org/10.1016/j.obhdp.2004.06.003. https://www.webofscience.com/wos/woscc/full-record/WOS:000223901300005.

Libet, Benjamin. 2004. *Mind time: The temporal factor in consciousness*. Cambridge, MA: Harvard University Press.

Libet, Benjamin, Curtis Gleason, Elwood Wright, and Dennis Pearl. 1983. "Time of conscious intention to act in relation to onset of cerebral activity (readiness-potential)." In *Neurophysiology of consciousness*, 249–268. Boston: Springer.

Miller, Jeff, Peter Shepherdson, and Judy Trevena. 2011. "Effects of clock monitoring on electroencephalographic activity: Is unconscious movement initiation an artifact of the clock?" *Psychological Science* 22 (1): 103–109. https://doi.org/10.1177/0956797610391100. https://journals.sagepub.com/doi/10.1177/0956797610391100.

Milyavsky, Maxim, Ran Hassin, and Yaacov Schul. 2012. "Guess what? Implicit motivation boosts the influence of subliminal information on choice." *Consciousness and Cognition* 21 (3): 1232–1241. https://doi.org/10.1016/j.concog.2012.06.001. https://www.webofscience.com/wos/woscc/full-record/WOS:000308685600015.

Newell, Ben, and David Shanks. 2014. "Unconscious influences on decision making: A critical review." *Behavioral and Brain Sciences* 37 (1) https://doi.org/10.1017/s0140525x12003214. https://www.webofscience.com/wos/woscc/full-record/WOS:000332474000001.

Nisbett, Richard, and Timothy Wilson. 1977. "Telling more than we can know: Verbal reports on mental processes." *Psychological Review* 84 (3): 231–259. https://doi.org/10.1037/0033-295x.84.3.231. https://www.webofscience.com/wos/woscc/full-record/WOS:000294404300011.

Schurger, Aaron, Jacobo Sitt, and Stanislas Dehaene. 2012. "An accumulator model for spontaneous neural activity prior to self-initiated movement." *Proceedings of the National Academy of Sciences of the United States of America* 109 (42): E2904–E2913. https://doi.org/10.1073/pnas.1210467109. https://www.pnas.org/doi/full/10.1073/pnas.1210467109.

Schurger, Aaron, Myrtos Mylopoulos, and David Rosenthal. 2016. "Neural antecedents of spontaneous voluntary movement. A new perspective." *Trends in Cognitive Sciences* 20 (2): 7–79. https://doi.org/10.1016/j.tics.2015.11.003. https://www.sciencedirect.com/science/article/pii/S136466131500279X?via%3Dihub.

Smith, Kerri. 2011. "Taking aim at free will." *Nature* 477 (7362): 23–25. https://doi.org/10.1038/477023a. https://www.webofscience.com/wos/woscc/full-record/WOS:000294404300011.

Soon, Chun Siong, Marcel Brass, Hans-Jochen Heinze, and John-Dylan Haynes. 2008. "Unconscious determinants of free decisions in the human brain." *Nature Neuroscience* 11: 43–45. https://doi.org/10.1038/nn.2112.

Tennen, Howard, and Jeanette Sharp. 1983. "Control orientation and the illusion of control." *Journal of Personality Assessment* 47 (4): 369–374. https://doi.org/10.1207/s15327752jpa4704_6. https://www.webofscience.com/wos/woscc/full-record/WOS:A1977DE32100001.

Verwijmeren, Thijs, Johan Karemans, Wolfgang Stroebe, and Daniel Wigboldus. 2011. "The workings and limits of subliminal advertising: The role of habits." *Journal of Consumer Psychology* 21 (2): 206–213. https://doi.org/10.1016/j.jcps.2010.11.004. https://www.webofscience.com/wos/woscc/full-record/WOS:000289596700014.

Wegner, Daniel. 2002. *The illusion of conscious will*. MIT Press.

Additional Readings

Aarts, Henk. 2007. "Unconscious authorship ascription: The effects of success and effect-specific information priming on experienced authorship." *Journal of Experimental Social Psychology* 43 (1): 119–126. https://doi.org/10.1016/j.jesp.2005.12.006. https://www.webofscience.com/wos/woscc/full-record/WOS:000243646900011.

Alloy, Lauren, and Lynn Abramson. 1979. "Judgment of contingency in depressed and non-depressed students: Sadder but wiser." *Journal of Experimental Psychology-General* 108 (4): 441–485. https://doi.org/10.1037/0096-3445.108.4.441. https://www.webofscience.com/wos/woscc/full-record/WOS:A1983RE75800007.

Bear, Mark, Barry Connors, and Michael Paradiso. 2020. *Neuroscience: Exploring the brain, enhanced edition: Exploring the brain*. Burlington, MA: Jones & Bartlett Learning.

Blackmore, Susan. 2007. "Mind over matter?" *The Guardian*. https://www.patheos.com/blogs/monkeymind/2007/08/susan-blackmore-on-ben-libet.html.

Fried, Itzhak, Roy Mukamel, and Gabriel Kreiman. 2011. "Internally generated preactivation of single neurons in human medial frontal cortex predicts volition." *Neuron* 69 (3): 548–562. https://doi.org/10.1016/j.neuron.2010.11.045. https://www.webofscience.com/wos/woscc/full-record/WOS:000287609700015.

Hergenhahn, Baldwin Ross, and Tracy Henley. 2013. *An introduction to the history of psychology*. Boston, MA: Cengage Learning.

Karemans, Johan, Wolfgang Stroebe, and Jasper Claus. 2006. "Beyond Vicary's fantasies: The impact of subliminal priming and brand choice." *Journal of Experimental Social Psychology* 42 (6): 792–798. https://doi.org/10.1016/j.jesp.2005.12.002. https://www.webofscience.com/wos/woscc/full-record/WOS:000241366900009.

Kassin, Saul. 2017. "Internalized false confessions." In *Handbook of eyewitness psychology*, 175–192. New York: Psychology Press.

PART V

Most Moral Philosophers Are Not Welfare Consequentialists, so What Are They?

Except for Chapter 4, Parts I–IV were individual-centric. Chapter 4 identified welfare economics as a subset of WC—only consequences matter, and the consequences that matter are the WB (welfare) effects on society's members.

CHAPTER 12

A Primer on Welfare Economics vs. Other Ethics

Quoting Hicks,

> If one is a utilitarian [welfare consequentialist] in philosophy, one has a perfect right to be a utilitarian in one's economics. But if one isn't...one also has the right to an economics free of utilitarian assumptions.[1]

Moral philosophy studies, builds, and compares theories about right and wrong. Are your actions right (morally right) or wrong (morally wrong)? Right as they affect you? Right as they affect others? As noted, an ethic is "a method to test right from wrong." All agree right is right and wrong is wrong but disagree on how both should be defined and measured. Welfare economics (introduced in Chapter 4) determines whether a policy is right or wrong. It is an ethic based on one objective—maximizing societal WB—an objective many reject. As in Chapter 4, I mostly avoid the words "good" and "bad": both can mean many things besides "right/moral" and "wrong/immoral".

An ethic can be as straightforward as a list of specific right and wrong actions (e.g., The Ten Commandments). Such lists can, however, be unsatisfying: they can get long, mine is different from yours, and the question arises, "Why is that on your wrong list?" leaving you to answer,

[1] While Hicks used the word "utilitarian" he meant, in our parlance, WC.

E. R. Morey, *Deconstructing Behavior, Choice, and Well-being*,
https://doi.org/10.1007/978-3-031-36712-0_12

"Just because" or "God said so". So, most non-religious ethics start not with a list of right and wrong actions but with foundational axioms/ assumptions. Then the ethic derives, through deduction, whether an action is right or wrong. Kant, for example, got it down to a single axiom, which he called a *precept*.

Most people (but not necessarily moral philosophers) judge acts as moral or immoral based on overlapping criteria. These include how it makes them feel, religious beliefs, perceived rights, intentions, consequences, whether the act is natural (human nature), process (how it was decided upon), disgust (Yuk!), and inherent value (value for its own sake)—to name a few (see Chapter 4). In this chapter, ethics based on different criteria for judging are contrasted with WC and welfare economics.

An aside: Why be ethical?

This chapter critiques contrasting ethics (proposals for determining right from wrong actions and being the right kind of person). It does not do justice to why one should behave ethically.

Welfare economists, unlike most ethicists, need not worry about the "right kind of person" side of ethics: every economicus must experience their highest-ranked available path, HRAP, whether they happen to be Mother Teresa, Donald Trump, or a sociopath who pleasures in the pains of others—NBT says you are constrained to do what you got to do.

Welfare economists worry about whether behaviors and policies will increase or decrease societal WB. Policies that increase societal WB should be imposed on society's members by making paths that don't either unavailable or unattractive.

In contrast, ethics that admit that the individual can select more, rather than less, ethical actions and live more, rather than less, righteous lives must deal with why an individual would want to.

Many individuals buy into a specific ethic—often a religious ethic. My aunt Edith lived a Christian ethic (King James Bible: Lutheran interpretation). Why? She wanted to be accepted by individuals of her faith and did not want to go to Hell. Faithful Buddhists and others live their lives trying to increase aggregate WB by reducing suffering. Buddhists claim being ethical will lessen the suffering of you and others.

But what about the skeptics: *Ethical Skeptics* are individuals skeptical of all ethical reasoning.[2] What if you don't believe in Hell? Don't accept the Socratic claim that being virtuous is our nature or the Kantian claim that you are duty-bound to behave ethically? Why shouldn't I cheat, lie, and cause mayhem if it increases my WB or fulfills my wants and desires? Why should I try to be the right kind of person?

I start my brief survey of ethics by discussing a few that give WC a role in determining right from wrong but not the only role. Buddhist ethics is an excellent place to start because it, like welfare economics, emphasizes welfare consequences while being quite different from welfare economics. Then I summarize other ethics that give welfare consequences a role but not the only role. Discussed then is the liberalism of John Stuart Mill.

Then I move to ethics where WC plays little or no role in determining right from wrong.

But before I discuss Buddhist ethics, I elaborate a bit more on WC and its particular case, welfare economics.

Processists vs. Consequentialists

In Chapter 4, consequentialism was discussed—WC. Welfare economics judges right from wrong solely based on consequences. An act should be judged based on its outcome, not what caused it (Mill 1879/2004).[3] Hume was an early consequentialist. In contrast, *processists* deem an act right or wrong based on whether the process used to choose was a right or wrong process, independent of the result.

A *welfare consequentialist* would judge the killing of a child by a sadistic pedophile moral if that child were destined to be a Hitler or Pol Pot—millions would have been saved. A processist would disagree, arguing that the intention and the process (the desire to sadistically, sexually

[2] "...to be skeptical about ethics is to be skeptical about the force of ethical considerations" (Williams 1985/2006 and Chapter 3). The individual does not necessarily behave unethically, rather, her behavior is not influenced by ethical considerations. "A skeptic, after all, is merely a skeptic."

[3] Qualifying a bit, a welfare consequentialist would say the process is important if it is enjoyed or disliked. Imagine you love to eat chocolate ice cream and would choose to eat it, but your mother says you must. You might get less WB in the latter case. Economists don't consider the consumption process. We do not say things of the following sort, "We need to take into account that chocolate is enjoyed more if you take your time and concentrate on its taste and mouth feel."

murder) is wrong, making the killing of baby Hitler wrong. As discussed in Chapter 4, processists and welfare consequentialists would disagree about Lucretia's rape.

Kant was a processist believing acts not based on a duty to behave morally are not necessarily of moral value—right is determined by your will/intention to do your duty, not what you actually do.

Processes are typically judged right or wrong based on their fairness or justness. For example, some advocate majority voting because they believe it is a fair and just process for group decision-making. If it happens to increase WB, that's frosting on the cake. If the outcome decreases WB, that does not make the process wrong. The US founding fathers chose majority voting as a way for the people to elect their representatives and for those representatives to make policy. Still, they limited the influence of voting by requiring that decisions can't violate the *US Constitution* or *Bill of Rights*.[4] They rejected majority voting by itself as the best process, though at the same time, judged decisions by a process based on the will of the people superior to decisions by The Monarch and The Church. Implicit is the idea that constitutional policies chosen by voting are right policies.

A process is deemed fair and right if everyone has agreed to it. Picture the Gary Larson cartoon with four desperate, starving individuals in a lifeboat, you, two other humans, and a golden retriever. You all agree to draw straws to determine who will be slaughtered for everyone else's dinner.[5] You lose. An observing processist would have no problem with the outcome. A welfare consequentialist may argue that the dog should be dinner: since dogs have a shorter lifespan than people, there is less future WB to lose.[6]

Most of us judge on both process and outcome. My students believe happiness without effort is wrong—"it is important to earn your WB." In

[4] This statement is not quite correct. There is the Electoral College.

[5] Some might question whether the dog was capable of agreeing to the process. There is a large philosophical literature on dogs in lifeboats. See the debate between Singer and the rights theorist Tom Regan, "Dog in the lifeboat: an exchange," *New York Review of Books*, April 1985. And "Rights, justice and duties to provide assistance," by the environmental philosopher Dale Jamieson.

[6] But eating you, rather than the dog, could increase aggregate WB. The dog might be a happy dog and you might be a depressed individual incapable of experiencing WB. And, while you might be racked with guilt for eating the dog, the dog would not sweat eating you.

1974 the philosopher Robert Nozick cooked up a thought experiment: a virtual-reality pleasure machine—you are wired up and have the experience of living a life of immense enjoyment, all the while sitting in a sealed black box.[7] (We discussed artificial pleasure in Chapter 4.) Most people say they do not want that kind of pleasure. Nozick interprets most peoples' disdain for the machine as a rejection of WC.

Legal systems typically judge guilt and determine punishment based on the consequences (the victim is dead) and the process (how did you kill him and your intent). We excuse you or limit your punishment if your action was an accident, in self-defense, if you are insane, or if it was a mistake (e.g., you reasonably thought the sex was consensual).

Consider the Role of WB in Different Ethics

Ethics differ by how much WB counts for determining right from wrong. Foremost, either WB is important, or it isn't. For example, for a pure processist, it isn't.

If WB does play a role in determining right from wrong, there is the extent of that role. At one extreme, only WB counts; this is WC. In one large subset of WC, the objective is to maximize aggregate WB; Benthamite utilitarianism is a subset of this maximize aggregate WB subset. While welfare economics is a subset of WC, it isn't necessarily a subset of the maximize aggregate WB subset.[8] Chapter 4 labeled ethics where WB is important but not the only determinant of right from wrong as *NotOnlyWB ethics*. Many ethics are NotOnlyWB.

A common view among welfare consequentialists and NotOnlyWB ethicists is that self-awareness conveys a greater capacity for enjoyment and suffering. Additionally, so does the ability to consciously imagine your future and mortality. Pigs have more capacity for enjoyment and suffering

[7] You are suspended in darkness and silence, and your brain is stimulated such that you perceive a happy life. None of my students ever want to live in his Pleasure Machine but have a hard time explaining why saying, "it isn't real happiness." Philosophers use "authentic". In the 1973 Woody Allen movie Sleeper, did Woody and Diane Keaton have orgasms in the Orgasmatron or think they did, but does it matter? It would matter to a processist. As an alternative to the chamber, consider happiness pills (SSRIs)—millions take them daily.

[8] In contrast, the objective of preference utilitarianism is to maximize societal preference-fulfillment, not societal WB. So, if want and desires, and WB don't matchup, preference utilitarianism isn't necessarily an ethic where WB counts.

than spiders and humans more than pigs. This, however, does not imply every human is capable of more WB than every pig. So, even if every human and pig count equally, it might be OK aggregate-WB-wise for humans to eat pigs. Still, it may be even better if we ate dogs—supposing they taste about the same. Dogs are arguably less self-aware, so they have less capacity for suffering. Then again, dog lovers get WB from having a live dog around and would experience a decrease in WB from hearing about humans eating dogs—we should eat the dog and get a pig for a pet?

Most ethicists who care about WB agree that individuals who were once alive and are now dead (George Washington and Smokey the Bear) can't experience WB. The same goes for individual entities for which life was never an option (Rocky the rock and Ralph the refrigerator). Most ethicists seem to believe that plants can't experience WB. [The ethical implications of plant WB are drastic if WB enhancement is the goal. Plants desire to survive, seeking water and nutrients with their roots and energy with their leaves. And they use chemicals to fight off pests. Few ethicists argue that individual plants should have moral standing. Peter Singer would have to write *Plant Liberation*.]

Should All Types of WB Count

Different NotOnlyWB ethics differ in whether some kinds of WB should be excluded when WB is aggregated, excluded because they are false, unreal, or generated by unacceptable behaviors or thoughts. Welfare economists don't parse acceptable and unacceptable bearers of WB; they do consider that behavior can reduce the WB of others: *negative external effects*. And many NotOnlyWB ethicists reject the welfare economists' view that it does not matter how WB is generated. One example is John Harsanyi, mentioned in Chapter 4, who argued that WB derived from hatred and prejudice should not count. Another is the Canadian philosopher and welfarist L.W. Sumner, the author of *Welfare Happiness and Ethics* (1996), who argues that happiness does not necessarily produce WB. His example: imagine that you are happy and have been for years because you have a devoted and loving spouse. And it is all a deceit: he never loved you, and his affairs started right after the honeymoon. Sumner argues that whether your happiness contributes to your WB, and in turn aggregated WB, depends on how you would have reacted if you had found out the truth. If with "C 'est la vie", your past happiness should count. If instead, you would have concluded your life was a farce of your priorities, a life not your own, then your past happiness should not be part of WB aggregation. A welfare economist would say enjoyment is enjoyment and suffering is suffering.

Whose Welfare Counts (Who Gets Moral Standing)?[9]

Related to the issue of what kinds of WB should count is whose WB should count.[10] Jane Austin referring to the casualties in a far-off war,

> How horrible it is to have so many killed, and what a blessing that one cares for none of them (Lord Brabourne edition of Jane Austen's letters)

There are billions of people and animals currently alive or coming down the pike, so who counts is critical for anyone who argues that whether an action is right or wrong depends, at least in part, on how it affects the WB of individuals. For example, to give moral standing to Happy, a specific elephant, would mean what? At a minimum, it would mean her WB should count.[11] Most economists limit moral standing to

[9] Distinguish between moral and legal standing. A party has "legal standing," *locus standi*, if they can bring a suit in court—the party can challenge another party in court. For example, Donald Trump, Tesla, Alabama, and Switzerland have it. Some believe fetuses should have it. Neither legal nor moral standing implies the other. Legal standing is not limited to living things. With a few exceptions, the animate entities with legal standing are humans. Historically, despite being human, women, children, and slaves did not have legal standing. Some countries are pursuing legal standing for non-human animals such as great apes, elephants, and whales (Lawrence Wright 2022).

[10] Introduced in Chapter 4.

[11] You might argue that an elephant's WB is difficult to measure. I agree. I would add it is easier to determine what affects an animal's WB than it is to determine what affects yours: you are more complicated. My dog, Sofie, was a simple creature, rarely deceptive or unclear; she wanted to play ball, run, pounce, and have her stomach rubbed and preferred meat to cheese and cheese to bread. In recent years, lawyers have argued in a few US courts that a few specific animals should be granted legal standing—release from captivity under habeas corpus (a "person" must be released from detention unless a court decides there are legal grounds for the detention). Like in all legal cases, the animals were represented by humans. A famous example is Happy, a lonely elephant residing at the Bronx Zoo (L Wright 2022). In 2020, Judge Allison Tuitt of the New York State Supreme Court, while expressing sympathy for Happy's plight, ruled that she was not a "person," so habeas corpus does not apply.

humans, though not all humans. Recollect that Bentham was species-inclusive, and so is Peter Singer. They argue for including everyone, and anything, who/that can feel pleasure and pain. Other modern ethicists require a degree of self-awareness. As noted in Chapter 2, research suggests dolphins, elephants, humans, and magpies are self-aware.

The Harvard philosopher Christine Korsgaard requires, as did Kant, that to count, one must have the ability to be "aware of the grounds for one's beliefs and choices" and of our "reasons for thinking and acting as we do". To count, we must be able to "step back" and "evaluate". "And this enables me to take responsibility for what I do." because "we are not completely governed" by our instincts, desires, and emotions. She believes only humans have this ability to think about themselves abstractly and symbolically. Kant argued that individuals incapable of taking responsibility for their behavior have no right to moral standing. Other animals do not have this capacity, so our obligations are to humans. Korsgaard argues that because humans are the only moral animals, we have obligations to ourselves and other animals because we share sensations.[12] Aristotle and Aquinas also made purposefulness and the ability to evaluate your actions requirements for moral standing.

That economists limit moral standing to humans is simply an ethical choice.[13] If it's just humans, the enjoyment and suffering animals experience can have influence if their experiences cause human enjoyment or suffering.[14] A few environmental and ecological economists include other sentient creatures; fewer include all individuals who can experience pain.

There is then the question of whether all the individuals in an accepted species should have standing. I imagine most welfare economists would say deciding whether to include or exclude foreigners isn't part of their expertise. So, a fundamental contrast between welfare economists and other welfare consequentialists is welfare economists assert that they have

[12] For more on our duties to animals, see M. Nussbaum on the complexity of animal values. See Nussbaum and Korsgaard on an extended Kantian perspective that animals should not be treated as a mere means-to-an-end, a resource (Korsgaard 2004).

[13] Rawls further limits society to citizens of a sovereign state who "share a commitment to a norm of fairness" (Runciman 2014).

[14] In A.D. 184, The Roman Emperor Commodus (161–192) played gladiator in the Colosseum. "The dens of the amphitheater disgorged at once a hundred lions; a hundred darts from the unerring hand of Commodus laid them dead as they ran raging around the *Arena*." (Edward Gibbon 1776/1906)—all for the amusement of himself and the citizens of Rome.

no expertise, or opinion, as to which humans count. Most NotOnlyWB ethicists argue that all humans should count.

Next, I summarize a few ethics and contrast them with WC and welfare economics. While there is a logic to the order in which I present them, feel free to jump around or skip a few. Try to get a flavor for the diversity. I start with Buddhist ethics because it shares much with welfare economics.

Is Buddhist Ethics Welfare Economics for an Economicus Who Suffers from the Quirks?

Buddhism is an ethic in that it outlines how you should live your life and behave toward others. It also lays out criteria for distinguishing between right and wrong behaviors—for most occasions. The following is based on my understanding of secular Buddhism, sometimes referred to as humanistic Buddhism.[15] My emphasis is on how secular Buddhism is both like and different from WC and welfare economics. For Buddhists, welfare consequences are critical, and right-process (*Right View* and *Right Thought*) is a path to increasing WB (reducing ill-being). WB is the goal, and right-process is how you get there.

While increasing WB is right; the emphasis is on reducing *dukkha* (suffering, unsatisfactoriness). [Chapter 6, the section *Decreasing Your Ill-Being by Being Less Reactive*, summarized the Buddhist path to increasing an individual's WB (reducing their ill-being).] Here we turn to the WB of a group consisting of all beings that can experience pain, where the WB of all counts equally. Quoting from a Buddhist text

> Through actions of body, speech, and mind, the Bodhisattva sincerely makes a continuous effort to stop all present and future pain and suffering, and to produce present and future pleasure and happiness, for all beings (Śāntideva as translated by Charles Goodman 2014)

[15] Whether Historical Buddhism is a religion depends on how you define religion. Traditionally, Buddhism has monks, monasteries, rituals, and a belief in reincarnation, but it has always been non-theist: there is no god, or gods, that created us and oversee us. Reincarnation was the norm in Classical India. Unlike, Christianity, beliefs are questioned rather than taken on faith. Taken alone, Buddhist ethics is not a religion. Many individuals who self-identify as religious Buddhists, Christians, Jews, or Muslims behave immorally as Buddhism would define the term. A current example of bad behavior is Buddhists in Myanmar.

This sounds like the utilitarianism of Bentham. But the process, including the intention, gets more emphasis, and intention sometimes trumps the WB consequences in determining right from wrong. According to legend, a follower generously gave the Buddha food. It killed him; it was spoiled. Dying, he insisted that the act was right because the giver did not know the food was contaminated (Goodman). Given that both WB and intent matter, Buddhists are NotOnlyWB ethicists.

While suffering and unsatisfactoriness exist and not all of it can be eliminated (bad shit happens), there is an emphasis on reducing the unnecessary suffering of you and other creatures. As summarized in Chapter 6, your ill-being will diminish if you understand impermanence and no-self. This will reduce your cravings and make you react more appropriately to the remaining ones. Thousands of years before Berridge found separate neural pathways for wanting/desiring and liking, Buddhists built their ethic on the distinction: asserting that seeking and getting what you want isn't the way to greater WB. Buddhists believe the default and wrong criterion is to base your ordering on wants and desires rather than liking: Assumption 9b rather than 9a:

Assumption 9a: *An economicus's ordering of paths is based on its WB (well-being) ...*

Assumption 9b: *An economicus's ordering of paths is based on its wants and desires.*

Buddhism outed *loss aversion* thousands of years before Kahneman and Tversky labeled the term. Buddhist impermanence (everything is impermeant: everything will be lost) makes loss central to suffering. Given loss aversion, if one wants to minimize suffering, avoid the lesser gains associated with acquiring things. Buddhism recognizes that our (false) sense of self affects how we value what we possess and how what we possess affects our sense of self (ownership/self-effects). It argues that these associations lead to false choosing and, in turn, suffering (less WB).[16] As discussed in Chapters 7 and 8, while *loss aversion* and *ownership/self*-effects cause false choosing, neither of these common quirks violates Assumption 9a.

[16] According to Buddhism, this aspect of false choosing is based on one's sense of self and the constructs one uses to assess one's self-image (*self-construal*, see Chapter 9). False choosing is caused by independent self-construal (the Western tendency). If the notion of a permanent and unchanging self is abandoned for *no-self* (*anata* in Pali) ownership/self-effects diminish.

As noted in Chapter 6, a difference with NBT is that the Buddhist view of human behavior permits the individual to forsake their highest-ranked available path, HRAP, violating Assumption 7 of NBT. While the individual is inclined to choose their HRAP in terms of wants and desires (Assumption 9b), they are not required to. Neither must they choose their HRAP in terms of their personal WB. So, Buddhist ethics includes how to live an ethical life.

Buddhist practice is geared toward affecting the WB of the practitioner and others. First, practice is geared to the practitioner learning that constantly reacting to wants and desires is a route to less rather than more personal WB. Why? Because we are loss averse, and everything acquired will be lost. Recommendations for increasing your WB: like what you have while you have it, don't buy things on credit that will be repossessed (you will suffer loss aversion), don't pursue and obtain things and relationships simply because you desire them, and be aware of impermanence.

Buddhism, like the Bible, has rules for how to behave toward others (refrain from killing (humans and other creatures), stealing, sexual misconduct, lying, and drunkenness). Rather than obeying them to please God, the Buddhist view is that following them will increase your WB and the WB of others.[17] Example, lying stresses the liar; besides, lying causes trouble (sounds like Epicurus). It is recognized that behaving in a Buddhist manner is something to aspire to, not a commandment without exception.

To the extent that an individual can increase their WB without decreasing the WB of others, doing so is Buddhist morally preferred. While Pareto improvements, PIs, are not part of Buddhist terminology, it seems they would advocate for them to the extent they are possible. Complicating, not negating, is whether your WB is separable from mine.

Note the adjectives "your" and "mine": no-self means there is no real you or me. Rather than constant and enduring, you are your current thoughts. And they are only weakly connected to your past and future thoughts and experiences, much as your experiences are linked to the experiences of other creatures. Suffering becomes less personal; the

[17] Their purpose is to increase WB—akin to *rule utilitarianism*, so unlike the Ten Commandments where the objective is fulfilling God's rules. Religious Buddhists who believe in reincarnation might worry that treating others badly will generate bad karma, causing them to come back as an animal with low WB, a reason why a Buddhist who has not achieved Enlightenment might behave ethically.

connection between you and your future "self" is no stronger than the link between you and others. The effects of your actions on your future self are no more relevant than their effects on others, both now and in the future.[18] So, suffering is ownerless for the enlightened, making their objective to decrease aggregate suffering (increase aggregate WB).[19]

Ethics is a progression for Buddhists: first, you realize that the path you desire and select causes you unnecessary suffering; you then learn to order paths differently by abstracting from your desires. Farther along the progression, your self-concept expands and evaporates: you become less of a permanent individual, and suffering becomes ownerless. Ideally, and eventually, you can't separate your WB from the aggregate WB of all living creates, so live your life to maximize aggregate WB by reducing suffering—and you like living this way.

In contrast to NBT, Buddhism teaches that you can, with effort, choose your ordering of paths. Hopefully, it converges to a Buddhist ordering: an ordering not based on attachment to desires but based instead on impermanence and ignoring the self—it would skew toward an ordering based on an integrated and aggregate view of WB.

Buddhism is consistent with emotion-specific orderings and the emotional empathy-gap (see Chapter 8): part of impermanence is the impermanence of your current emotional state. This means your ordering is impermanent, which violates the spirit of Assumption 4. In addition, Chapter 6 argued that the Buddhist view of humans violates Assumption 7. Other than those two, no other NBT assumptions are violated. While

[18] Economists use discount rates to mathematically specify the extent to which you discount your future WB relative to your current WB. They don't consider your discount rate for the WB of others relative to your personal WB. [If asked, they might suggest it is, of course, infinity.] In contrast, a Buddhist might argue that the two rates should be the same because your future self is not more connected with you than you are to others. It isn't clear to me whether a Buddhist would discount their future WB more or less than a typical Western consumer. Impermanence and lack of self suggest a high rate of discount—the older you isn't the same self you are today—so why worry about him? On the other hand, a concern for the WB that others experience now and, in the future, might suggest a low personal discount rate. Robert Wright's Chapter 7 in *Why Buddhism is True* mentions personal discount rates but does not discuss what rate a Buddhist would use, rather the chapter discusses how one's discount rate can be manipulated. I continue to look for articles on discounting and Buddhism.

[19] Buddhism argues that benevolence follows, logically, from the premise of no-self, but not everyone buys their logic (see, e.g., Siderits 2019).

it does not violate an NBT Assumption, the emotional empathy-gap does lead to *flawed choosing*.

You could be a true-blue economicus (adhere to all of the NBT Assumptions) and follow a Buddhist path. Your ordering would be different from that of the average Western consumer: it would be a Buddhist ordering based on interdependent, rather than independent, self-construal. That is OK because NBT is silent on the source of your ordering, and welfare economics is OK with any ordering. You would view work and leisure as two sides of the same coin (the concept of *Right Livelihood*). Work, done correctly, would be a way toward greater WB. This is quite different from the assumption that having more is the way to greater WB and that work is simply the unpleasantness you must endure to consume more. Right livelihood is described as having a job where you have goals to achieve that are within your reach, though not easy; you have autonomy and responsibility; you are part of a greater whole, a team.[20]

Higher-ranked paths would involve fewer negative *external effects* and more positive ones. Given the Buddhist view of no-self, "external" is not the best adjective (external to what?). Paths that involve making or using alcohol, drugs, or guns would not be high in your ordering because the Buddhist view is that their production and consumption produce suffering. They would also include producing and eating meat, arguing that killing and eating animals is neither good for them nor us.[21] In this regard, Buddhism predates both Bentham and Peter Singer, the names that come up if asked to name a utilitarian.

In Chapter 6, flow was described as a type of happiness: pursuing goals and activities that are challenging but not too challenging, causing you to enter a state of flow (losing your sense of self and time, being in the zone, a feeling retrospectively described as happiness). Producing flow experiences is consistent with NBT and welfare economics, and Buddhism advocates for its production. Unlike the Western concept of flow, which

[20] Your highest-ordered available path would involve work, but not 24/7, and it would not involve you choosing the available path with the highest income, unless your plan were to give much of it away.

[21] Tibetan Buddhists, including the Dali Lama, eat meat. On the high plains of Tibet, there was not much to eat in the winter, just sheep and yaks (Goodman 2014). Now that more food groups are available, some Tibetan Buddhists are advocating for a more vegetarian diet.

can be achieved by activities that only produce WB for you, Buddhist flow is achieved by flow activities that enhance aggregate WB. Playing a video game alone can produce Western but not Buddhist flow. Online games with hundreds or thousands interacting are another matter.

So, is Buddhist ethics welfare economics for economici who suffer from the endowment effect and other common psychological quirks? Not quite. But if the ethical objective is to maximize aggregate WB, and if one admits flawed choosing caused by common quirks (loss aversion, ownership/self-effects, salience effects, empathy-gaps), the policy recommendations of the two ethics align.

John Stuart Mill: A Backward-Looking Utilitarian and a Forward-Looking Liberalist

I was taught that he, Bentham, and James Mill (John's father) founded what I called in Chapter 4 Benthamite utilitarianism. That characterization is incorrect and disserves both Benthamite utilitarianism and Mill. Over his life, Mill argued as both a utilitarian (Mill 1879/2004) and a liberalist (Mill 1859/2011), but neither view requires the other. Mill suffered from a dissociate-personality disorder: there was Utilitus Mill, the back-looking devoted son of James Mill and the godson of Bentham, and there was the more passionate forward-looking Liberace Mill, committed to liberty; the two mostly coexisted without openly condemning the other, but rarely appeared together in public, and Liberace appeared more as Mill aged (Fig. 12.1).

Mill wrote *On Liberty* eight years before *Utilitarianism*. *Utilitarianism*, however, was a look back, "the ideas contained in *On Liberty* underpinned his future actions as both a politician and public intellectual.... *On Liberty* illuminated his future" (Reeves 2008). First, I present Utilitus Mill, then Mill's liberalist ethic.

Utilitus Mill, the Utilitarian?

For Utilitus Mill, right behavior, typically not achieved, is directed toward increasing aggregate happiness. And such behavior can be inconsistent

Fig. 12.1 Liberace—not Liberace Mill

with maximizing personal happiness. Mill was raised as a Benthamite utilitarian but did not write *Utilitarianism* until late in life.[22] In the view of his modern biographer, Mill wrote it as a tribute to his father and Bentham, not because of any great passion for Benthamite utilitarianism.

[22] Mill's childhood was tough: rigorously educated in an "intellectual petri dish" by his father and godfather; it resulted in a nervous breakdown. They hoped to make him the torch bearer for utilitarianism (Reeves 2008).

> From Mill's perspective, utilitarianism marked an end rather than a beginning. In it [Utilitarianism] he finally laid to rest the ghosts of his father and Bentham. The essay looked backwards, offering a final settling of his Benthamite accounts, and scarcely featured in his thoughts or actions in the remaining dozen years of his life... Utilitarianism illustrated Mill's past... (Reeves)

But in the honoring, Mill fundamentally deviated from Benthamite utilitarianism. Bentham argued all pains and pleasures were commensurable, a univariate cardinal concept—to judge the morality of a policy, one only had to put all its pain and pleasure effects on the correct scale and see which way the needle moves. Mill mucked up this simplicity by stating that pleasures generated by more valuable activities (intellectual pursuits) should count more than trashy ones, making his measure of WB multidimensional.[23,24] Bentham utilitarianism is a single metric for judging activities. In contrast, Mill introduced a second qualitative element into the equation, raising the thorny question of who was to say which activities produce more valuable pleasures. Mill preferred reading Socratic dialogues to having sex with strangers, but it is hard to find grounds for why Mill's pleasures should be the valuable pleasures (Reeves). For Mill, like Bentham, pleasure was a cardinal concept, so possibly comparable across individuals.

According to Mill, a virtuous man is a man who, with some success (intent is immaterial), increases net happiness, not necessarily the man who maximizes his own.

> The standard isn't the agent's own greatest happiness, but the greatest amount of happiness altogether. (Mill 1879/2004)

[23] Mill found "superiority of mental over bodily pleasures...It is better to be a human being dissatisfied than a pig satisfied; better to be Socrates dissatisfied than a fool satisfied." Would a foolish pig agree? Disagreeing with Mill, the Greek philosopher Aristippus (435–336 BC) claimed bodily pleasures are better. In 1823 Bentham, under a pseudonym, argued that the pleasures of male-with-male sex should be included in the felicity calculus, so such acts should not be illegal (Bentham 2013) Not Paul, but Jesus: Volume III.

[24] For Mill, mental pleasures are cheaper and safer than the bodily sort. Compare home in bed reading Homer to having sex with a prostitute in Hyde Park, the latter a popular Victorian pastime. "In 1857, the Metropolitan Police estimated that the capital contained 2,825 brothels and 8,600 prostitutes. Evening visitors to the Haymarket were treated to what was popularly dubbed the 'Haymarket march past'. Dostoevsky, in 1862, commented on 'mothers bringing their young daughters to do business' (Reeves)."

For Mill, a human was free to choose any available path, so not constrained to experience their highest-ranked available path, HRAP (Assumption 7 of NBT).

Freedom to Choose: Liberace Mill and Liberalism

In contrast, John Stuart Mill's *liberalism* judges an action or policy as right if it gives the individual more freedom and wrong if it restricts it: "pursuing our own good in our own way" (Mill 1859/2011). The classic work is his *On Liberty*. Liberalism isn't libertarianism. [Mill's role for the government goes far beyond what U.S. Republicans would accept—his advocacy of social programs has caused some to label him a socialist.]

From their license plates, we know New Hampshirers want to Live free or die.

Liberalism differs from WC and welfare economics in that individual liberty is right, even if the individual uses it to rain misery on his head. Summarizing *On Liberty*, you should be given the freedom to flourish in the manner of your choosing unless your actions harm others—a moral life is a life the individual chooses and should be allowed and encouraged to choose. Autonomy—literally self-governing—gets closer to what Mill meant than the word "liberty." When talking to a French correspondent, Mill used the phrase "l'autononomie de l'individu" to describe the central theme of *On Liberty* (Reeves). [Applied to non-human, non-domestic animals, liberalism is living and dying in their natural state.]

Liberalism as an ethic gives precedence to freedom—a process for achieving things—rather than consequences—what the individual achieves. If an economist assumes individuals are incapable of acting contrary to their WB, as economists typically do, giving you more freedom can't reduce your WB. And the line between liberalism and WC blurs.

For the modern Tea Party and a subset of Trump supporters, freedom (fewer restrictions on their choices) is the primitive measure of right. Welfare economists also believe more choice is better than less, but not for its own sake, but because (1) more choice allows you more opportunities to better yourself, and (2) economicus always takes full advantage of every opportunity to better himself.

But what does it mean to say you should be given the liberty to flourish unless your actions harm others, in which case they should not be permitted? In the language of economics, when does a *negative external effect* (an act that directly and negatively affects others) rise to a harm? Quoting

> That principle is that the sole end for which mankind are warranted, individually or collectively, in interfering with the liberty of action of any of their number is self-protection... That is, the only purpose for which power can be exercised over any member of a civilised society, against his will, is to prevent harm to others. His own good, either physical or moral, isn't a sufficient warrant." Mill (1859/2011)

Strictly interpreting the term "self-protection," it would seem that Mill would judge the internalization of many externalities a violation of his principle.[25] But, reading further, Mill broadens the principle:

> Those principles, I contend, authorize the subjection of individual spontaneity to external control, only in respect to those actions of each, which concern the interests of other people. ... Acts, of whatever kind, which, without justifiable cause, do harm to others, may be, and in the more important cases absolutely require to be, controlled by the unfavorable sentiments, and, when needful by the active inference of mankind. The liberty of the individual must be thus far limited; he must not make himself a nuisance to other people.

Mill excludes from his principle children and "barbarians." You get a better feel for what Mill considered harmful through his examples. "Fornication...must be tolerated" meaning prostitution should be legal (Reeves). Reacting to the argument that society can limit drinking simply because it decreases security and weakens and demoralizes society, Mill angrily responded that if this is harm, then we would all, wrongly, have an interest in everyone's "moral, intellectual and physical perfection" (Reeves). So, if I get drunk and offend you with my free speech and offensive behavior, Mill would have said I am at liberty to do so, but if I get in my car drunk and run you over, I have crossed the line.

[25] *An externality* is an *external* effect that is being produced at an inefficient amount. If the external effect is produced at its efficient amount, and that amount is greater than zero, there is an external effect but no externality. For example, second-hand cigarette smoke is an external effect (a negative one), but if it is regulated or taxed, so the efficient amount of second-hand is produced, there is still an external effect, but no externality.

I am tempted but hesitant to summarize that for Liberace Mill, your freedom ethically trumps your WB in the sense that more personal freedom and less WB trumps less freedom and more WB. And—it is OK to restrict your freedom if it leads you to harm others less, keeping in mind that for Mill, many reductions in the WB of others don't rise to harm.

The US Declaration of Independence conveys the right to life and liberty but only the right to pursue happiness, suggesting that the founding fathers thought liberty trumped happiness. Another interpretation is that the founders believed that giving you more liberty would always increase your WB or, at a minimum, generate more WB than if the Monarch and Church were calling the shots. The research discussed in Parts II and III finds that the founding fathers had it wrong if they assumed you and I always know what's in our best interests.

Consider the following thought experiment on the freedom to choose: You can live in World X or Y. In World X, you choose your highest-ranked available path. In World Y, all is the same, except the government forces you to consume the path of goods and services you would have chosen in X: your eats and drinks are the same, and what you would have chosen, but you don't have the freedom to not eat and drink them. Which world would you choose, and why? It depends on (1) how much you directly value choice[26] and (2) how the freedom to choose your experiences affects your enjoyment of specific goods and services. Mill, the liberalist, would judge World X better than Y, even if you would prefer being told what to do: Mill asserts that thinking and choosing are of inherent value. Mill does not address (2): the issue of how an ice-cream cone tastes might depend on whether you choose it or were required to eat it, given you would have chosen it. Economists ignore the possibility that the enjoyment you get from consuming a good is influenced by how you came by it. Economists don't talk much about choice being valued for its own sake, independent of what is chosen, but there isn't a thing in NBT that precludes it either. Thinking back to the path definition (in Chapter 2) and Assumption 9a

> Assumption 9a: *An economicus's ordering of paths is based on its WB (well-being) ...*

[26] This issue is discussed by the economist Frank Hahn (1925–2013) who argued that the exercise of choice might enhance WB.

Freedoms (or their lack) are components of every path and could be a critical determinant of how you order paths. For example, if freedom were paramount to your WB, you would order paths with more freedoms above those with fewer, independent of their other components. Or, more nuanced, while appreciating freedom, you may be willing to trade away a particular one for more ice-cream cones or less global warming. Liberace Mill would say paths where you have more freedom are ethically better for you, even if you don't think so. It is a juxtaposition: freedom to choose is right for you—but you are not free to choose ice cream over freedom.

Philosophers disagree on how freedom/liberty influences WB. Foundationally, one view is while specific freedoms exist (e.g., free speech or the right to an abortion), freedom itself is not well-defined. Related is what it means to have more or less freedom: maybe on Path j, Fred would be freer to speak than on Path k, but on k, he would be freer to drink alcohol and divorce. So, on which path is Fred freer? An answer necessarily requires that, for Fred, all types of freedoms are WB-comparable. And while economists don't distinguish between *freedom* and *freedom-to-choose*, others do.

Nevertheless, suppose freedom is a meaningful concept; how does more (less) freedom contribute to more (or less) WB?[27] Adding to the set of available paths increases the probability of a newly available path with more WB. Some argue that this is the only way freedom affects WB—indirectly. Mills is not in this camp.

Others believe freedom can also enhance WB simply because it comes with more available paths, even if none of these WB-dominate. You would experience more WB if you selected Path j from the set of paths, X, than if you had selected that same Path j from the set subset $X - \Upsilon$. Why might this be? The more alternatives available to you, the more influence you have on others, and you like the power and responsibility? For example, you want to marry, and if Wanda is willing, you will marry her. Consider three cases: just Wanda is willing, Wanda and Shirley are both willing, or Wanda, Shirley, and Bob are. All else constant, you would rank the Wanda/Shirley/Bob path highest and the just Wanda path lowest because the more paths available, the more you can say "No" and "to be responsible for that fact that 'no' was said" (Thomas Hurka 1987). "The more times we can say no, the more impact we will have on the world when

[27] More freedom could also decrease WB.

we choose, and, hence, the value there is in our situation" (Ian Carter 1995). You get WB from having Shirley and Bob as marriage options even though you would marry neither if Wanda is available—because you have more influence, particularly on Shirley and Bob. [I leave it to you to decide whether this argument is consistent with the NBT Assumptions.] When I wrote this paragraph, Biden was sworn in as the 46th US President. For Biden supporters who would never have voted for Trump, having Trump on the ballot allowed them to not just vote for Biden but also to vote against Trump.

Another view is that freedom is a primary type of WB: it has independent value and, possibly, ***unconditional value***. "Our freedoms have value independently of the value we attach to the particular things they leave us free to do" (Carter 1995). Moreover, freedom has unconditional value if paths with more freedom are always ranked higher than paths with less—paths are lexicographically ordered by degree of freedom ("Live Free or Die.").

Another view is freedom is a bearer of a type of WB, not WB-commensurable with other kinds of WB.

A familiar view is freedom is good "just because"—no explanation needed.

Liberace Mill would embrace some of these views, but maybe, like me, he would have trouble drawing the boundaries between them. He might have argued that freedom is not a component of WB but is still important.

Freedom and its role have drastic implications for governance, particularly in our current climate of Trumpism, the pandemic, and the right-wing view that liberty is paramount and at risk.[28]]

Neither Enjoyment, Suffering, nor Freedom is Primary (Deontological/duty Ethics)

Numerous ethics reject determining the right or wrong of an action by how individuals are affected. They argue right and wrong aren't defined by increases or decreases in society's WB, or by whether it gives its members more freedom, but by God, or the supreme leader, or by what

[28] Reading on how freedom affects WB and one's life include Ronald Dworkin (1979), Rawls (1971/1999), Raz (1986), Hurka (1987), Will Kymlicka (1990/2002), Sen (1988), and Carter (1995).

Fig. 12.2 Immanuel Kant

is natural, or by what provides an evolutionary advantage, or by rights, or by doing one's duty. Start with duty.

Kantian Ethics: The Universality Principle and More

Kant's ***universality principle***, the bedrock of his ethic, is that your actions are right if you want everyone to behave like you and wrong if you would not—you would be happy to make your behavior the law.[29] For example, your stealing is right only if you agree with a law requiring everyone to steal. You have a duty to behave according to his universality principle—Kantian ethics is duty-based (***deontological***: from the Greek words for duty (*deon*) and study (*logos*) (Fig. 12.2).

Kant's universality principle is similar to but not the Golden Rule ("Do unto others as you would have them do unto you."). The convicted

[29] "Act only according to that maxim whereby you can at the same time will that it should become a universal law." This is the first formulation of Kant's *Categorical Imperative*, a commandment/imperative with no exceptions for how to live your life.

murderer advocates the Golden Rule when he says to the judge, "Sentence me as you would have me sentence you." But he is violating the universality principle—even the murderer does not want everyone murdering.

Kant would want us to agree/contract to abide by his universality principle. Kantian ethics is a type of *moral contract*: society's members enter into contracts/agreements, often implicit, and behaviors that violate these contracts are wrong.[30]

Kantian ethics rejects right from wrong based on consequences. So increased WB can be moral but isn't universally moral.

Kant considered his universality principle an obligation all rational beings have an ethical duty to follow. It is the sole foundation of morality and is derived from pure reason and logic, or so he thought. It is not inferred by observing the world (according to Kant, observation can tell us how people act but not how they should act). And it is derived without regard to its influence on the world. Kant was incorrect about it being the result of pure reason and logic.

Kant is the guy who wrote,

> Fiat justitia, pereat mundus (Let justice be done, though the world perish)

For Kant, intention was paramount, and for an action to be unequivocally moral, it had to be based on the intent to do one's duty. Kissing your partner is a moral act only if you and the partner do it out of a sense of duty—how it makes the two of you feel does affect whether the kiss is moral or immoral. [This sounds close to what Sunday school taught me about sex. You have a duty to procreate, but it being fun does not make it right or wrong].

Not everyone has duties, only rational, self-regulating, autonomous individuals. So non-human animals are duty-free and unable to act morally or immorally.

Kantian ethics and ethics based on WB judge on opposing criteria. It is difficult for economists to get their heads around Kantian ethics: whether

[30] A modern version of right and wrong based on a Kantian-type moral contract is Thomas Scanlon's 2000 book, *What We Owe to Each Other?* The premise is that an action or principle is right if can be justified to reasonable others; it is a rule of behavior we should be able to agree on. See the section "Contract Morality".

an action is right or wrong isn't based on its effect on WB, and consequences either don't matter or are secondary. For a Kantian, a policy that increases the WB of some and decreases the WB of no one (a PI) isn't necessarily a moral improvement. Economists need to know that people believe people have duties and should fulfill them. There are more living Kantian philosophers than welfare consequentialists. Haidt and others find that duty-based morality is more common among conservatives than political liberals.

Kantian Choice Theory

A kanticus is similar to an economicus, except it has a superpower, the ability to not choose its HRAP. Both have a complete ordering of paths based on WB. Like an economicus, it gets to select a path from the available set, so both have free will or not (see Part IV). However, a kanticus can voluntarily constrain itself from choosing its HRAP. It does so based on self-imposed rules/duties: if you are a kanticus, you can choose to resist your own WB and desires. So, "one's preferences are not a reliable guide to proper decision-making" (White).

To predict the behavior of a kanticus, the model needs to account for duties, responsibilities, and obligations, even if self-imposed. Kanticus isn't a slave to its ordering—it can act contrary to it.

Of course, an economist can dismiss the distinction between economicus and kanticus, asserting that self-imposed duties and rules are simply determinants of your ordering. We can get away with this because we are vague about "preference", so we can argue along the following lines. "Linda likes to abuse puppies but does not because she feels it is wrong, and this feeling of wrongness is sufficiently unpleasant that her chosen path never includes puppy abuse." Or, "She is afraid that if she abuses puppies, she will end up in Hell where she would burn forever, which would hurt like hell." That's the thing about NBT; there are no behaviors inconsistent with it. If I abuse, it is because my HRAP includes abusing, and if I don't, the same is true, even if I would enjoy the experience. This becomes circular nonsense. For economists, my decision to not abuse can't simply be because I have decided it is unacceptable behavior.

The Kantian economist Mark White posits a behavior model with two distinct orderings of paths: one reflecting only your inclinations, the other with the caveat that paths that violate the universality principle are not included. The latter is consistent with doing your duty. If your will is strong, you choose to use your duty-based ordering. If your will is weak, you use the ordering based only on your inclinations. White defines the strength of your will as the probability you behave consistently with your duty-based ordering. Moral is choosing based on your duty-based ordering.

Two Kants

Arguably, there are two Kants: the duty-based, textbook Kant, as just described, and a more human, caring Kant. The above Kant of Wikipedia and college-classroom fame can be pretty unappealing ("cares more about rules than about ends". "eschews all feelings", "insists on duty for its own (incomprehensible) sake", "cold fish" (Uleman). He comes across as someone who does not care about people. Uleman's book on Kant's morality describes the more human Kant.

> The interpretation of Kant's moral theory that I [Uleman] offer cuts against the grain of interpretations that emphasize Kant's commitments to formal rules and rationalism... Kant was deeply committed to a kind of formalism, and was deeply committed to rationality. But if these commitments are overemphasized, or emphasized in the wrong ways, we are left with a view that is less engaging and more academic than Kant's...Kant does insist that diverse human aims and ends, to be morally acceptable, must conform to the 'form of universality'—that is, that they may be pursued only if they could be universally endorsed. Described thus, Kantian morality does not endorse any particular aim or end—it just insists that we pursue our aim and ends only if they pass a formal test. Because it does not dictate particular aims or ends, Kantian morality seems to endorse good human lives lived across circumstances and historical time and place: it seems pluralistic and inclusive. Because it insists on universal acceptability, it seems to respect the value of hearing from everyone, or at least of imaginatively trying to; by putting yourself in other people's shoes (would it be OK with everyone): it seems deeply democratic...

Kant

> Demands much more than accord between ends and aim and a certain form; he demands that we embrace, as intrinsically and ultimately good, the free rational human will itself. Embracing the free rational will as good means organizing our individual and collective lives in ways that actively honor this good. As a consequence, Kantian morality rejects projects, the ultimate object of which is to serve God or to alleviate material suffering: these projects, for Kant, unacceptably subjugate free rational will to other ends…The free will that Kant values is one that is fundamentally legible to others, and committed to a radically shared rationality…emphasizing the aim or end—free rational willing.

The primitive for this more humanistic Kant isn't the universality principle; it is *free rational-willing*: doing one's duty and following the universality principle is the collective path to free rational-willing. Free rational-willing is Uleman's term for Kantian autonomy and is the heart of his morality. Since economists are more comfortable with the word choosing, they might change her phrase to *free rational-choosing*: people are rational and, in Kant's view, should live in a world where they can freely choose their actions, including the ability to not adhere to their liking nor wanting ordering. And a will is a real thing that resides in every human adult, the thing that chooses an alternative and then causes you to do what it takes to experience that alternative; it is the choosing center—willing is choosing. Your will is free if it gets to choose "on grounds that are its own, and not on grounds given to it by something or someone external to it" (Uleman).[31]

The Kantian ethic shares a primitive similar to the primitive in Millsian liberalism (free choice by rational individuals should be encouraged). However, it differs in that Kant believed the way to achieve this was for each individual to rationally choose to subjugate their freedom to their

[31] Kant relied on dualism to argue that your will can be free (Uleman). He viewed the body as physical, controlled by the laws of physics. And he believed that if what you will is determined by the laws of physics, what you will isn't freely willed. At the same time, he believed that if what you will is constrained by reason, your will isn't free. [For example, if constrained by reason, you can't freely will that three plus three equals eight.] Taken alone, these beliefs imply that the will is not free. However, this argument is materialist. Kant got his will freed by imagining will isn't something subject to reason or the laws of physics; it is a spiritual thing—the opposite of materialism. An analogy is God's Will which isn't subject to anything; otherwise, it would not be God's Will.

duty to the universality principle. This is the logical way for everyone to consider that their actions affect others. You might think of it as Kant's universal way of internalizing externalities.

Kantian ethics, like many ethics, is dependent on man being rational and having free will, both of which are questionable. For more on Kantian ethics from an economics perspective, see *Kantian Ethics and Economics* by Mark White.

My Rights (and Your Duty to Uphold My Rights)

Rights Theory judges individual behavior assuming the individual has certain rights: your action is moral if you had the right to take that action, wrong if you lack the right, and wrong if your action violates the rights of another.

A *right* is an entitlement, a prescribed protection (Kramer). For example, a "right to life" means your life is protected from assaults by others.[32] If you have a right to life, others have a duty to not take your life. Rights impose duties on others: you must uphold my rights. Advocates of a specific right emphasize it, playing down the duty side. Rights are typically thought of as unconditional in that the right holder has the right under all circumstances.

An action is moral if the actor has the right to do it, even if it makes everyone miserable. And I behave morally if I dutifully uphold your rights, even if doing so makes me miserable.

Rights are asserted: human rights, women's rights, right to life, abortion rights, civil rights, the right to remain silent, and even property rights—these are rights of individuals. [In contrast, environmental ethicists assert every species has a right to exist (not go extinct), a right conveyed on the species, not on any member of the species.[33]] Rights often conflict, for example, "The Right-to-life" versus "A Women's Right to Choose." A standard view among rights theorists is that rights are primitive and do not require justification. In this view, a right that exists

[32] A right, a protection, can be contrasted with a *liberty*, another type of entitlement: a liberty is a prescribed freedom, for example, a freedom to sing in the shower. It is a lack of a duty; as in, I am not duty-bound to keep my mouth shut in the shower.

[33] Giving a non-human species the right to exist, independent of human welfare, and in an environment suited to their species, has drastic implications for humans. If this right exists, then humans have a duty to preserve the species, an obligation. Humans would be required to fulfill this obligation before they worry about their own WB. Such a duty perspective on animals is alien to welfare economists.

because it achieves a goal isn't a right. Despite that, there is a compulsion to justify a right. Justifications include God, the Laws of Nature, the interests of society, and "Just because".

The most influential early account of rights theory is that of the seventeenth-century British philosopher John Locke; he argued that the laws of nature mandate that we should not harm anyone's life, health, liberty, or possessions. For him, these are our natural rights, given to us by God. Following Locke, the United States Declaration of Independence, authored by Thomas Jefferson, recognizes three foundational rights: life, liberty, and the pursuit of happiness. Jefferson and other rights theorists maintained that we deduce other more specific rights from these, including property rights, movement, speech, and religious expression.

Four features are often associated with moral rights. First, rights are natural, not invented or created by governments. Second, they are universal insofar as they do not vary by country. Third, they are equal in the sense they are the same for all people, irrespective of gender, race, or handicap. Fourth, they are inalienable, which means I can't hand over my rights to another person, such as giving up my right to freedom by selling myself into slavery for tuition money for the kids.

Suppose the right is bestowed by God or the laws of nature (a natural right). There is no presumption that exercising a right makes the right holder better off or that violating someone else's right makes them worse off—rights are right, and violating one is wrong. Bentham considered natural rights "nonsense on stilts".

Consider property rights—the right to possess and control. Most economists are big fans, but why? Locke considered the right to possess (have possessions) a natural right bestowed by God. Economists don't claim the right to own property is God-given but argue that property rights are rights justified by consequence, a WB justification, not a God or law-of-nature justification, so not an actual right. Economists are not rights theorists; they think about the efficient amounts of things, not absolute rights. For example, there is an efficient amount of free speech, likely less or more than the current amount.

Your right to free speech and your property rights constrain me—I can't consume what you own unless you offer. Rights typically increase the choice set of the right holder and decrease the choice sets of everyone else. Economists could model behavior with rights as a constraint: choose the highest-ranked path subject to the constraint that all include free speech.

Millsian liberalists abhor unconditional rights except for the right to choose. The principle of liberalism is the right to choose to live as you please, presuming your choices don't cause too much harm, so it is a conditional right. The right to liberty is problematic because I have less liberty if I must uphold your right to liberty.

Complicating: there are two views on rights (what they do for the right holder): *will theory* and *interest theory*. Both are problematic:

> The function of a right is to give its holder control over another's duty…will theorists believe that all rights confer control over others' duties to act in particular ways…To have a right is to have the ability to determine what others may and may not do, and so to exercise authority over a certain domain of affairs. (Wenar 2011)
>
> Interest theorists maintain that the function of a right is to further the right-holder's interests. An owner has a right, according to interest theory, not because owners have choices, but the ownership makes owners better off. (Wenar 2011)

Why is this distinction important? For *will theorists*, a right is only a right if the holder can waive it: capable of choosing to not exercise the right. This implies individuals unable to waive their rights (e.g., infants, animals, and comatose adults, have no rights. By this logic, I do not have a right to freedom because I can't legally waive my right to it under US law and become your slave, and Australians don't have the right to vote because they are legally required to vote. In contrast, *interest theorists* do not require rights to be waivable, partly because they want infants, animals, and comatose adults to have rights.

In interest theory, you are only eligible for a right if you would be made better off by having it—you can have no right to free speech unless having it will make you better off. Those incapable of being better or worse off can't have rights. In this scenario, all living individuals capable of suffering could have a right not to suffer, but not rocks. However, interest theory does not say that you have a right to everything that would make you better off. People who reject animal rights worry that interest theory argues for animal rights.

The Word of God, or the Supreme Leader

Divine-command theory posits that God is the decider regarding moral or immoral thoughts and behaviors (sins). With God as the decider, cursing one's parents is immoral:

> Whoever curses his father, or his mother shall be put to death. Exodus 21:17

To operationalize this ethic requires the ability to figure out God's rules. Is God cool with my becoming a suicide bomber against the heathens? Religion is ethics for millions, but easy to criticize. Quoting the Harvard psychologist Steven Pinker, writing for the Sunday *N.Y. Times* magazine:

> Putting God in charge of morality is one way to solve the problem, of course, but Plato made short work of it 2,400 years ago. Does God have a good reason for designating certain acts as moral and others as immoral? If not—if his dictates are divine whims—why should we take them seriously? Suppose that God commanded us to torture a child. Would that make it all right, or would some other standard give us reasons to resist? And if, on the other hand, God was forced by moral reasons to issue some dictates and not others—if a command to torture a child was never an option—then why not appeal to those reasons directly?

Most people are not as quick to dismiss morality based on God's Will; most are religious, at least to an extent.

The God I learned about ruled clearly on the morality of numerous activities, such as parent-honoring and wife-of-neighbor lusting. I was told that God declared, he never told me this directly, "Sex before marriage, or simply for fun, is immoral." But God provides no guidance for most activities—is it better to play baseball or read comic books?—suggesting I could decide, within limits, what was best for me—maximize my enjoyment—as long as no Commandments were violated. Nevertheless, my nature would lead to lots of sinning (being immoral).

For the Christian God, intent and remorse are more important than actions: when my time has come, if I believe and ask for forgiveness, I am off to heaven, no matter how many I lusted after or smote along the way. I am unsure whether this makes the Christian God a processist or a consequentialist. I am also unsure whether my childhood God would want us to save the whales or even if she cares. Religions and gods differ on the value of the environment: Buddhism, for example, would view the whales and us as inseparable parts of the system, making both whales and humans worth preserving. Morality based on the word of God is fundamentally different from ethics based on WB: your sin may make you happy and no one unhappy, but in the eyes of God, it's immoral.

The Will of Nature

Actions are moral if they follow the natural order—you and your dog having sex is immoral, even if you both enjoy it; it isn't natural.[34] Natural-law ethics assume all men have a common human nature, which is moral, so behavior consistent (inconsistent) with it is moral (immoral). To be moral is to do what is in your nature.

Operationalizing this ethic requires identifying human nature (behaviors and characteristics common to all humans). Religious thinkers, philosophers, anthropologists, and primatologists have collectively spent thousands of years on whether there is a human nature and, if so, what. Is it bestowed on us by God (our creator), genetics, or stuff that every culture teaches? For example, while observed in a few primate groups, the making and use of tools aren't observed in all of them, so it isn't part of primate nature. On the other hand, it is part of human nature, so it's a moral activity for humans but not for chimps. Within-species sex is human nature, so moral. Is lying to and killing human nature?

Rousseau believed in human nature and thought it moral, making him a proponent of Natural-law morality. Others argue that people are inherently immoral: Hobbs is the arch-type. Some assert that genetic engineering is immoral for the same reason that Frankenstein's monster

[34] Consider the following story devised by Haidt (2012): "Julie and Mark are brother and sister. They are traveling together in France on summer vacation from college. One night they are staying alone in a cabin near the beach. They decide that it would be interesting and fun if they tried making love. At very least it would be a new experience. Julie was already taking birth control pills, but Mark uses a condom too, just to be safe. They both enjoy making love, but they decide not to do it again. They keep that night as a special secret, which makes them feel even closer to each other. What do you think about that, was it OK for them to make love?" Respondents say no. despite the fact that their reasons for why it was not ok are assumed away by the story. In the end, people say it is bad but can't articulate why. The sex was a PI (both were better off and no one else is worse off).

was immoral; it's unnatural. Environmentalists have argued that saving nature is moral simply because nature is natural. Welfare and environmental economists are too quick to dismiss such thinking as illogical; it isn't.

This ends my brief discussion of deontological/duty ethics.

Virtue Ethics

In virtue ethics, moral versus immoral is determined by your character and your inclinations: to be moral is to have virtuous (moral) inclinations. Your behavior and its consequences are secondary. Duties and rules are secondary, and so are social contracts. If you maintained a virtuous character throughout your life, you had a moral life. Plato and Aristotle were virtue ethicists, and so was Aquinas—virtue ethics was the predominant ethic until the Renaissance. The economist historian McCloskey (2008) argues that Adam Smith was a virtue ethicist, and much in Smith's *Theory of Moral Sentiments* supports this. Economists who have not read it may imagine Smith a WC; he was not.

In the nineteenth and early twentieth centuries, virtue ethics was eclipsed by Kantian ethics and WC. It reemerged in 1958 with *Modern Moral Philosophy* by the British philosopher Gertrude Anscombe[35]—it had never lost its street appeal. Anscombe's article rejected WC because "it commits one to endorsing evil deeds" and concluded that Kantian ethics … is just incoherent" (Driver 2014). Whether she intended to resurrect virtue ethics is debated—but she did.

The three pillars of virtue ethics remain the Aristotelian concepts of *arête* (excellence or virtue), *phronesis* (practical or moral wisdom), and *eudaimonia* (true happiness/flourishing)—(Hursthouse 2013). Virtue ethicists distinguish between primary and secondary virtues: the secondary ones are implied by the primary ones. There is disagreement about which are primary, but all agree that generosity, honesty, compassion, and courage are primary. To possess a virtue means that it is part of your core. Taking honesty as an example, always telling the truth is neither necessary nor sufficient to possess this virtue. Having it simply means you strive to be, for its own sake, an honest and truthful person, not that you blurt out the truth on every occasion.

[35] She coined the term "consequentialism."

Practical and moral wisdom is the knowledge and experience you need to do what you intend—for example, you know what it takes to be generous or courageous. Teenagers lack practical and moral wisdom—they intend to be virtuous but muck things up. If you possess the virtues, are experienced enough to have practical and moral wisdom, and are lucky enough to have some wealth, you flourish and experience eudaimonia.[36] It is easier to say what this does not mean than it does. It does not mean your WB is maximized; a virtuous person would not maximize their personal WB.

Non-humans can be neither virtuous nor non-virtuous: they are incapable of virtue: it requires the ability to evaluate your actions, so your dog can't be a bad dog, but you can be in the doghouse for lacking virtue.

Welfare consequentialists, including welfare economists, complain that virtue ethics produces no objective criteria or rules for judging behaviors and policies. Virtue ethicists agree but think pursuing an objective, such as increasing societal WB, is folly.

Looking back to Buddhist ethics, Damien Keown, Professor of Buddhist Ethics at the University of London, thinks Buddhism is a type of virtue ethics, arguing that following the Buddhist way makes one a virtuous person, one of its end goals. The debate in Buddhism is whether it is an end goal or simply an effective way to reduce suffering (increase WB).

Evolutionary Morality Theory

An ethic could be based on evolutionary biology: genes for being good: see Dawkins (1976) and Steven Pinker (2008). We get along, and most of us don't behave in ways that drastically reduce the WB of others—at least not all the time—because gene containers that get along have a better chance of passing their genes on to the next generation.[37] It seems that empathy and *reciprocal altruism* are in our genes. Empathy is the ability to put yourself in another's shoes. Reciprocal altruism is when I do something to help you even though it temporally weakens me: I do it because I expect you to return the favor. Empathy contributes to our caring for

[36] See the discussion of eudaimonia in Chapter 4.

[37] Genghis Khan is the dramatic exception: he did not "get along" and his genes are in .5% of the male population of the world (Hillary Mayell 2003).

others (those weaker), and reciprocal altruism contributes to our sense of fairness and justice. [In a related vein, the economist and game theorist Ken Binmore in his book *Natural Justice* (2005), argues that the ethics a society practices result from cultural, rather than biological, evolution; it is a solution to repeated games.]

Contract Morality (*Contractualism*)

Using an agreed-upon process, members of a society enter into contracts/agreements with one another; a few are explicit (e.g., written law against killing people), but most are implicit. Behaviors that violates a contract are wrong/immoral. Both Rawls and Kant can be viewed as contractualists: Rawls is more a political than a moral contractualist; Kant is a bit of both. Kant and Scanlon (the modern voice of contractualism) argue that the contract is motivated by everyone's mutual respect, and it is rational to respect others. Quoting from *What We Owe to Each Other* (2000):

> An act is wrong if its performance...would be disallowed by any set of principles [rules]...of behavior that no one could reasonably reject...

An act is wrong if no reasonable person could argue that the rule against it isn't justified. Morality is about contractual relationships between rational individuals (explicit and implicit). In his review of Scanlon's book, the philosopher Thomas Nagel describes the idea behind Scanlon's contractual rule.

> The idea is that if our aim is to be able to justify our conduct to others, we will want it to conform to principles that none of them could reasonably reject, because then everyone who shares our interest in justification would in effect be prepared to license what we do insofar as it accords with those principles. If we deliberately do something that is in this sense wrong, we are in effect saying we don't care about its admissibility to reasonable others.

Contractualism differs from WC and welfare economics. It is concerned only with how we behave toward others, while WC also worries about how we treat ourselves. WB does not play the leading role in contractualism. Its objective isn't to maximize societal WB, and it does not require that all kinds of WB are commensurable.

In contrast to contractualism, Hobbs (*Leviathan* 1651) believed you are motivated by self-interest. You would commit to a social contract limiting what you can do, but only because it would limit the bad shit other people could do to you—such as shooting or shunning you. The economic Nobel laureate James Buchanan (1919–2013) thought the same: entering into a social contract that outlines good behavior is motivated by self-interest rather than respect. To distinguish it from the mutual-respect camp, this camp is referred to as *contractarianists*. The contractarian philosopher David Gauthier believes you want to maximize only your WB but that this is sometimes achieved by behaving in ways that will make you worse in the short run. For example, you don't break your promises or bully even though it would increase your current WB; behaving ethically is a good practice because it will influence how others deal with you in the future when you want something from them.

Ethics Based on Group Rights, Things Having Rights, and Inherent Value

Most ethics convey moral standing to individuals; in which case, a group of individuals only has moral standing because its members have it. E.g., consequentialists want to maximize an aggregation of the members' WB. Contrast that assumption with the group having moral standing or value, but the individual members of the group do not. So the group has the right, and the objective is to maximize the WB of the group. And the group's welfare isn't an aggregate of the WB of its members.

For example, you may posit that a non-human species has the right to not go extinct or, in addition, the right to prosper in its natural state. E.g., elephants have the right to exist undisturbed in their natural habitat. Such a *group right* conveys neither rights nor moral standing to specific elephants. In fact, the prospering of the species in its natural environment might require the suffering of all its members: wild animals continuously struggle. Nevertheless, this group right conveys a duty toward elephants, making us wrong if we do not provide them with sufficient natural habitat.[38] [What amount of natural habitat is adequate?].

[38] In 1981, in Palila (an endangered species of bird) vs. the Hawaii Department of Land and Natural Resources, US Court of Appeals, the species successfully sued for habitat protection under the Endangered Species Act, effectively granting the species limited legal standing. Their habitat was being destroyed by feral goats and the species successfully

Or you may posit that future humans have a right to exist with sufficient resources, so current humans must make this happen. Given such a right, we must provide for them even if no future individual has rights. Or you might posit that an ethnic, cultural, or religious group has the right to exist without giving moral standing to any of its specific members.

If it is the group, rather than the individuals in the group, that has moral standing, it is foreign, at least for an economist, to talk about the WB of the group, but it is possible. One, for example, may consider the WB or integrity of a family that has a right to exist and prosper independent of the WB of its members. Still, economists typically don't think like this.

There is the question of which groups get group rights. At a minimum, a group has to have a persistent identity. For example, a crowd is a group of people who do not have a persistent identity. In contrast, Canadians, fetuses, squirrels, and cloggers are groups with persistent identities. There are many.

Equally alien to economists, ecological systems (e.g., the Everglades or a redwood forest) and natural formations (e.g., the Grand Canyon) could have rights.[39] "It is good to preserve and maintain the

sued for their removal. https://scholar.google.com/scholar_case?case=8158542596159694344&hl=en&as_sdt=2&as_vis=1&oi=scholarr.

[39] *Should trees have standing?—toward legal rights for natural objects* (Christopher Stone 1972) is the foundational legal treatise for affording them legal standing. In a 1972 Supreme Court dissenting argument, echoing Stone, Justice William Douglas famously wrote, "Inanimate objects are sometimes parties in litigation. A ship has a legal personality, a fiction found useful for maritime purposes. The corporate soul—a creature of ecclesiastical law—is an acceptable adversary, and large fortunes ride on its cases. The ordinary corporation is a 'person' for purposes of the adjudicatory process...So it should be as respects valleys, alpine meadows, rivers, lakes, estuaries, beaches, ridges, groves of trees, swampland, or even air that feels the destructive pressures of modern technology and modern life...The river, for example, is the living symbol of all the life it sustains or nourishes..., including man who are dependent on it or who enjoy it for its sight, its sound, or its life. The river as plaintiff speaks for the ecological unit of life that is part of it. Those people who have a meaningful relationship to that body of water, whether it be a fisherman, a canoeist, a zoologist, or a logger—must be able to speak for the values which the river represents, and which are threatened with destruction." (https://en.wikisource.org/wiki/Sierra_Club_v._Morton/Dissent_Douglas). The case was the "Sierra Club v. Morton": the Sierra Club was trying to stop the Disney Corporation from building the Mineral King ski area in the Sierra Nevada wilderness. The Court dismissed the suit, concluding that neither the Sierra Club nor the wilderness had legal standing. See, Elizabeth Kolbert (2022). The ski area was never built: the proposal led to some of my initial research. At the moment (May 2022): Mary Jane Lake in Florida, along with a few other

Everglades and immoral to destroy or diminish it." In this view, you behaved immorally if you turned part of it into a golf course. The Wisconsin forester Aldo Leopold 1887–1948) published in his now-famous A Sand Country Almanac (1949).

> A thing is right when it tends to preserve the integrity, stability and beauty of the biotic community. It is wrong when it tends otherwise.

He did not explain why the biotic community has a right to be beautiful. From this perspective, the suffering or pleasure of an individual animal or plant has no relevance. Leopold's reason is neither an animal-rights justification nor a justification based on preserving it for humans. This designation is mostly for natural entities. Still, it could be applied to a built entity such as the Sistine Chapel, the German language, or Venice ("Venice has value and should be preserved because it is unique and a remarkable creation."). A justification for attributing value to a natural or environmental resource is that, unlike a truck, it did not come into existence to make humans better off (Brennan 1984). Another justification was put forward by the philosopher Richard Routley/Sylvan. He hypothetically asked if it would be OK for the last human to destroy, for fun, the Sistine Chapel and the Grand Canyon. He thought most of us would conclude it was wrong to push the button that would blow them up, even though there would be no humans around to experience them.

The common denominator is *inherent value*: a thing or group has value in and of itself, independent of how any living individual (human or otherwise, including that thing) experiences the world: it is a value that no individual experiences, *experience-less value*. Economists understand experiential value (value experienced) but don't understand or believe in inherent value—for them, it makes no sense.[40] Consider a tree. Assuming

water bodies, has filed suit in Florida State Court arguing that a planned development of homes and office buildings (Beachline South Residential), which will fill in wetlands, will "adversely impact the lakes and marsh that are parties to his action," causing injuries that are "concrete, distinct, and palpable" (Kolbert 2022; Smith 2022).

[40] I must qualify: economists believe that humans have inherent value and nothing else does.

I was tempted to use the word "intrinsic" rather than "inherent" but will stick with "inherent" because while inherent value is a type of intrinsic value in the philosophical sense, there are other types of intrinsic value. "Intrinsic" in philosophy typically means axiomatic, as in the hedonistic assumption that pleasure is the only determinant of right,

the tree is incapable of experiencing, a welfare economist would say it has value only if its existence can influence the experiences of individuals with societal standing. For example, I have standing, and the tree makes for a lovely view from my home, or it can be used to build an addition or sequester carbon dioxide, making the earth more pleasant for society's members. Or the tree has value because two magpies, Heckle and Jeckle, both card-carrying members of society, nest in it.

If those with standing no longer care about the tree, or all die, The welfare-economic view would be that the tree no longer has value. But the tree still could have inherent value. If inherent value exists, it is independent of whether people believe in it; it isn't determined by us.[41]

Making the distinction clearer: if society's members get value, for example, from simply knowing that an ecosystem is thriving, this is economic value, not inherent value. Why? Because one or more individuals experience the value. Above, I assumed the tree is incapable of experiences, but a polar bear can experience pleasure and pain. So if a bear is a member of society, their experiencing pleasure is an economic value, not an inherent value. In contrast, the inherent value of a bear isn't something the bear or anyone can experience.

Note the distinction between a species' inherent value and its right to exist. Either can be used to motivate preserving polar bears, but they are not the same reason: a "right" is simply the "right thing to do"; it does not imply that doing the right thing needs value. If a group has inherent

and pain is the only measure of wrong. This implies, for example, that ice cream can't be intrinsically moral or immoral because ice cream is neither pain nor pleasure, but it could be extrinsically moral if its consumption produces pleasure, the intrinsic moral good. Acts and things have extrinsic value if they produce intrinsic value. Not everyone agrees on what are the intrinsic values. The inherent value of an object or system is a type of intrinsic value because its existence is axiomatically defined as morally right. The philosopher G.E. Moore (1873–1958) suggested that when determining whether something was intrinsically valuable, you consider whether it would be valuable if it were the only thing in existence. If you answer yes, you think, according to Moore, that thing has intrinsic value (SEP on *Intrinsic vs. Extrinsic Value*). If you would say that pleasure (or a species) is valuable even if it is the only thing that exists, then you believe pleasure (or that species) has intrinsic value. Not everyone buys Moore's test. What is intrinsic value and what has intrinsic is a prominent topic in moral philosophy.

[41] God has been invoked to motivate inherent value, as in "Polar bears have inherent value because God values the creatures he created." This is faulty reasoning. If God is an individual who experiences something because his creatures are prospering, then his experience has economic value—if God has moral standing.

value, this could be used to argue for the group's right to exist (not go extinct). And a thing or a group could have a right to exist even if it has no inherent value. For example, one might posit that it would be wrong to destroy a distant star simply because it is part of the physical universe.

When I teach environmental economics to environmental-studies majors, they express the belief the environment and planet have inherent value. They reject the idea that the management of environmental resources should be based only on the values experienced by individuals. Even though I have sometimes accused them of being crazy, their belief is logical if one starts with the axiom that environmental resources have inherent value.

All This Said About Ethics:

In the eighteenth century, Hume pointed out that while there are reasons supporting different ethics, there is no one correct ethic based on "Reason". As Mill wrote,

> What proof is it possible to give that pleasure is good? (1879/2011)

The bottom line is there is no logical reason to prefer one ethic over another. It all comes down to how moral and immoral are axiomatically defined.

For example, there can be no logical argument against axioms such as "We should improve the environment because improving the environment is the right thing to do." Or "Giving individuals with moral standing more freedom to flourish is morally right." Or "The only metric of right behavior is doing one's duty." Ethical axioms can't be judged based on logic.[42]

But facts influence how to implement an ethic. For example, as noted earlier, a WB consequentialist would advocate complete freedom for Robinson Crusoe if they believed he would always choose his HRAP. And

[42] Axioms can be judged on whether they contradict fact, though axioms that define the essence of an ethic are typically not of that sort. An ethic based on a set of axioms can be judged wrong if those axioms are self-contradictory. Example, if one axiom is more freedom is the one measure of good and another is more happiness is the one measure of good.

will advocate interference in Robin's life if they believe he will exhibit flawed choosing.

You can be an economist modeling choice without being a WB consequentialist. You can also speculate on the role of choice theory if you adopt a different ethic, as in Mark White's book.

Now that I have briefly reviewed other ethics, the next chapter, the next to last, returns to welfare economics, getting specific about its limitations as an ethic. It ends with economic ethics that are not welfare economics.

References

Anscombe, Gertrude. 1969. "Modern moral philosophy." In *The is-ought question*, 175–195. Springer.

Aquinas, Thomas, and Fathers of the English Dominican Province. 1265–1274/1947. "The Summa Theologica." Benziger Bros. https://www.ccel.org/a/aquinas/summa/FS.html.

Ashford, Elizabeth, and Tim Mulgan. 2012. "Contractualism." Stanford Encyclopedia of Philosophy. Stanford University. https://plato.stanford.edu/.

Batchelor, Stephen. 2015. *After Buddhism: Rethinking the dharma for a secular age*. Yale University Press. https://yalebooks.yale.edu/book/9780300224344/after-buddhism/.

———. 2017. *Secular Buddhism: Imagining the dharma in an uncertain world*. Yale University Press. https://yalebooks.yale.edu/book/9780300234251/secular-buddhism/.

Bentham, Jeremy. 2013. *The collected works of Jeremy Bentham, volume iii: Not Paul but Jesus*. Edited by Bentham Project. London: Faculty of Law, University College London. https://discovery.ucl.ac.uk/id/eprint/1392179/.

Bentham, Jeremy, and John Bowring. 1839. *The collected works of Jeremy Bentham, volume 2 part i*. https://www.google.com/books/edition/Works_of_Jeremy_Bentham_Volume_2_Part_1/98FdDQEACAAJ?hl=en.

Binmore, Ken. 2005. *Natural justice*. Oxford University Press. https://www.webofscience.com/wos/woscc/full-record/WOS:A1984SH48000003.

Brennan, Andrew. 1984. "The moral standing of natural objects." *Environmental Ethics* 6 (1): 35–56. https://doi.org/10.5840/enviroethics19846118. https://www.webofscience.com/wos/woscc/full-record/WOS:A1984SH48000003.

Brennan, Andrew, and Yeuk-Sze Lo. 2011. "Environmental ethics." Stanford Encyclopedia of Philosophy. Stanford University. https://plato.stanford.edu/.

Brown, Claire. 2017. *Buddhist economics: An enlightened approach to the dismal science*. New York: Bloomsbury Press.

Carter, Ian. 1995. "The independent value of freedom." *Ethics* 105: 26.
Cudd, Ann. 2012. "Contractarianism." Stanford Encyclopedia of Philosophy. Stanford University. https://plato.stanford.edu/.
Dawkins, Richard. 1976. *The selfish gene*. New York: Oxford University Press.
De Waal, Frans. 2008. "Putting the altruism back into altruism: The evolution of empathy." *Annual Review of Psychology* 59: 279–300. https://doi.org/10.1146/annurev.psych.59.103006.093625. https://www.webofscience.com/wos/woscc/full-record/WOS:000253283000011.
Driver, Julia. 2014. "Gertrude Elizabeth Margaret Anscombe." Stanford Encyclopedia of Philosophy. Stanford University. https://plato.stanford.edu/.
Dworkin, Ronald. 1979. "Do we have a right to liberty?" In *Liberty and the rule of law*, edited by R.L. Cunningham. College Station, TX: Texas A&M University Press.
Fleischacker, Samuel. 2013. "Adam Smith's moral and political philosophy." Stanford Encyclopedia of Philosophy. Stanford University. https://plato.stanford.edu/title/.
Gethin, Rupert. 1998. *The foundation of Buddhism*. Oxford: Oxford University Press.
———. 2008. *Sayings of the Buddha*. Oxford: Oxford University Press.
Gibbon, Edward. 1776/1906. *The history of the decline and fall of the roman empire, vol. 1*. New York: Fred de Fau and Company. https://oll.libertyfund.org/title/gibbon-the-history-of-the-decline-and-fall-of-the-roman-empire-vol-1.
Goodman, Charles. 2014. "Ethics in Indian and Tibetan Buddhism." Stanford Encyclopedia of Philosophy. Stanford University. https://plato.stanford.edu/.
Grey, William. 2009. Last man arguments. In *The Encyclopedia of Environmental Ethics*.
Hahn, Frank. 1982. "On some difficulties of the utilitarian economist." In *Utilitarianism and beyond*, edited by Amartya Sen and Bernard Williams. Cambridge: Cambridge University Press.
Haidt, Jonathan. 2008. "The emotional dog and its rational tail: A social intuitionist approach to moral judgment." *Reasoning: Studies of Human Inference and Its Foundations*: 1024–1052. https://www.webofscience.com/wos/woscc/full-record/WOS:000305482200055.
———. 2012. *The righteous mind: Why good people are divided by politics and religion*. New York: Pantheon Books.
Hicks, John Richard. 1975. "Value and capital: An inquiry into some fundamental principles of economic theory." *OUP Catalogue*.
Hurka, Thomas. 1987. "Why value autonomy?" *Social Theory and Practice* 13 (3): 21.
Hursthouse, Rosalind. 2013. "Virtue ethics." Stanford Encyclopedia of Philosophy. Stanford University. https://plato.stanford.edu/.

Jamieson, Dale. 2017. "Rights, justice, and duties to provide assistance: A critique of Regan's theory of rights." In *Animal rights*, 177–190. Routledge.

Jaworska, Agnieszka, and Julie Tannenbaum. 2013. "The grounds of moral status." Stanford Encyclopedia of Philosophy. Stanford University. https://plato.stanford.edu/.

Jones, Peter. 2014. "Group rights." Stanford Encyclopedia of Philosophy. Stanford University. https://plato.stanford.edu/.

Kant, Immanuel. 1785/2003. *Groundwork of the metaphysical of morals*. Edited by Mary Gregor. Cambridge: Cambridge University Press. https://books.google.com/books/about/Kant_Groundwork_of_the_Metaphysics_of_Mo.html?id=Ibcy57Hz4tcC.

Keown, Damien. 1992. *The nature of Buddhist ethics*. New York: Palgrave.

———. 2005. *Buddhist ethics: A very short introduction*. Oxford: Oxford University Press.

Kolbert, Elizabeth. 2022. "A lake in Florida suing to protect itself." *The New Yorker*, April 18.

Korsgaard, Christine. 2004. *Fellow creatures: Kantian ethics and our duties to animals*. Vol. 24. *The tanner lectures on human values*. http://nrs.harvard.edu/urn-3:HUL.InstRepos:3198692.

———. 2007. "Facing the animal you see in the mirror." Facing Animals, Harvard University.

Kramer, Matthew. 2008. "Matthew Kramer on legal rights." In *Philosophy Bites*. https://philosophybites.com/2008/07/matthew-kramer.html.

Kreeft, Peter. 1990. *A summa of the summa: The essential philosophical passages of St. Thomas Aquinas' Summa Theologica; edited and explained for beginners*. Ignatius Press.

Kymlicka, Will. 1990/2002. *Contemporary political philosophy*. Oxford: Oxford University Press.

Leopold, Aldo. 1949. *A sand country almanac*. Oxford: Oxford University Press.

Magnuson, Joel. 2022. *The dharma and the socially engaged Buddhist economics*. Palgrave Macmillan.

Mayell, Hillary. 2003. "Genghis Khan a prolific lover, DNA data implies." *National Geographic*, February 13.

McCloskey, Deirdre. 2008. "Adam Smith, the last of the former virtue ethicists." *History of Political Economy* 40 (1): 43–71. https://doi.org/10.1215/00182702-2007-046. https://www.webofscience.com/wos/woscc/full-record/WOS:000253416700002.

Mill, John Stuart. 1859/2011. *On liberty*. London: Walter Scott Publishing Company and Project Gutenberg. https://www.gutenberg.org/ebooks/34901.

———. 1879/2004. *Utilitarianism*. 7 ed. London: Longmans, Green, and Company, Project Gutenberg. https://www.gutenberg.org/cache/epub/11224/pg11224-images.html.

Nagel, Thomas. "One-to-one." *London Review of Books*, 3.

Nussbaum, Martha. 2007. "Facing animal complexity." Facing Animals, Harvard University.

Philosophy, The Internet Encyclopedia Of. Ethics. Edited by James Feiser and Bradley Dowden. The Internet Encyclopedia of Philosophy.

Pinker, Steven. 2008. "The moral instinct." *The New York Times*, January 13. https://www.nytimes.com/2008/01/13/magazine/13Psychology-t.html.

Rahula, Walpola. 1959. *What the Buddha taught*. New York: Grove Press.

Rawls, John. 1971/99. *A theory of justice*. Cambridge, MA: Harvard University Press. https://www.webofscience.com/wos/woscc/full-record/WOS:000281657300017.

———. 1981. "The basic liberties and their priority." The Tanner Lectures on Human Values, University of Michigan. https://tannerlectures.utah.edu/_resources/documents/a-to-z/r/rawls82.pdf.

———. 2001. *Justice as fairness: A restatement*. Harvard University Press.

Raz, Joseph. 1986. *The morality of freedom*. Clarendon Press.

Reeves, Richard. 2008. *John Stuart Mill: Victorian firebrand*. London: Atlantic Books Ltd. https://atlantic-books.co.uk/book/john-stuart-mill/.

Regan, Tom. 1985. "The dog in the lifeboat: An exchange." *The New York Review of Books*.

Richard, Kraut. 2014. "Aristotle's ethics." Stanford Encyclopedia of Philosophy. Stanford University. https://plato.stanford.edu/.

Runciman, W.G. 2014. "The kind of dog he likes." *London Review of Books*, 2.

Scanlon, Thomas. 2000. *What we owe each other*. Cambridge MA: Harvard University Press. https://archive.nytimes.com/www.nytimes.com/books/first/s/scanlon-owe.html.

Siderits, Mark. 2007. *Buddhism as philosophy: An introduction*. Indianapolis/Cambridge: Hackett.

Sen, Amartya. 1988. "Freedom of choice: Concept and content." *European economic review* 32 (2–3): 269–294.

Siderits, Mark. 2019. "Buddha." Stanford Encyclopedia of Philosophy. Stanford University. https://plato.stanford.edu/.

Singer, Peter. 1975/2009. *Animal liberation. Animal rights*: Springer. https://www.webofscience.com/wos/woscc/full-record/WOS:000329385300023.

. 2011. *Practical ethics*. Cambridge University Press.

Smith, Adam. 1759/2022. *The theory of moral sentiments*. Vol. 1. Ireland: J. Beatty and C. Jackson and The Gutenberg Project. https://www.webofscience.com/wos/woscc/full-record/WOS:000283912100003.

Smith, Wesley. 2022. "Natural rights: A lake sues." *National Review*, April 12.

Southwood, Nicolas. 2009. "Moral contractualism." *Philosophy Compass* 4 (6): 11.

Stone, Christopher. 1972. "Should trees have standing?—Toward legal rights for natural objects." *Southern California Law Review* 45: 51.

Trivers, Robert. 1971. "The evolution of reciprocal altruism." *Quarterly Review of Biology* 46: 22.

Uleman, Jennifer. 2010. *An introduction to Kant's moral philosophy*. Cambridge University Press.

Wenar, Leif. 2011. "Rights." Stanford Encyclopedia of Philosophy. Stanford University. https://plato.stanford.edu/.

———. 2017. "John Rawls." Stanford Encyclopedia of Philosophy, Spring. Stanford University. https://plato.stanford.edu/title/Wenar/.

White, Mark. 2011. *Kantian ethics and economics: Autonomy, dignity, and character*. Stanford, CA: Stanford University Press.

Williams, Bernard. 1985/2011. *Ethics and the limits of philosophy*. Routledge (2006/2011): Fontana Press (1985).

Wright, Lawrence. 2022. "The elephant in the courtroom." *The New Yorker*, February 28.

Wright, Robert. 2017. *Why Buddhism is true: The science and philosophy of meditation and enlightenment*. Simon and Shuster.

Zimmerman, Michael. 2014. "Intrinsic vs. Extrinsic value." Stanford Encyclopedia of Philosophy. Stanford University. https://plato.stanford.edu/.

Zsolnai, Laszio. 2009. "Buddhist ethics for business." In *Ethical prospects: Economy, society, and environment*, edited by Zsolt Boda, et al. Dordrecht: Springer. https://link.springer.com/book/10.1007/978-1-4020-9821-5.

CHAPTER 13

A Bit More on Welfare Economics, External Effects, and Interpersonal Comparisons of Well-Being

Chapter 4, which introduced welfare economics, briefly discussed external effects. However, it did not detail their practical significance in judging specific behaviors, institutions, and processes. For example, it did not address the common belief that unregulated competitive markets are the ethically best mechanism for determining what is produced and who consumes what.

Some welfare economists advocate for free markets and freedom of choice; so do many others. Their reasoning is often tautological. For example, if efficiency is the goal, and one makes assumptions that guarantee that unregulated competitive markets are efficient, unregulated competitive markets achieve the goal.

To keep things simple, initially assume Assumptions 1–9 hold, and there are neither incorrect beliefs nor flawed choosing—an idealized world in which to judge welfare economics as an ethic. But, even then, it has problems.

E. R. Morey, *Deconstructing Behavior, Choice, and Well-being*,
https://doi.org/10.1007/978-3-031-36712-0_13

The Ethical Goal of Welfare Economics is Maximizing Societal WB, not Achieving Efficiency

According to welfare economics, actions that increase the WB of some members but don't decrease the WB of other members (PIs) are right. And actions that decrease the WB of some members but don't increase the welfare of other members (Pareto deteriorations) are wrong.

In contrast, an act is *efficiency increasing* if those whose WB is increased could hypothetically compensate those whose WB was decreased. If the compensation occurred, no one's WB would be lower, and some would have more WB. I use the following phrase with my students, "An act (or policy) is efficiency increasing if the gain to the gainers is greater than the loss to the losers."[1]

PIs are efficiency increasing and, by definition, increase societal WB. But most efficiency-increasing actions are not PIs. A synonym for efficiency increasing is *potential* Pareto improvement, *Potential* because there is the potential for the gainers to compensate the losers and turn it into a PI. If the compensation occurs, then the act with the compensation is a PI

Efficiency increasing does not imply societal WB has increased. It might increase societal WB, and it might decrease it. Efficiency increasing is neither necessary nor sufficient for societal WB to increase. Unfortunately, this does not preclude overzealous economists from wrongly declaring, "More efficient is better."

Most things are not Pareto Improvements: someone usually ends up worse off. Every government policy decreases someone's WB. So the dictate that a PI increases societal WB, while correct, isn't of much

[1] Economists claim efficiency is a positive concept, yet it becomes an operational concept only after one judges who is and who isn't a member of society—a foundational normative judgment. Of course, we believe our society should not include French people or other foreigners, because they do not belong to our tribe. The Israelis exclude the Palestinians, and the Palestinians exclude the Israelis. Another critical question is whether future animals (humans and other creatures) should belong. For example, if future individuals do not count, why sweat global warming? Besides, whether an action is efficiency increasing) depends on how society's wealth is distributed. Usually, there will be gainers and losers, so an action is more likely to be efficiency increasing the more the wealth of society is held by those who gain from that action, and the less the wealth is held by the losers. That is, how wealth is distributed affects whether an action is efficiency increasing: an action is more likely to be efficiency increasing if it helps rich people and hurts poor people than if it hurts rich people and helps poor people.

practical use for parsing right from wrong government policies. And most people's behaviors negatively affect somebody. This is also true for animal behavior. [There are woodpecker holes in my stucco, dog poop is widespread, and animals eat plants and animals.] In the real world, few changes hurt no one, so implementing Pareto improvements will require the losers to be compensated.

Two additional facts further muddle the PI criterion for judging actions. (1) One can typically make any action a PI by adding or subtracting individuals from the roles of society. I play this game with my students. If the action isn't a PI and you want to make it one, ban from society those made worse.[2] On the other hand, if the action is a PI, and you don't want it to be, find one individual who is made worse off by the action and enter him into society's roles—it is as simple as that.

In conclusion, whether an act or policy is efficiency increasing (a potential PI improvement) isn't a welfare-economic criterion for parsing right from wrong. Increasing efficiency may decrease aggregate WB, and decreasing it may increase aggregate WB. Remember rich Donald, the guy who stole your dead mother's ring.

But Doesn't Welfare Economics Imply That Unregulated Competitive Markets Are the Right Mechanism for Allocating Resources and Distributing Goods and Services?

No, it does not—it demonstrates that if certain assumptions hold, properly regulated competitive markets are preferred, on efficiency grounds, to unregulated competitive markets.

The First Theorem of Welfare Economics proves that if a specific list of assumptions holds, the equilibrium in an unregulated competitive market system will be efficient. The equilibrium will have the property that the only way to increase the WB of one member of society will require that the WB of other members decrease. A corollary is overall efficiency is necessary for maximum societal WB. This has led many, including some economists, to wrongly conclude that markets are always ethically

[2] For example, if you assume that Muslims or Lutherans are not members society, how their WB is affected by a policy plays no role in determining whether the policy is a PI or a potential PI.

preferred for allocating resources and distributing goods and services. And wrongly conclude that unregulated, competitive markets are better than regulated ones.

The First Theorem was anticipated in Adam Smith's *Wealth of Nations* (his invisible hand) but was not formally proven until the 1950s. The theorem does not support the conclusion that unregulated competitive markets are the right way to organize economic activity. While beautiful, it only proves that equilibrium in an unregulated competitive market system will be efficient in an idyllic world. And efficient does not imply that societal WB is maximized.

The proof of efficiency requires that everyone's behavior is consistent with Assumptions 1–9 of NBT. And it requires complete information and certainty so incorrect beliefs and flawed choosing are not admitted. Unfortunately, the real world isn't this idyllic: human behavior deviates from Assumptions 1–9. Besides, since there is incomplete information and uncertainty, we all hold numerous incorrect beliefs and practice flawed choosing.

For example, the proof requires that the WB of all parties to all market trades are made better off by every trade—but often, they are not. I'm watching late-night TV and see your ad for the BowFlex trainer. I want the six-pack abs like the dude and dudette in the ad. I call the number on the screen, provide you my credit card ($29.99/month for 24 months), and the nuts, bolts, and rubber bands arrive two weeks later. You, the seller, are better off, but I'm not because I incorrectly believed the machine would produce muscles like the couples'. Or, the X-rated movie I watched put me in an emotional state that temporarily made the device more attractive. Or perhaps I had done my research and decided that a Mr. Universe weight set was better for me, but right before the Bow Flex ad, there was something in the movie that cued me to temporarily concentrate on the fact that one of Mr. Universe's free weights could fall on my foot.

But, even if everyone always maximized their realized WB, the proof also requires no external effects: it requires the assumption that no one's behavior directly influences the WB of others: there are no external effects.[3] But much of what we do directly affects others. Rather than listing specific examples of how an individual's behavior can affect others

[3] One can't even conclude a voluntary trade between two individuals is efficiency increasing.

(as I did earlier), try to think of something you do that you are sure does not affect anyone else, negatively or positively—I can't.[4] The proof also requires that when a good is produced (e.g., a BowFlex machine, electric power, or organic broccoli), its production has no direct effects on the production of other goods or people's WB.[5] Some days the hours I spent on this book made my wife better off; other days worse off. And reading this paragraph could easily affect how you interact with others, affecting their WB.

To summarize, using the First Theorem as proof that unregulated competitive markets pursue WB-efficiency requires there are neither flawed choosing nor external effects. And, even if the competitive market equilibrium outcome were efficient, there is likely another outcome, either inefficient or efficient, that generates more societal WB. Fairness is an issue, and market systems did not evolve to achieve fairness. In market economies, those who start with a big pile of resources end up with lots of goods and services; those who begin with few consume much less.[6]

If one supposes no flawed choosing but admits external effects—a common position among welfare economics—government intervention in the market (taxes or regulations) can increase efficiency. For example, economists advocate for a tax on carbon emissions because there are

[4] Can you? Consider some possible candidates: an act done alone, and no one else ever finds out you did it (watching Bugs Bunny cartoons at 3 a.m.; trying my left shoe on my right foot). Or I daydream of dancing with the NYC ballet and keep my dreams to myself. Each act might later affect how I behave toward my wife, my students, or my dog. And this might affect their WB. E.g., my imagining dancing with the NYC ballet might make me aware that we all have both strengths and weaknesses, and this might make me more inclined to forgive students who exhibit the typical weaknesses of eighteen-year-olds. A forgiven student is typically a happier student.

[5] The smoke from my power plant makes it more difficult for the laundry next door to produce clean air-dried underwear. And the bees I employ to produce honey pollinate your fruit trees, making is easier for you to produce your apples—a famous example.

[6] Mistakes and luck can cause those who start with nothing to end with riches and those who start with a lot to end up poor. You might counter my conjecture that the market does not redistribute wealth by arguing that in a market system, with enough hard work, you will get ahead. Fair enough, though I would counter that a propensity to work hard is a resource that you either did or didn't get in the parental/genetic draw. I got lucky by being born with intelligence and then adopted by parents who were not financially rich, but who were willing to spend all that they had on their children's educations. And my anxiety genes have caused me to work hard to keep the wolf at bay.

negative external effects when carbon-based fuels are burned. A properly regulated competitive market system is preferred to an unregulated one on efficiency grounds.

As Lionel Robbins (1898–1984) pointed out in 1938:

> It was not possible to say that the economic science showed that free trade was justifiable.[7]

External Effects Caused by Relative-Position Effects and by Abhorrent Behaviors

I shudder at the implications for welfare economics.

External effects include everything directly affecting third parties, including those caused by people taking offense simply because they find certain behaviors objectionable.

An example should suffice: Suppose I'm not fond of public displays of affection by people with red hair, so my WB declines whenever I witness such displays. I don't even need to see it; just knowing it is happening makes me miserable. Imagine many rich people feel this way, whereas people with red hair tend to be poor. Reducing their public displays of affection (hand-holding, kissing, etc.) could increase efficiency. And a ban may even increase societal WB. But, of course, it would depend on how different distributions of WB are judged. Efficiency might even require those with red hair to have their own neighborhoods and schools so individuals of my ilk are less offended.

I, and others, become livid when ignorant people practice free speech. So, efficiency may require less free speech, particularly if the speakers are poor. People get upset by others: their inappropriate sex, fun, and weight; their beliefs (religious, political, and other); and everything thing else the beholders find disgusting.

[7] Putting this quote in context, Robbins was reacting to Mr. Harrod's conclusion that if we can't make interpersonal utility comparisons, economics has little to say. "But I confess that at first, I found the implications very hard to swallow. For it meant, as Mr. Harrod has rightly insisted, that economics as a science could say nothing by way of prescription. It could say whether a certain course of action could lead to a desired end. It could judge the consistency of different policies. But, in itself, it passed no verdict of good or bad. It was not possible to say that economic science showed that free trade was justifiable..." See footnote 27 in Chapter 3.

You might believe that negative external effects that result from an objectionable ordering on the part of the impacted should not be considered, but for welfare economists, orderings are sacrosanct. What does and does not increase societal WB depends on everyone's orderings, but welfare economists, unlike ordinary people, show no inclination to draw a line between appropriate and inappropriate orderings.[8] An implication is that racial and gender discrimination, and other offensive acts, will increase societal WB if enough people are prejudiced.

Consider the pleasure of causing others to suffer: all else constant, one ranks higher paths that inflict suffering. More sadism could be efficiency increasing. For welfare economists, the WB the pedophile gets from pedophiling counts toward aggregate WB, the same as the WB you get from eating ice cream, and the same as the WB loss to their victims. This is an extreme example, but you get the point.

Chapters 4 and 5 considered relative-position effects, but Chapter 4 did not consider their implications for welfare economics. A relative effect occurs when your welfare depends not just on what you consume but also on how much your friends and neighbors consume. Evidence presented in Chapter 5 indicates substantial relative-wealth effects. Chapter 6 discussed other relative-position effects (faster runner, more attractive spouse, more sex than your peers).

Relative-position effects are external effects, so efficiency and societal WB require that they be considered. E.g., efficiency dictates that such direct effects on others must be produced in efficient amounts, and to accomplish this, behaviors must be manipulated with taxes or regulations. For example, if my striving to work more to have more isn't regulated, I will strive an inefficient amount (too much): I won't consider that my striving to have more stuff will decrease your WB. So, efficiency requires my behavior to be manipulated, so I strive only the efficient amount—manipulated with income-tax rates or work restrictions. If you train and become faster on your bicycle, I am now relatively slower, so worse off, and efficiency requires that your training be limited. Few people think about the implications of relative-position effects on efficiency and societal WB: behavior manipulations would be needed

[8] Economists would argue on efficiency grounds that without regulations or laws, there will be an inefficient amount of child molestation—too much. Nevertheless, their argument is the same efficiency argument one could use to restrict minorities to certain neighborhoods.

to internalize these external effects. Of course, one could declare that relative-position external effects should not be considered, making one not a welfare economist.

What If We Add Common Quirks, Incorrect Beliefs, Violations of NBT Assumptions, and Flawed Choosing?

With these, the welfare economist can't even conclude that you will do what is right for you: you will do things that will decrease your WB. In a world of common quirks, incorrect beliefs, and flawed choosing, a welfare economist can't logically argue that more freedom is morally preferred to less. If increasing societal WB is the goal, correctly applied paternalism is morally preferred. In that world, the welfare economist is ethically obligated to stop me, or at least most people, from trying heroin.

The Practical Value of Welfare Economics Is Limited Because It Refuses to Compare My WB with Yours or Even Accept That They Are Comparable

It can't determine, in practice, whether most actions are right or wrong. [In its defense, most ethics share this deficiency.] Suppose it is impossible to compare your WB to mine (make interpersonal WB comparisons). If so, whether a policy or act increases societal WB is unanswerable. If WB isn't comparable across the members of society, aggregate WB is, most of the time, a meaningless concept. The same is true of societal WB.

The idea that we can't compare the WB increase to some with the WB loss to others goes back, at least, to Jevons, who, referring to interpersonal comparisons of WB, stated in 1871:

> I see no means whereby such comparisons can be accomplished. Every mind is inscrutable to every other mind and no common denominator of feeling is possible. (Jevons, as quoted by Robbins [1938])

Quoting Broome (1988):

> This idea [the refusal to make interpersonal comparisons] gave rise to a style of welfare economics that still lingers. In the United States, indeed, it still predominates. Virtually everything that happens in an economy is good for some people and bad for others. The dogma says economics cannot compare the benefit to some with the loss to others. So, it cannot judge whether a change is good or bad on balance. Economics, then, is unable to judge the merits of virtually any economic event.

The Default to an Efficiency Criterion: The Big Switcharoo

Despite all this, applied economists, myself included, have spent hundreds, thousands of hours estimating dollar measures of WB changes. We do this to add them up and publish them in a journal. Or we do it because we were asked to (and paid) by a policymaker or lawyer, for example, one suing a PRP, a *potentially responsible party* (e.g., British Petroleum for the oil spill in the Gulf). Such behavior suggests our estimates can be used to determine whether a policy will make society better off. They can be used to estimate whether an action will increase or decrease efficiency, but not whether it would increase aggregate or societal WB.

A way out of this dead-end is to make the goal maximizing efficiency rather than maximizing aggregate or societal WB (see R. Posner in Chapter 4). If asked directly, welfare economists would say the objective is to increase WB, but still, some say "more efficient is better than less". Repeating a quote from Broome (1988):

> They [welfare economists] have slipped from identifying efficient states, which can be done without interpersonal comparisons, to claiming that efficient states are better than others, which generally cannot. Robbins was right about this...

Welfare economics, in practice, concentrates on identifying efficiency because, unable to adopt a fairness metric and insisting that WB can't be compared across individuals, it had nothing else to do. From that, it has slipped into pursuing efficiency regardless of other goals.

WB Is Cardinal

Most welfare economists reject this; instead, they assume that WB has only an ordinal meaning. But, making interpersonal WB comparisons almost always requires that WB is cardinal for each member of society, and each member's WB can be compared. Recollect from Chapter 2 that if your WB is cardinal, you can determine whether a move from path j to path k will increase your WB more or less than a move from path s to path t. If your WB is only ordinal, you can't do this.

Societal WB allows for your WB to count more or less than mine. So, in addition to assuming cardinal WB, one has to decide what is fair: decide how much my WB counts relative to yours. Unfortunately, welfare economists refuse to make fairness judgments; ordinary people make them all the time but disagree on what is fair.[9]

In my principles of economics course, I tell my students that there are no objective criteria to judge whether one distribution of WB is more or less fair than another—it is simply a matter of what you choose to believe. I have read, heard, and taught this so many times I give it no thought. Yet, this economic view that fairness is subjective is a subjective assumption that many reject.

For example, most people find it unfair that the combined wealth of the world's eight wealthiest men equals the wealth of the world's bottom 50%. And they believe that a policy whose only effect on WB is to increase the WB of one of the eight would decrease societal WB even though it would increase aggregate WB and be a PI

What people think is fair typically depends on why they think people do what they do, including how much behavior is chosen. So, for example, if you believe the poor could have been prosperous but chose, instead, leisure, while the rich are rich because they chose hard work, then you view as unethical policies that take from the rich and give to the poor—doing so would decrease societal WB.

Alternatively, if you believe whether you are rich or poor is mostly a matter of dumb luck (who bore you, where you were born, and what happened to you when you were a baby), you believe it is ethical to take from the rich and give to the poor—doing so would increase societal WB.

[9] An economist might assert that economics is a science and specifying a criterion for fairness is unscientific. It is true that parts of economics follow the scientific method. Economic ethics isn't one of them.

A question that economics, psychology, and neuroscience are designed to answer is how much we control our actions and destiny. The findings, to date, suggest not as much control as we would like to think.

* * *

Our ability, as welfare economists, to distinguish right from wrong comes down to the following. If we can agree on who is and who isn't a member of society, actions that increase the WB of some members and decrease the WB of no members are right, and those that reduce the WB of some members and increase the WB of no members are wrong. Of course, this isn't saying much.

Interpersonal WB Comparisons Are Making a Comeback Among Economic Ethicists: Rawls, Sen, and Dasgupta

The dearth of welfare-economic predictions has led a few economic ethicists to search for additional criteria to make economic ethics more useful. Their works are studied more by non-economists than economists and less by American economists than those in Europe. Rawls, Sen, and Dasgupta propose and defend specifics on what is fair. For example, Rawls believes ethical is what is contractually acceptable to society's members.

I limit my discussion to them: they are the predominant economic ethicists of the last fifty years. They are neither utilitarians nor welfare economists.[10,11] Each is happy to make interpersonal comparisons, and none define societal WB as aggregate WB. And they care about what is fair.

Rawls

His ethic is both process and consequence; the great Harvard political economist envisioned a group of reasonable people choosing how society should be organized (the form of government, the laws, and how

[10] In contrast, Yew-Kwang Ng is a welfare economist who endorses interpersonal comparisons.

[11] Expanding beyond these three, consider Bowles, Jeffrey Sachs, and the late Anthony Atkinson. Also, Broome who might not have considered himself an economist.

economic activity is organized). The group must decide how to organize society before each member knows their position in society (wealth, intelligence, parents, abilities, etc.). This is choice behind a *veil of ignorance*. He argues this is a good process because it causes good consequences—the process eliminates self-interest bias by the deciders, so Rawls is both a *contractualist* and a *process consequentialist*. The Rawlsian process will result in an ethical social contract, so adhering to it will be ethical, and deviating from it will be unethical.

Rawls specified fair, arguing that the organization of society's institutions and the distribution of its wealth must be perceived as fair if it is to be accepted by its citizens.[12] He limits his analysis to societies with sufficient resources to meet everyone's basic needs.

Social cooperation will make the goods-and-services pie bigger. However, to get their cooperation, the citizens must know in advance that the pie will be sliced fairly. For Rawls, it is unfair for me to get more stuff simply because I was born rich or with more than average talents. So, he argues that income should be equally distributed unless distributing it unequally would be better for everyone, including the least well-off. Rawls expressed this in two principles. The first takes precedence over the second.

The first principle affirms for all citizens familiar basic rights and liberties: liberty of conscience and freedom of association, freedom of speech and liberty of the person, the rights to vote, to hold public office, to be treated in accordance with the rule of law, and so on. The principle ascribes these rights and liberties to all citizens equally. Unequal rights would not benefit those who would get a lesser share of rights, so justice requires equal rights for all in all normal circumstances...

Rawls's second principle of justice has two parts. The first part, fair equality of opportunity, requires that citizens with the same talents and willingness to use them have the same educational and economic opportunities regardless of whether they were born rich or poor.

The second part of the second principle is the difference principle, which regulates the distribution of wealth and income (Wenar 2017).[13]

[12] If a system is accepted as fair by all of its citizens, then behaviors that violate the rules of that system are unethical.

[13] Quoting Rawls, "First Principle: Each person has the same indefeasible claim to a fully adequate scheme of equal basic liberties, which scheme is compatible with the same scheme of liberties for all." "Second Principle: Social and economic inequalities are to

The difference principle is that society can only choose an unequal income distribution if everyone has more income under the unequal distribution. And, if it can choose between several unequal distributions (all preferred by everyone to an equal distribution), the fair choice is the distribution that provides the highest income for those at the bottom.

"The [second] principle does not allow the rich to get richer at the expense of the poor" (Wenar 2017). Ethical (unethical) economic policies are those consistent (inconsistent) with the two principles. Rawls clarifies that if a government action affects incomes, it is only ethical if it increases the incomes of the worse off. And actions that increase their incomes are ethically preferred.

Rawls defined fairness with rights, opportunities, and income, not WB. This is added evidence that Rawls was not a utilitarian. In addition, income is easier to measure than WB, making his principle easier to apply than ethical principles based on WB.[14]

What do his two principles imply about living an ethical life? I speculate. Choosing an ethical mechanism for organizing economic activity requires that the choosers choose behind a veil of ignorance. So, Rawls must have felt that without the veil, individuals would choose the system personally best for them. He believed that an individual is incapable of deviating from their highest-ranked available path, HRAP. Or thought deviating is possible but only with difficulty.

Suppose Rawls thought individuals are capable of deviating from their HRAP. Would he say each choice I make (e.g., going skiing, selling real estate, working in a food bank) is unethical unless it increases the WB of the worst off? While that would be a noble goal, most of us would not live up to it. Alternatively, would he say that to the extent I am capable, I should live my life—not necessarily choice by choice—but overall, in a way that will increase the WB of those worse off than me? The London School of Economics philosopher Alex Voorhoeve says yes, concluding,

> ... certain principles for individual conduct—including a principle requiring relatively advantaged individuals to sometimes make their economic choices

satisfy two conditions: (a) They are to be attached to offices and positions open to all under conditions of *fair equality of opportunity*. (b) They are to be to the greatest benefit of the least-advantaged members of society (the *difference principle*)" (Rawls 1971/1999).

[14] It is easier to identify those who are worst off in terms of income than in terms of WB.

> with the aim of maximising the prospects of the least advantaged—are an integral part of a Rawlsian political conception of justice. (Voorhoeve 2005)

Rawls argued that if reasonable citizens choose behind his veil of ignorance, they will select a society based on his two principles, not utilitarian principles.[15] [He viewed utilitarianism as his competition. Rawls' principles are based on an agreed-upon social contract, not maximizing aggregate WB or aggregate want fulfillment, so they conflict with Benthamite and preference utilitarianism.]

Sen

Sen argues that the nineteenth and twentieth-century purge of interpersonal comparisons from economics was misguided. And to be useful, economics must judge the gains of some against the losses of others. He argues that economics can and should propose criteria for interpersonal judgments. Like Partha Dasgupta (1942-), Sen is particularly interested in the WB of the poor in developing countries. Both offer a quality-of-life approach for identifying WB. Sen equates WB with what you do and achieve (are capable of and choose to do) and your unrealized capabilities (what you could do but choose not to do).[16] More capabilities are ethically preferred—you have more freedom (more options).

Feeling happy is of value, but it's not all of WB. Other aspects are achieving or having the capacity to achieve a long life, enough to eat, knowing there will be enough to eat, and literacy—all these expand what one is capable of. These, for Sen, are components of WB (intrinsically good) even if they never increase your emotional or life-satisfaction WB. And emotional WB does not contribute to WB if it is *inauthentic,* such as living in dire circumstances but being happy because you were born with happy brain chemistry. Of course, having happy brain chemistry is better than depressed brain chemistry, but happy neurons do not imply more WB, as Sen defines WB. And if you are in dire straits, happiness

[15] His argument restrictively assumes that the citizens do not care about relative income and that citizens are risk neutral. Chapter 4 discussed data that shows people do care about their relative position.

[16] This view of well-being goes back to Adam Smith and Karl Marx (Sen 1988).

because something worse did not happen when you expected it would, is not increased WB.

For Sen, components of WB are objective and easily measured, or, at least, are easier to measure than emotional or life-satisfaction WB. Sen also asserts that fulfilling desires does not necessarily increase WB. He puts forth two reasons: we don't always like what we desire, and the oppressed have such limited desires that fulfilling them will not increase their WB. Sen admits flawed choosing, rejecting the assumption that choosing Path *k* over Path *j* necessarily means path *k* gets you more WB. Sen's conclusions are in step with recent developments in neuroscience on wanting versus liking, discussed in Chapter 5. Sen is neither a Benthamite nor a preference utilitarian.

Recently, Sen (2009a), following in the step of John Rawls (Sen was his student), proposed a philosophy of social justice (*The Idea of Justice*). While Rawls laid out his just society—*perfectly just* (what Sen refers to as *transcendental justice*), Sen finds Rawls's tack impractical for actual judgments in the real world. Instead, he views justice as a continuum (*comparative justice*). The goal is not to make the world just, only less unjust.

Sen equates justice with fairness, and while indicating there are different notions of fairness, he wants to judge fairness from an impartial perspective, a global observer who takes account of all points of view. In practical terms, gross injustices such as slavery and unnecessary starvation are unjust. The implications are less clear if one must choose between two states of injustice, neither grossly unjust. That, in a way, is his point; often, there is no clear answer. Sen is outlining a process for deciding, not the answer.

Dasgupta

For Dasgupta (*Human Well-Being and the Natural Environment*), a better society is a wealthier society: wealth is broadly defined to include not only manufactured capital but also the natural-resource stock, the environment, education, knowledge, freedoms, and society's institutions. An action is right if it adds wealth because greater wealth leads to greater societal WB.[17] For Dasgupta, societal WB depends on both average WB and how WB is distributed, and the poor have a greater claim to additions to the pie.

Dasgupta equates personal WB with a "well-lived life" (to achieve an admirable character, a successful family, warm friendships, a meaningful job, and a life free of coercion). [As Aristotle pointed out, you can't live well without wealth.] Components of WB include human rights and not being treated based on one's name, caste, or political, religious, or ethnic affiliation. Dasgupta is not a pure rights theorist. He feels these rights need to be justified in terms of human flourishing, so they are not absolute.

A problem is how to measure and weigh these different components of wealth. Doing this starts with identifying the properties of an acceptable index, the topic of his book. For Dasgupta, societal WB is an aggregate of the WB of individuals, and an individual's WB depends on both his material WB and his "ability to exercise various kinds of freedoms". Democracy, civil liberties, and sustainability enhance welfare. Intergenerational WB is important but threatened because we are using our natural resources too quickly.

* * *

Rawls' principles are rights, opportunities, and income; Sen's and Dasgupta's principle is WB, defining WB more broadly than emotional and life-satisfaction WB, including rights and capabilities. A difference is Rawls uses income directly rather than indirectly through its influence on WB. All three argue that bettering the poor should have more weight than bettering everyone else. Sen and Dasgupta are more specific about what constitutes WB. Sen and Dasgupta consider what is ethical in our world of poor societies with immense suffering—agreeing that more command over goods and services, either individually or collectively, isn't always the best way to increase WB. Rawls is more abstract and limits his two principles to societies with enough resources to provide everyone with food and shelter.

[17] Dasgupta was an early arguer that income measures of wealth ignore our dependence on natural resources. He is an eminent natural-resource economist. He notes that he ignores animal welfare.

Nevertheless, their ethics have a lot in common: (1) emphasizing making the worst off better off. As a Buddhist would say, reduce suffering. (2) Each requires that we all have the same rights and freedoms. Each requires that our educational opportunities and ability to live a long and healthy life should not depend on our wealth, gender, ethnicity, or race. And (3) none directly addresses how an individual could live a more ethical life or whether an individual can choose to live more ethically.

References and Sources

Broome, John. 1988. "What's wrong with poverty?" *London Review of Books*, 2.

Rawls, John. 1971/1999. *A theory of justice*. Cambridge, MA: Harvard University Press. https://www.webofscience.com/wos/woscc/full-record/WOS:000281657300017.

Robbins, Lionel. 1938. "Interpersonal comparisons of utility: A comment." *Economic Journal* 48 (192): 635–641. https://doi.org/10.2307/2225051. https://www.webofscience.com/wos/woscc/full-record/WOS:000203610800002.

Sen, Amartya. 1988. *The standard of living*. Cambridge: Cambridge University Press.

———. 2009a. *The idea of justice*. Cambridge, MA: Harvard University Press.

Voorhoeve, Alex. 2005. "Incentives and principles for individuals in Rawls's theory of justice." *Éthique et Économique Ethics and economics* 3 (1).

Wenar, Leif. 2017. "John Rawls." Stanford Encyclopedia of Philosophy. Stanford University, Spring. https://plato.stanford.edu/title/Wenar/ .

Additional Readings

Binmore, Ken. 2010. "Arguing for the achievable: Sen's theory of justice." *Science* 329 (5997): 1286–1286. https://doi.org/10.1126/science.1194620. https://www.webofscience.com/wos/woscc/full-record/WOS:000281657300017.

Dasgupta, Partha. 2001. *Human well-being and the natural environment*. Oxford: OUP.

Econlib. "Vilfredo Pareto." https://www.econlib.org/library/Enc/bios/Pareto.html.

Mullany, Gerry. 2017. "World's 8 richest have as much wealth as bottom half, Oxfam says." *New York Times*, January 16, 2017. https://www.nytimes.com/2017/01/16/world/eight-richest-wealth-oxfam.html.

Ng, Yew-Kwang. 1997. "A case for happiness, cardinalism, and interpersonal comparability." *The Economic Journal* 107 (445): 1848–1858.

Sen, Amartya. 1999. "On ethics and economics." *OUP Catalogue*.
———. 2009b. "The idea of justice: A reply." 26th International Social Philosophy Conference, St Joseph's Univ, Philadelphia, PA, July 30–August 01.
———. 2013. "Ideas of justice: A reply." *Critical Review of International Social and Political Philosophy* 16 (2): 305–320. https://doi.org/10.1080/13698230.2012.757919. https://www.webofscience.com/wos/woscc/full-record/WOS:000212892900011.
———. 2015. "The idea of justice: A response." *Philosophy & Social Criticism* 41 (1): 77–88. https://doi.org/10.1177/0191453714553501. https://www.webofscience.com/wos/woscc/full-record/WOS:000348857600010.
Wolff, Jonathon. 2010. "Philosophy bites." In *On John Rawls: A theory of justice*. http://philosophybites.com/2010/02/jonathan-wolff-on-john-rawls-a-theory-of-justice.html.

CHAPTER 14

Epilogue: Do You Make Choices, and if so, Has Your Choosing Made You Happy?

To summarize, my book is an exercise in wondering why we do what we do. I distinguish between behavior and choice (chosen behaviors). The economic default is to assume that much of what we do, we first chose to do. Economists call their behavior model "choice theory," not "behavior theory". And everyone desperately wants to believe that if they have an experience of choosing, it was that conscious, cognitive experience that determined why they did what they then did—we did it because we consciously chose to do it.

Effort was directed at defining what is meant by a "choice". If choice requires the ability to select an alternative different from the one selected—the lay definition—economici don't make choices. For economists, there is choice unless external constraints result in only one available path. Humans, mollusks, and plants all make choices in this weak sense.

I proposed a definition of choice. The whole philosophical debate about free will comes down to defining a choice and whether humans and other animals are capable of it.

My objective was to get you interested in the psychology, neuroscience, and philosophy of behavior and choice and their implications. I did this against the backdrop of how economists think about behavior, provoking you to think about the premises of neoclassical choice theory, NCT, and where they came from. I asked you to question the theory's ability to

E. R. Morey, *Deconstructing Behavior, Choice, and Well-being*,
https://doi.org/10.1007/978-3-031-36712-0_14

predict your behavior and the behaviors of others (humans and other animals).[1] And to cause you to contemplate the practical relevance of welfare economics, the predominant ethic of economics.

One aspect of NCT has excellent predictive power—you can't do what you can't afford: you cannot have what is not available. In Principles of Microeconomics courses, the budget constraint reigns—you can't consume a path of goods that costs more than you have to spend. It generates NCT's big prediction: demand goes down when a price goes up—except when it doesn't. If a price increases or your income falls, you can no longer afford your consumption path, so you need to cut back. Unfortunately, economists don't explicitly consider other equally important constraints imposed by age, health, culture, skills, and obligations. I suspect economists do this because they are fuzzier and difficult to mathematically model. So, rather than tackling the difficult job of modeling them, they get lumped into a hodgepodge called *preferences*. NCT then assumes that this ordering of paths is given and fixed, making it your ultimate constraint. When I assert this, colleagues look at me funny. Modern preferences are a hodgepodge of likes, desires, and constraints.

When my behavior is different from yours and can't be explained by us having different constraints, the difference is attributed to different preferences. As George Stigler and Gary Becker noted in 1977, "No significant behavior has been illuminated by assumptions of differences in tastes."—something that can explain everything explains nothing. The full range of constraints needs to be explicitly modeled, and to the extent tastes do differ, it is essential to ask why and try to model why.

As I was taught, NCT assumes that you will choose your most-preferred path subject to your constraints; you maximize your utility subject to your constraints. As noted, what "more preferred" means is hard to say; it isn't much discussed. One conjecture is that if path *t* is preferred to path *d*, you associate more WB with *t* (more emotional or life-satisfaction WB). I discussed emotional WB (happiness) in depth, how what it means has evolved, and what makes you happy and unhappy (and for how long). A significant raise will make you happier, but not forever, or as long as you predict it will—unless it permanently raises your income relative to your peers.

[1] Economicus, the imagined individual in neoclassical choice theory, was born out of the religious belief that man was created in the image of God, so rational and non-erring. It is not a product of evolution.

I discussed the diverse literature on the relationships between income, consumption, emotional WB, and life-satisfaction WB—it's complicated. But, generally speaking, more money does not necessarily increase emotional WB in the long run unless you start critically poor. Average WB in the developed West has not increased much over the years, even though average incomes have significantly increased. Why? Research indicates your absolute income and wealth are not the main determinants of your WB. In addition, relative-position effects are important: you compare yourself with others and your former self on multiple dimensions, including income.

Research in psychology and behavioral economics (if you believe it) indicates your choosing is often flawed. The good news is your flawed choosing is often predictable and avoidable. For example, when something significant happens, there is pleasure or misery—a deviation from your norm—but it wanes over time. Unfortunately, we don't anticipate the waning. Instead, we incorrectly believe that our current feeling will persist, whether happy or miserable. For example, the new freshman drops out of college after a week because she is anxious and incorrectly believes the anxiety will never diminish. Or you buy a new car because you imagine the pleasure of having a new car will last, forgetting that it will soon be your old used car. Systematic mis-assessment of an action's benefits and costs causes flawed choosing. Being aware that you suffer from it makes you less prone to err but does not guarantee it. You may want your friends, family, or government to nudge you away from flawed choosing. Duration bias should be taught in elementary school. While common quirks cause flawed choosing, they don't all violate the assumptions of NBT, and NBT is consistent with flawed choosing.

And sometimes, what appears to be flawed choosing is not. For example, If the anticipated loss in the endowment effect is realized, as some research and theory suggest, the endowment effect does not cause flawed choosing.

I also believe I don't violate the NBT Assumptions or practice flawed choosing. I do this despite the research indicating everyone is a victim of it but believe they are not. And I believe the research. Go figure!

Your ordering of paths is based on your wants and desires. It varies with your emotional state. It is also affected by cues, observed and subliminal. These findings make it difficult to pretend your ordering is stable. And it deviates from your ordering if it were based on WB. The empirical question is how much and when.

While most people, including most economists, believe that which alternative you experience is determined by your conscious experience of choosing that alternative; it is not required to explain behavior. NBT is consistent with everything determined by your unconscious. And that the choosing experience is only window dressing. One could add the assumption that what you experience is always driven by conscious choosing (Assumption 12), but the evidence does not support this.

Substantial research in neuroscience and psychology indicates that the unconscious generates the choosing experience to make you feel responsible for and accept what you then do (buy the new car, divorce the old guy, ski). If the hypothesis is correct, the choosing experience does not determine what you next do, but this does not mean conscious thought does not influence behavior. A choosing experience, while it does not affect what you already unconsciously selected, can influence how your unconscious will select next time. More generally, conscious thoughts affect what the unconscious will later decide. The experience of conscious choosing is a critical component of our sense of self. And it makes you believe that other people are responsible for what they do and should be treated accordingly—execute the killer and reward the humanitarian.

Even though I intellectually understand that my choosing experiences don't influence what I do next, I stumble through life imagining/fantasizing that they do. For example, I fantasize that I drink wine rather than beer because I consciously choose wine. I believe that which I think is false, so I suffer from what philosophers term *involuntary fictionalism*, *involuntary choice-fictionalism*.[2]

It's tough to conceptually separate NCT and economic ethics. NCT assumes you know what is best for you, and subject to your constraints, you achieve it. This, combined with the welfare-economic assumption that right actions increase the WB of individuals (betters them), implies that you should be free to pursue your interests as long as doing so does not hurt others. In contrast, welfare consequentialists who believe that humans often get it wrong advocate strong or weak paternalism. [The sexy term for weak paternalism is *nudging*.[3]] While most people believe

[2] The philosopher William Irwin, a co-sufferer, calls it *free-will fictionalism*.

[3] "Nudge" as you are nudged toward the alternative in your best interest. Richard Thaler and Cass Sunstein have a well-known book, *Nudge*.

the effect on WB is a factor in determining right from wrong, few believe it should be the only factor.

Most moral philosophers are not even welfare consequentialists—a surprise to economists. Many modern moral philosophers adhere to a duty-based ethic or a process ethic. The book included a primer on ethics. It is common for economists to mash up WC and liberalism (more freedom is better). But more freedom being better than less, only follows from WC if we behave in our best interests and do not hurt others. Liberalism, in contrast, argues that freedom is good even if it allows you to make yourself worse off.

A century ago, NCT abandoned cardinal utility, and welfare economics forsook comparing utility across individuals. So, it now provides little guidance for those trying to parse right from wrong behaviors and policies. Desperately, welfare economics default to "More efficient is better than less efficient," but as I tell my students, "Efficiency is like sex; more is better except when it's not." Economic philosophers such as Amartya Sen and Partha Dasgupta argue that if economic ethics is to be more prescriptive, it will need to embrace more criteria for judging than each individual's ordinal WB.

Additional Readings

Irwin, William. 2015. "How to live a lie." *The New York Times*, November 2, 2015. https://archive.nytimes.com/opinionator.blogs.nytimes.com/2015/11/02/how-to-live-a-lie/.

Stigler, George, and Gary Becker. 1977. "De gustibus non est disputandum." *American Economic Review* 67 (2): 76–90. https://www.webofscience.com/wos/woscc/full-record/WOS:A1977DA61600007.

Thaler, Richard, and Cass Sunstein. 2008. *Nudge: Improving decisions about health, wealth, and happiness*. New Haven, CN: Yale University Press. https://www.webofscience.com/wos/woscc/full-record/WOS:000249349000005.

Index

E. R. Morey, *Deconstructing Behavior, Choice, and Well-being*,
https://doi.org/10.1007/978-3-031-36712-0

C

O

P

Q

R

Y

Z

SPRINGER NATURE

GPSR Compliance

The European Union's (EU) General Product Safety Regulation (GPSR) is a set of rules that requires consumer products to be safe and our obligations to ensure this.

If you have any concerns about our products, you can contact us on ProductSafety@springernature.com

In case Publisher is established outside the EU, the EU authorized representative is:

Springer Nature Customer Service Center GmbH
Europaplatz 3
69115 Heidelberg, Germany